"Make the..." adjustment to a decelerated mode of living" 144

Type A Behavior — 161

Eisenhower's Heart Attack

❖ ❖ ❖ ❖ ❖ ❖ ❖ ❖ ❖ ❖ ❖ ❖

Eisenhower's Heart Attack

How Ike Beat Heart Disease and Held on to the Presidency

Clarence G. Lasby

UNIVERSITY PRESS OF KANSAS

Published by the University Press of Kansas (Lawrence, Kansas 66049),

which was organized by the Kansas Board of Regents and is

operated and funded by Emporia State University, Fort Hays State

University, Kansas State University, Pittsburg State University,

the University of Kansas, and Wichita State University

Library of Congress Cataloging-in-Publication Data

Lasby, Clarence G., 1933–
  Eisenhower's heart attack : how Ike beat heart disease and held on
to the presidency / Clarence G. Lasby.
    p.   cm.
  Includes bibliographical references and index.
  ISBN 0-7006-0822-2 (alk. paper)
  1. Eisenhower, Dwight D. (Dwight David), 1890-1969—Health.
2. Presidents—United States—Biography. 3. Myocardial infarction—
Patients—United States—Biography. I. Title.
E836.L35 1997
973.921'092—dc21
[B]   96—45407

British Library Cataloguing in Publication Data is available.

Printed in the United States of America

10 9 8 7 6 5 4 3 2 1

The paper used in this publication meets the minimum requirements of

the American National Standard for Permanence of Paper for

Printed Library Materials Z39.48-1984.

For my beloved Geri

Illness is the night-side of life, a more onerous citizenship. Everyone who is born holds dual citizenship, in the kingdom of the well and in the kingdom of the sick. Although we all prefer to use only the good passport, sooner or later each of us is obliged, at least for a spell, to identify ourselves as citizens of that other place.

—*Susan Sontag,* Illness as Metaphor

Contents

❖ ❖ ❖ ❖ ❖ ❖ ❖

ACKNOWLEDGMENTS / xi

LIST OF ILLUSTRATIONS / xiii

INTRODUCTION / 1

1. The Nation's Number One Killer / 7

2. The Man Who Felt Like Tarzan / 19

3. Misdiagnosis and Cover-up / 57

4. Treatment and Recovery / 113

5. "When the Going Gets Tough, the Tough Get Going" / 155

6. The Politics of Illness / 200

7. The Life Apart / 247

8. The Struggle to Stay Alive / 293

9. The Meaning / 324

NOTES / 333

BIBLIOGRAPHY / 369

INDEX / 377

Acknowledgments

❖   ❖   ❖   ❖   ❖   ❖   ❖

I am indebted to Gene Gressley for leading me into this study by arranging access to the papers of Dr. Howard Snyder at the University of Wyoming, and to Emmet Chisum for guiding me through them; to James Leyerzapf at the Eisenhower Library, who is helpful to everyone who appears in Abilene and directed me to health material in unexpected places; and to Richard Wolfe, curator at the Countway Library of Medicine at the Harvard Medical School, whose professional skills are immediately apparent and of lasting benefit.

I owe special thanks to Dr. Oglesby Paul, emeritus professor of medicine at the Harvard Medical School, a marvelous biographer and writer as well as an eminent cardiologist, who read four chapters of the manuscript and some old electrocardiograms and whose advice was invaluable; and to Dr. Thomas Mattingly, a gracious gentleman who gave me a considerable amount of his time to explain the complexities not apparent in the documentary record.

I am forever grateful to Robert Divine and Lewis Gould, two of my colleagues in the history department at the University of Texas. Distinguished scholars who encourage by example, they read the entire manuscript and made it better than it was. I also thank Stephen Ambrose, who offered to read the work of a stranger and responded to it like a colleague.

I am fortunate to have worked with Michael Briggs at the University Press of Kansas, because he believes in this book and understands what I have tried to convey.

Above all, I want to thank my wife, Geri, who traveled to many archives with me, who participated in the research and improved the writing, and who has offered encouragement for a lifetime.

I am solely responsible for the judgments and opinions expressed in the book.

Illustrations

❖ ❖ ❖ ❖ ❖ ❖ ❖

Captain Dwight Eisenhower at Camp Meade, Maryland,
Tank Center in 1919. / 22

The army chief of staff relaxing in Hawaii in 1946. / 31

Dr. Paul Dudley White leaning forward at a press conference in 1955.
With him are General Snyder, Colonel Mattingly,
and Major Walter Tkach. / 89

On the sundeck at Fitzsimons Army Hospital in October 1955
wearing the message "MUCH BETTER THANKS." / 123

Returning to Washington, D.C., on Veterans Day, after
seven weeks in the hospital. / 133

Leaving Walter Reed, thin and weak, after surgery for ileitis. / 224

Strolling with Secretary of the Interior Stewart Udall minutes after
signing over his Gettysburg farm to the U.S. government. / 310

Visiting with Nixon at Walter Reed two months before his death. / 319

Introduction

❖ ❖ ❖ ❖ ❖ ❖ ❖

Canst thou not minister to a mind diseased;
Pluck from the memory a rooted sorrow;
Raze out the written troubles of the brain;
And with some sweet oblivious antidote
Cleanse the stuft bosom of that perilous stuff
Which weighs upon the heart?

Therein the patient must minister to himself.
   —William Shakespeare, Macbeth

"Two events in my lifetime shook me severely," wrote Dr. Leonard Scheele, surgeon general of the United States, in October 1955. "One was the announcement of the president's coronary thrombosis, and the other was the announcement of the Japanese raid on Pearl Harbor." Scheele surely was alone in according parity to such disparate events, and scarcely a hint of his sentiment has entered the annals of recent American history. Hundreds of books and articles have chronicled the "day of infamy," but no author has written with thoroughness and care about the "heart attack of the century." The president's rapid recovery and his completion of a second term undermined journalist Raymond Moley's claim that on that autumn day "a little raw onion on a hamburger altered the course of history."[1]

I came to this neglected subject largely by indirection. I was collecting information for a book on coronary heart disease in twentieth-century America, hoping to explain how a society could for so long and so persistently ignore the most ravaging epidemic in its history. I had planned to include a page or two on the Eisenhower attack and its object historical lesson—that one of the most busy men in the world, working under constant stress, could survive his coronary and return to normal life. But a chance encounter at the home of a colleague led me in 1982 to the University of Wyoming and the papers of Dr. Howard McCrum Snyder, who served for sixteen years after World War II as Eisenhower's personal and presidential physician. Those documents were so revealing and suggestive as to inspire me to search further—in the Eisenhower Library at Abilene, Kansas; in collections widespread in relevance and geography, of Drew Pearson, Dr. Paul Dudley White, and the American Heart Association; and finally, in the monumental assortment of materials eventually brought together for deposit in Abilene by Dr. Thomas Mattingly, the president's army cardiologist. By the end of the decade I had access to what is by far the most extensive and impressive collection of medical data for any president in our history.

Increasingly over the recent past, scholars have searched for medical records in order to explain the impact of illness upon our leaders. There is still controversy regarding the effect of cerebrovascular disease on Woodrow Wilson's performance at Versailles and during his fight for the League of Nations; there is still partisan rancor as to whether hypertensive heart disease led a "sick" Franklin Roosevelt to a "sellout" at Yalta; there is still amazement at John Kennedy's success in hiding his Addison's disease; and there has already been attention to the ailments of Ronald Reagan and George Bush. My study does not add significantly to this area of interest. Even with virtually complete documentation for all of Eisenhower's illnesses—the heart attack, ileitis, and stroke—there is no telling evidence to connect them with his specific decisions or policies. Clearly, he was less active and less personally aggressive during his second term, but that is not unusual. And, too, when certain issues threatened his deeply held principles, as when "reckless" spending threatened to cause budget deficits, he became vigorous and combative.

The Eisenhower medical files are rife, nonetheless, with new information that challenges old understandings—whether concerning medicine, politics, or press relations—and my attention gravitated at first to these revisionist aspects. Instead of the excellence of medical treatment we assume is customary for our presidents, I found a shocking misdiagnosis in the crucial hours after the heart attack. Contrary to all existing historical accounts, I contend that in the early morning hours of 24 September 1955 Dr. Snyder mistook a coronary thrombosis for a gastrointestinal problem, waited for ten hours before he recognized his mistake and called for help, and conducted an unremitting cover-up of his error for the rest of his life.

In a similar way, the newly available documentation moves Dr. Snyder to the forefront among those physicians who influenced the president during his illness, especially in his most important decision—to seek a second term. Journalists at the time and scholars thereafter variously praised or condemned Dr. Paul Dudley White, the eminent civilian cardiologist whose name had become a household word, as the prime mover in that decision. Recently one of them put it bluntly: "February 14, 1956, Paul Dudley White chose the next president of the United States." The evidence suggests otherwise. Within a month after the attack, Dr. Snyder was planning for the president to run again, and through insight and guile he created the circumstances to make it possible. Dr. White, in contrast, wanted the president to retire, and told him so. Only reluctantly, and belatedly, did he accede to the arguments of the military physicians.[2]

The new evidence alters somewhat the most robust of the historical interpretations surrounding the heart attack—that the Eisenhower administration was far more open with regard to the president's health than any in the past, so much so as to constitute a "dramatic change" or a "watershed." There was unprecedented openness and candor, but there also was an assiduous effort on the part of the president and his staff to prevent the disclosure of health information that might adversely affect his political prospects. Even as the press secretary was dispensing an avalanche of medical data, Eisenhower was working—in a way that sometimes gave credence to the concept of the "hidden-hand" presidency—to ensure that his physicians were circumspect and would leave his future to him. The Eisenhower White House was relatively truthful, but it had to hedge on its promise of the "whole truth."[3]

I have made these findings, together with other health information not hitherto available, an integral part of this book. But my primary focus is on the relationship between a man and a disease, in the most personal sense. Shortly after World War II, coronary heart disease entered the public consciousness as a major threat to the well-being of the American people. Experts proclaimed its death toll—hundreds of thousands a year and rising, until it reached a high point of 539,000 in 1968. It was truly "captain of the men of death," and the policy elite mobilized for an attack. Their strategy, based upon decades of faith in the germ theory of disease and driven by the conquest of infectious diseases and the achievements of science during the recent conflict, was to fund research to the highest amount possible in order to find an appropriate "magic bullet."

Eisenhower's coronary, as *Newsweek* noted, "placed a powerful mass stethoscope on everyone's organ of life—the heart," which in turn brought forth a vigorous and spontaneous desire to find a cure, and a hope that the president would take charge of the war against his disease. But even though his own heart had faltered, risking his life and threatening his career, he would not endow his illness with any special, historical meaning. Instead of a Franklin Roosevelt fighting to save his people from polio, or a Richard Nixon declaring war on cancer, he kept faith with his belief that "money alone isn't going to keep him or anyone else from having a heart attack."[4]

Eisenhower would not take command of the national crusade against heart disease, but he became a supreme commander, and a hero, of a different sort. He took a model from his nineteenth-century past—the self-sufficient individual seeking to control his own destiny—and he lived the maxim his mother taught: "The Lord deals the cards; you play them." Decades before his contemporaries, he made a commitment to preventive medicine, and he made the required changes—and sacrifices—in his everyday life. For much of his adulthood he had to be attentive to his health, but during his second term he became consumed with it. Indeed, had the American people known the full story of his medical life, some caustic and unschooled oberver surely would have observed his diet and his dieting and called him a "health nut"; counted the times he practiced and played golf and proclaimed him an "exercise freak"; disparaged his and his doctor's never-ending concerns about his blood pressure and pulse and named him a hypochondriac; and smiled at his attempts to control his anger, wondering what it was all about.

After 1955 the president had to play his "heart disease" card, and by virtue of the rich collection in Abilene, I have tried to construct a meaningful portion of what Arthur Kleinman, a Harvard psychiatrist, has called an "illness narrative"—a "story the patient tells, and significant others retell, to give coherence to the destructive events and long-term course of illness." In thousands of queries, decisions, and actions, Ike and Mamie, together with their family doctor, sought to understand and cope with the powerful undercurrent of coronary disease. They searched for its source in his personal past and their contemporary culture; they monitored its progress through daily symptoms and readings; and they dealt with anxiety, frustration, and fear as central conditions of his life. In a very private, human world on the margins of the presidency, they gave credence to the aphorism of the famous physician William Osler: "It is much more important to know what sort of a patient has a disease, than what sort of disease a patient has."[5]

By the time he entered office in 1953, Dwight Eisenhower had decided that even though he was the recipient of the most attentive medical care in the world, he still would have to "minister to himself." Forty years later his country was struggling to do the same. As a prelude to Heart Month in 1993, the president of the American Heart Association estimated that 70,020,000 of his fellow citizens suffered from some form of heart disease, at an annual cost to the nation of $117.4 billion. He understandably admonished that "it's time all Americans take what responsibility they can to lower their risk of cardiovascular disease." A month later the First Lady advised that the "responsibility ethos" would be a crucial part of her husband's health program and "that individuals are going to have to also be responsible to take care of themselves and to have an understanding of what causes health as opposed to illness." Soon thereafter journalist Bill Moyers, speaking of his popular PBS series and book *Healing and the Mind*, was urging Americans to rely more on exercise and meditation and less on drugs and surgery. "We can change behavior to prevent illness, reverse illness, and manage illness," he said. "We can be agents of our own well-being."[6]

Every person's illness is distinctive, and his or her response to it is a matter of time, place, position, knowledge, personality, or some other factor beyond comprehension. Eisenhower's response was extraordinary; he was a pioneer in preventive medicine, and his future biographers will have to give attention to his preoccupations and prescriptions. My hope is that this study of his experience will be instructive. For through it all, he perceived and adhered to a single defining lesson—that *he* must be the caretaker of his life.

✳ WES ALLES SAYS 1 OF EVERY 4 CALIF CITIZENS (INCLUSIVE OF ALL AGES) HAS SOME FORM OF HEART DISEASE.

1

The Nation's Number One Killer

❖ ❖ ❖ ❖ ❖ ❖ ❖ ❖ ❖ ❖ ❖ ❖ ❖ ❖ ❖ ❖

*In this secret and fell disease there is a fascination to which no physician is a
stranger, a fascination in its dramatic events and in the riddle to be read.*
  —*Clifford Allbutt,* Diseases of the Arteries

*Certainly the disease did not suddenly leap into existence about 1920, fully
armed for destruction like Athena from the brow of Zeus.*
  —*Howard Sprague, "Environment in Relation to Coronary Artery
  Disease"*

"Adam quite possibly died a coronary death," surmised cardiologist Dr.
Paul Dudley White in 1952, as he sought to call attention to the remote
origins of what his generation had come to call coronary heart disease. If
the dread malady was present in the Garden of Eden, however, it was slow
to make a discernible entrance into recorded history. There is some circumstantial evidence of its existence throughout the centuries. Egyptian mum-
mies revealed arteries with atherosclerosis; Greek, Roman, and medieval
physicians wrote of aches, anguish, tightness, paralysis, and pain in the
heart, of restricted vessels and sudden death; and Leonardo da Vinci
sketched wondrous specimens of the coronary arteries, including some
with sclerosis. But the signs and symptoms that appeared over thousands
of years in the literature, the case histories, the anatomical drawings, and
the pictorial representations were individually isolated, infrequent, and
imprecise. They did not depict a disease, even dimly, and all of them
together were immaterial when compared with the astonishing percep-

tions and descriptions of a small group of English physicians during a twenty-five-year period in the last half of the eighteenth century.[1]

In 1768, at a time when King George III was facing off against the American colonists, his personal physician read the nine-page paper "Some Account of a Disorder of the Breast" before the College of Physicians in London. William Heberden described a complex of symptoms never before mentioned by medical authors, and because of the sense of strangling and anxiety that attended the disorder, he named it angina pectoris (literally, chest pang). It was a grave matter, "For if no accident intervene, but the disease go on to its height, the patients all fall down and perish immediately." In his elaboration of the morbid entity, he gave such a striking description of heart pain following exertion that it became a classic that has lasted for more than two hundred years:

> They who are afflicted with it, are seized while they are walking (more especially if it be uphill, and soon after eating), with a painful and most disagreeable sensation in the breast, which seems as if it would extinguish life, if it were to increase or to continue; but the moment they stand still, all this uneasiness vanishes.[2]

Heberden's essay on angina pectoris, published in 1772, inspired some of his younger countrymen to further inquiries. John Fothergill proposed that such "gusts of passion" as anxiety and anger, as well as exertion, could bring on the pain. As if to prove it, the famous surgeon John Hunter, who suffered from angina and bemoaned that "his life was in the hands of any rascal who chose to annoy and tease him," fell dead after a heated argument with the governors of his hospital. Edward Jenner, who later gained renown for his research on the smallpox vaccine, examined the heart of one of his patients who had died from the disease and made an amazing discovery: "I was making a transverse section of the heart, pretty near its base, when my knife struck against something so hard and gritty as to notch it. I well remember looking up to the ceiling, which was old and crumbling, concerning that some plaster had fallen down. But on a further scrutiny the real cause appeared; the coronaries were become bony canals. Then I began a little to suspect." The coronary arteries were the source of the disease, he deduced, and his hypothesis gained support from a boyhood friend, Caleb Hillier Parry of Bath, who wrote in the last year of the eighteenth century that the coronaries might become "so obstructed as to intercept the blood, which should be the proper support of the muscular fibres of the heart, that the organ becomes unequal to the task of circulation."[3]

The collective inquest of the English group gave the world a new disease, located in the area of the heart, brought on by exercise and emotion, marked by terrible pain and sudden death, and seemingly caused by a lack of blood flowing through the coronary arteries. Quite unbelievably, the medical profession added almost nothing to these initial insights for more than one hundred years thereafter. Angina pectoris was not sufficiently prevalent to command attention among the many other novelties presented to the medical world, whether of such diseases as tuberculosis, diphtheria, malaria, pneumonia, and meningitis, or of the revolutionary developments in antisepsis, surgery, anesthetics, and bacteriology.

The disease did remain within the public consciousness during the nineteenth century because of its two predominant clinical features—terrible pain and sudden death. No picture was more clearly forthcoming than that of the helpless victim in the throes of an anginal attack, and throughout the world physicians strained to give a fitting description of the pain. The Germans spoke of *Der Teufel's Knotte* (the Devil's grip); the French favored *epouventable* (dreadful and frightening); and the English and Americans taxed the resonance of their language, characterizing the pain as ruthless, fierce, cruel, tearing, piercing, squeezing, stabbing, burning, excruciating, agonizing, a paroxysm of torture, a vice-like oppression, the boring of a red-hot drill, the scraping of a huge steel comb, and a saber thrust through the heart.[4]

The most celebrated case of individual suffering was that of Senator Charles Sumner of Massachusetts, the inveterate foe of slavery before the Civil War and the loyal friend of the freedmen during Reconstruction. He was an expert on pain, for in the aftermath of a spinal injury in 1856 he sought a remedy in Europe known as the *moxa,* the application of burning cottonwood along the length of the back until it turned the spine into a blister. The *moxa* was reputed to be the worst suffering that could be inflicted upon mortal man, but Sumner found his first attack of angina to be even worse, "so severe as to make the fire seem pleasant." It was "much like the sudden grasp of a cold hand," he wrote of one such seizure, "which gradually tightened, until it felt like a clasp of steel crushing his heart to atoms," so devastating as to make him feel that "life at this price is not worth the having."[5]

The pain of angina pectoris had its companion in the fearful sense of the nearness of the angel of death. The possibility that even a first attack could be fatal led the world-renowned Canadian physician William Osler to comment that angina began where other diseases ended—in death, that without warning there could come "a rapid change, a sudden unconsciousness, a stony stare, a slight change in the facial expression, and then in two or three gasps it is all over." For him the most historic and telling case was that of the distinguished English educationalist Thomas Arnold of Rugby, who, in the summer of 1842, feeling himself to be in perfect health, early one morning felt a severe pain in the left side of the chest that extended down the left arm. He immediately summoned his doctor, who detected a feeble pulse, took note of the beads of perspiration on his forehead, put a mustard plaster on his chest, and administered brandy and water. After a brief discussion about the disease, the doctor was dropping some laudanum into a wineglass when he heard a rattling in the throat and a convulsive struggle. Arnold was dead within minutes, a fact that led his son to memorialize that his father arose

> . . . to tread
> In the summer morning, the road
> Of death, at a call unforeseen,
> Sudden.[6]

Osler, who spent much of his career and earned his fame at Johns Hopkins and after 1904 at Oxford, was so fascinated by the disease that in 1897 he made it the subject of a book, *Angina Pectoris and Other Allied States,* and in 1910 chose it for the topic of his distinguished Lumleian Lectures before the College of Physicians of London. He did not set forth any new understanding of its origins or its progress, but he did present an incomparable portrait of its likely victims, one that was to persist in the public memory from that time forward. His 268 case studies were most often "the well 'set' man of from forty-five to fifty-five years of age, with a military bearing, iron-grey hair, a florid complexion," and "the robust, the vigorous in mind and body, the keen and ambitious man, the indicator of whose engines is always at 'full speed ahead.'" Among this type were the physicians, engaged in "the incessant treadmill of practice," for whom hard work and worry were "too much for a machine with an ever-lessening reserve"; the "gifted race" of Jews, whose intense absorption in life, pleasure, and family taxed their nervous energy to the utmost and subjected their systems to stress and strain; and members of the upper classes in general, beset by the high-pressure life of modern days, "aggravated by worries, particularly the possibility of not carrying through some big scheme or the onset of a financial crisis." Osler also gave a nationalistic flavor to his demographic portrait—one that would likewise persist—when he suggested that although the disease originated in England, in the typical angina patient there "was incarnate the restless American spirit which drove him into a premature grave."[7]

Osler's insights and interest were exceptional; most physicians considered angina a disease of an elite few and simply ignored it. They were aware, however, that "heart disease" was becoming a problem. Sometime around 1905 it displaced tuberculosis and pneumonia as the United States' greatest killer, and by the 1920s had seized the role of "captain of the men of death." But it was a capacious umbrella that covered congenital heart disease, syphilitic heart disease, hypertensive heart disease, arteriosclerotic heart disease, and especially rheumatic heart disease, the dreaded scourge of the young and the most deadly form of all. The latter had its source in rheumatic fever, an infection that began with a sore throat or tonsillitis, marked its pathway with painful, swollen joints and a heart rate of around 120, smoldered within the body for months and even years, seriously damaged the valves of the heart, and killed 50 percent of its victims by the age of forty. For at least the first forty-five years of the twentieth century, the "rheumatic heart" claimed nearly all of the physicians' time and attention.[8]

Angina remained a mystery, as was strikingly evident in 1923 when "heart experts" failed to diagnose the disease in President Warren G. Harding. On a campaign trip south from Alaska the president suffered severe stomach pains, which his ill-trained homeopath and close friend, Dr. Charles Sawyer, blamed on tainted crabmeat. In Seattle the president nearly collapsed from weakness, and on the way to San Francisco the pain persisted, but he stubbornly insisted on walking to his limousine and into a hotel. In the Bay City five physicians, including the president of the American Medical Association and an acclaimed heart consultant, reviewed Harding's recent health history: pain in the chest, radiating down the arms, particularly the left arm; several attacks of indigestion suggestive of gallstones; indigestion most often at night with pain and distress; attacks of dyspnea (difficult breathing) at night; and chronic weakness. They suspected the problem was the gallbladder, but four days later death "came like a thunderbolt," as one of the doctors explained. "All at once he went," wrote another. "Just like that. Something just snapped. That's all." After some debate the physicians announced that the president had died of "apoplexy or a rupture of a blood vessel in the axis of the brain near the respiratory center" (in modern terms a stroke.)[9]

Despite the confusion about coronary disease—even among the nation's foremost medical experts—a quiet revolution in understanding and perception was under way. The first breakthrough came from the insight of a practicing internist in Chicago, Dr. James B. Herrick, who made a startling assumption about the events occurring in the coronary arteries (so named because they compose a crown of vessels sweeping down over the heart). As researchers had done before him, he began by comparing his bedside observations and case histories with autopsy results. From them he discerned a clinical entity in which the total occlusion of a coronary artery by a thrombus (blood clot) led to the failure of the heart muscle nourished by that artery, with symptoms similar to those historically associated with angina. But unlike his predecessors, he reasoned that such occlusions need not be fatal, and that the symptoms and outcome should depend on the size of the vessel occluded, the condition of the heart muscle, and the ability of other "collateral" arteries to maintain an adequate circulation. In 1912 he excitedly published his paper, "Clinical Features of Sudden Obstruction of the Coronary Arteries," in the influential *Journal of the American Medical Association,* where it "fell like a dud."[10]

Herrick's initial failure to gain an audience (later his paper would become a landmark) did not deter him from his missionary work, which was furthered immensely by the advent of a new machine, the electrocardiograph, introduced by a Dutch physician in 1901 and brought to the United States in 1914. The EKG, as it came to be known, provided a record of the electrical currents generated within the heart, with each beat producing waves on the paper designated universally as P, Q, R, S, and T. "The little strips of paper," as one doctor described it, "imprinted by the disease itself, form permanent and unquestionable testimony of events which have occurred." By making an association between a specific lesion in the heart muscle with an inversion of the T wave on the newly available EKG, Herrick was able to diagnose a "coronary thrombosis" during the life of the patient. Others complemented his research and by the early 1930s were able to present a complete electrocardiographic picture of coronary artery disease and, after heated debate, to force the acceptance of a clinical distinction between angina pectoris and coronary thrombosis. The former came to denote those temporary but recurring episodes of pain stemming most often from a reduction of the blood supply to the heart, known as myocardial ischemia; the latter to define the longer-lasting, more intense, and more lethal pain, resulting from a deprivation of blood so acute as to kill a portion of the heart muscle, or myocardial infarction.[11]

Cardiologists during the decade of the Great Depression also were able to reach a consensus regarding the pathology of coronary disease. Early in the lives of most human beings, they came to believe, the walls of the coronary arteries developed atherosclerotic lesions composed of cholesterol. In some these lesions changed into plaques and, as the disease progressed, led to the scarring and even calcification of the arterial wall, converting the vessel into a rigid tube. The process could be diffuse or restricted to a single artery—most dangerously the left anterior descending artery, which feeds the pumping chamber of the heart and came to be known as the "widow-maker"—but in either event it would narrow the caliber of the vessel, thus restricting the flow of blood. In such manner, as the great Osler had suggested some forty years before, the "avenger comes through the arteries." The thickened walls could cause angina pectoris; if they became the site of an acute obstruction because of a thrombus, or clot, they could lead to an infarction—the death of a section of the muscle of the heart. In the worst cases, infarction would give rise to ventricular fibrillation, a rapid, uncoordinated twitching of the heart muscle that almost always ended in sudden death. "The cardiac pump is thrown out of gear," a scientist explained, "and the last of its vital energy is dissipated in the violent and prolonged turmoil of fruitless activity in the ventricular wall."[12]

These new insights into coronary disease had little effect upon laymen, who were still attuned to the view expressed by a Cleveland physician in 1932 that it was a natural part of the aging process, that "deterioration of the arteries appears to be a favorite method of Nature to eliminate us after our biological responsibilities have been fulfilled." The general public remained fatalistic in the face of the increasing number of heart attacks, as did most practitioners, one of whom wrote in 1940: "What can the individual do to prevent his dropping over with heart disease at the most productive period in his life, that is, between forty-five and fifty-five years of age? The answer to this question in the vast majority of cases is—nothing. The signs of this dramatic episode were written, so to speak, on his birth certificate, but like other items in his destiny it was not possible to read it there." The small number of cardiologists, in contrast, were far more optimistic; they no longer considered the disease as a natural accompaniment of old age and no longer looked upon it as necessarily fatal. "We have learned that heart disease is now often reversible," one of them proclaimed excitedly. "This will indeed go down in history as a golden age in cardiology."[13]

There was little time for research on heart disease during World War II, but the conflict actually became a turning point in that it drove coronary disease to the center of the stage. In the narrow sense, cardiologists became aware that the wonder drugs so widely introduced during the war offered a means to control rheumatic fever and thus would put an end to their most dangerous enemy to date, rheumatic heart disease. In the broader view, they recognized that the widespread use of sulfa drugs and penicillin also meant an end to the infectious diseases that had killed so many in the past, and would thereby move the spotlight to the nation's newest challenge, the chronic plagues of cancer and coronary disease. Thus they were in a transitional stage between "infection and infarction," as one of the experts described it, and they had no doubts about making that transition quickly. Indeed, they shared the unprecedented confidence of the American people that they could accomplish anything, a euphoria based upon the spectacular triumphs of wartime science, especially the development of the atomic bomb.[14]

The cardiologists' first postwar response to the new challenge was to reorganize. In 1945 the American Heart Association (AHA) was still an elite club with a very small budget and a limited perspective, whose major function was to conduct an annual scientific meeting and to publish the research-oriented *American Heart Journal*. In 1946, sensitive to the estimate that 658,000 Americans would die from heart disease compared with only 183,000 from cancer, the cardiologists decided to convert their organization into a voluntary public health agency that could make the people "heart-conscious," with a membership that included interested laymen and an agenda that featured a national fund-raising campaign to be used in support of research.[15]

While the cardiologists were launching their private and voluntary crusade against heart disease, a remarkable woman was mobilizing the U.S. government for the same purpose. Mary Woodward Lasker was a successful businesswoman who founded Hollywood Patterns during the Great Depression, as well as the wife of advertising tycoon Albert Lasker, who sold his agency in 1942 for a fortune that allowed them to pursue a mutual interest in health. Certain that heart disease had become the number one killer of her countrymen, Lasker used her friendship with presidential aide Clark Clifford, her access to President Truman, and her influence with Congress to orchestrate the establishment in 1948 of the National Heart Institute.[16]

The testimony before Congress on behalf of the Heart Institute was a firestorm filled with anger, frustration, amazement, and passion. Lasker had prepared and distributed a "fact sheet" that was to dominate the congressional debate (and virtually all other discussions) for years to come. She explained how the American people were "assaulted by killers from within, whose victims from these diseases total twice as many persons each year as were lost by our armed services on all fronts during the last war." General William "Wild Bill" Donovan, the superspy wartime director of the Office of Strategic Services, thought it "incredible that a nation which could spend more than a quarter of a billion dollars a day to fight a military war permits a common enemy within its midst to victimize and murder almost six hundred thousand of its citizens every year." Senator Claude Pepper, a Florida Democrat who considered the enemy "far more dangerous than Hitler ever was, so far as the lives of our people are concerned," demanded action: "Suppose an external enemy were reaching here as a gigantic monster and killing one out of three of our people. We would not be sitting in the Congress debating." Advertising executive Emerson Foote was so excited he could not remain seated; he proclaimed: "I tell you, as the clock on the wall ticks by, people are dying of cardiovascular diseases. These people cannot be saved! . . . Let not that tragedy go on." And Dr. Leonard Scheele, the surgeon general of the United States, agreed, insisting that "the important thing is to hit that problem and hit it fast, because if we wait a year, six hundred thousand people die."[17]

Despite all of the excitement, there were no reliable statistics to determine the number of heart disease deaths caused by coronary thrombosis as opposed to the other forms of the disease. It was not until 1948 that the International Classification of Diseases, Injuries and Causes of Death even included "arteriosclerotic heart disease." Until then most coronary deaths were listed in the published mortality statistics under the vague and meaningless rubric "chronic myocarditis." When experts gathered in 1950 for the First National Conference on Cardiovascular Diseases, they knew almost nothing about coronary disease. They used only 8 pages of their 255-page conference report to review the causes, symptoms, and treatment of the "anginal syndrome" and "cardiac infarction," and stated their belief that "one of the chief scourges of our day" was increasing because of an aging population and better diagnosis. The only evidence they had was anecdotal.[18]

Even the most skilled cardiologists were unable to offer more than a blurred picture of those disease mechanisms. In the two years spanning the midcentury a flourish of important studies appeared—the celebrated fourth edition of Paul Dudley White's *Heart Disease,* a new edition of Samuel Levine's *Clinical Heart Disease,* Ernst and Norman Boas's *Coronary Artery Disease,* and H. M. Marvin's *You and Your Heart*—and all of them appeared mystified about causation. These experts believed that the disease usually affected those over forty years of age and that it most often struck men rather than women, usually men of a "mesomorphic" body type—muscular, stocky and strong. They acknowledged the powerful role of heredity and family history, and they recognized a relationship between hypertension and heart failure, although they could not explain it. They were much less certain about other factors associated at one time or another with the etiology of coronary disease—race, climate, and use of coffee, tea, alcohol, and especially tobacco.[19]

The professionals were likewise uncertain about diet, although it was emerging as the most likely cause. Since the deposits on the lining of the arteries consisted largely of cholesterol, research naturally focused on that firm, yellowish-white substance. As early as 1908 a Russian investigator produced atherosclerosis in rabbits simply by feeding them meat, milk, and egg yolks, and a colleague subsequently achieved the same result by adding pure cholesterol to their food. But most scientists remained skeptical about generalizing from the rabbit to humans, and were unwilling to assume that the same mechanism was at work. They were unsure, as well, about the relationship between the cholesterol produced by the body for essential human needs and that taken from the diet. They acknowledged the important relationship between the serum cholesterol level and atherosclerosis, but they were not prepared to insist on a low-cholesterol diet as a preventive measure, except for those individuals who had the disease. On the other hand, they were intrigued at midcentury by a new discovery, by Dr. John Gofman of the University of California at Berkeley, of some giant molecules that seemed to be responsible for transporting cholesterol to the coronary arteries. A breakthrough seemed imminent.[20]

The authorities were struggling with another explanation that had been in vogue for many decades, namely, that the increasing incidence of heart disease (and many other afflictions as well) was a result of the "stresses of modern living," as a panel discussion of the New York Heart Association described it as late as 1950. During the nineteenth century many believed that disease was endemic in the United States because of the nation's hectic life and culture, and the change and tumult of the twentieth century gave support to this perspective. In 1930 a cardiologist trying to explain the increase in coronary disease found a new factor to be "the mad pace of American life today. . . . The tone, the pitch, the rhythm accompanied by the rapid tempo wears and tears and tugs at that reserve meant to be conserved for those declining years." Twenty years later Dr. Samuel Levine of the Harvard Medical School was asking: "Has there been some specific deleterious influence at work during these past decades, such as the telephone with its terrorizing clang, or the motor car with its noxious fumes, or a dietary defect with an overabundance or lack of some element, or the prevalent habit of smoking? . . . or is it merely the hustle and bustle of the twentieth century?"[21]

Although they remained puzzled about the effect of environmental stress, most cardiologists still gave credence to the argument that coronary disease occurred more often among certain types of individuals, especially the overworked businessmen at the prime of their lives and the top of their careers. The concept of a "coronary type" went back to the English group in the eighteenth century, found enrichment in the writings of Dr. Osler, and fit well with the general belief that many Americans were too hard-driving, ambitious, competitive, rushed, and worried. The stereotype had strongly positive connotations, however, because those men who suffered heart attacks were considered leaders and builders who drove themselves —even sacrificed themselves—to attain success for their families and their nation. Dr. Helen Flanders Dunbar suggested that coronary occlusions came most often to hardworking persons who were "driving themselves without mercy and apparently enjoying it" and who were or would like to be "top dogs in their own worlds." Dr. Paul Dudley White, the most influential cardiologist of his day, even perceived the increasing incidence of heart attacks as "a potent force in retarding the progress of civilization," for "frequently men of great ability and experience, important factors in the life of the country, are dramatically removed from the scene at their prime by death or invalidism."[22]

Whatever its cause, in the public mind by the middle of the century heart disease had come to mean "coronary" disease; the people knew it was on the increase, and it inspired the same sense of fear as it had a hundred years before. "The name 'heart' and 'heart disease' is enough in the daily papers to put the fear of the Lord into anyone who knows the meaning of it," wrote one cardiologist, and the American people did read in the rising number of "coronaries" the shocking truth that no one was immune. "The average man or woman has read or heard so much of sudden death resulting from coronary disease or has had a close relative or friend who has succumbed to this disorder," wrote Boas and Boas, "and he is stricken with terror when he learns that he himself is suffering from the same condition." When the popular author Catherine Marshall learned that her husband was experiencing pains in his chest and arms and would have to leave work, she wrote: "Now with a sickening, deadly persistence, one thought kept recurring. I tried to ignore it but it could not be dismissed. . . . No one of us would voice the thought, but as we waited, watching for the car bringing Peter home, the two words might as well have been written on the wall in neon lights—HEART ATTACK."[23]

Dwight Eisenhower was one American who surprisingly had given little thought to coronary heart disease. On the eve of becoming president, he was exceptionally attentive to his health; he was well aware of the danger of chronic disease; and he fit the portrait of a prospective heart attack patient—a man of great ability and a "top dog" in his own world. But his lifelong concern had been with his stomach and not with his heart.

2

The Man Who Felt Like Tarzan

❖ ❖ ❖ ❖ ❖ ❖ ❖ ❖ ❖ ❖ ❖ ❖ ❖ ❖ ❖

No one could come in contact with Ike without being impressed by all sorts of things—his vitality, that grin, his intelligence, his self-confidence, his knowledge and experience, his love of life and of people, his curiosity, his bearing, among many others—but one attribute stood out above them all. It was the pleasure he took in living.

Surely this author is not alone in thinking that it must have been a wonderful thing to be Dwight Eisenhower.

—*Stephen Ambrose,* Nixon: The Triumph of a Politician, 1962 to 1972

I think an Eisenhower with a terrible bellyache fighting for enough strength to throw out the first pitch of the major [league] baseball season may be a more revealing picture of the man than some of his speeches or his face beaming from a television screen.

—*Merriman Smith,* Meet Mr. Eisenhower

In his 1967 book, *At Ease: Stories I Tell to Friends,* the seventy-seven-year-old Eisenhower reminisced about the "fairly good health" he had enjoyed up until his sixty-fifth birthday. "A good constitution, a gift of my forbears," he wrote, "and a reasonably active outdoor life, a requirement of my profession, combined to give me months on end without the slightest ache or pain." The old soldier's recollection was in accordance with his health history only insofar as he qualified his evaluation with the word "fairly" and because he acknowledged one very important exception: "Stomach aches . . . of sharp intensity were known to me." In fact, even before he entered the White House, the beloved war hero with the sprightly step, the vigor of youth, the easy smile, and the seeming glow of physical well-being, had known and suffered a full measure of illness.[1]

During childhood Dwight Eisenhower contracted the usual diseases such as measles, chicken pox, and mumps; had his tonsils removed; and suffered one serious mishap—a fall that caused an abrasion on his knee and led to a two-week period of "blood poisoning," during which he was delirious and the doctor advised amputation of his leg. This experience became part of the Eisenhower legend, embellished by the various accounts of a fourteen-year-old boy determined to die rather than live as a cripple, a brother sworn to guard him from that fate worse than death, parents praying night and day throughout a period of two weeks, a doctor so frustrated by a family averse to his advice as to mutter the word "murder," and finally, the miraculous recovery. Even without adornment the episode was dramatic and, as Eisenhower's first biographer suggested, reflective of his early and deep attachment to the values of the frontier: "To be a cripple, an object of pity, to be incapable of full participation in life, was worse than death. For on the frontier life was almost wholly physical. On the frontier one could not be truly alive, truly a man, unless he were physically whole, strong, self-reliant."[2]

By his own account sixty-three years later, this childhood experience reflected an even more fundamental truth. "I'd rather be dead than be crippled," Eisenhower recalled having told his brother Ed during his illness, *"and not be able to play ball"* (italics mine). Dwight's daydream of "bathing in glory" was to excel in athletics, to be a sports star. He wrote later about his high school years that it "would be difficult to overemphasize the importance that I attached to participation in sports" and that he "could not imagine an existence" in which he was not playing either baseball or football, or both. His teenager's dream was not unusual, for he came of age at a time when Americans had placed a special focus on fitness and had determined that exercise and sport were essential activities for the middle-class male. Theodore Roosevelt practiced the "strenuous life" as a way to revitalize the individual and the nation, and Bernarr Macfadden sold "physical culture" as the means to purify the body and the mind. These and other heroes pointed the way to health and success—through the foremost national games of baseball, football, and boxing, or through such personal efforts as gymnastics, calisthenics, and exercise with dumbbells.[3]

The difference between Eisenhower and most of his fellow Americans—and his biographers have failed to stress this sufficiently—was that to a large extent he fulfilled his dream and *became* an exceptional athlete and, by virtue of that, a special kind of man. At Abilene High School he was a good lineman in football, a good outfielder in baseball, and outstanding as a boxer, the latter of which made him a town hero as the result of a courageous fight with a larger, stronger, and faster opponent. After graduation he worked at building his strength, choosing the most physically demanding work at the local creamery and continuing to play baseball, but when he appeared for entry into West Point at the age of twenty-one, he was still small for an athlete—five feet, eleven inches tall, weighing 152 pounds.

His physical endeavors at West Point provided the final sculpting of a body image—the mental picture of one's appearance that changes and evolves from childhood on—that approached the ideal "body beautiful" within the masculine society of his time. He worked hard on the track to build up his legs, developed a gymnastics regimen to develop his arms and shoulders, grew thicker in the chest, gained twenty-four pounds, and emerged with the physique of the robust and muscular mesomorph. He was as strong as any of his fellow cadets and in his second year developed into an excellent running back on the football team. After a game against Rutgers the *New York Times* called him "one of the most promising backs"; after he played Colgate the *New York Herald Tribune* wrote that the "work of Eisenhower brought joy to the army rooters"; and against Carlisle he played well against the legendary Jim Thorpe, after which the *New York Sun* named him a "rattling good back."[4]

On 16 November 1912 Eisenhower sprained a knee in a game against Tufts and his football career was over. The injury caused a deep depression and a sense of shame for a time. "I was like a man with his nose cut off going out into society," he explained. The misfortune also put an end forever to the joy he derived from the rugged sports—the "small-town baseball" and "big league football," as he described it, and the boxing, which had enabled him to "lick" any of his peers in Abilene. But it did not alter his perception of himself as an athlete; he had advanced in sports far beyond his expectations, and he would always walk as a man among men. Nor did it adversely affect his body image or the confidence that devolved from it. For the rest of his life he tried to keep his weight at his West Point optimum of 172, and he continued to build his body through calisthenics, through work in gymnastics, where he learned to chin himself five times with his right hand alone and three times with his left, and through par-

Captain Dwight Eisenhower at Camp Meade, Maryland, Tank Center in 1919.
(Courtesy Dwight D. Eisenhower Library: U.S. Army photograph)

ticipation in less physical sports, especially golf. His physical strength and athletic demeanor remained apparent to everyone. When Mamie met him in 1915 she described him as a well-built "bruiser"; in 1918 a young soldier praised him to his mother as "a giant for build" who at West Point was "a noted football player and physical culture fiend"; in 1926 George S. Patton called him a "*he*-man"; and thirty years later Richard Nixon considered him "a superb specimen of a man who believed in keeping himself phys- ically fit."[5]

Eisenhower's athletic prowess was a matter not only of exceptional physical endowment but also of will. "I believe that football, perhaps more than any other sport," he wrote, "tends to instill in men the feeling that victory comes through hard—almost slavish—work, team play, self- confidence, and an enthusiasm that amounts to dedication." On another occasion he compared football to war, noting that both required "guts, brains, physical power, skilled teamwork, and heart." All of these were attributes he had displayed in full, and that knowledge gave him a self- pride that would last a lifetime. He had honored one of the foremost precepts of his generation—that an individual is responsible for his own condition, or, in the words of Bernarr Macfadden, "It lies with you, whether you shall be a strong virile animal . . . or a miserable little crawling worm."[6]

There was a correlative maxim that Eisenhower took from the early twentieth-century American culture—that a strong body is an avenue to good health and that a man has only himself to blame if disease or sickness strikes him down. For the most part he had no reason to question the verity of this proposition, but his faith was tested over time by recurring episodes of gastrointestinal discomfort and disability. They apparently began at West Point, causing two brief periods of hospitalization, and became more serious during his residency in the Panama Canal Zone between 1922 and 1924, with bouts of crampy abdominal pain associated with loose, watery stools and a weight loss of fifteen pounds. The young captain's symptoms suggested "tropical dysentery," a complaint familiar to the area, but he made a self-diagnosis and decided that the "culprit" was his appendix, which he arranged to have removed when he made a trip to Denver in 1923 to be present for the birth of his second son. "Whether they agreed with me or not," he explained many years later, "the doctors were cooper- ative. They removed my appendix, possibly on the theory that no harm would be done, that it would shut me up, and if a cure was not effective, I might be more hesitant in the future about invading their field. The cure did not take. Three decades would pass before I would learn the cause of my repeated distress, when doctors described it as a 'young man's disease,' ileitis."[7]

During those three decades abdominal upsets periodically tormented Eisenhower. His official medical files portray a history of pain, distress, and anxiety, and because a career officer would be reluctant to voluntarily create a record of chronic health problems, they almost certainly understate the extent of his suffering. In 1927, while he was in Washington writing a guidebook to the American battlefields in Europe under General John J. "Black Jack" Pershing, he appeared at the general dispensary for an evaluation that covered two weeks, with the resulting entries: "Uncomfortable feeling in the right upper quadrant of the abdomen for the past two weeks. Slight nausea associated. . . . Improved, but not entirely free from pain. . . . The gallbladder is normal in size and position but is sluggish in its emptying." In 1928 he was spending a relaxed year at the Army War College, with plenty of time for golf and friends, but he still worried about his health. During his annual physical examination, an outstanding army internist, Dr. George Beach, searched for intestinal parasites and for the possibility of an amoebic or bacillary dysentery. After performing a barium enema study of the colon, he had to settle for an observation of "diseases of the rectum and colon." The following year, when the thirty-nine-year-old major was in France to revise his guidebook for the American Battle Monuments Commission, he had to check into the American Hospital in Paris because of continued periods of abdominal discomfort and loose bowels. Again the physicians found no meaningful evidence, but they did treat him for amoebic dysentery.[8]

Back in Washington, where Eisenhower was extraordinarily busy and under stress with an assignment to the office of the assistant secretary of war, his symptoms returned and persisted for several years. The records for 1931 report: "For some time he has had sudden cramps, then followed by an intense desire to defecate." The following year—after hospital visits in April, July, August, and November—brought similar entries: "Long history of GI symptoms of an indefinite nature. He has mild cancer phobia. The complaint runs through his records. He has had complete gastrointestinal studies where all studies were reported negative except a delay in emptying of the gallbladder. A week ago he had a pain in the epigastrium. . . . Same pains. Consider a neurotic element. Thinks he has something wrong with his bowels." For Ike the stomach problems, together with a newly developed stiffness in his back, were more than an irritation. He was fearful that the army might retire him at an early age.[9]

Eisenhower, at a loss to explain his abdominal ailments, wrote in his diary, "Lots of troubles with my insides lately. Have been bothered five to six years with something that seems to border on dysentery. Doctors have come to the conclusion that it is a result of nervousness, lack of exercise, etc. Am taking some medicine at the moment that for a day or so seemed to be exactly right—but now am apparently no different from usual." At another time he noted, "Doctors report after long ex-ray [*sic*] exam, that they can find nothing wrong with my insides." He was correct. In 1934, when Eisenhower entered Walter Reed General Hospital for a survey to find the cause of his stomach and back ailments, the admitting officer summarized: "Since 1926, has had loose stools, three to five daily, without an acute diarrhea and no mucus or blood, no epigastric distress. Has noticed that sudden desire to defecate follows nervous tension. No known idiosyncrasies." Even after X-ray studies and gastric analyses, the experts could find no cause for his problems.[10]

In October 1935 Eisenhower sailed aboard the SS *President Harding* for the Philippines, where he would spend four years working under Douglas MacArthur, among other things trying to prepare a seemingly impossible plan for the defense of the islands. In March 1937 he was in the hospital at Camp John Hays for six days with a discharge diagnosis of "enteritis, acute, cause undetermined." The following year he spent five days in Sternberg General Hospital in Manila for what he called a "strange intestinal ailment," with an exit diagnosis of "constipation, acute, cause undetermined." His memory of the hospitalization, offered some twenty years later, was far more vivid. He went to the hospital with an extremely painful abdomen distended like "a dying frog," he recalled; after losing consciousness, he awoke on an operating table, where doctors, having diagnosed a "stoppage of the bowels," were about to place an ether cone on his nose. At that point, suffering "the tortures of the damned," he said he would like to go to the toilet, and the physicians, happily surprised, let him try. He was able to expel gas and gain some relief, and after spending a further embarrassing period of time with a nurse standing at his bedside listening for the passage of flatus, and hearing it, the doctors folded their towels and decided that no operation was necessary.[11]

The doctors suspected nervousness and lack of exercise were somehow associated with Eisenhower's problems; he wondered about hard work and ambition. "The other day I read a comment by an eminent Chinese educator," he wrote in 1937. "He said that the Oriental is satisfied with things that are good, but that the American is always striving for the best with resultant bad effects upon his blood pressure, happiness and longevity." Neither explanation was a good portent, for the years following Eisenhower's return to the United States were the most stressful and busy of his life. In 1940, while serving as chief of staff of the Third Division at Fort Lewis, Washington, he had an attack of shingles, the only one he ever had. "The doctors thought it serious enough to recommend hospitalization," he recalled. "I managed to dodge, for I was less miserable when I had something to occupy my mind. But straight thinking, in the midst of physical pain and a disturbing query, was a little difficult." Thereafter he moved on to a series of "backbreaking" jobs, in which he was so busy as to complain in 1944, "I seem to live on a network of high tension wires."[12]

The war taught Eisenhower early, as he put it, that a commander must have "an inexhaustible fund of nervous energy." He "runs into strange personalities, weird ideas, glory-seeking, enemy reaction, and all the other incidents of war." He has to "wheedle, demand, cajole, order, follow up, inspect, urge, listen, and talk." You can well imagine, he explained to Mamie, "the pounding that one must take in a position like this; the worries, fears, doubts—sometimes the hysteria of subordinates all sifts up to the 'Old Man'—and I've got to find some way of bolstering courage and speeding effort." Toward the end of the war his nervous tension and exhaustion were evident to everyone around him. General Walter "Beetle" Smith at one time told him, "Look at you. You've got bags under your eyes. Your blood pressure is higher than it's ever been, and you can hardly walk across the room." And his driver, Kay Summersby, commented, "The general's physical and mental condition was worse than we had ever known it. . . . Beetle was positive that he was on the verge of a nervous breakdown."[13]

The official army doctrine, to which Eisenhower claimed to subscribe, was that when commanders faced endless pressures, they had to tend to their health. Just before Christmas of 1942, he came to the "dismaying realization that there are certain limits of physical stamina that cannot safely be exceeded." Until that time he had been somewhat arrogant, feeling that he could "lick Tarzan," for as he explained in his memoirs of the war: "I inherited a hardy constitution from sturdy forebears and, heretofore always careful of health requisites, I had come to believe myself immune from the fatigues and exhaustions that I frequently observed in others. Long hours and incessant work were easily enough sustained, I thought, so long as one refused to fall victim to useless worry or to waste his strength in any kind of excess." But the long hours of work with little sleep led to "an unaccustomed nervousness" and "a deterioration in vigor" that he could not overcome, and on Christmas Day he contracted a severe case of flu, serious enough for the doctors eventually to put him to bed. "For four days they would not let me move," he recalled, "and during that time I not only recovered my health, I learned a lesson I did not thereafter violate: a full measure of health is basic to successful command. I did not have another sick day—aside from minor accidents—during the war."[14]

The truth was actually different in two important respects. For one, he violated the lesson almost from the time he learned it by failing to tend to his health. He took almost no time for exercise, he ate too many starchy foods and gained weight, he smoked too much, and he drove himself too hard. General George C. Marshall, who tried to get him to arrange for regular exercise and "to do things that relax his mind and body," eventually ordered him to Washington for a furlough. For the most part, however, Ike did what he believed he had to do, and with confidence in his health. "I think my greatest asset these days," he told Mamie, "is a strong basic constitution. I cannot remember when I've had any exercise—and I continue to be plagued with a half cold (or too much smoking), but I seem to stand up pretty well."[15]

The supreme commander also was ill much more often than he admitted in his memoirs, mostly with a cold, the flu, a sore throat, or a recurrence of his shoulder and knee problems. In the summer of 1943 he also had to spend several days in bed when, on the occasion of a physical examination for promotion, the dispensary physician ordered him to his quarters because of hypertension. There are no military medical records referring to gastrointestinal problems during the wartime period, but the symptoms certainly persisted to some extent. In the fall of 1942 Ike complained of being "dizzy in the head and weak in the stomach," and attributed it to a long trip to Scotland. In the summer of 1943 he had something that he wrote "is variously known here as Mediterranean tummy, Algerian pip and African trots," and which he believed everyone had periodically. The doctors were more concerned and ordered him to bed for three days for a rest, after which he complained, "Recently I had two or three days of the doctors hounding me for a bad intestinal upset, but I am feeling fine again." In January 1944 he apparently had a more serious episode, for as he mentioned to Mamie, "I'm having a flare-up with my insides, accompanied by some shooting pains! I *think* it's just the old trouble, but at times it's worrisome." His stomach troubles were probably more frequent than his informal comments indicate, for nearly everyone close to him knew about them. When Richard Nixon was traveling in Australia in 1953, he met Field Marshal William Slim, who had served with Eisenhower during the war. "How's Ike?" Slim asked, and then continued, "How's his tummy? Ike always used to have trouble with his tummy."[16]

Even while Eisenhower found it impossible to tend to his health in a meaningful way, he still worried, especially about the lack of exercise, about getting fat, and about aging too fast. "I must begin to get a little bit of exercise daily," he told his son, "or I'm going to suffer for it. Long and confining hours, seven days a week . . . finally produce a load that can be carried only if a man keeps in fine physical shape." He sometimes joked with Mamie about pressure causing him to grow old faster, fearing that "at this rate I'll be something like the equivalent of ninety-two when I get back to the U.S. Maybe you'll have to meet me at the pier with crutches—or a litter." More seriously, he explained, "The eternal pound, pound, pound seems a burden, but when it once ceases it is possible that many of us will be nigh onto nervous wrecks, and wholly unfit for normal life." And he told his wife to "be sure you're in blooming health when I come home. You'll have the job of nursing me back to health."[17]

Eisenhower's hectic pace of activities diminished only slightly upon his return from Europe on 11 November 1945, for he had agreed to serve as army chief of staff at the worst of all possible times. In the troublesome months ahead he was unhappy with a president and a Congress hell-bent on demobilization; he was angry at military leaders engaged in acrimonious rivalry; and he could not win on issues important to him, such as universal military training. He also had very little time for relaxation, as the American people flooded him with invitations for speeches and politicians flattered him with prospects for the presidency. "Each day brings a succession of troubling and worrisome problems," he complained to a friend after less than a year in Washington.

There never seems to be a piece of good news. Such of these matters as are inescapable and inherent in current chaotic conditions, I can take in my stride. When they result from stupidity or negligence or complete lack of cooperation on the part of some of the other people with whom we have to deal, my patience and temper both give out. I will be more than delighted when the time comes that I can retire to a cabin somewhere and take it easy and let others worry about budgets and all the other things that are constantly on my desk.[18]

During these early postwar years Eisenhower became far more conscious than ever before about his and his wife's health. As for himself, he believed that the war years "may have taken a much greater toll out of me than even I suspected." As for Mamie, he was so concerned that soon after victory in Europe he made a special request to General Marshall to let her join him in England—citing "trouble with her general nervous system for many years"—a request denied by President Truman on grounds of equity. Mamie had valvular heart disease with involvement of the mitral and aortic valves, apparently the result of rheumatic fever during childhood, a condition that caused chronic fatigue, especially noticeable after 1942. In addition, she was not sleeping well because of "horrid" dreams and nightmares, experienced some palpitations during which her heart would beat like a "trip hammer," and had occasional shortness of breath and a persistent cold. Shortly after Ike's return to the United States, on the occasion of the couple's trip to her birthplace in Boone, Iowa, she came down with an acute case of bronchopneumonia, and had to spend two weeks in the local hospital.[19]

During Mamie's illness Eisenhower met Major General Howard McCrum Snyder, who became the most important physician in his life. Snyder had treated Mrs. Eisenhower on numerous occasions during the war at the request of General Marshall, and when she fell ill in Iowa, Eisenhower called him for help. Snyder rushed to Boone, and after assuring himself that Mamie was in good hands, he accompanied Ike to Chicago for a speaking engagement, where the general developed "speaker's throat." The doctor went on to Washington, where Eisenhower testified before a congressional committee despite a severe sinus infection. Snyder arranged on 22 November 1945 for his new patient to enter Ashford General Hospital in White Sulphur Springs, West Virginia, where he spent ten days recovering from an acute case of bronchitis that verged on pneumonia. Eisenhower left the hospital to become chief of staff. One of his first decisions was to ask General Snyder to join his small advisory group, where his foremost responsibility would be to tend to his and Mamie's health.[20]

Snyder was born in 1881 in Cheyenne, Wyoming, the son of a pioneer family. He left home at the age of eighteen to attend the University of Colorado. From there he went to Jefferson Medical College in Philadelphia, and after an internship at the city's Presbyterian Hospital, he served as a contract surgeon at Fort Douglas, Utah. His experience was so favorable that he decided on a future in military medicine and accepted a commission as a first lieutenant in the Army Medical Corps. Apart from assignments in Puerto Rico and the Philippines, he spent most of his career in the United States, although he did travel extensively during World War II as assistant inspector general for the War Department. In 1945 Snyder had just reached retirement age and was looking forward to a promising financial opportunity as a civilian. Instead, he accepted Eisenhower's offer. That decision led to a relationship—as doctor and friend—that lasted for more than twenty years. In 1948 Snyder resigned from the army to accept an appointment and join Ike at Columbia University; three years later he returned to active duty with an assignment to join the general at Supreme Headquarters of the Allied Powers in Europe (SHAPE); and in 1953 he became physician to the president, a position he held until 1961.[21]

When Eisenhower hired Snyder he was doubtless thinking primarily about Mamie's problems, but very soon his own health became a matter of the doctor's intense scrutiny, and it remained so ever after. In January 1946, even before Snyder had a chance to familiarize himself with his patient's medical history, he had occasion to observe an episode of gastrointestinal pain:

The first attack I witnessed began early one morning shortly after the Eisenhowers had taken residence at Fort Myer. The symptoms were nausea and slight vomiting, colicky pain and moderate distention of the abdomen. The pain was generalized but not severe. There was tenderness in the lower right quadrant near the midline, but not rebound tenderness. I did not think this attack was unusual because I had been with the general at a dinner gathering the preceding evening. He had indulged very heartily in a Mexican dinner prepared at the home of one of his friends. I felt certain that had I indulged as heartily as he did, I would have suffered a like aftermath. Neither the general nor Mamie made any reference to the fact that abdominal disturbances

The army chief of staff relaxing in Hawaii in 1946.
(Courtesy Dwight D. Eisenhower Library)

of this nature had been experienced by the general upon frequent occasions over an extended number of years.[22]

In the following months Snyder made a study of his patient's medical history and found nothing disturbing in the family background. Eisenhower's father died at eighty, presumably having had arteriosclerosis for some time prior to his death, and his mother died suddenly at eighty-four from an unknown cause. Old medical records gave evidence of the knee problem, a chronic painful condition in his left shoulder, a recurrent ringing in the left ear, and a tendency toward high blood pressure. The latter was troublesome enough that a urological consultant tried to "increase the arterial tone" by administering testosterone during the latter part of the war. Snyder also studied the general's personality: "I attempted to learn by osmosis all that I could about his characteristics," he recalled, and one lesson came quickly—"that although his emotional control was excellent, it was well to keep out of his way when he was angered." The Eisenhower temper was always a shock to initiates, and Snyder happened to be present during the first postwar meeting between Ike and Mamie, at which time he experienced the rising voice, the reddened face, and the protruding blood vessels across the temple. He immediately feared an "intracranial" accident, his term for a stroke, and such a possibility continued to be a source of silent anxiety for him.[23]

None of these problems was of as much immediate concern to the physician, however, as the pattern of alarming abdominal disturbances, another of which occurred in August 1946 shortly after Eisenhower arrived home from a trip to Latin America. "I was so worn out on my return," the general wrote, "that upon being overtaken by a slight attack of indigestion, I developed an illness that lasted for twenty-four hours, which was one of the most distressing things I have ever gone through." The first symptom was pain in the lower abdomen, beginning shortly after midnight, for which Mamie gave him a small dose of milk of magnesia because such treatment had, in years past, often relieved abdominal distress. This time it did not, and the pain was accompanied by an accumulation of gas and distention of the abdomen, which persisted for hours without relief. Mamie called Dr. Snyder, who, Ike explained, "stayed with me constantly, and so far as I know, tried everything on me except the atomic bomb." The doctor was able to relieve the distress after about five hours, and thereafter, the patient remembered, "My recovery was about as quick as was my contraction of the trouble, and while I was left weak, I could still come to the office and go to work."[24]

In the late summer and early autumn of 1946 Eisenhower also had a nagging case of bronchitis, a bothersome ringing in his left ear, and, worst of all, a recurrence of bursitis in his left shoulder, which was so painful that if he wished to lift the telephone to his left ear, he had to use his right hand to raise the sleeve of his jacket. His various problems put him in Walter Reed General Hospital in October for a thorough physical examination. The neurologists and orthopedic specialists concluded that he was suffering from rheumatoid arthritis, which, because of his age, was slow in progress and warranted a course of medical treatment involving injections of vitamin A. The internists were less successful regarding his gastrointestinal system; they were unable to identify a cause for the symptoms he had put up with for so many years, even after an evaluation of the gallbladder, an upper gastrointestinal series, a barium enema, a proctoscopy, and laboratory studies for bacteria and amoebas. Snyder was especially anxious about the collective inability to discover the source of the problem and felt that only his own opportunity to travel kept him from going "nuts" thinking about it.[25]

During the last two months of 1946 the general's arthritic complication and bursitis worsened, to the point that, as he put it, the "constant pain and nagging aches get me a bit upset and irritable and I suppose it is high time I let the doctors have a field day with me." It would be the first extended period of rest from his military work since 1935, so he decided to seek a hospital equipped to provide a combination of rest and outdoor recreation with therapy and treatment. He found such a place in Coral Gables, Florida, where during the war the army had converted the old Biltmore Hotel into Pratt General Hospital. He remained there between 8 December and 12 January for the purpose, as he expressed to various friends, of giving the doctors "a full four weeks shot at me"; letting the doctors see if "they can find the source of infection inside me"; and giving them about a month "to straighten out something cock-eyed about my blood." The doctors kept Eisenhower's work to a bare minimum, but they failed again to find any answers to his arthritic and gastrointestinal problems, even though the relaxation and exercise—fishing and golfing, especially—were beneficial. After only a week, an aide noted that he "looks rested, is clear-eyed and tanned, and if the treatment prescribed for his bursitis proves successful, we can say—'Mission Accomplished.'" After his return to Washington, Ike wrote to a friend: "It was difficult for me to understand that I had a whole month in which to do as I please, subject only to minor interruptions. I came back much improved in health."[26]

Even though the five weeks in Coral Gables represented Eisenhower's first extended break from his military activities since 1935, he was sensitive about the potentially adverse implications of his hospitalization. He asked friends to keep the matter "sub rosa" because people and "publicity hounds" immediately "jump to the conclusion that I am on the edge of a collapse." He took great care to keep his secret; in one instance, after preparing a telegram to some old friends in which he spelled out his plans, he changed his mind and decided to inform them by an airmail, special delivery letter, in order to maintain the confidential nature of the contents. The official hospital press release also was careful to mention bursitis as the reason for the stay, and to place emphasis on the rest instead of the therapy. Although Ike's plans for the future were nebulous at this point in time, he clearly was thinking of future opportunities, perhaps even the presidency. His experience in the army had taught him that ill health could foreclose a career, so he chose to ensure that information about his problems would not close off any of his opportunities.[27]

The general's optimism after leaving the hospital was tested only a week later, on the early morning of 21 January 1947, when he left his car for his office and felt wobbly, as if he might fall. He walked with difficulty to the elevator and had to support himself against its side to keep from collapsing. On reaching his office the vertigo continued; he could not look continuously at the papers on his desk but could relieve the dizziness temporarily by supporting his head on his hands or by leaning far back in his chair with his head extended. He summoned Dr. Snyder and left at 9:45 A.M. for Walter Reed General Hospital, where he spent the night. Snyder thought immediately about the possibility of a stroke, but after an EKG, X-rays, and other tests the experts decided he had experienced a mild case of Ménière's disease, a syndrome characterized by ringing in the ears, dizziness, and nausea. Snyder was not satisfied with the diagnosis, and two days later, when Eisenhower was in New York City to address the American Heart Association, he arranged for an unpublicized consultation with Dr. David Barr, physician in chief of New York Hospital and professor of medicine at Cornell University Medical College. It was Ike's first time in a civilian medical center, and he found it "most interesting."[28]

Dr. Barr studied the clinical records Snyder had assembled over the past fifteen months, examined the patient, and found no physical defects of serious significance. He attributed the recent attack of giddiness to toxic or functional causes rather than any significant organic disease, and he proposed a series of leukocyte counts and stool examinations to be taken over the next several months. Overall he judged the general to be in "unusually good physical condition," but he was concerned about his daily lifestyle and the arduous duties and constant demands upon his time and energy. He emphasized such in a letter to Snyder: "Perhaps it would be well also to suggest to him that he restrict considerably his use of cigarettes. Certainly a man of his temperament will be sounder if he can each day obtain some exercise. In the long run, it is important that he cut down on unnecessary activities and that he protect himself more than he has in the past."[29]

After the examinations by eminent experts on three different occasions, Snyder was content that he had not overlooked anything serious, but he still worried about the general's intestinal problems. He was no stranger to this type of affliction, having begun his inquiry into dysentery and other tropical diseases early in the century as a member of the Tropical Medical Board in the Philippines, and his search for the causes of inflammation, pain, soreness, and tenderness in the abdomen had covered forty years. He considered himself an expert in palpating and percussing the abdomen, but he had never confronted a case like Eisenhower's, and the mystery continued to perplex him.[30]

Snyder was very pleased, nevertheless, that "the press had not picked up a whisper regarding the abdominal disturbances." In fact, an article in the *New York Herald Tribune* in February 1947 proclaimed "Ike's Golf and Health Both Good." Citing "medical advisors to the five-star general," which could only mean Snyder, the story attributed the first of Eisenhower's three physical examinations during the last few months to bursitis, "a not serious but nevertheless irritating condition"; the second to a "toxic upset or stomach ache"; and the third "just to be sure the other two were correct." All of the doctors agreed that "Ike is in first-class physical condition for a man of his age," the newspaper reported, but what it did not mention was that one of them, Dr. Snyder, was already at home in his role as assistant manager of the general's "good health" image.[31]

The chief of staff did feel well for some time, but another episode of acute abdominal distress struck him in September 1947. He was on a fishing trip with friends in Savannah, Georgia, and after a large meal of fried chicken he experienced nausea, vomiting, and diarrhea of a prolonged and exhausting nature. A private physician, an acquaintance of his friends, attended him during the night and administered hypodermic medication that ended the symptoms within twenty-four hours. He remained weak, anorexic, and prostrated for two or three days thereafter. Seven weeks later he entered Walter Reed for a six-day annual checkup, and because of his three acute abdominal disturbances within two years, the physicians made an extensive gastrointestinal survey, making use of every special test available. They still found no abnormalities and offered no explanations. "My stay in Walter Reed was for check-up purposes and so far as I know I came off with a very good verdict," he explained to General Smith. "My 'ringing' ear bothers the doctors a lot and of course my tendency to run up a bit of blood pressure when I get angry or irritated causes them to shake their heads. Aside from these things they seem to think that for an old fellow I am plugging along pretty well."[32]

The spate of medical problems while he was chief of staff had their effect on Eisenhower. He knew that he could no longer keep up the pace he had followed during the war and noted when he entered Pratt General Hospital that it was "to correct things I have done to myself by reason of high-pressure activity over a number of years." He settled on a new approach, which he explained to his brother: "Activity must be paced to the capacity of the physical machine to support it." And his intent when he left the army, he wrote to his father-in-law, was to not undertake any activity or employment that would keep him "confined to a desk and working under high pressure," lest it be "detrimental" to his health.[33]

Snyder was prepared after two years of close observation to give advice to his patient. In the broad sense, he considered Ike an "active, vital, dynamically functioning individual" who rarely seemed fatigued, and who had an excellent appetite and great reserve ability. "He recovered from all illness rapidly and he really recovered," the doctor remembered, "snapped back without any evidence of harboring a disability." Snyder was also optimistic because his patient appeared to have a very healthy heart. Eisenhower's first EKG in November 1945 was normal, as were those taken in June and December 1946 and November 1947. At both Pratt General Hospital and Walter Reed the experts put him through complete cardiovascular examinations, including fluoroscopic studies and EKGs taken after exercise on the Master's Two-Step Test (one of the first stress tests), with completely positive results. At Walter Reed in November 1947, Colonel James Taylor, chief of cardiology, detected a rather rapid pulse rate but found no symptoms of coronary or myocardial insufficiency. He did suggest a decrease in cigarette smoking but otherwise concluded: "Cardiac examination this date reveals a well developed and nourished white male, approximately fifty-seven years of age, with no external evidence of cardiac disease."[34]

The cardiologists saw no problems, but Howard Snyder still worried about his patient's temperament. Those who worked closely with Dwight Eisenhower shared a knowledge that would have surprised the American people—the "man with the glowing smile had a thunderous temper." Ike suspected that he might have taken it from the awesome temper of his Pennsylvania Dutch father; in whatever event, he displayed it at an early age. If things failed to go his way when he was a child, he would bloody his head or beat his fists against a tree. He remembered a Halloween when his parents would not allow him to go trick-or-treating and he ended up in the stump of an apple tree. "For some reason I guess I thought the apple tree was to blame," he explained, "and I was there crying as hard as I could, beating the apple tree with my fists." On another occasion he "flared up in sudden violent anger" over an incident with his brother, and before he could gain control of himself he seized a brick and threw it violently at Arthur.[35]

Ike listened to his mother's moral precept that "he who conquers his temper is greater than he who taketh a city," but he never was able to live up to it. When he was in Panama learning to play tennis at General Fox Connor's private court, he was not able to master the game; Mamie noted that "when he found he could not control his tennis strokes he used to beat his head literally against the wall." In the Philippines General MacArthur had an angry dispute with his subordinate, after which he said, "Ike, it's just fun to see that damn Dutch temper. It's just fun to see that Dutch temper take you over." And John Eisenhower supposed that his father's reluctance to lay a hand on him as a boy "stemmed from a fear that, strong as he was, he might inflict serious bodily harm when his temper was aroused."[36]

In the spring of 1942 Eisenhower confided to his diary, "Yesterday I got very angry and filled a page with language that this morning I've 'expurgated.'" His emotion turned his mind to General Marshall's temper, which was often fired in the face of stupidity, but which was also fleeting. "At least he doesn't get angry in the sense I do—I blaze for an hour," Ike wrote. By that time he had also arrived at an insight: "Anger cannot win, it cannot even think clearly. . . . So for many years I've made it a religion never to indulge myself, but yesterday I failed." It was not his final failure, as he admitted six months later in a letter to Mamie: "I'm so d—— mad today that I shouldn't write to you; but it occurred to me that the scribbling of a note might reduce the heat of anger and get me on an even keel again."[37]

In fact, the tensions of the war served as a red flag for the "terrible-tempered Mr. Bang," as one journalist described him. Ike mused in the middle of the war, "As I grow older I think I indulge my irritations and occasional fits of temper more than I should," but he thought he was doing a good job of controlling them. Those in close proximity would have wondered. Omar Bradley noted at a dinner one night "another aspect of Ike new to me: a deep-seated, barely controlled anger. The public perceived him as smiling and genial. But I saw that he had very thin skin, a short fuse and an explosive temper." Kay Summersby catalogued various occasions of his anger and temper in her postwar memoir: his "rare temper flared only when the coffee was cold"; he "blew up one day when I mentioned to a press correspondent . . . that the general smoked a certain brand of cigarette"; "Butch told me that the general raked him over a thousand hot coals" and that another similar occasion "might blast the earth right out from under his very feet"; the "Eisenhower temper really came to a boil"; he "erupted into the granddaddy of all tempers"; and "he has a temper which should be accompanied by red hair and an Irish or Italian ancestry."[38]

During the first eighteen months after the war, when relations between Ike and Mamie were strained because of rumors about an alleged wartime affair with Kay Summersby, Snyder took note of several of the general's "anger explosions" with the "twisted cord-like temple arteries standing out on the side of his head." The doctor had observed that even when Ike tended to suppress his anger, it was "at the expense of his blood pressure." He remained fearful, especially of a cerebral accident, as when his patient had his siege of vertigo. "I thought immediately that he might have had a vasospasm of the middle cerebral artery," Snyder recalled. "I didn't feel it wise to quiz him as to whether or not there had been any upsetting incident immediately before he left the house. Had I referred to it, it might have exaggerated the reaction had that been the cause." But there was nothing in the physical examinations to support his worries. The general's blood pressure since 1922 had ranged from slightly elevated to high normal, even though his staff during the war had often referred to his "high blood pressure," especially following times of anger. Snyder obtained numerous readings and evaluations, and the specialists determined that although Eisenhower had shown a long history of labile blood pressure, manifest at times of stress, there was no persistent arterial hypertension.[39]

Snyder concluded from his observation of Eisenhower's personality that what he needed basically to stay well was careful attention to his diet, regular exercise such as golf, and frequent relaxation to lower pressure and stress. He understandably continued to worry every day about the source of the abdominal problems, wondering if there was some condition causing a temporary paralysis or obstruction in the intestinal tract. His concern in that regard was soon justified, for 1949 brought an alarming attack marked by a week of severe illness, a total of seven weeks and two days away from the office, a "hush-hush" hospitalization, and rumors that the general's problem was not with his stomach but with his heart.

On 7 February 1948 Eisenhower left the army, looking forward to a retirement both pleasant and profitable. He stayed on for several months at Fort Myer to write his memoirs, which netted him over half a million dollars, and took a month's vacation at the Augusta National Golf Club. Then he moved in June to New York City to become president of Columbia University, where a condition of his employment was more time for leisure and recreation than in the past. He was able to adjust to his new position, but he could not escape his old frustrations. As a five-star general he was, by law, on active duty for life, and he gave in to President Truman's request to serve as a consultant to James Forrestal, the secretary of defense, and as the informal chairman of the Joint Chiefs of Staff. Thus the early months of 1949 were anxious ones, as he had to depart almost every week from the relaxed atmosphere of Morningside Heights to the contentious halls of the Pentagon.[40]

Forrestal was trying—without much success—to unite the military services as required by the National Defense Act of 1947, and Eisenhower found the quarreling among the admirals and generals increasingly troubling. He felt pressure from the president and the secretary, who, he believed, "apparently assume that I have some miraculous power to make some of these warring elements lie down in peace together." In one of the rare instances in his lifetime, he was unable to make any significant difference. "I am so weary of this interservice struggle for position, prestige and power that this morning I practically 'blew my top,'" he wrote on 14 March. "I would hate to have my doctor take my blood pressure at the moment." Five days later he noted in his diary that the "situation grows intolerable."[41]

Then on the afternoon of 21 March, in the midst of two days of conferences on defense, he became ill with a stomach disorder. The press gave few details about the illness. On 26 March the *New York Herald Tribune* and the *New York Times* carried short columns, based upon an official Defense Department release, about Eisenhower being sick during the week with what his physician diagnosed as "a severe case of acute gastroenteritis." He had reportedly canceled all official and social engagements and would leave Washington within a few days for "a complete rest." Three days later the *Times* noted that Eisenhower was going to Florida "to recuperate from an illness which has confined him for the last week," defined by Dr. Snyder as "an inflammation of the stomach." He climbed without assistance aboard President Truman's private plane, but newsmen thought he looked pale and weak and asked him about it. "I'm not as puny as I look," he replied, and he told them that after a rest he planned to call the Joint Chiefs of Staff together for a conference. Brief reports out of Key West over the next several days said that Ike was tired from the plane trip and was resting comfortably indoors; they quoted Dr. Snyder's opinion that the "general is picking up. When he came here he was a very sick man." On 31 March the *New York Times* announced that he was well enough to practice golf for thirty minutes. Thereafter press coverage was virtually nonexistent, noting on 13 April his arrival in Augusta, Georgia, to recuperate; on 12 May his return to Washington; and on 15 May his trip to Columbia University.[42]

An interested reader might well have derived from the news announcements that the general had suffered a severe stomach problem of a temporary nature and that, once it was under control, he had taken an extended vacation before reporting back to Columbia. This was somewhat more than the usual stomach upset, however, as Eisenhower revealed nearly twenty years later in his anecdotal *At Ease.* He recalled the sense of tension in those months, exacerbated by Secretary Forrestal's wavering decision to resign and by his own immoderate use of tobacco and hard-driving work habits. "I was, when working, driven by the need to go at top speed, day after day, starting early and continuing past midnight," he confessed. "This was rough on my staff and several times during the war it might have been fatal to me. But the climax did not come until the peaceful days of 1949."

That climax, as he described it, came on the evening of 21 March, when he was stretched out in his room at the Statler Hotel and "was struck with an attack of a most distressing kind (one that foreshadowed the ileitis attack of 1956)." General Snyder treated him "as though I were at the end of the precipice and teetering a bit. For days, my head was not off the pillow. . . . I was so ill that I lost touch with events. I read no papers and simply lay in bed. After a week or so, the doctors felt I was sufficiently recovered to go down to the warmer climate of Florida and try to shake off the aftereffects of these debilitating attacks." After the doctors transferred him to Key West, he remembered, "I remained on the sick list, forbidden solid food and cigarettes. During most of that time, I was so ill that I missed neither." After the "collapse," as he referred to his experience, he had to spend "a month or so of recuperation at Key West."[43]

Ike's story has served until recently as the basis for every historical account of the illness. Now the papers of Howard Snyder (deposited at the Eisenhower Library) offer elaboration because the doctor discussed the episode at some length in the late 1950s in the unfinished draft of a book in which he planned to present a health history of Eisenhower. When he arrived in Washington in response to a call from the general, Snyder recorded, the patient was complaining of "colicky pains" throughout his middle abdomen.

> He had no temperature, his pulse was not accelerated, I palpated his abdomen and found that there was tenderness in the lower right quadrant just external to the line of the appendectomy scar. . . . There was no rebound tenderness; there was beginning distention of the lower abdomen, particularly to the left of the midline. . . . The general was not nauseated, and he had had a bowel movement. As was frequently the case, the contents of the general's dinner with Forrestal on the evening before had been hot Mexican food; that is, food prepared according to the Texan manner.[44]

Snyder checked his patient's lungs and heart, both of which were fine, as he explained in his account, and he found no evidence of any pathology except for the abdomen. He interpreted the upset as another in the long history of intestinal problems with which he had dealt so many times before, and he did not consider it necessary to call in any consultants. Friends sent delicacies to tempt Ike's appetite, and by Thursday he was eating fairly well. President Truman, equally solicitous, offered his plane, *The Sacred Cow*, to take the general to his vacation resort in Key West. Shortly after his arrival he underwent (on 29 and 31 March) a detailed series of laboratory tests focusing upon his blood, urine, and stools, and thereafter his convalescence went rapidly, assisted by dietary restrictions, an end to smoking, and Metamucil. After his "month sick leave," he was in "splendid shape" again.[45]

Snyder did not prepare his draft history simply from memory. He was relying, in large part, on information from a long and confidential letter he had written from Augusta, Georgia, on 13 April 1949 in response to an inquiry from the Doud family physician in Colorado, Dr. Herbert Black. In the letter he had described the illness as a "simple, though very acute, gastroenteritis, induced by indulgence in a Mexican supper of chile con carne and tamales. The reaction was much more severe than should have been anticipated and must have been influenced by the exhausted physical condition present at the time of this incident." The letter also described the blood chemistry, urine, cardiogram, and other laboratory tests taken at Key West as normal, and discussed the convalescence at some length. "The general did not indulge in anything during his first week at Key West except complete rest and relaxation," Snyder related. "During the second week he got out for a bit of practice of golf balls with his approach clubs, and during the last three afternoons he played nine holes of golf without undue fatigue and certainly with no signs of exhaustion." The patient was on a high-protein diet, his blood pressure was lower than usual, he required no specific medications, and, as the doctor concluded, "I believe that after two weeks [of] further relaxation and recreation, that the general will return to active participation in his field of activities in better physical and mental shape than he has been [in] for many months past."[46]

Snyder's account of the 1949 illness, written a decade after the event, eventually served as the starting place for another unpublished "history" of Eisenhower's health written by Dr. Thomas Mattingly in the 1980s. Mattingly, a distinguished cardiologist at Walter Reed General Hospital, had served during the early 1950s and during the 1955 heart attack as Howard Snyder's and Dwight Eisenhower's favorite military consultant. For thirty years thereafter he reflected on and researched the possibility of Eisenhower's having had an additional heart attack *prior* to becoming president. By 1987 he had concluded that Dr. Snyder's diagnosis of gastroenteritis in 1949 was a "deceptive diagnosis" and that the general probably suffered a mild heart attack.

Mattingly went further. He claimed a cover-up, as "both Eisenhower and Snyder were purposefully withholding the occurrence of this illness from the public and from the consulting cardiologists." Snyder, he charged, "definitely belonged to the old school of physicians" like Vice Admiral Ross McIntyre (who for twelve years had hidden the ailments of Franklin Roosevelt) and was more interested in protecting the "political life" of

Eisenhower than he was in providing the truth to the public. Mattingly liked and respected Eisenhower, but he believed he had "sanctioned and collaborated in" the deception. "As an ambitious army officer," the cardiologist deduced, "he, like many others with aspirations of becoming high-ranking officers and leaders, made special effort to keep his records free of any disease or physical abnormalities which might interfere with subsequent promotions and assignments." In this instance, the lure of the presidency supposedly required the general to mislead the public.[47]

Mattingly had arrived at his conclusion after thirty years of committed detective work. His first inkling about an earlier heart attack had come during the coronary thrombosis of 1955, when he was flying to Denver to serve as a cardiological consultant. During the trip he talked with another passenger, Merriman Smith, a highly respected White House journalist, who heartily subscribed to and mentioned the rumors about such a previous attack. Mattingly firmly denied them, and although he wrote off the incident as an example of untrustworthy journalism, it continued to tease at his mind. There was not even a hint of any cardiovascular problems in the official medical records of the president, however, nor in any of the many discussions Mattingly had had over many years with both Eisenhower and Snyder. But in 1967 Mattingly became interested again when he was reading his inscribed copy of *At Ease* because Ike's description of the "collapse" and the "climax" in 1949 implied to him something more than a gastrointestinal illness. He broached the subject gingerly with Eisenhower during a medical examination and learned nothing. Then he visited Dr. Snyder, by then partially impaired by a series of strokes, and left "empty-handed." Snyder had insisted that the intestinal tract was the only important problem he had with the general before 1955, and that he had never found evidence of coronary disease.[48]

Fifteen years later, Mattingly returned to the subject with a passion. While attending the 1982 annual meeting of the Association of Medical Consultants of the Armed Forces, he chanced to talk with a retired internist, Colonel Charles Leedham, who boasted that when he was chief of medicine at Oliver General Hospital in Augusta, Georgia, between 1947 and 1950, he had treated Eisenhower for a heart attack. Mattingly tried doggedly then and later to get Leedham to elaborate, but he "clammed up." The following year Mattingly decided to compile documents concerning the entire life health record of Eisenhower; he gained access to Snyder's papers from his heirs, and to all existing military medical records from the

Office of the Surgeon General of the Army. Upon studying the material, he found evidence of laboratory reports documenting Eisenhower's admission to Oliver General Hospital in Augusta, Georgia, in April 1949—a fact never mentioned by the general or his doctor in the official medical record and one that fired his suspicions.[49]

In his monumental "Life Health Record of Dwight D. Eisenhower," a compilation of documents and comments deposited at the Eisenhower Library in 1989, Mattingly admitted his inability to locate any definitive proof of a 1949 heart attack. But driven by Colonel Leedham's statement that he had treated the general for one, he had gone on to find enough circumstantial evidence to convince himself that there was a coronary and a subsequent cover-up. He found, for example, a comment by Clare Booth Luce that Eisenhower had told her in 1950 that he had quit smoking because he "had a little heart trouble, a little warning from my doctor, and so I quit," which led Mattingly to the conclusion that Ike stopped smoking only out of a desire to avoid another heart attack. He suspected that the claims of Snyder and Robert Schulz, Eisenhower's military aide, about Ike playing golf shortly after the illness were falsehoods meant to further the deception; and that Snyder's explicit letter to Dr. Black in Colorado was a "plant," a part of the cover-up. After having studied Snyder's draft chapters and having found "omissions, errors and embellishments" in all of them, Mattingly no longer trusted his former colleague, least of all about what actually happened in 1949. Above all, he theorized that Snyder's use of the diagnosis of gastroenteritis to hide coronary disease was part of a larger pattern—a pattern of deception that included another case of reported food poisoning in 1953 and the initial period after the heart attack in 1955.[50]

Mattingly's shocking and incriminating theory unfortunately has found favor among academics. Historian Robert Ferrell, after "looking at all the signs, and a very considerable body of medical evidence," and acknowledging that "no final proof has appeared, and perhaps none ever will," concludes: "It seems almost certain it was a heart attack." Political scientist Robert Gilbert believes this "new and startling interpretation" of the "mystery illness" may well be on target, and that "Eisenhower suffered from potentially life-threatening cardiac problems both before and throughout his presidency (although this fact was carefully concealed from the public)." In his 1995 volume in the American Biographical History Series, Professor William Pickett elevates the fallacious speculation to doctrine, claiming that the 1949 event "was in fact a heart attack."[51]

The evidence is overwhelming, and common sense dictates, that the cardiologist and the scholars are wrong, and that despite Mattingly's personal research and suspicions, for which there are credible alternative explanations, the problem really was with the stomach and not with the heart. The available medical records show that immediately upon arrival in Key West, Snyder arranged for Eisenhower to go as an outpatient to the U.S. Naval Hospital for a thorough gastrointestinal checkup. Indeed, the specialists repeated urine and blood tests—to measure albumin, globulin, blood sugar, chlorides, calcium, acetone and diacetic acids, leukocytes, bile, and the sedimentation rate—on four days during the first week. We also know from the existing medical records that after Ike moved to Augusta for his vacation, Snyder was still focusing on the stomach. His patient entered Oliver General Hospital on four different days during the week of 18-26 April to undergo a broad range of tests—blood chemistry, hematology (including a malaria smear), serology, urinalysis, stool cultures (because he was "suspected of having amebiasis or other type of localized gastrointestinal pathology," the medical record states), and radiographic examinations (a barium enema, gastrointestinal series, and chest X-ray). The tests were all normal, although the radiologist did note: "There is some irregularity of calibre of the small bowel. . . . A small bowel series is recommended if symptoms persist."[52]

Snyder also arranged for an EKG at Key West on 4 April, exactly two weeks after the onset of Eisenhower's illness, which the attending cardiologist interpreted to be within normal limits. In 1984, when Mattingly first studied this isolated EKG, he also considered it to be normal; he noted that an "elevation of ST and a terminal dip of the T wave in the anterior lead" were suggestive of heart wall damage, but he explained to Colonel Leedham that he had detected similar indications in a 1947 and a 1952 EKG, "thus indicating that these were chronic configurations and not the result of resolving changes of a recent myocardial damage." But years later, having formulated his theory about Snyder's proclivity for deception, Mattingly claimed that he and unnamed "other reviewing cardiologists" determined that the EKG *could* fall into the category of "an abnormal electrocardiogram suspicious of myocardial damage" (italics mine).

There is no way to resolve this technical issue with absolute certainty. One could speculate wildly, of course, that Ike could have had a coronary that did not record clearly on the EKG; or that Snyder, like so many physicians before him, could have mistaken the symptoms for those of acute

gastroenteritis, and that his patient could have survived despite his exceptionally early ambulation and exercise. What we know for certain, however, is that Mattingly's belated reading of the EKG is at odds not only with
that of the attending cardiologist back in 1949 but also with those of two
distinguished cardiologists (one from the Harvard Medical School and the
other from the Brigham and Women's Hospital in Boston) who in 1993
reviewed Eisenhower's 1946 and 1947 EKGs together with the disputed EKG.
They concluded that none of them justifies a diagnosis of new or old
myocardial infarction. "In particular," one of the experts wrote, "I consider
that the tracing of April 5, 1949, is within normal limits; there is some S-T
segment elevation in the precordial leads (as there was in 1947), but this
may be and usually is a normal finding when of the modest degree present
and when there is no serial change."[53]

What is absolutely beyond question is that neither Snyder nor Eisenhower *believed* the illness to be a heart attack. Otherwise their behavior
at the time would have been strikingly different. A heart attack in 1949
was an extremely serious issue for both patient and doctor. As two cardiologists wrote in that year: "A person who first discovers or believes
that he has a heart ailment suffers serious and often permanent emotional disturbance; if he is told that his illness is the result of coronary
artery disease, or hardening of the arteries, the psychic shock is often so
great as to lead to a serious anxiety state." Two years later a congressman
testified that most of the people he met who had suffered heart attacks
"seem to give up hope as soon as they have one of these attacks. They
do not seem to think there is any future for them; that they are going to
be bedridden for the rest of their lives and are just waiting to die."
Eisenhower's activities—walking up the steps of an airplane unassisted
eight days after the "attack," practicing golf on the tenth day, and returning to work and to extensive golfing in the weeks thereafter—give no
indication of such anxiety or hopelessness.[54]

In like manner, a heart attack imposed momentous responsibility upon
a physician. Even after the emergency period, an expert explained to Congress in the spring of 1948, there was a need for stringent management of
a cardiac patient: "When the coronary gets out of bed at the end of six
weeks, that is just the beginning of his problem. . . . That man has to be
decompressed, just like a sandhog working under the river has to become
decompressed when he comes up to sea level." For any doctor in 1949—a
time when the standard treatment for a coronary thrombosis was extensive

bed rest, customarily from four to eight weeks—to have so much as suspected a heart attack and then to have allowed his patient to walk, work,
and play golf within a period of several weeks would have constituted
criminal negligence. Snyder allowed Ike to do all of those activities.[55]

Indeed, Eisenhower's personal correspondence and desk calendars during this time period (which Dr. Mattingly did not have an opportunity to
study and the scholar-critics simply failed to consider) provide compelling
evidence of an increasingly active schedule of work and play. On 30 March,
nine days after his illness began, he wrote a letter in longhand to the new
secretary of defense regarding Marine Corps participation on the Joint
Chiefs of Staff, and the following day he sent to Washington his opinions
after a careful review of the draft report of a special board to consider the
establishment of an air force academy. On 7 April, two and one-half weeks
after becoming ill, he held an afternoon business meeting with General
Alfred Gruenther, director of the joint staff of the Joint Chiefs of Staff, and
General Lauris Norstad, deputy chief of staff of the air force; later that
evening he dined at the Little White House with all of the members of the
Joint Chiefs of Staff, after which they watched a film, *The Secret Life of Walter
Mitty*. The group had traveled to Florida to discuss the stressful issue of
the military budget for the next fiscal year, and Eisenhower met with them
for brief periods every day between 8 and 12 April, after which they
sometimes dined together or watched a movie. In subsequent weeks he
spoke often to each of them by telephone.[56]

Any physician would have prevented such an early work schedule for
any recovering heart patient, and *even more*, would have forbidden golf
completely (which the doctors did in 1955, when Eisenhower really had a
heart attack, for a period of *five months*). But Snyder told the press that the
general practiced thirty minutes on 31 March, only ten days after the onset
of the illness, and informed Dr. Black that he practiced and played nine
holes on three occasions during the second week at Key West. Eisenhower's
correspondence indicates that he played nearly every day thereafter—between 12 April and 11 May—while he was at the Augusta National Golf
Club. On 20 April he informed the secretary of defense, "I feel stronger
every day though I must admit the 'drives' are somewhat short of expected
destination." A week later he wrote to his close friend Swede Hazlett that
he had been miserable for a time but that for the past two weeks, "I have
been puttering around with a bit of golf every day."[57]

Could these references by Snyder and Eisenhower have been part of a grand deception, manufactured to make it appear that the general was not really ill with something as serious as a heart attack, and thus was able to play golf? Eisenhower's private correspondence defies any such likelihood. The day after his return to Washington he wrote to a local member of Augusta National, "It is a shock to wake up in the morning and find that I have a schedule to keep—instead of drifting out to a practice tee for some instruction under my friend, Ed." He was referring to the golf professional Ed Dudley, to whom he wrote later that same day to thank him for his "patient instructions" during "the past month," and to insist that he submit a statement to represent "some decent remuneration to yourself for the time you spent on me." Four days later he wrote to a former personal aide that "I have frequently played eighteen holes of golf a day during the past month and on one or two occasions even went twenty-seven holes. This did not seem to bother me in spite of the fact that I take a great many more strokes than the average person does in getting around the course."[58]

There can be no reasonable doubt, as one of Eisenhower's aides later explained to Mattingly, that Ike "played golf 90 percent of the time" he was at Augusta, and that "weather took care of the rest." At the time he was playing golf, he could not have been in the Oliver General Hospital recovering from a heart attack, as Colonel Leedham claimed. We can never know for certain why the colonel made his charge. It may have been nothing more than braggadocio, for, as Mattingly relates, Leedham first presented the subject to him and others with a "very boastful statement" but a year later had only "vague memories." Leedham also may have been susceptible to the rumors that were already going around about Ike's health. One held that he had "something like a heart attack" during his "long rest" in his chief of staff period; another (one that the secretary of defense, Louis Johnson, repeated) that he suffered an attack sometime after 1945, although not in 1949 when he went to Key West because, as the secretary authoritatively revealed, on that occasion he had "peeling of the stomach lining."[59]

In the real world of 1949, Eisenhower's return to work and to golf did not conform to the behavior expected of a recovering heart patient, who ordinarily would have been fearful about his future and anxious about his fate. To the contrary, his optimism about his illness—which he described in letters to friends as a "severe digestive disorder," a "queer sort of digestive or stomach disorder," or "quite a spell of sickness"—never wavered. And his understanding of why he became ill was the same as it had been in the past—he had been working too hard, this time by accepting an inordinate number of speaking invitations. Even before leaving Key West, he advised General Smith not to repeat his experience, lest he face the choice between a flat decision to accept no invitations or a "physical break-down." Do not become "as I was for several months," he warned, "the slave of your calendar and the victim of every organization that needs a top-flight drawing card," or "you will be taxed so heavily and the drain on your vitality will be so endless that the game will not be worth the candle." Speaking from the special vantage point of his "present situation," he felt qualified to elaborate: "I used to think that people could not wear me down unless I let them. I know now that if they come bearing invitations and leave with acceptances, they can wear me out in no time at all. I hope this will be a lesson to you. . . . I am proof, fortunately still living, of the dangers of the so-called ptomaine circuit."[60]

All of Eisenhower's personal papers, all of his medical records, and everything we know about the behavior of heart attack patients and their physicians point to one conclusion—he did not have a heart attack in 1949 and did not participate in a cover-up. It is difficult on the face of it to believe that a man who practiced the values of honor, integrity, and duty would have lied to the American people about such a critical issue and persisted in that lie for a lifetime. It is understandable, on the other hand, that he would have tried to avoid undue publicity about his digestive problems— as he had as early as November 1946—because "people immediately jump to the conclusion that a fellow is really on the verge of collapse." Part of his motivation was personal; he did not wish to be seen as sickly. A larger part was political, as Snyder intimated in his account a decade later: "I feared that if the general got into politics, someone would surely pin upon him the label that he was a chronic invalid and couldn't stand the strain of office."[61]

Eisenhower's political calculations after the defeat of Thomas E. Dewey in 1948, when the presidency suddenly became a distinct possibility, are still fuzzy. As biographer Stephen Ambrose has pointed out, "There is not a single item in the massive collection at the Eisenhower Library prior to late 1951 that even hints that he would seek the job or that he was secretly doing so." But he adds that "his actions could not have been better calcu-lated to put him into the White House. . . . No professional politician could have plotted a campaign for the general as successful as the one he directed himself." At the very least, his actions were inspired by a persistent ambi-tion and an expanding sense of duty, and the need to keep his options open. Consequently, Snyder did not volunteer information to the press about his illness beyond what he had told them at the outset—that Ike was "a very sick man" with a "severe case of acute gastroenteritis." He was telling the truth, and he saw no reason to elaborate about the details.[62]

Should Eisenhower's health have been a negative factor in his considerations about public office? Several critics, all of whom conclude that he had a severe health problem in 1949, believe so. One argues that he "probably should not have run for the presidency in 1952." Another suggests that "peaceful retirement" would seem to have been "the most desirable" choice, but "duty and ambition would not allow it." A third writes, "Whether his 1949 illness was a heart attack or a severe intestinal disorder, it seems to have been due to the pressures of the positions he held at the time. It was foolhardy, therefore, for him to become president of the United States a few years later since the burdens of office would be much heavier and the danger to his physical well-being much greater—unless, of course, he welcomed that danger." The point the critics miss is that Ike did not sense any unusual danger. Stomach problems had been plaguing him since the 1920s, and they were not serious enough to prevent him from serving his country, even at the highest level. He had recovered from this illness as from all the others; the only difference was that this time he determined to do more to stay healthy in the future.[63]

The illness in 1949 was a turning point for Eisenhower. He finally recognized that he was no longer a "Tarzan," that he had been careless in exceeding his limits, that he was complicitous in his illness, and that he had to avoid a recurrence. He never doubted that it was his personal responsibility to take the initiative. He believed strongly in the power of his own volition, and he was always leery of the phrase "With the help of God." As he once explained, "I never say that. I won't say that. I don't believe that. I believe that the Lord deals us a hand, that's right, but he expects *us* to play it." He was especially confident of playing his hand at this moment in time because he was coming off a great victory of willpower. He had stopped smoking.[64]

Ike was a tobacco addict. He started the habit at least as early as his attendance at West Point, where he was a rebellious, "roll-your-own" smoker who indulged in excess of what the regulations allowed. By World War II he had worked up to a customary four packs of Camels a day, and the chain-smoking was a necessary part of his life. When he arrived in London and attended his first dinner party, arranged in his honor by Ambassador John Winant, he unknowingly embarrassed the guests by smoking prior to their toast to the king, which went against the British custom. When he learned of his indiscretion from the ambassador, he was furious and responded, "Last night was the end of my attendance at formal dinners in London." Thereafter those wishing his company—as well as clubs and dining rooms with bans against smoking who wanted his business—had to conform to *his* custom. "This was a silly performance on my part, I guess," he admitted later, "but as I've often said, my smoking in those days was not just a habit; it was a continuous performance."[65]

Eisenhower was not a fan of tobacco. In the fall of 1940 he went so far as to make a deal with his son to pay him $1.50 per week for as long as he did not smoke, up until the age of twenty-five. Likewise, he was not happy with his habit, but he could not break it. "I find myself smoking incessantly—all the time," he wrote to Mamie during the war, "and I try to cut down and one hour later find I've burned up more cigarettes than usual." He decided a bad cough in 1943 came from too many cigarettes, "which I don't seem able to do anything about—but I always excuse myself by saying 'It's the only bad habit I have.'" He blamed a cold in 1944 on "cigarettes as much as germs," and then admitted that "it simply seems impossible for me to be truly moderate in the matter of smoking. I'm just a weak sinner." Nor was he susceptible to the importunings of his doctors. Toward the end of the war a physician gave him "a stinging lecture" about the number of cigarettes he smoked; and in 1947 both Dr. Barr and Dr. Taylor urged him to *restrict* his habit, but to no avail. Biographer John Gunther, who interviewed Eisenhower when he was chief of staff, wrote, "He smoked like a furnace. . . . I asked him what brand of cigarettes he liked and he replied that it didn't matter in the slightest—he smoked anything."[66]

Because of the illness in 1949, Ike had to give up smoking for ten days, after which he asked for a package of cigarettes and Snyder pleaded with him to reduce his consumption to about twelve per day. "I used many arguments," the doctor remembered, "among them telling him the story of how Willkie lost his voice when in the midst of his campaign because his throat played out on him. . . . I cited the fact that he might become very dependent upon his voice in the midst of a campaign for a public office." Snyder also told his patient that the nose and throat specialist who had treated him had blamed his condition on smoking.[67]

Ike had already decided that cigarettes were doing him no good whatever and, because of his public speaking schedule, were like sandpaper on
his vocal chords. He still was not eager to cut back. He rebelled "at the
prospect of a life in which cigarettes would be counted and smoking regulated by the clock" and realized that "some afternoon when the pressure
would be particularly severe, I'd find that I had already exhausted my
day's quota and would have to suffer the agonies of deprivation or start
again on the four-pack-a-day road." Snyder remained adamant, however,
and Ike at that moment "wanted above anything else to avoid another
collapse." So he made his decision: "If I had lived for ten days without a
cigarette, I could get along without them for another ten days, ten years,
or ten decades." He quit cold turkey and never smoked another cigarette.[68]

Having conquered smoking, it was a small challenge for Ike to work
with his doctor to institute a regimen of preventive medicine. Snyder had
retired from the army and was employed by Columbia University, but his
primary responsibility was still to look after Ike and Mamie, and he
stopped by their home regularly. He gave his primary attention to the
stomach problem not only because of its danger in a political sense but
also because he found his patient "now becomes alarmed and apprehensive at the first indication of abdominal distention and cramps."[69]

Since the various experts had failed over many years to discover the
cause of the upsets, Snyder fell back upon his own observations, which
were that the attacks "usually develop after a period of nervously exhausting work, and have been precipitated by eating a highly spiced or 'rich
and rough' meal, or a meal of spare ribs and sauerkraut." His prescription
was to have the general take a tablespoon of Metamucil every day to quiet
the symptoms and to eat a "reasonable" diet, including "yogurt and other
dairy products, proteins, and green and yellow vegetables, with elimination of fats and starches and sugars insofar as this is possible." In the
summer of 1950, just before the Eisenhowers left for their Denver vacation,
the doctor sent them a memorandum spelling out precisely what they
should eat at each meal, asking only that Mamie watch her fats more
carefully than Ike. It is telling, in light of the allegations about a heart
attack, that Snyder paid little attention to Eisenhower's cholesterol, getting
only one reading in each of the years 1949, 1952, 1953, and 1954. After the
1955 heart attack, he obtained an average of ten each year.[70]

Ike's prescription for himself drew upon his wartime experience. After
returning to Columbia, he was pleased to have made a "splendid come-

back" from his recent illness and was confident that he could remain in "fine shape" if "I do not again become neglectful of exercise and proper care of myself." He had "thoroughly tested and proved the virtues of a complete and absolute rest" through his "health-seeking trip to the South," and he informed his brother that in the future he intended to take not less than a total of ten weeks of vacation every year. "If I am not able to keep up to this leave schedule," he wrote, "I will simply quit all my jobs except that of helping out in Washington." He felt so strongly about the value of good health that he urged Milton to give up his job in UNESCO, adding: "My experience this spring convinced me that there most certainly is such a thing as overwork—for the rest of my life I am going to work at avoiding that particular disease."[71]

In an attempt to control his activities, Eisenhower tried to reserve every Saturday afernoon and every Sunday for relaxation, and in 1950 he vowed to reserve one full week out of every two months when he would leave the city or "lock the front door of my house." There was another way to deal with overwork and tension, however, he would play more golf. By this time in his life he was a devotee of the game, or, as Snyder put it, "He ate, drank, and slept golf." The general was a member of the Blind Brook Golf Club and also played on weekends, as frequently as the weather permitted, at several other of the elite courses in and about New York City. Every April he left for his favorite course at the Augusta National Golf Club, where most of his close friends joined him. Snyder was delighted with the general's increased exercise, convinced it kept him in "better health, both physically and mentally." He also believed it had "re-made" him, and boasted: "His shoulders had broadened and firmed, he could hit a golf ball fifty yards farther by 1950 than he had been able to do in the early years following his return from Europe." During the campaign, when advisers urged him to stop playing golf, he became irate, complained that he was more a "slave" than ever before, and continued to play.[72]

Whether by design or through good luck, Eisenhower remained exceptionally healthy for several years after 1949—in sharp contrast to the previous four years—despite his decision to take a leave of absence from Columbia at the end of the following year to serve as the first commander of NATO and then to undergo the demands of a political campaign. His blood pressure remained reasonably stable (135–145 over 85–90), his pulse was slower than normal, and he kept his weight at the magic number 172, even though he was "hungry as a bear most of the time and was ready to eat the china on which the food was served." He worked conscientiously at staying healthy; even on his trip to Europe he used the time aboard ship to exercise every day and to start a truly rigid diet, from which he did not depart for several weeks. He was more confident about his physical condition than he had been for years, and in the fall of 1951 he was boasting, "Ever since I stopped smoking . . . my only complaint, aside from an occasional cold, has been the difficulty of reminding my appetite to have some consideration for my girth."[73]

During these several years the general not only tended to his own health but felt so literate about the subject that he became a practitioner dispensing health advice to his friends. He had an ongoing wager and a "weight contest" with the rotund, rollicking George Allen, trying to get him to lose twenty pounds. He advised Cliff Roberts that there was no easy way to quit smoking, but that if he could throw out of his mind any feeling of self-pity or privation or hardship "I think that you will be amazed how quickly you can accustom yourself to a new regime." And he became so concerned about the physical condition of his closest friend, Bill Robinson, that he wrote him "the kind of letter I have never written to any other person." He advised him to lose considerable weight, to smoke and drink in moderation, to exercise regularly, to get lots of sleep, and to "eat wisely." But he was not content to dispense mere superficial advice; he offered details. As for eating, he sent his own "invariable daily diet," noting that the "secret is to do without any butter, sauces, sugar, creams, or anything of that kind, and never take more than one small piece of toast as a daily diet of bread." As for exercise, golf was helpful, but not sufficient by itself. He proposed having something in the office, such as one of the large rubber bands advertised for the purpose, for use frequently if only for a few seconds at a time, or a niblick (a number nine iron with a steel head), for swinging about ten or fifteen times six times a day. "On top of this," he recommended, "frequently raise your chest to the fullest extent, stretching up on the abdominal muscles; and, when you have occasion to walk, walk very rapidly, swinging the arms fairly high and with the chest raised. You may think you look ridiculous, but who in New York ever looks at what anybody else on the sidewalk is doing?"[74]

That the NATO commander—or "Dr. Ike," as his personal physician dubbed him—was so intent on getting a friend into "tip-top condition" surely would have surprised the American people. But his assiduous attention to the requisites of good health, although decades ahead of his time, had become an integral part of his way of life and very likely a part of his decision to seek the presidency. And on the eve of the election of 1952 he was confident that his concern had served him well. When he returned from his European assignment in May, he went to Walter Reed for an evaluation of his blood pressure and cardiac status, both of which were normal. During his summer vacation in Denver, and after spending several days in the mountains fishing, he noticed that he was more short of breath than usual and had a mild gastrointestinal upset. He went to Fitzsimons Army Hospital for another checkup in August, including a cardiovascular examination, after which the chief of cardiology, Colonel Edwin Goyette, happily reported:

> While this patient's blood pressure has tended to be on the high side of normal, showing some elevation of the systolic pressure on excitement, the fact that there has been no marked or significant change in thirty years is indicative of a good cardiovascular system. In view of the benign course, the still normal electrocardiogram, still normal heart size, and good retinal vessels, I do not think that there is sufficient evidence to warrant any diagnosis of any cardiovascular disease. I believe that this patient's blood pressure is entirely compatible with his age. The mild elevations noted in the past are probably indicative of some stress reaction.[75]

During the political campaign, when a rumor spread that some mysterious disease made his election too risky, Snyder told the former editor of the *Stars and Stripes* that Ike was in "excellent" condition, with no problems whatever. In a similar vein, *U.S. News and World Report* published a long article, with information that could have come only from Dr. Snyder, proclaiming Ike to be less fatigued at day's end, despite the "increasing tempo" of the daily grind, than most of the younger men traveling with him. There were good reasons for his superior health, the story explained. He always had kept close watch upon his physical condition by guarding his diet, arranging for plenty of sleep and exercise, and getting a daily checkup from his personal physician. In addition, he knew how to relax and avoid exhaustion, and was even-tempered by nature, with only "occasional flashes of anger," which subsided quickly. The journal concluded that if Eisenhower won the election, he could survive four years in the White House.[76]

Howard Snyder undoubtedly agreed with that impression in its broadest sense; indeed, he had worked hard to create it. But he was not completely free from worry. He had a reminder on the campaign train of a danger he had sensed many times before. He was sitting in the lounge car with Mamie and speechwriter Kevin McCann while the candidate was reading aloud the draft of a presentation for a huge rally in Detroit. Mamie interrupted time and again for twenty minutes, insisting that the speech was out of character. "Finally Ike gave up," McCann recalled. "He threw the speech down and slammed his way into the bedroom of the train so hard I thought he'd throw the train off the track." Since 1945 Snyder had watched Ike's irritation turn to anger and, on some occasions, to this kind of "vein-popping rage." The presidency, he knew, could be the source of unparalleled irritations.[77]

3

Misdiagnosis and Cover-up

❖ ❖ ❖ ❖ ❖ ❖ ❖ ❖ ❖ ❖ ❖ ❖ ❖ ❖ ❖

A man who has early risen and late taken rest, who has eaten the bread of carefulness, striving for success in commercial, professional, or political life, after twenty-five or thirty years of incessant toil reaches the point where he can say, perhaps with just satisfaction, "Soul, thou hast much goods laid up for many years: take thine ease," all unconscious that the fell sergeant has already issued the warrant.

    —*William Osler*, Lectures on Angina Pectoris

The episode is unmatched in American history. The president was lying in a room in a house in Denver in the middle of the night with a heart attack. Only one person in the world, Howard Snyder, knew it, as he informed neither the president nor Mrs. Eisenhower of his tentative diagnosis. No oxygen supply was available. He did not summon an ambulance. Snyder was not a heart specialist. No second opinion was immediately sought, no consultation arranged.

    —*Robert J. Donovan*, Confidential Secretary

At precisely 9:10 P.M. on 9 January 1953, Dwight Eisenhower entered the Starlight Room of the Waldorf Astoria Hotel. Only days before his own inauguration, he was stopping for a surprise appearance at the inaugural dinner of the American Heart Association. He greeted the honorary chairman, Governor Thomas E. Dewey; the principal speaker, Dr. Milton Eisenhower; and an audience of 850 guests, mostly wealthy industrialists with a scattering of blacks, labor leaders, and disease fighters. He had come, he said, to applaud them "for helping us to defeat a dread enemy in our midst."[1]

The association had hoped for more than a brief appearance. After the election of 1952, it invited the general to "spearhead" its campaign against heart disease as the guest of honor at a public banquet, only to have him suggest his brother as a substitute. The association persisted, hoping to enlist his prestige against one of the nation's "most important domestic problems." His participation, the association told him, would go far to record his support of voluntary health agencies, in contrast to Harry Truman's "drive for socialized medicine." The sales pitch failed to enroll Ike as a guest of honor, but it induced him to stop by and "greet the people."[2]

The general made the evening a "momentous occasion" that surpassed the hopes of its sponsors. Departing from his prepared text, he shared something of himself. He spoke of his early life among "six rather lusty and tough boys," of "riding the lead horse on the binder" in the hot Kansas sun, and of the joy of the "ten o'clock drink out of that old water jug wrapped in a wet gunny sack under a shock of wheat." Leaving the rural past, he turned to the problem at hand—a scientist, "working over his tubes and studying," on the verge of saving life, forced to shelve his project for a lack of funds. He asked his audience, among whom he noticed the "white ties, beautiful ladies, wonderful jewels," to go home, listen to their consciences, and send twice the amount they had pledged. It is like Americans, he proclaimed, to give "cheerfully and happily, because it is the right thing to do and because we are free."[3]

Eisenhower's speech represented far more than the opening salvo for an annual campaign. It was an acknowledgment—by a president-elect—of the need to join in battle against the nation's number one killer. As the war in Korea began to wind down, a powerful bipartisan lobby called for an unprecedented research effort to find a cure for heart disease, and Ike was alert to the popular demand for action. "If the annual toll for coronary heart disease were revealed to the American people as a casualty list from a battlefield," he told a group of doctors some months later, "the effect would be one of national shock and a demand that something be done." But the old soldier's leadership was more symbolic than real because he had no personal feelings about the dread disease. Indeed, while others were raising the specter of an "enemy loose within our country," he was enjoying a period of exceptionally good health.[4]

The president's first three years in office were his best ones. The war in Korea came to an end, the economy was booming, the federal budget was balanced, Joseph Stalin died, there was peace in much of the world, and scientists achieved a victory over poliomyelitis. He did have some unpleasant struggles over McCarthyism and civil rights; he was often frustrated about politics and politicians; and he was increasingly conscious of his age, so much so that he asked his secretary to watch him carefully for any sign of physical deterioration. But he enjoyed his work, and more than ever before he had time and opportunity to enjoy the pleasure of family and friends. One of the latter recorded the "gratifying and heart-warming" joy of the Eisenhowers during a visit to Gettysburg: "The president had cooked breakfast for the grandchildren that morning in the kitchen. He is active every minute, trying to crowd in as many games of golf, hours of fishing, fun with the children, and bridge with his friends as he can during his brief vacation."[5]

During both work and play, Dr. Snyder's responsibilities and presence were enhanced, and he seemed eminently well prepared for his new role as physician to the president. He was the best-liked man on the White House staff, and in the words of a medical colleague, "He was a gentleman of very easily recognized gentility." He was strikingly handsome—an erect, even stately, six feet, three inches tall with "a full head of beautiful, gray-white hair, and so distinguished looking that you'd turn around and look at him two or three times." He exuded a confidence that came from knowledge, experience, and, above all, the trust and affection of the Eisenhowers. He was really "an old-time general practitioner," a friend put it, "who just had a knack of sensing dangers; particularly good with the president because he'd been with him for many, many years." He and his wife lived in a luxurious Connecticut Avenue apartment, and they were often at the White House in the evening hours playing cards or watching movies. They were more than friends with the Eisenhowers; they were part of the family.[6]

Unlike his predecessors, Snyder made the health of the chief executive his full-time job. His office, only a short distance from the president's own, consisted of two well-equipped rooms with shining cases of drugs and instruments, with a view through the garden toward the Washington Monument and the Jefferson Memorial. Snyder accompanied Eisenhower nearly everywhere—on trips overseas, on parades at home, and on weekends to Gettysburg. On a few occasions Ike chose to go on vacation without a physician present, but that ended early in 1955 when he caught a cold at

George Humphrey's plantation and his irate press secretary insisted on greater caution. "I think it is criminal to have the president go traveling around the country without a doctor," James Hagerty wrote. "Some day something serious will happen unless we change this tendency of the president to think that he does not need a doctor along." Thereafter Snyder went everywhere, and he carried two black bags—one in preparation for terrible emergencies, packed with special probes and compresses, "the grim reminders that mad men might lie in wait for his boss," the other armed with supplies designed to meet any medical ailment or crisis.[7]

Not everyone was satisfied with Howard Snyder as the president's physician. Some doctors questioned whether his age (he was seventy-three in 1953), his experience, and his ability were appropriate for such a grave responsibility. He was not a specialist, and his education and training were in some respects outdated. This uneasiness extended to some of those close to the president. In November 1954, when Lucius Clay was charting the course of a second term, for which the candidate's health would be crucial, he advised Ike of a feeling among some of the gang that Dr. Snyder was too old and not really capable of providing the medical care and advice that a president of the United States should have.[8]

The president disagreed. In his 1955 "efficiency report" on his physician he gave him a superior rating. "It is almost presumptuous for me to comment on General Snyder's professional qualifications," he attested. "They are of the highest order and are, of course, a matter of record in the Army Medical Corps. As I have said previously, in addition to his medical competence, General Snyder is a personal friend. His devotion to me and to our family is selfless and complete. . . . Certainly I hope he continues in his present post for the remainder of my time here." Members of the Eisenhower family, including Mamie and her mother, Elvira "Min" Doud, who found the doctor very helpful and solicitous, could not have been more supportive. Mamie had always considered Snyder her doctor, kidded about sharing him with Ike, and never lost her deep respect for him. As she put it: "I'm not worried about Ike at all. My gracious, nothing could happen . . . the way Dr. Snyder is always poking at him."[9]

As he had for some years past, Eisenhower worked closely with Snyder to carry out a program of preventive medicine. He tried to avoid a recurrence of stomach distress by watching his diet, and he had the doctor review menus with Mamie or the cook. He also acceded, with delight, to another feature of Snyder's program—to exercise as often as possible. Ike was not the first president to play golf, but he was the first to make the game virtually synonymous with his name. He played whenever possible on Wednesdays and Saturdays at Burning Tree, an exclusive club in suburban Maryland; several times a year at Augusta National, the home of the famous Masters Tournament and the site of "Mamie's Cottage," a three-story house built for the first couple by the membership; during summer vacations at Cherry Hills Country Club in Denver; at the nine-hole "cow-pasture" green at Camp David; and on occasion, as travels dictated, at courses around the country and the world. For an aging athlete still sensitive about his physical appearance, golf was a way of keeping fit and staying young; for a busy executive, it was a contribution to good health. "We want the president to have all the rest and relaxation he can," Dr. Snyder explained. "People sometimes forget that his job is more than a matter of eight in the morning until six or seven in the evening . . . . Golf is fine for him, so I say he should play whenever he gets a chance." Estimates were that he played some seventy-five times in both 1953 and 1954, as a result of which golf professionals gave him credit for creating a golf boom, Democrats griped about his spending too much time away from his job, and physicians speculated that the game was beneficial for the relief of tension and thereby good for his health.[10]

It was not a cure-all, however. Even before Eisenhower was comfortably ensconced in his office, he received an unwanted reminder from the past—one that was to teach him that his health suddenly had become a matter of public relations. In the past if he became ill the repercussions were personal; as president they could have implications for his country and the world, and most definitely for politics.

On the evening of 15 April 1953, following a brief vacation in Georgia that included a round of golf with Ben Hogan, Ike ate a large portion of heavily spiced fish in the exclusive dining room of the Augusta National Golf Club. Later that evening he became ill with a stomach problem. He was still ailing the next morning and running a slight fever when he had to fly to Washington for a luncheon speech before the American Society of Newspaper Editors. Dr. Snyder had given him "medicines and sedatives," but he had to deliver his talk, as he recalled in his memoirs, "under great difficulty, experiencing one of the most miserable periods, physically, of my life."[11]

His speech, "The Chance for Peace," in which he described the terrible cost of the arms race, was one of the two most impressive of his presidency. It also was one of his most courageous because while he was delivering it, as he remembered, "the pain was such as to cause heavy perspiration on my face and head, and at the same time, chills of a very disturbing kind. The result was that I could concentrate on the text only by supreme effort; at times I became so dizzy that I feared I would faint."

The president's special counsel, Bernard Shanley, noticed how the "perspiration started to roll down his face and he started to shake," so he got him off to a side room and tried to get him to cancel his appointments. Ike was willing to skip the lunch awaiting him at the head table, explaining to the host that his digestion was still upset, but he insisted on meeting two additional commitments—to throw out the first ball at Griffith Stadium to open the American League baseball season, and to help celebrate the two-hundredth anniversary of Rowan County in North Carolina—because he felt it would be "putting too important an interpretation on what I thought was a temporary illness if I should cancel the engagement." At the baseball game a bitingly cold wind was blowing, but to please the photographers he tossed off his coat and hat; at a park pavilion in Salisbury, again with a very cold wind, he did the same, much to the dismay of Dr. Snyder. "As the ladies say," the doctor wrote to a mutual friend, "I could have killed him."[12]

After returning to Augusta by plane around 9:00 P.M., the president went immediately to bed, and even the next day he felt too weak to play golf. His midriff was still so sensitive, he told reporters, that if he brushed his arms across his stomach on the downswing, it caused some pain. For some time in the afternoon he sat in the sun watching a golf game, and Dr. Snyder had him up at 5:00 P.M. for bridge. His fever was gone, and thereafter he improved rapidly. But the episode was for everybody, as Shanley put it, "a scary day and for two days we wondered what the result was going to be."[13]

From Augusta Hagerty announced to the press that the president had suffered a "slight attack of food poisoning." Ten days later Snyder described the illness in a letter to his and Ike's close friend, General Alfred Gruenther, as "a severe gastrointestinal upset" that lasted for about thirty-six hours. "It was a terrifically exhausting day for a man who had suffered his first physical upset since becoming president," the doctor explained, "but there was no way out of it." Ike went back to playing golf and bridge with the gang with no lasting effects, and in his memoirs he compared the attack to "one that several years later was diagnosed as the same kind that occasioned a serious operation for ileitis."[14]

Every piece of evidence we have—the press reports at the time, the correspondence of Dr. Snyder then and later, and the president's memoirs—describes the illness as a severe intestinal problem. Unfortunately, these contemporary reports have come into question. Dr. Mattingly came to the conclusion decades later that the episode was "an impending heart attack" or a "mild heart attack for which a deceptive diagnosis of food poisoning was announced to the press and public." Scholars have accepted his suspicions, as they have with regard to the 1949 "attack." One described this "heart attack" as "much less difficult, only a slight affair, not in any sense requiring the nearly two months of recovery that followed the attack of 1949." Another, recognizing the impossibility of determining whether Snyder or Mattingly was correct in his diagnosis, nonetheless found evidence to suggest that the subsequent 1955 heart attack "may have been Eisenhower's third." In fact, there is not a shred of evidence to suggest the April illness was anything other than a gastrointestinal upset, and it is impossible to imagine that Snyder would have given a "deceptive diagnosis" and then allowed the president, the supposed victim of a heart attack—however mild—to return to work in a few days. This "new interpretation" defies logic, and it is as baseless as were the rumors that sprang up at the time.[15]

The health of a president was a far more alluring topic than that of a general, and in the aftermath of this first, brief presidential illness, as one journalist explained, "A new batch of stories circulated through cocktail parties and sewing circles. Among the things Ike had, according to the boys with the inside dope, was stomach ulcers." The most notable purveyor of the rumors was Drew Pearson, the popular radio commentator and author of the "Washington Merry-Go-Round." Pearson had dismayed Eisenhower initially in 1943 when he broke the sensational story kept secret by other correspondents in Sicily—that General George S. Patton had slapped a battle-weary soldier. The two men maintained a polite relationship after the war, but the columnist—who had tried throughout the war to expose the truth about Franklin Roosevelt's condition and, having failed, resolved to fulfill his newspaperman's obligation to make clear the facts about the health of every president in the future—claimed a particular interest in

Eisenhower's condition, often coming up with questionable information. As early as April 1949, he heard a rumor that the general had cancer, and shortly after the 1952 election he accepted the view of a heart specialist that the newly elected president "could not possibly live out his four years," ostensibly because he had to have a scooter carry him between golf holes at Denver. Pearson believed the "truth" should have come out before the election, and he had wanted to mention Ike's "heart condition" on the air, but ABC balked. "I hinted at it as best I could," he wrote in his diary, "but tempers run so high that people won't believe you even if you do try to report a candidate's health."[16]

By the spring of 1953 Pearson was bothered by "how little time Eisenhower spends at work," especially by his playing golf "at least three times a week" and his frequent three-day weekends. He confided to his diary: "The newpapermen protect him. I think it boils down to the fact that Ike is really not at all well, also probably rather lazy. I understand he has colitic poisoning, as well as high blood pressure." In April he gave voice to his suspicions when he wrote in his newsletter that the president had a long history of intestinal problems, and in August he charged that Ike had high blood pressure, "the first symptom of heart disease," and was hiding it from the people.[17]

The administration was at odds over how to deal with the rumors. Jim Hagerty, along with most Republicans, had bitterly resented the concealment of Franklin Roosevelt's illness in 1944, but as press secretary he did not favor a policy of full disclosure of health information. When journalists approached him for more details, he issued a brief but emphatic denial of Pearson's story but would not give them any further information. He believed that to do so would only add fuel to the "rumor fire" and thus spread it, and he was confident that Ike's public appearances and travels around the country would convince reporters and the American people of his well-being.[18]

Dr. Snyder was less constrained. He knew the rumors were lies, and he was not happy with the policy of silence. So he leaked information about Ike's health to *U.S. News and World Report* and gave private "backgrounders" to selected reporters—noting the low-calorie diet, the regular exercise, the "dynamic" blood pressure, the "slightly vulnerable" digestive system, and the "good" heart. As if intent upon squelching every rumor, he stated bluntly to a conference of the New York Heart Association that his patient was not suffering from heart disease. "The president's cardiovascular system has been thoroughly examined by specialists—in the army, the navy, and civilian life—at approximately annual intervals since I made supervision of his health my responsibility in October 1945," he insisted. "In all of these examinations the findings indicate that our president shows less evidence of the ravages of time and stress than is anticipated in a man of his age." He added, "I am not so prideful of my own competence that I have not consulted with many heart and vascular disease experts in this connection."[19]

By the fall of 1953 the president's health had become a public issue, and Robert Donovan of the *New York Herald Tribune,* a newspaper friendly to the administration, put the question directly to Ike at his news conference: "Sir, in view of certain published accounts which seem to have caused some concern in the country, I wonder if I could presume to ask you how you are feeling these days?" The president and the other reporters burst into laughter, and Ike replied, grinning, "Well, I will tell you: As you people know, or some of you know, I have had sort of a sore elbow which has prevented me from getting my exercise to which I am accustomed, which I think I need, and which I love. Aside from that, if I am not in good condition, the doctors have fooled me badly, because I feel fine and, as a matter of fact, I underwent quite a series of tests just before we came back from Denver, and the reports given to me were cheering to a man of my age."[20]

Ike's humor ended the speculation for the time being, but his administration did not formulate a clear policy on the broad issue of what the public had a right to know about the health of their president. Jim Hagerty did not want to respond to any misinformation lest he give credit to it. As a general approach, Snyder also was opposed to parading the president's health before the public. He conceded it would be wise and necessary shortly before the end of his term—if Ike chose to run again—to issue a "dignified review" of his health history and his current condition, but nothing more. The rumors, however, led him to abandon his policy of silence and to "leak" the medical news because it was all good news. The larger issue regarding secrecy versus openness remained unresolved and would plague the White House for the next seven years, the more so at times when the administration wanted to hide the president's ailments from his people.[21]

In these early years of the first term, Snyder's program of diet and exercise seemed so successful as to give him great confidence about his patient's general well-being. He did not keep an official record of his ongoing evaluations, but his correspondence gives a sense of what he was thinking. "The president seems to be able to take the daily blow-ups by one or another member of the Congress in stride," he explained to General Al Gruenther in the summer of 1954. "He keeps his equanimity and his health. As you know, he looks older than he did when he took hold of the reins as chief of staff of the War Department and evidences of fair wear and tear are necessarily noticeable. However, from my careful observation, I believe that in some ways he is in better shape than he was during that period. I am sure his great responsibilities have not had the deleterious effect that is implied by the many whispered rumors that become current regarding his physical condition."[22]

The official medical records, even though scant for this early period, bear out Snyder's optimism. The doctor made use of the full range of military medical facilities for outpatient and inpatient evaluations of the president, especially Walter Reed, where a presidential suite was always available, and Fitzsimons Army Hospital, which Ike had used many times before when he was in the Denver area, where his two children were born, and which was convenient during summer vacations when he had his temporary White House at Lowry Air Force Base. In 1953 the president chose to have his annual physical examination at Fitzsimons, an outpatient evaluation by Colonel Goyette, who essentially repeated his favorable report of the previous year. He found no evidence of a persistent hypertension and no abnormalities of the cardiovascular system.[23]

In the summer of 1954, just after he had returned from a fishing trip in the Rockies, Ike chose again to have his physical at Fitzsimons, and this time he stayed overnight to facilitate Snyder's request for laboratory tests and a barium enema study. There were no gastrointestinal or cardiovascular problems, but Colonel Goyette did find the president's resting blood pressure higher than in the previous two years. He recommended follow-up evaluations after his return to Washington and suggested to Dr. Thomas Mattingly at Walter Reed that if the elevations persisted, he might consider some form of antihypertensive drug therapy. Back in the White House on 15 October, Snyder watched the blood pressure carefully for a week and found it to be lower. He wondered if the higher readings in Colorado—the diastolic as high as 110 on several occasions—had been caused by the elevation, as Ike and Mamie had come to believe. He asked the cardiologist about his experience in the mile-high altitude in Denver.[24]

Colonel Goyette did not consider altitude to have any affect on blood pressure, but he did have some thoughts about Eisenhower's condition:

I think the wide swings in the president's blood pressure are better explained on the basis that he is an early labile hypertensive. His history indicates that he has always been a hyperreactor in that his blood pressure tended to go up somewhat during periods of stress. During the past two years he has been subjected to a great deal more stress and at more frequent intervals. As you have said, he gets somewhat impatient and feels frustrated because his program is not progressing through the Congress as rapidly as he would like to have it. During these periods he builds up a great deal of internal tension, which is manifested in part by an elevation of his blood pressure. He probably does not relax as quickly as he formerly did, which causes his periods of maximum elevation to be more sustained. This is the pattern that we see in patients who are first developing hypertensive vascular disease. They react more violently to certain stimuli and the effect is more prolonged.[25]

Colonel Goyette's evaluation was worrisome enough to lead Snyder to discuss the issue at length with Dr. Mattingly, the chief of cardiology at Walter Reed, who would become the second most important physician in Eisenhower's life. Mattingly was a graduate of Georgetown University Medical School who had entered the Army Medical Corps in 1935 because he lacked the funds to fulfill his dream of studying cardiology at Massachusetts General Hospital. He finally did manage in 1949 to get to Harvard Medical School for a refresher course in cardiology, where he coauthored a paper with Dr. Paul Dudley White. The two men developed a friendship such that upon his return to Washington, Mattingly served as White's "man Friday" to help organize the Second World Congress of Cardiology. During the early 1950s his official army duty was to develop a diagnostic cardiac laboratory and a residency program for cardiologists at the Walter Reed General Hospital. He also established one of the earliest hypertensive and peripheral vascular clinics in the military, and for his various activities he earned a national reputation as a true professional, an example of army medicine at its very best—intelligent, thorough, honest, experienced, and trustworthy.[26]

Mattingly had served at times as a consultant for various members of the White House staff during the Truman administration and beginning in

1952 had participated in some of Eisenhower's physical examinations at Walter Reed. Early in 1954 he won Ike's trust and respect through his treatment of General Pete Carroll, a longtime friend and a favorite assistant of the president. Mattingly diagnosed the aide's chest pains as a mild heart attack, and after reviewing his medical and family history gave an unusually dire prognosis, even though the patient was only forty-three years old. Fearful that he might have been too pessimistic, he asked permission to have Dr. Paul White consult on the case. In early 1954 White examined the patient, concurred with Mattingly, and passed his findings on to the president. In October of that same year General Carroll died of a heart attack.[27]

As to the president's own health, Mattingly asked Snyder to obtain a series of early morning blood pressure readings in addition to the midday readings, all of which proved to be satisfactory. He also examined Ike in December 1954, in March 1955, and again just before he left for vacation on 1 August 1955. The cardiologist found no chest discomfort suggestive of angina, no symptoms of dyspnea, and no indications that Eisenhower's occasional fatigue had a cardiac element. "On repeated examinations of the cardiovascular system," he concluded, "I have found no abnormality on auscultation of the heart, no evidence of valvular heart disease, cardiac enlargement, abnormality of heart sounds or undue enlargement or increased density of the great vessels." He agreed with Colonel Goyette that Eisenhower had a labile blood pressure, but he found no evidence of hypertensive vascular disease and he opposed any drug therapy. He was content for the time being to have Snyder remain with the preventive program of weight control and periodic relaxation.[28]

Even after the careful evaluations by the army's foremost cardiologist, Snyder was uneasy in the summer of 1955 because one reality continued to plague him—the president's outbursts of anger had increased in both number and volume during his years in office. John Eisenhower made the observation that real outbursts of temper were rare with his father, and that he almost always recovered immediately, but when he did become angry he was "spectacular." Those who served him during the early White House years agreed. Bryce Harlow told of an occasion in 1954 when the president jumped on him for rewriting a speech that he did not want changed. It was like "looking into a Bessemer furnace," and at first it was so exciting to see, so dramatic a sight, that he leaned forward to see deeper into the "flaming furnace." Suddenly he realized the president was speaking to him, and he knew he had better answer "because, after all, life is short at best." But once he explained the reasons for his action, he saw the "furnace door clank shut completely and totally, the fires all turned off." It was "like an Oklahoma thunderstorm or tornado—whish, and it was gone."[29]

The temper did not improve with greater experience in the White House. Bernard Shanley recorded a progressive worsening in the months building up to the Geneva Conference in July 1955. The special counsel, who had heard his boss tell the story about Ida Eisenhower selecting Bible passages to induce her son to curb his boyhood temper, concluded that the mother had done a poor job. Ike blew up in meetings if they did not go just as he wished; he "bawled out" his devoted secretary, Ann Whitman, when she failed to deliver his medicine to him at the exact time he expected it; and by May he was angry every fifteen or twenty minutes. Shanley recalled that he and Mrs. Whitman went "through a period of almost 2½ months, which no other person knew about, which at times became almost unbearable for both of us. I saw Ann in tears more times than I care to say. At one time I didn't think it was a possibility, if things stayed the way they were, that she would last out a week." He compared the president to a trial lawyer preparing a case, who is "disgustingly grumpy and takes out all his nervousness and upset on his family and partners," who "is impossible to live with [until] finally his partners and children are ready to shoot him." Even after Ike made his case at Geneva, he gave the two a "pretty rough time," and he did not relax until he went to Denver for his vacation.[30]

For ten years Howard Snyder had worried that one of the president's fiery displays would cause a stroke, and he did everything he could to prevent them. Some imagined another health repercussion, as speechwriter Emmet Hughes described: "But an unwelcome report of some baseless criticism or some unfinished labor or some blemished performance could ignite an explosion of temper almost fiercely physical. His voice would shout, his cheeks flame with rage, his arms wave threateningly. And I recall one of his oldest White House associates murmuring, after witnessing one such scene, 'My God, how could you compute the amount of adrenalin expended in those thirty seconds? I don't know why long since he hasn't had a killer of a heart attack.'"[31]

In contrast, the president gave no indication whatever in these early years of any personal concern about a heart attack, and for good reason. He had none of the accepted conditions or signs that might portend heart disease—no family history, no high cholesterol, only marginally high blood pressure, no abnormal EKGS, and no overweight. In addition, he had been serious about his health, tending to it in every way he knew how, and the experts said that his heart was perfectly normal. It seemed beyond the realm of possibility that the nation's number one killer could affect its number one citizen.

After the stress of the Geneva Conference, Eisenhower needed a rest, and the days of late summer 1955 were exceedingly pleasant for him. There were no crises in the world, the economy was booming, Congress was in recess, the "spirit of Geneva" was still aglow, the Gallup poll had measured his popularity at a record high of 79 percent, and he was on vacation. He left Washington on 14 August for Denver, a city he had favored since his marriage there in 1916, where he could stay at the home of his mother-in-law and conduct affairs of state from a summer White House at nearby Lowry Air Force Base. Never before in his presidency had there been so much time for those things that brought him contentment—time for fishing, painting, golf, and bridge, and time especially to meet with old friends.

Ike had no regrets about staying away from Washington for so long, feeling that "there are so few people who have any real conception of the need and difficulty of keeping 'fit' in this position." Indeed, the day after a stag party that included golf, skeet shooting, and fly casting, he left on a fishing trip to the Byers Peak ranch of his friend and Denver banker, Aksel Nielsen. The ranch was eighty-two miles from the city, 8,900 feet high on the western slopes of the Continental Divide, with a stream flowing through it. The president remembered the excursion as "one of the finest trips I ever made to the mountains," as an "idyllic existence" with delightful weather and good fishing. He enjoyed the stillness and repose, and worked on one of his best paintings, a small winter scene of his favorite fishing hole on St. Louis Creek. Dr. Snyder was elated, for these five days "were as full of contentment as I had ever seen come into the life of the president during the many years that I had been with him."[32]

Back in Denver on 23 September, Eisenhower spent the early part of the beautiful Friday morning at his desk at Lowry Field. He left a stack of correspondence for his secretary, on the top of which was a letter to the Senate majority leader, Lyndon Johnson, who had suffered a heart attack in July 1955. "I am delighted to have your encouraging report on your

ALL THE "A" SIGNS: EXCESSIVE EXERCISE, HIGH ALTITUDE, STEADY + HEATED ANGER, POOR DIET, CONSTANT TENSION

recovery," the president wrote. "I most earnestly hope, for your sake, that you will not let your natural bent for living life to the hilt make you try to do too much too quickly." At about 11:00 A.M. Ike went to the golf course at Cherry Hills Country Club for an eighteen-hole match with the club professional. Scarcely were they under way than he was called to the clubhouse for a telephone call from Secretary of State Dulles. By the time he could reach the telephone, Ike was told that Dulles was en route to an engagement and would call back in an hour. He left the course and returned to the clubhouse at the appointed time only to learn that there was difficulty with the telephone circuits, so he returned to play. Finally, after the third interruption, he was able to speak with the secretary. He was visibly upset because he considered the call unnecessary, and after the fourteenth green his game went downhill. He finished the match in a sour humor.[33]

Because the morning's golf had been "badly broken up," in the president's words, he decided to stay for a late lunch and play an additional nine holes in the afternoon. At about 2:30, after hurriedly eating a huge hamburger sandwich garnished liberally with Bermuda onions, he was back on the course. At the end of the first tee he was called to the clubhouse again, ostensibly because Dulles wanted to speak with him. "At this point," his physician recalled, "his anger became so real that the veins stood out on his forehead like whipcords." After a period of waiting by the telephone, he learned that someone had made a mistake and that the secretary was not on the line. "My disposition deteriorated rapidly," he remembered. "I was made the more unhappy by an uneasiness that was developing in my stomach, due no doubt to my injudicious luncheon menu." It was on the eighth hole that he complained of indigestion. "Maybe I can't take these onions anymore," he told the club pro, "Rip" Arnold. "They seem to be backing up on me. I seem to have a little heartburn." So he quit the game and headed home. It was no proper ending for such a magnificent week.[34]

The Eisenhowers' "second home" was an unpretentious three-story gray brick house on broad, tree-shaded Lafayette Street, about four miles from downtown Denver. It was there that Mamie had grown to womanhood, where she had sometimes sought solace from the requirements of military life, where the young couple had lived at times when they were moving from one army post to another, and where they could always feel comfortable. "It was a happy place to go," wrote Robert Cutler, chairman of the

National Security Council, "for it was a dear, remembered home for all of them; where you felt as much at ease as if in comfortable slippers. It gave you a solid feeling of touching the real thing in life." When Ike arrived from the golf course at about 4:30 P.M., he spent several hours painting in the paneled basement game room, where he was joined at 5:00 by George Allen, who was there with his wife for dinner, and Dr. Snyder, who was stopping by to check on Eisenhower's condition. After dinner Snyder offered to mix drinks for his two friends, who were now playing billiards. Both declined; they were tired and expected to retire early.[35]

At dinner the president's indigestion had disappeared, but he still ate very little of the roast lamb and assorted vegetables. After the meal he prepared some milk of magnesia for George Allen, who felt ill. The two took a short walk, and the Allens left shortly thereafter. Ike went to bed at about 10:00 P.M. and fell asleep. Sometime between 1:30 and 2:30 A.M., he was awakened by a "severe chest pain" and thought immediately of the onions and the afternoon distress of the day before. Mamie, who was sleeping in an adjoining bedroom, heard him stirring and asked if he wanted anything. He was looking again for the milk of magnesia, he replied, and she found it and gave him a dose. She also turned on the light and, after looking at him, decided that he was quite ill. As she had done many times before when her husband was sick in the middle of the night, she called Dr. Snyder, who had decided fortuitously not to attend his fraternity reunion and was staying at the bachelors' quarters four miles away at Lowry Field. Snyder slipped on his clothes over his pajamas and arrived at the Doud home at about 3:00 A.M. for what was to be the beginning of the worst day of his life.[36]

Ike remembered very little of what happened then. "General Snyder arrived shortly thereafter and gave me some injections," he wrote in his memoirs, "one of which, I learned later, was morphine. This probably accounts for the hazy memory I had—and still have—of later events in the night. I do remember that one or two doctors came into my room and that later I was helped into a car and taken to a hospital." The president did not mention that it was 2:30 P.M. before he made that trip to the hospital, nearly twelve hours from the time he received his injection of morphine. He would never know, or probably even suspect, that there was almost certainly a cover-up concerning the events of that night and the following morning. He believed what his doctors and his associates told him, as did every journalist and every historian of his day—and after. But new records and plain common sense suggest that, like so many times in the past, the disease confused the diagnostician, and left the patient at risk.[37]

When Snyder arrived at the Doud home in the early hours of Saturday morning, there is no doubt that he gave the president some shots, certainly of morphine. But what happened thereafter is open to question because of three very different accounts that eventually emerged. Dr. Snyder gave the first explanation during the eleven hours before he told anyone about the heart attack; press secretary James Hagerty and cardiologist Paul Dudley White put forth a second and completely new interpretation during the week after the attack; and Dr. Snyder proposed a third, entirely different scenario over the next ten years.

Secret Service records show that at 6:20 A.M. Dr. Snyder called James J. Rowley, the special agent in charge of security, and told him not to bring the cars to the house because the president did not feel well, and to stand by until called. A few minutes later the doctor telephoned the president's secretary, Ann Whitman, who had come to refer to him affectionately as "old duck," to say that her boss would not be in early, though he might be in at 10:00 A.M. or so. The doctor also phoned Murray Snyder, the president's assistant press secretary and former reporter for the *Brooklyn Eagle,* who held a press conference at 8:00 A.M. at Lowry Air Force Base, and announced that the president had suffered a "digestive upset" in the night, that Dr. Snyder was with him, that he was still in bed, and that if he went to his office, it would not be until considerably later. The journalist said he did not know whether it was the kind of indigestion the president had experienced before. At another press conference at 9:30 A.M., Murray Snyder reported that he had spoken with the doctor some thirty minutes earlier but insisted that he had learned nothing more specific than he had announced before. He added that he would be talking to the doctor again during the morning. At about 11:00 Ann Whitman received a call from Bob Clark of the International News Service to tell her that because Murray Snyder was reluctant to say the upset was not serious, the wires were blowing it up into some serious illness. She called Dr. Snyder about forty-five minutes later, and he informed her that the illness was not serious and that the president was asleep.[38]

At 12:15 P.M. two important events took place. The assistant press secretary called the newsmen to the conference room again and made the following statement: "I just talked with General Snyder and he tells me that the president is resting. He said that this indigestion is not serious and he says that it is the same type of indigestion that many people have had. It is not serious. I asked him when the president became ill. He said he was called at 2 o'clock." When asked if the president would leave the house on that day, the assistant secretary replied: "He does not plan to leave the house. This is the kind of 24-hour stuff many people have had, and I am not going to predict how long it will take him to shake it off. He is resting in bed now." He said that he did not believe the president would attend church Sunday, but that he expected he would meet his appointments on Monday. No stomach specialists had been called in, and "the fact that Dr. Snyder will not remain in constant attendance is a good indication that it is not considered serious."[39]

Almost simultaneously, and of signal importance, Mrs. Whitman called the Secret Service to say the president would not need them that day, a directive that could have come only from Dr. Snyder, who earlier had told the agents to stand by with the automobiles. It was not until 2:10 P.M., slightly more than two hours later, that Dr. Snyder called the Secret Service again with a complete reversal of plans. He spoke to agent Rowley, who had returned to his quarters, and asked him to bring the cars immediately to the Doud house for the purpose of moving the president to the hospital. Upon arrival the agents parked at the side steps of the front porch. In the meantime, Dr. Snyder, assisted by Major General Martin Griffin, the commanding general of Fitzsimons Hospital, and Dr. Byron Pollock, its chief of cardiology, had supported the president down the stairs. At 2:30 P.M. Rowley and the president's valet, Sergeant John Moaney, assisted the patient from the front entrance to the car, with the agent entering the car first to help the president get into the rear seat. Dr. Snyder slipped in beside him, with Dr. Pollock on the opposite side, the agent picked up the doctor's two bags, and they left. They took a circuitous route in order to avoid the press, which the Secret Service thought might have established a motor watch on the house (by way of patrolling in their cars at certain intervals) after the 8:00 A.M. announcement.[40]

The presidential limousine arrived undetected at the rear entrance of Fitzsimons Hospital, where General Griffin had gone ahead to be ready with a wheelchair. The special agents wheeled the patient ten feet to the elevator which ascended to the eighth floor, the tower part of the hospital, where they rushed him to Room 8002. In a hurried mobilization they took over the entire eighth floor of the hospital and established posts with military police and Secret Service agents in the main lobby, at the front and rear elevators, and at the stairway on the seventh floor.[41]

Dr. Pollock, one of the pioneers in the use of anticoagulant therapy, was the physician in charge of the patient by virtue of his position as chief of cardiology at Fitzsimons, and he quickly made use of the few weapons in his armamentarium that might help keep the patient alive. He administered several drugs—morphine, which took its name from Morpheus, the Greek god of dreams, and which had been the doctors' constant companion for more than one hundred years as a magical drug to kill pain; papaverine, a nonaddictive white powder derived from opium, which was enjoying a brief popularity as an antispasmodic (or coronary dilator), and which some physicians had found useful in reducing pain; and atropine, a poisonous alkaloid derived from belladonna and other plants, which purportedly offered some protection against arrhythmias. The doctors also hurriedly placed Ike in bed under an oxygen tent, which they believed might decrease the work of the crippled heart, facilitate breathing, lessen pain, and prevent acute arrhythmias and shock.[42]

Simultaneously the medical staff was seeing to the necessary laboratory tests, the most important of which was to determine the prothrombin time, a measurement of the time it takes for blood to coagulate, which normally was thirteen or fourteen seconds. The usual treatment for a coronary was to administer anticoagulant drugs to lengthen the prothrombin time to above twenty seconds, so as to combat the tendency of the blood to clot. In less than an hour the test had shown Ike's prothrombin time to be normal (at fourteen seconds), and at 3:50 P.M. Lieutenant Colonel John Sheedy administered heparin, which had become the most widely used and quick-acting of the anticoagulants. Twenty minutes later he gave the patient his first dose of Coumadin, a miracle drug derived from unspoiled sweet clover, which after World War II had become the choice for long-term treatment to reduce blood clots.[43]

In the meantime, actions were under way to inform the world of the heart attack. Slightly before 2:00 P.M., just prior to leaving the Doud house for the hospital, Dr. Snyder had called Murray Snyder, who was lunching with Ann Whitman and two secretaries at the Famous Chef Restaurant, to inform him of the new developments. The latter quickly arranged a press conference for 2:30 P.M. at Lowry Air Force Base and immediately telephoned his boss, Jim Hagerty, who was on vacation in Washington, D.C.

On that day the press secretary had spent a cold, rainy afternoon in the capital playing golf at the Columbia Country Club. When he returned home, he glanced at the early afternoon edition of the *Washington Star* and read in a two-column box on the bottom of the page that the president had suffered a digestive upset and had not gone to work. It was too bad about the upset stomach, he remarked to his wife, but it was probably the result of the president's eating something too fast before he rushed out to play a round of golf.

Hagerty then took a nap but awoke at the incessant ringing of his White House phone. It was his assistant in Denver, his voice strained and choked with emotion, calling with the news. Snyder related that he had already called for the press corps at the Brown Palace Hotel to come to the White House press room for a briefing. "Jim, I intend to play this straight and give the fellows everything as fast as I can get it," he told Hagerty. "Okay?" His superior agreed: "Play it your way and give them everything you can. We've got a hell of a responsibility on our shoulders now."[44]

"I hung up the phone and for a few seconds felt as if I'd been slugged," Hagerty recorded in his diary. "The president of the United States had had a heart attack, I kept thinking. What will happen to him and the country?" But there was no time for contemplation. Murray Snyder had scheduled his press conference for 2:30 Denver time (5:30 Washington time), which left Hagerty less than thirty minutes to contact key government officials. He spoke first to vice president Nixon. "Oh my God," the vice president remarked, and then he uttered the words of consolation that others would repeat. "I know many people who have had heart attacks and have had complete recoveries. We all need the president. I'm sure he'll be all right." The operator broke in with another call from Denver, and Murray Snyder read the bulletin he planned to issue. A few minutes later Ann Whitman called from Denver, in tears, with two messages: Dr. Snyder wanted Dr. Mattingly, who had been responsible for all of the president's cardiovascular examinations since 1953, to come to Denver; and Mrs. Eisenhower, who would personally call her son, wanted Hagerty to call Ike's brothers. Hagerty dropped all other calls to speak with Milton Eisenhower, then president of Pennsylvania State University, and proceeded to call other government officials as quickly as he could.

At 5:15 P.M. in Washington Hagerty took another call from Murray Snyder and learned that the president was under an oxygen tent and was doing well, and that Dr. Snyder had asked Dr. Paul Dudley White of Boston to enter the case as a consultant. Hagerty was pleased, but he was also disturbed at Dr. Snyder's conflicting reports, ranging from a mild digestive upset to a mild coronary thrombosis. "Sooner or later," he thought, he would have to "straighten it out." At present, however, he had dozens of calls to make and he had to arrange for a plane to get him to Colorado as quickly as possible.[45]

Back in Denver, Murray Snyder held his press conference at 2:30 P.M. and made a very brief announcement: the president had just had a "mild" coronary thrombosis, he had been driven to Fitzsimons Army Hospital in his own car, he had walked from the house to the car, and Dr. Snyder had accompanied him to the hospital. As the news was flashing throughout the world, Dr. Snyder hurriedly attended to other important matters. At the president's request, he called the army's surgeon general in Washington, asking him to send Dr. Mattingly to Denver. Sometime in the midafternoon he also gave a report to the Secret Service on what had taken place on Lafayette Street. "After the president was settled," agent Rowley wrote,

Dr. Snyder informed the writer that at 2:30 A.M. this morning he was summoned by Mrs. Eisenhower and that on his arrival his examination of the president showed the president's condition as a coronary thrombosis attack, anterior type. Dr. Snyder administered the necessary medicine and remained on watch. He stated that the president slept well from 5:00 A.M. to 11:00 A.M. At 1:15 P.M. he summoned Dr. Pollock and General Griffin from Fitzsimons and they took an electrocardiograph. At 2:00 P.M. they announced the cardiograph disclosed a coronary thrombosis condition and they all concluded it would be best to move the president to the hospital where there were [*sic*] all necessary equipment available.[46]

Snyder likewise sat down to apprise Dr. Pollock of the treatment given in those early hours for the official hospital admission note, which the latter signed at 4:00 P.M.:

For the past few days Gen. Eisenhower has been vacationing in Fraser, Colo. He has felt in excellent health, pulse has been averaging about 60/min. Blood pressure 140/80. He had hamburger for lunch yesterday, and a few hours thereafter began to feel mildly upset in upper abdomen, so that he had poor appetite for supper. Mild distress continued as patient retired, and about 0300 hrs. this morning he suffered severe chest pain substernal in location, somewhat squeezing in character and persistent. He was seen By Gen. Snyder, who found pulse somewhat fast—about 85–90 min., blood pressure 160/120, administered morphine gr. ½, repeated in 45 min., papaverine (IM) gr. 1. Gen. Eisenhower received symptomatic relief, BP returned to 140/80. Pulse remained somewhat increased. Patient remained in bed. This morning the substernal discomfort continued. At 1230 hrs. Gen. Snyder requested that EKG be taken. I saw Gen. Eisenhower at 1315 hrs., took electrocardiogram, which revealed QS deformity with marked RS-T segment elevation in leads reflecting LV activity. (See tracing.) Diagnosis was made of acute massive anterior myocardial infarction and arrangements were made to move the patient into the hospital.[47]

There was no respite for General Snyder during these hectic first few hours at the hospital. After tending to the most pressing demands, he had to deal with another especially sensitive issue of inviting a civilian cardiologist to serve as a consultant on the case. It is impossible to determine from the records who was the first to propose bringing an outside expert to Fitzsimons Hospital; many people were involved, and they very likely came to a simultaneous decision. Milton Eisenhower proposed calling in a civilian specialist during his early telephone conversation with Jim Hagerty, arguing that it would increase greatly the public confidence in the handling of the illness. Fitzsimons was an army hospital, he noted, and Dr. Snyder, Dr. Mattingly, and the Fitzsimons doctors were all army medical men. "Good men, that was sure, but still army officers." Ellis Slater, a close friend of Ike's, called Dr. Snyder as soon as he heard of the attack over the radio and asked him to call in Dr. Cowles Andrus of Johns Hopkins University. Snyder received other nominations (among whom were Dr. Samuel Levine of Boston, Dr. Francis Chamberlain of San Francisco, and Dr. Gilbert Blount of the University of Colorado School of Medicine), discussed the list with the surgeon general of the army, and, with the latter's approval, decided to invite Paul Dudley White to journey to Denver.[48]

General Snyder was less decisive about what information he should give to Murray Snyder, who held eleven press conferences before the day was out. He revealed only that the president had mild indigestion Saturday evening, that the first symptoms of an occlusion or thrombosis appeared at about 2:45 A.M.; that he held up the announcement of the heart attack because he "wanted to wait until the diagnosis was complete"; that the First Lady had arrived at Fitzsimons not because of any change but because she "felt she would be more comfortable being near" her husband; and that Paul Dudley White had agreed to serve as a consultant. Further clarification would have to come from Hagerty, who was to arrive later in the evening with Dr. Mattingly.[49]

The patient, in the meantime, remained in critical condition. He dozed for much of Saturday afternoon, awoke at 5:00 P.M. and was very alert, and mentioned some mild substernal pain. At 7:00 he was perspiring moderately, his color was flushed, and he complained of an increase in chest pain, though it was not severe. The doctors quickly took another EKG and gave him another shot of morphine and atropine. Thereafter he rested more comfortably, sleeping at short intervals; he awoke briefly at midnight, with no complaints except for a slight "itchy feeling." It was an eerie ending to a momentous day.[50]

The second day, Sunday, 25 September, began with the arrival in Denver of Dr. Mattingly and Jim Hagerty, press secretary to the president, the man who would ostensibly clear away the confusion. The forty-six-year-old, stocky, bespectacled Irishman had begun his journalistic career at Columbia University as campus correspondent for the *New York Times* and had joined that paper after graduating in 1934. Nine years later he resigned to handle press relations for Governor Dewey, which eventually involved two unsuccessful presidential campaigns. He did not know Eisenhower before 1952, but after he joined the team the two developed what approached a father-and-son relationship. "If the president had a single close friend," wrote one observer, "a man whom he could trust, it was Hagerty." As press secretary, and as a confidant to Ike, Hagerty had earned the respect of the White House press corps as a man of great energy, honesty, and competence.[51]

Hagerty had left Washington at 7:50 Saturday evening on a military air transport plane with Mattingly, who was carrying the president's medical records, and journalist Merriman Smith of United Press International, the dean of the White House press corps. Smith had called to ask if he could hitch a ride and agreed not to report any conversations Hagerty might have with Mattingly during the flight. In those discussions the army cardiologist told Hagerty, whom he thought was "a picture of all gloom and doom," that he was "mystified" about the cause of the heart attack. No previous examination of the president had revealed any sign of a heart disorder, and his examination on 1 August indicated that, with the exception of bursitis in the right shoulder, he was in "first-class" condition. Hagerty was also a silent bystander to a heated argument between the cardiologist and the journalist. When Mattingly said there had been no previous signs of heart trouble, Smith refused to believe it and repeated the rumors about Ike having suffered an earlier heart attack. Mattingly offered to show Smith the official records, resented being called a liar for the first time in his life, and acquired an immediate distaste for the press.[52]

The "three very serious and sober guys," as Hagerty described them, arrived in Denver near midnight in a blinding rainstorm; they flew over Lowry Air Force Base twice trying to get in but had to land at Stapleton, the commercial airport. Hagerty rushed to the hospital, where he found among the physicians "an air of concern you could almost cut with a knife. The president of the United States was in their charge, and they realized the deep responsibility that they had." They were not fearful about their situation, but they all seemed to be looking forward to the arrival of Dr. White the next afternoon.[53]

Hagerty spoke briefly with the doctors and reviewed the transcripts of the press releases. Then Dr. Snyder asked to see him alone in his room. The doctor was visibly upset and related that the president, on hearing that his press secretary was on the way, had said, "Good. Tell Jim to take over." Hagerty noted, "I knew exactly what the president meant by that remark. He meant that he wanted me to give as full reports of his illness as I could give and to give the doctors all possible assistance in the handling of this, the first case in history of a president of the United States in office suffering a heart attack. That direction from the president from the very first day I went to the hospital was one which I consistently followed throughout the time he was at Fitzsimons." Later Ike told him that his interpretation had been correct, and he explained in his memoirs, "I had been one of those who during President Wilson's long illness had wondered why the public was kept so much in the dark about his real condition, and thought that the nation had a right to know exactly the status of the president's health. So now I had a quick reply: 'Tell the truth, the whole truth; don't try to conceal anything.'"[54]

With Hagerty now in charge, one of the journalists in Denver remembered, the "change in tone was dramatic. The reporters liked Murray Snyder and thought well of him, but he was not varsity. With Hagerty came brisk, unsentimental efficiency and the first freshets of information that quickly swelled to a mighty flood." But there was not much efficiency during the secretary's first hours in Denver. He called his first press conference at 1:12 A.M. Sunday at Lowry Air Force Base, and another at 8:00 A.M., but in both instances he had to defer to the reporters' questions, promising only to try to get the answers. There was a need for clarification because the Sunday morning papers were openly critical of what they presumed was a deliberate deception on the part of the administration. "The president's attack was a closely guarded secret until the decision to take him to the hospital," wrote the *New York Times*. "During the twelve hours between the time the symptoms first occurred and the trip to Fitzsimons, General Snyder insisted that the president was merely suffering a common digestive upset."[55]

Dr. Mattingly, arriving at the eighth floor shortly after midnight, received a briefing from Snyder and Pollock, and then examined the president briefly. He met with the hospital staff and Snyder again, and then entered his findings in the clinical record at 1:00 A.M. His description of the president's status during the early hours of the attack was virtually the same as Pollock's, but with some important new information:

> About 0230 hrs. he was awake and complained of severe epigastric distress. He was seen by Gen. Snyder at 0300 hrs. and after antispasmodics and morphine he slept and rested well from 0500 to noon. He was seen in the afternoon by Col. Pollock and brought to hospital. Chest pain has never been absent since early AM at times when awake. *There has been no period of shock even during movement to hospital, pulse and blood pressure have remained stable with no arrhythmias.* (italics mine)[56]

Mattingly was unable to get any sleep, although he dozed briefly; he arose for an early mass at the post chapel, where he prayed for guidance. At 8:00 A.M. Dr. Snyder approached him, so deeply shaken by the local Sunday morning newspaper reports that he was almost in tears. "Tom, the press is trying to crucify me," he said, "accusing me of delaying calling Fitzsimons and getting the president in the hospital—that he could have died in the Doud home, that we should not have let him walk down stairs." Snyder gave only one explanation for his actions—that he wanted to be sure he would not panic the nation by announcing a presidential heart

all true !

attack at 2:30 A.M. Mattingly decided not to press for any further details about why his friend had waited so long the next morning to contact the hospital and get help. He had never seen Snyder, who was ordinarily calm and stoic, so upset, and he suspected he was having trouble with his conscience. In any event, Mattingly recognized his colleague's need for support and tried to assure him that Dr. White would not pick up these sensitive questions and, even more, that he would support Snyder's early management of the illness.[57]

Snyder was still under the gun with Hagerty, who asked to meet with him again on Sunday morning to seek answers to some of the "contradictory statements" that had been made during the first few hours of the attack. The men talked at length, and Hagerty asked for clarification on the time of the announcement and the "walking" by the president from the house to the car. He then held a press conference, shortly before noon, with a few "fresh-ets" of information. He explained that Mrs. Eisenhower had called Dr. Sny-der at 2:00 A.M.; that Dr. Snyder had called General Griffin and Dr. Pollock at about 12:30 P.M.; that the cardiograph was "the confirming diagnosis"; that Dr. Snyder, assisted by Dr. Pollock, made the decision to announce that the president had had a heart attack; that the president was assisted and supported as he walked from the house to the car because the doctors thought it was easier for him than being carried on a stretcher; and that Dr. Snyder had made the decision to call in Dr. White.[58]

"All of these questions caused a little confusion in the press," Hagerty recorded in his diary, "and while I cannot blame anyone for it, I do think they could have been avoided if Murray and Dr. Snyder had been working more closely together. For example, I do not blame the doctor for wanting to wait *until the morning* before exciting Mrs. Eisenhower or Mrs. Doud and until he could get cardiograph equipment to the house" (italics mine). Hagerty did not mention, at least not in his diary, what he thought about Snyder waiting *until the afternoon* before asking for cardiographic equip-ment. He was more concerned about the public relations aspects than the historical record, noting that "all of these instances had caused consider-able concern among the president's friends, and it was necessary for me to get them straightened out." He still was perturbed that the two Snyders had identified the problem as a mild digestive upset. "What they could have said," he thought, "was that the president was not feeling well, that the doctor was at the house and just as soon as he had diagnosed it, he would let them know."[59]

The president's Sunday morning was also less than perfect. He awakened at 1:45 A.M. sweating profusely about the head, shoulders, and upper chest and had to have a change of pajamas. Thereafter he was restless, sleeping at fifteen- to thirty-minute intervals until 6:35 A.M., when he complained of pain in the chest. Dr. Pollock administered morphine, atropine, papaverine, and milk of magnesia, after which the patient slept until 8:30 A.M., at which time he complained again of chest "soreness." After another EKG he remained restless, sleeping only occasionally, but his color improved. At 10:00 A.M. he had his first meal, a glass of milk and a small dish of oatmeal.[60]

Everything seemed better on Sunday afternoon with the arrival from Boston of Dr. Paul Dudley White. It was not surprising for the military doctors to select White; he had earned the highest respect of Tom Mattingly, his name was familiar to the president because of General Carroll's case, he had ties to leading staff members Sherman Adams and Robert Cutler, and he was the most widely recognized heart expert in the United States. In many ways his career paralleled the rise of and recognition of coronary heart disease as a clinical entity. After graduating from Harvard Medical School in 1907, he journeyed to London to study the new EKG machine under the direction of the world-famous cardiologist Dr. Thomas Lewis. In 1914 he returned to Massachusetts General Hospital with the innovative machine, feeling "like a lonely adventurer entering an unexplored and unknown country planning to spend my life in a new and as yet unrecognized specialty." From then until the 1950s, he had an exceptional influence in several different capacities. He was a pioneer founder of the American Heart Association in 1924, the first executive director of the National Advisory Heart Council two decades later, and the politicians' favorite witness to testify before congressional committees about the virtues of medical research.[61]

White was also a prolific author, with more than four hundred articles in medical journals, most of them related to patients rather than basic laboratory investigations, and his 1931 textbook, *Heart Disease,* quickly became the standard for students everywhere. His fame as a practitioner extended beyond his homeland to the world, and among the eminent he had treated were Pablo Casals, Albert Schweitzer, Andrew Carnegie, Cornelius Vanderbilt, William Randolph Hearst, Alben Barkley, and the presidents of Nicaragua, Colombia, and the Philippines. It was fitting for him now to treat the most prominent man in the United States, and early Sunday morning he left Boston as the only passenger aboard a U.S. Air Force Constellation (though not before telling reporters the president might be able to run for reelection!). His plane arrived at Lowry Air Force Base at 1:30 P.M., blew a tire upon landing, and stopped at the edge of the airport in a haze of black smoke. Waiting to greet him was Hagerty, who later said, "I liked him the moment he came off the plane."[62]

White talked with Mattingly on the way to the hospital. Upon arrival, he quickly consulted with the other physicians and reviewed the past and present history, the laboratory findings, and the EKGs as far back as 1947. He noticed that the military doctors were keeping very careful records, "in apple pie order, with as little fuss as possible," and at 2:30 P.M. he filled out his own consultation note about the attack. After giving some background information, he wrote of the president:

> Got home at 4:30, painted till 7:30, light supper, bed by 9:30. Soon asleep. Awoke at 2:30. Complained of increasingly severe low substernal nonradiating pain for which General Snyder saw him at 3:00 & gave [morphine sulfate] ¼ gr. s.c. Second dose at 3:45. Then slept from 4:30 to 11:00 A.M. *Papaverine started at 3 P.M.* 1 gr. IM ev. 4 hrs. ECG taken at 1 P.M. showed [coronary thrombosis]. Dull pain continued. (italics mine)[63]

At 3:30 P.M. White went in with Colonel Pollock for a brief examination of the president, hoping to put him at ease about his condition. When he left he informed the assembled physicians of his complete agreement with the present regimen and said that he had no additional therapeutic suggestions to make. He rated the heart attack "a 3 out of a possible 5" and issued a bulletin: "The president yesterday had a moderate attack of coronary thrombosis without complications. His present condition is satisfactory." White also asked Hagerty to stress to the news media that "moderate" meant "neither mild nor serious," a definition which was in all the leads and headlines of the stories the next morning. White also met with Mamie and John Eisenhower, and later with Nixon and Adams, and was able to reassure them. Everything did seem better with a world expert on hand, and Hagerty decided to take advantage of the situation by asking the Bostonian to give a press conference the following day. White was the kind of man, he decided, who would have a soothing effect on the patient, the press, the American people, and, not least of all, the president's friends like Bill Robinson and Cliff Roberts, who were still worried about Ike being surrounded by military doctors.[64]

In the meantime, White had an opportunity to talk at length with his old friend, Tom Mattingly, about the criticism the press had leveled at Dr. Snyder, especially about walking the president down the stairs in the Doud home, and the delay in giving out the diagnosis of "heart attack." In the late afternoon White went to Lafayette Street to explore the stairs, after which the two met again and agreed that walking the patient was preferable to strapping him to a stretcher and tilting it awkwardly down a narrow, winding stairway. The sleuthlike cardiologists returned to the hospital for a quick check on the patient and then decided to walk to dinner at the officers club, where they were sharing a room. On approaching the entrance, White spotted a tee of the nearby golf course and proposed a moonlight stroll around the greens, where he initiated a discussion that continued at dinner and late into the night. They talked about long-term management of the case, about the eventual movement of the patient back to Washington, and about the "rough time" the press was giving General Snyder because of his delay in calling for help. There were some reasons for criticism of his handling of the patient, they agreed, but recognizing his position as a surgically trained physician and not knowing his real thinking, they found it difficult to evaluate. Perhaps this was a poor example of treatment, but what gave the press the right to criticize? And why make an issue of it now, when everything seemed to be proceeding satisfactorily?[65]

White and Mattingly did not want to hurt Snyder, but at the same time they wanted to assure the press that once the true diagnosis had been established there had been no attempt at a cover-up and that now they were giving out the real facts. They decided on a plan to "take the heat off" the general and "cool the press" by leaving it to Hagerty to explain the situation. If there was a direct question, White would respond that Snyder did what he considered best for the president, and that the cardiologists would neither compliment him for his management nor condemn him for mishandling the case. Otherwise during the news conference White could state at least in a general way that the delay in diagnosis and hospitalization had not harmed the patient or altered the outcome. The latter judgment would sound reasonable because the patient was now in the hospital and had suffered no apparent ill effects from the delay. And, too, as White told his friend, "I shall give the press and the nation a course on myocardial infarction. They will get so interested, the press will not raise the question of management before hospitalization, especially if in the morning he continues to be doing satisfactorily."[66]

The cardiologists honestly believed that for the moment, at least, no harm had been done, and their proof was in the general well-being of the patient. After his Sunday afternoon examination by White, Pollock, and Mattingly, the president ate an evening meal of milk toast, custard, Jell-O, and milk and had a visit from his son, during which time he appeared cheerful and communicative. He slept for long intervals until 10:00 P.M., and although he continued to perspire, he did not complain of any more pain when he was awake. Dr. Sheedy was slightly concerned about his irregular heartbeat, about every four beats, but overall Ike was doing fine.[67]

Monday, 26 September, the third day after the attack, might well have been named "Paul Dudley White Day" in Denver because of the sixty-nine-year-old cardiologist's brilliantly successful 10:00 A.M. news conference. Even before the conference began, the day looked bright. At 9:00 White (together with Mattingly, Pollock, and Snyder) examined the patient and was very pleased because Ike had awakened with a hearty appetite, ate a breakfast of fruit, cooked cereal, egg, toast, and milk, and had a bath, a shave, and a bowel movement. When the doctor discussed with him the nature of the disease, its prognosis, and a course of treatment, Ike was cheerful and mentally alert; he definitely seemed to be on his way to recovery. White knew he was still "seriously and acutely ill," as he wrote on his record card, and although he did not like the heart sounds, the rather fast pulse, and the many premature beats, there had been no complications. After leaving the hospital room, White returned to Lowry Air Force Base and sat down with Hagerty to review the many questions that were still hanging fire, especially concerning Dr. Snyder's treatment and diagnosis of the president, how long Ike would have to remain in the hospital, and whether he would be able to run for reelection. White was confident he could handle any questions, and he did so well that shortly after the conference was over Hagerty expressed his "deep personal appreciation" for the "wonderfully informative" performance.[68]

Unlike Hagerty, who used a press conference to inform, White sought to educate. With his full mustache, rimless glasses, mild manner, and timely use of the vernacular, he made an impressive instructor. Sitting in the oak-paneled room ordinarily reserved for military briefings, with a plane standing by for his return to Boston, he overwhelmed his audience. He might have been addressing a class of medical students as he explained the complex terms and processes of coronary thrombosis, the "commonest important illness that besets a middle-aged man in this country today." It was first of all a disease of the arteries, not of the heart. The process begins "insidiously" on the coronary arterial walls as a thickening impinges "on the bore of the artery—the caliber of the artery itself, like a tube." As the wall narrows, the condition of angina pectoris sometimes develops, though not with the president, and if the blood clots at the narrow part, the disease is acute. "So coronary thrombosis is simply the laying down of a clot in the coronary artery." Since the arteries branch out like a tree over the surface of the heart and penetrate it "like roots going into the ground," the clot prevents an adequate blood supply from flowing and a part of the heart muscle "aches." Some of the muscle fibers die, causing an "infarct," and have to be taken away. "This process, you see, is like a little damaged area, like an abscess, without any germs or infection. But that has to be taken care of, the dead muscle carted away. Then actually these little wrecking cells come in and take away, after the first week. With the removal of the dead muscle, a scar forms with new building cells, and after about two weeks, the scar becomes "strong."

White spiced his lecture with observations on the possible causes of coronary thrombosis—inheritance, body build, exercise, stress and strain, diet, alcohol, and tobacco—and insisted that neither golf nor the high altitude was involved in the president's attack. He mentioned some of the more arcane aspects—the oxygen tent, EKG, and leukocytes—and talked about the patient. Eisenhower had experienced no earlier signs of the disease; he had had a "bad pain" on Saturday night but none since; he had "wonderful morale"; and he had had "a good bowel movement," an item the doctor insisted on including because "the country is so bowel-minded anyway" and because it was important. He dodged questions concerning a second term. When asked about his statement in Boston that it was conceivable the president could run again, he pointed out that many people "can not only live out this condition but can be normally active for many years thereafter." But he had never had a patient with presidential responsibilities, he conceded, and even with a complete recovery, the decision would have to be left with the president.[69]

White's performance made an incredible impression, and he definitely allayed most of the apprehensions about the president's care. "It swept away the rumors of impending catastrophy [*sic*]," wrote a retired military physician, "the fears that the published bulletins regarding the president's condition were not entirely true, and acted as a breath of fresh air in a darkened cellar." An editor of a newsletter opposed to smoking added, "Nothing ever published by any heart association holds a candle to your statement about coronary disease, from the standpoint of lucidity as well as authority." Shortly after it ended, Hagerty told White that "the newsmen covering here unanimously agreed that yours was one of the best, if not the best, conference they have ever attended"; years later a reporter wrote to Hagerty to rave about the "history-making" event.[70]

What was striking, apart from the stark clarity of the lesson on coronary disease, was that White addressed none of the questions that reporters had been asking for two days and that Hagerty had been turning around in his mind. The doctor focused on the disease rather than on Dr. Snyder's diagnosis, and none of the newsmen asked about the "digestive upset" or the "delay." The Bostonian was as elated as Mattingly had ever seen him after the conference, and said: "Tom, it worked!" In his 1971 autobiography he noted, "We quickly discovered that if we could distract the reporters for five to ten minutes at the beginning of these conferences we would have fewer difficult questions to answer." In fact, White did not go through any process of discovery; he was able to distract the press his first time around. Delighted with his accomplishment and the progress of his patient, he accepted the plaudits and left for Boston, in the perception of Mattingly, "as excited as a ten-year-old boy who had found his first bird's nest."[71]

The questions about Dr. Snyder did not disappear, however, at least not immediately. The next day, Tuesday, the reporters were after Hagerty again about the "twelve-hour delay." The secretary gave an extensive and, as it turned out, his final discussion of the issue. It constituted the official version of what happened at the Doud home and offered a reasonable explanation of the doctor's actions. When Dr. Snyder was summoned at about 2:00 A.M., he explained, it was impossible to diagnose the ailment for certain. The president had complained of severe pain, so the doctor gave him morphine. The president went back to sleep and slept soundly until around 11:00 A.M. When Eisenhower awoke, Dr. Snyder called in Dr. Pollock, and the two doctors made a cardiograph tracing and "confirmed" the diagnosis of coronary thrombosis. Since that time, Hagerty continued, Dr. White and others had made clear that the sleep the president was able to

Dr. Paul Dudley White leaning forward at a press conference in 1955. With him are General Snyder, right; Colonel Mattingly, center; and Major Walter Tkach. (AP/Wide World Photos)

get in the first interval was "very important and essential" to his ultimate recovery, and that rest is an all-important factor in the president's battle for life. The secretary was able to put an end to questions about the stretcher, pointing out that the doctors had decided it would require less physical exertion for the president, and be less "upsetting," for them to assist him than it would have been to have used a stretcher.[72]

The defense of Dr. Snyder ended several days later when Paul White, back in Boston, called a press conference in his office. No one at the White House or in Denver had asked him to comment "on the time lag before the cardiogram was taken," he volunteered, but he thought he could add something "helpful" about some aspects he had not discussed at length in Denver. In fact, he was simply following through on the discussion he had with Mattingly to help "take the heat off" Howard Snyder. "I issued a new statement this afternoon," he wrote to Hagerty, "which I hope may help take care of some of the criticisms that have been appearing recently. It is ridiculous, it seems to me, for these to be brought up anyway but I hope I have taken care of them."[73]

After an opening paragraph in which he praised the family doctor for being on the front line of battle against coronary heart disease, the Bostonian switched immediately to the central issue:

> The problem of the immediate diagnosis "indigestion versus a heart attack" is often difficult or impossible at the onset especially if the pain is low under the breastbone, as it was in President Eisenhower's case, or high in the pit of the stomach, that is, the epigastrium. General Snyder very quickly suspected coronary thrombosis and, therefore, gave the two hypodermic injections of morphine at 3 o'clock and 3:45. However, he didn't want to make such an announcement in the middle of the night to the world. It was evident that General Snyder thought coronary thrombosis probable inasmuch as he ordered an electrocardiogram to be taken on the spot before moving the president. This was incidentally taken after the president had waked up at 1 o'clock following the subsidence of the effect of the opiate. . . . General Snyder did not want to disturb him for several hours because he was in pain and mild prostration at the time and so he waited until he recovered from the attack before he had the electrocardiogram.[74]

White went on to say that "any family doctor would do well to follow Major General Snyder's procedure." Dr. Snyder had been correct in his diagnosis of a heart attack instead of indigestion, he explained, and in his administration of morphine. Conceding that "some physicians wondered about the delay" before the EKG was taken, he proclaimed it "just right," and added: "I'm surprised at the criticism. To me the procedure was a natural one." To have given the EKG immediately or to have moved the patient too soon "might have been fatal." He also supported Snyder for deferring the EKG and the hospitalization, because both were more effective after the immediate reaction of the attack had subsided. When he was finished, White sent a verbatim copy of his conference to Howard Snyder, who expressed his "great appreciation" for the helpful and timely words.[75]

White's voluntary generosity arose from his decency; he rarely criticized anyone, and he had no desire to denigrate Dr. Snyder. He also wanted to be a good soldier by endorsing the actions of his military colleagues, some of whom, like Mattingly, he respected. He also hoped to inspire confidence in Snyder and the others not only among the public but in particular with the patient, because over the long term they would be providing Eisenhower's primary care. He was accurate, too, in his acknowledgment that some physicians did choose to treat coronary victims in their own homes during the initial hours after the attack. Nonetheless, he was participating in a cover-up, although he would not have thought of it in that sense. He was not telling the press about his own early reservations about Snyder's care, and he was dissembling when he said that any "family doctor" would do well to follow Snyder's procedure when he knew that he would not follow it himself.

By the time the news magazines appeared in the week of 2 October with their first stories of the attack, the issue of the "twelve-hour delay" was fading. *Newsweek* left the question in limbo: "Whether Snyder at once realized that Mr. Eisenhower had suffered a heart attack is not known. The family was convinced that Mr. Eisenhower had merely suffered a flare-up of indigestion." *Time* accepted Hagerty's explanation that Dr. Snyder had detected the first symptoms after an initial examination and, upon completion of the diagnosis eleven hours later, decided to move the president. *U.S. News and World Report* explained that Dr. Snyder "was able to relieve the president's symptoms of shock and get him to rest. Dr. Snyder wanted the president kept in a state of rest." And in a section entitled "Questions People Are Asking—And the Official Answers," the magazine added an interesting comment about the deception: "Officials point out that the president's physician wanted complete verification before announcing a coronary thrombosis. He did not want a lot of 'leaks' to come out about the president's condition. So he told Murray Snyder . . . that the president had indigestion. He was not telling an untruth. The president did have indigestion before the heart attack."[76]

Had the press been more alert and aggressive, and better informed about coronary heart disease, they could have asked some penetrating questions about the Hagerty-White version of the medical treatment of the president of the United States. For example, they might have asked the press secretary the following: Did Dr. Snyder in the early morning of 24 September detect any of the symptoms other than pain that sometimes accompany a coronary thrombosis, such as dyspnea, cyanosis, heavy perspiration, or nausea? Why did the doctor not administer any drug other than morphine? Why did he not telephone the cardiologist at Fitzsimons Hospital in order to consult about the most recent treatment of coronary cases, the possibility of new drugs, or the need for EKG equipment at the Doud home? Why did he not immediately call his friend Tom Mattingly, the specialist most familiar with Eisenhower's cardiovascular health, since it was already daybreak in Washington, D.C.? Why did he not have a cardiologist on hand at least by early morning to be there when the president awoke? Why did the doctor not administer oxygen on Lafayette Street, if it was considered an immediate necessity at the hospital?

The journalists might have saved at least two questions for Dr. White: Did he really believe that it was only "natural" procedure for the physician to the president of the United States to diagnose a heart attack, give two shots of morphine, and then wait for ten or eleven hours before seeking the assistance of a cardiologist, before administering such additional drugs as heparin, papaverine, and atropine, and before arranging for an EKG and hospitalization? Could the nation's first citizen not expect better care than that?

The press was anything but aggressive, and after only a brief period of questioning it gave up forever its concern about Dr. Snyder and his diagnosis—with one momentary exception. At a presidential news conference nearly four months later, on 19 January, reporter May Craig asked Eisenhower if he thought it was right and proper for a White House physician to conceal the serious illness of a president for many hours and to refrain for many hours from calling in other physicians to consult on his diagnosis and early treatment. Ike replied, "Well, you are asking what I assume to be a hypothetical question—(laughter)—because in my own case my doctor was in close contact, I think, with others very rapidly, certainly as soon as daylight came, and it was determined what to do about it." When the reporter said she understood it was as much as ten hours before Snyder consulted with others, the president replied: "It may have been. But it probably may take some ten hours to determine whether a person is suffering from having eaten some bad food or some other cause, I am not sure. I am not a doctor, you are sure of that."[77]

That the press did not insist—in October—upon a complete explanation from the doctors reflected the shrewdness of James Hagerty. He handled the public relations aspects of the heart attack magnificently and deserved an accolade for the journalists' retreat. He simply ignored the initial story about indigestion put out by Howard Snyder and Murray Snyder, and replaced it with a second version—that Dr. Snyder needed the twelve-hour delay in order to "confirm" his diagnosis and allow his patient to rest. That version became almost foolproof when blessed with the prestigious imprimatur of the nation's most famous cardiologist. "There was some criticism of Presidential Physician Major General Howard Snyder last week for not taking a cardiogram until eleven hours after the attack and for giving no drugs except morphine at first," *Time* explained as it consigned the story to history. "But Boston's Dr. Paul Dudley White . . . called Snyder's treatment 'just right.'" The journalists were not willing or able to take issue with Dr. White; it was one thing to question a family doctor, another to challenge an international authority. And too, every day the president lived and improved was testimony to the doctors' competence and proof that no harm had been done. In the final analysis, there was no better defense than the good result.[78]

The issue disappeared, as well, because it quickly became yesterday's news as it was subsumed by a hundred new stories about the president's convalescence. This was particularly true because of Hagerty's decision to "tell them the truth, the whole truth." For the next six weeks he held several briefings every day for a press corps that grew from twenty-two to more than one hundred and slept on cots in the press room at Lowry Air Force Base. He overwhelmed them with details—about what Ike ate and what he avoided; how long he slept and how he felt; the decor of his room and the color of his pajamas; the books he read, the music he heard, his birthday gifts, the people he saw, and the decisions he made. James Deakin of the *St. Louis Post Dispatch*, a young reporter who stayed in Denver for twelve weeks and had a story on the front page of his paper every day, suspected the press secretary of hiding some truth behind the inundation. "Hagerty could not prevent a few questions about the delayed announcement," he opined. "But thereafter he swamped the reporters with information. He opened the bag for them. He told them so much that they had no way of knowing whether he was telling them everything. They could not discriminate; there was no time to find out whether any nuggets were missing from the avalanche. . . . He loved 'em to death."[79]

Ruminating about the Eisenhower illness some thirty years later, Deakin acknowledged that the newsmen at Lowry did not "seriously challenge" the secrecy of the early morning hours; they did do "some probing into the cover story and the delay, but it was just a light workout." He still looked upon the "indigestion" story as a "deception of the American people," and he still resented it, but he viewed it as one small episode in the historic conflict between journalists and officials. Administrations made it a practice to lie about the president's health, he thought, and one only had to recall the massive deceptions under Woodrow Wilson and Franklin Roosevelt to realize how much better the Eisenhower administration was than most. Hagerty was responsible for this change for the better, and after all, his was only a "little" cover-up. Or was it?[80]

The truth about the early morning of 24 September 1955 was very likely a victim not only of skillful official management of the news, but also of journalistic suspicion about the government. Smug in their assumption that "the administration" had lied to them from the very outset, almost as a matter of course, the press failed to ask the most obvious and promising question: What if Dr. Snyder actually had been telling the truth in the beginning and really believed the illness was only indigestion? The journalists filed 2.25 million words on the "big story" to newspapers, wire services, and magazines, but they were so blinded by suspicion of the executive branch that they deceived—and muzzled—themselves. By doing so, they may have missed the biggest story of them all—that the president of the United States suffered a heart attack that went undiagnosed for ten hours. Their myopia is understandable, at least in part, because Dr. Snyder was doing everything possible to silence their questions and their doubts, and to lead them away from the truth.

Nearly a month after the heart attack, Murray Snyder wrote to Howard Snyder to commiserate about the "dark hours" of 24 and 25 September, noting that he had shared some of the pressures and also "the blame of some of the quarterbacks who got on the scene Monday morning." He praised Dr. Snyder for his superb judgment, which he thought might be responsible for the "fact that the boss is still with us," and he suggested that for the sake of history, the doctor might want sometime to reconstruct the minute details of those first twenty-four or thirty-six hours. "There have been too many mistaken commentaries on this period, due perhaps for the most part to the fact that in this crisis those to whom was entrusted the precious life of the president were far too busy to watch clocks or calendars or keep diaries." Dr. Snyder replied that, in fact, he had been watching the clock: "During the long hours I sat at the president's bedside on the morning of September 24, I made a detailed note in pencil of all the events of that morning. I have those penciled notes. These facts will be incorporated in the confidential history I keep of this as in every other illness the president has suffered."[81]

The doctor was actually stretching the truth; he had not kept a confidential history of the president's other illnesses. In his extensive papers at the University of Wyoming and the Eisenhower Library, there is no record of the lengthy illness in 1949, and there are only scattered documents that bear upon the acute gastrointestinal attack in 1953 or any other ailment. He did intend to write about the heart attack, however. When the surgeon general of the army asked for his approval and suggestions for a project to provide an official, factual account of the president's sickness and convalescence, on the grounds that "it will go down as one of the milestones in the history of the presidency," Snyder simply took over the project. He continued to "reconstruct" the events that took place on the morning of 24 September, but in a very different sense from what Murray Snyder or General Hays intended. For the next ten years he wrote and rewrote, explained and embellished, covertly and publicly, until eventually fact and fiction began to merge. He achieved overwhelming success in his roles as apologist and historian; his version of the events displaced all others and found its way into every account written thereafter.[82]

It is impossible to imagine all of the emotions Dr. Snyder must have felt in the wake of the heart attack. Tending to the health of Dwight Eisenhower had been the very essence of his life for ten years, and he gave to it virtually all of his time, his energies, his friendship, and his affection. Suddenly the president was lying under an oxygen tent, his life in jeopardy. Little wonder that Hagerty found the doctor visibly upset, with his hands shaking badly, almost in tears, some ten hours after the hospitalization, or that Mattingly found him almost weeping, to the point that he offered him a sedative. In addition to the human feelings between a physician and his very special patient and friend, Snyder was sensitive about the tragedy happening on his watch. He knew fully what the price would be if many of those Americans, especially the friends or staff of the president, found reason to question his competence. There would be little sympathy, even from the gang, for a seventy-four-year-old practitioner who failed in a time of crisis.[83]

Snyder was also thrust into the spotlight and became the focus of questions and suspicions. He admitted lying to the White House staff, the press, and the American people with his initial report about indigestion, while he alone watched over the president. "I am sure the press at the Denver White House were much irritated," he wrote to White, "in that I did not make them acquainted with the true diagnosis until after what they considered an unwarranted delay. I, therefore, became subject to much criticism and moderate abuse." In addition, he had to submit to the interrogation of Hagerty, and when the press secretary's revised story went out to the world—that the doctor had "suspected" a heart attack but waited alone with the patient for nearly twelve hours before he confirmed it with an EKG—it raised questions about his judgment. Snyder also was well aware of what it meant to be a "military doctor," which to many Americans implied an inferior capability and performance. He wrote to the surgeon general of the navy in early October: "I also know that you have a pride in the service as I have and need facts to answer many allegations and wrong estimates that are made by many civilians, doctors and others, of the quality of the military medical services."[84]

At the very time he had to face perceptions about having let down his patient, his service, and his country, Snyder was further disheartened because others quickly took over the major responsibility for the president's care. Dr. Pollock had immediate control of the case, and he shared the medical decisions with Mattingly and White. This triumvirate of specialists selected White as their spokesman and Pollock as the one to see to their schedule of treatment. They also recruited two other physicians, Colonel George M. Powell and Lieutenant Colonel John Sheedy, so as to make possible a routine whereby a doctor would be on duty, awake, for twenty-four hours of every day. The cardiologists did not give Snyder a regular assignment, and after about a week, when he heard the president complain about "too damn many doctors visiting his room," he took the criticism personally and confined his visits to the morning and evening unless there was some special occasion.[85]

The displacement was more than physical. Snyder sensed that his advice now seemed superfluous, for "in the presence of these eminent cardiologists, the president probably very naturally paid little regard for any comment I made to him. As a matter of fact, he ignored my presence in the sick room. It seemed that I could have been a piece of furniture so far as he was concerned. This is readily understandable, because I represented, under the circumstances, something familiar, as did his wife." The doctor was sensitive to the new reality, but he did not welcome it or believe that he deserved it—certainly not after ten years of dedicated, sixteen-hours-per-day service.[86]

So Snyder stayed in the background, remaining nearby in the suite of rooms, night and day, studying the reports of the cardiologists and nurses, talking with Eisenhower's family and friends, and, above all, preparing and disseminating a defense of his actions on the night of the attack. This explanation had a very different tone and thrust from the story put out to the press by Hagerty and White (and, indeed, by Snyder himself in the early hours after the attack, when he told Ann Whitman that he "suspected" an attack and that he "renewed his suspicions that this was a serious thing" *after* the president awoke). In their version Hagerty and White had emphasized that the doctor only "suspected" a heart attack, gave two shots of morphine for the pain but no cardiovascular drugs, and waited for the president to awaken in order to take an EKG to "confirm" the diagnosis. In contrast, in Snyder's new account, he immediately diagnosed the illness as a coronary thrombosis, quickly administered not only morphine but also several exclusively cardiovascular drugs, and then delayed a call to the cardiologists and deceived the press in order to better protect the health of the patient and his family. In the Hagerty-White account, the doctor appeared uncertain and tentative; in the doctor's version, he was sure-minded, decisive, courageous, and humane.[87]

[handwritten marginal note: SNYDER REVISED VERSION]

It will never be possible to determine with absolute certainty which of these versions, if either, is correct. But any inquiry will have to begin with a startling document, in Dr. Snyder's handwriting, filed among his papers at the Eisenhower Library. It demands citation in full:

> Memorandum made at bedside between 7 a.m. and 11 a.m., Sept 24, '55 . . .
>
> 2:54 A.M. Mrs. Eisenhower called. Said pres. had pain in chest about 2:45 A.M. She had given milk of magnesia. No relief, pain getting worse. (Mrs. E. told me later that about 2:30 A.M. she had gone to the bathroom, passing the door to his bedroom on her return she heard him muttering in his sleep, she stopped at his bedside and asked him if he was having a nightmare—"Ike" replied, "No dear, but thank you" and smiled. About ten minutes later, she had returned to bed, he came to her bedside and said "I've got a pain in my lower chest." It was for that reason and because "Ike" had spoken of having indigestion the prior afternoon that she gave him the milk of magnesia, which frequently before had relieved such symptoms.
>
> 3:11 A.M. I arrived at the house (by chauffer's watch). As soon as I arrived, listened to the president's heart and took blood pressure, I realized it was a heart injury. BP 160/120, pulse 90—The president was

restless and alarmed. I broke a vaporole of amyl nitrite and gave it to him to sniff while I prepared and injected a 2cc ampule of papaverine hydrochloride (1 gr.)—I then prepared and injected immediately ¼ gr. morphine sulphate. The patient was still restless although his pulse had steadied and blood pressure was coming down. About 20 min. later, I gave him by intramuscular injection an ampule of heparin— 10,000 units. The pres. was still restless. I therefore gave him a second injection of ¼ gr. morphine sulphate—about 45 minutes after arrival. I had kept spygmamanometer [*sic*] on arm. Blood pressure had dropped to 130/80—pulse 68.

I asked Mamie about 4:30 A.M. to slip into bed with the president to see if this would not quiet him and assist in warming his body. He had developed a cold sweat in the meantime. Moaney had brought a couple of hot water bottles early, and we had used warm 195 proof alcohol to dry his skin. The president had desired to go to the toilet about 4:30 A.M. Mrs. E. and Moaney did not know where they could quickly find the bedpan. The pres. said he did not want to use it. I therefore supported him to the bathroom. He had a b.m. and expelled a good deal of gas. He felt more comfortable and shortly after Mamie got into bed, he was quiet.

5 A.M. President was quietly asleep.

7 A.M. Mamie slipped out and went to her bed and fell asleep.

5 A.M. to 11 A.M. The president slept quietly—on his back—mouth closed—no snoring—no air hunger. I took his pulse occasionally without disturbing him.

11:30 A.M. Began to awaken.

12:00 noon Pulse crept up to the upper 70s.

12:15 P.M. Called Gen. Griffin for a cardiogram. Asked them to come in civilian clothes.

1:00 P.M. Cardiogram confirms infarct in anterior wall of heart muscle.[88]

If Dr. Snyder actually wrote parts of this memorandum on the morning of 24 September, before his colleagues took the EKG, there is no question about his suspecting a coronary thrombosis. Amyl nitrite, papaverine, and heparin are cardiovascular drugs, and he never would have administered them for indigestion. One might wonder about his decision to use amyl nitrite, which was a treatment for angina pectoris rather than coronary thrombosis, and certainly question his walking the president to the bathroom when he might still have been in the throes of a heart attack, but these reservations would not challenge the basic soundness of his diagnosis. Indeed, so compelling is the doctor's handwritten note that it induced Dr. Mattingly to change his mind about the events.

In 1982, when Mattingly was gathering material for a health history of Eisenhower, he took note of the conflicting accounts about Snyder's actions and settled on one of two likely scenarios. In the first, Snyder, who was basically a surgeon with little previous opportunity in his clinical experience to witness the features of an acute heart attack, considered the problem an acute gastrointestinal attack, similar in character to those he had observed in the past. Only the next day, when it finally "dawned on him" that the symptoms were not gastrointestinal, did he call the hospital for help. He did administer morphine in the early hours, but probably did not give papaverine or heparin at all, or at least not until later in the day when he considered the possibility of a heart attack. In Mattingly's second scenario, Snyder considered the illness a mild heart attack, determined that it would subside and that insufficient damage or EKG changes would occur to recognize it as such later, and that neither the public nor other physicians need know about it. Only when the patient's condition failed to improve did he accept the need for hospitalization and call for help.[89]

Several years later, when Mattingly was able to review a copy of the handwritten memorandum, he accepted its validity, arguing that he had no reason to disbelieve the doctor's personal account about recognizing a heart attack and administering heparin and papaverine. His conclusion did not dissuade him from his opinion, however, that Snyder belonged to the "McIntire school" of presidential physicians—those who lied easily about their presidents' health, as Dr. Ross McIntire lied about President Roosevelt—and that in 1949 he had emulated his longtime friend, Vice Admiral Joel Boone, whom Mattingly believed had given a "deceptive diagnosis" of food poisoning when President Harding suffered his apparent heart attack. Indeed, Mattingly eventually theorized in his "health history" that Snyder had tried to cover up Eisenhower's 1955 heart attack in the same manner that he had concealed assumed heart attacks in 1949 and again in 1953—as part of a pattern—and he continued to believe it was entirely within Snyder's "character" to suppress, withhold, or "plant" information for such a purpose.[90]

The likelihood is overwhelming, despite Mattingly's theory, that Snyder wrote his "bedside memorandum" well after the events in order to cover up his own error in misdiagnosing the heart attack as a gastrointestinal problem. The document itself raises questions. It is not a running account of chronological events. It is clearly retrospective, at least in part, as when Snyder adds in parentheses following the 2:54 A.M. entry: "(Mrs. E. told me later . . .)." Nor was all of it written "during the long hours he sat at the bedside," as Snyder later claimed, or between "7 A.M. and 11 A.M.," as the memorandum states. The final entry is at 1:00 P.M., noting that a cardiogram had *already* confirmed a heart attack. Even more suggestive of a "plant" is the fact that the typewritten copy of this memorandum, also in Snyder's papers, has an *additional* paragraph, obviously added sometime later—almost certainly in 1958 when his secretary was preparing material for his book—and also meant to exonerate Snyder:

> During the morning after Mamie awakened, I informed her I would call Fitzsimons Hosp. and get a cardiogram as soon as the pres. began to awaken. Also had several requests from Murray Snyder for details and diagnosis for the president. I informed Murray he could say "indigestion" if he had to put out a diagnosis. I did not want the seriousness of the attack to be made public—to shock Mamie and Min and disturb the household until the president had gotten the full benefit of his sedation and a cardiogram would confirm and locate the area and approximate extent of heart muscle damage.[91]

Placed within the historical context of the time, the Snyder memorandum simply makes no sense, and raises serious questions. If the doctor diagnosed the illness correctly and administered the proper cardiovascular drugs, why did he not make it known to his colleagues? When he spoke with Dr. Pollock at the Doud home and later sat down with him to prepare the official hospital admission note and the patient's official medical history, why did he not hand him a copy of his memorandum, or at the very least indicate that he had given the patient heparin? When he was so distressed because of the questions from the press as to be virtually in tears, and sought out Dr. Mattingly for help, why did he not mention his notes or his treatment using cardiovascular drugs? When he had to answer to Hagerty about what happened on that morning, and met with him privately on two occasions, why did he not give the "true" account? When he was working with Dr. Pollock attending the patient, when he was talking with his friend Dr. Mattingly, and when he was meeting with the two of them together with Hagerty and White to prepare for the potentially threatening press conference, why did he not mention amyl nitrite or heparin? Why did he not challenge the story put out to the world by Murray Snyder, Hagerty, and White that only the EKG confirmed a diagnosis of a coronary thrombosis?

For Snyder to have administered heparin—as he claimed in his memorandum—without mentioning to any of the cardiologists that he had done so, would have been blatantly unprofessional and incomprehensible. Yet none of the *official* documents—the admission note or the patient's history written by Pollock on 24 September, the "interval history" of Mattingly on 25 September, and the consultation notes of White later the same day— mention heparin in their descriptions of Snyder's treatment. Hagerty does not mention it in his diary entry after his lengthy discussion with the doctor about the inconsistencies in the news reports, and White wrote in his "defense" of Snyder that he used *only* morphine.

It is equally incomprehensible that if Snyder did administer heparin, the most effective therapy available for a coronary thrombosis, that he did not continue to do so. Because the drug's anticoagulation time is short-lived, the customary treatment was to repeat the dosage of 7,500 to 10,000 units every six hours. If Snyder was knowledgeable enough to know the proper dosage, as he claims in his memorandum, he surely should have known enough to give the president a second injection at 9:00 A.M. because after that time the first would have become ineffective. As it developed, only after admission to the hospital did Pollock institute the acceptable regimen for heparin at six-hour intervals.[92]

There is a discrepancy among the cardiologists about whether Snyder administered papaverine. Pollock and Mattingly accepted his claim that he gave the president morphine *and* papaverine shortly after his arrival, and recorded such in their official notations. White, who was very careful in taking histories, contradicts Snyder by listing the first use of papaverine at 3:00 P.M. on 24 September, after Ike was in the hospital. It is possible, as Mattingly suspected at one time, that Snyder administered the drug in the late morning after recognizing that something was wrong. That likelihood comports with the fact that by Snyder's own admission he did not give a second shot after the customary four hours. As with heparin, it was not until the president was in the hospital that he received the proper dosage of the antispasmodic drug.[93]

The documentary evidence is compelling that Dr. Snyder wrote his "bedside" memorandum after the fact in order to protect himself from extreme humiliation and from charges of incompetence. He most likely wrote it about a week after the attack, at a time when he was sending a very similar, and equally astonishing, exculpatory message to dozens of important people. In the seven days from 26 September to 2 October, he mailed fifty-seven such letters, to the Eisenhowers, Arthur, Earl, Edgar, Milton, and John; to members of the gang, Al Gruenther, George Allen, Pete Jones, Cliff Roberts, Ellis Slater, and Bob Woodruff; to members of the staff and the cabinet, Robert Cutler, Jerry Persons, and Oveta Culp Hobby; to associates in the military medical establishment, Brigadier General George Armstrong, Dr. Frank Berry, Major General Raymond Bliss, Major General Silas Hays, and Rear Admiral B. W. Hogan; to leaders of the AMA, Drs. George Lull and Elmer Hess; to his son, Colonel Howard Snyder; and to assorted physicians, friends, and politicians all over the country.

Snyder explained that he administered papaverine, morphine, and heparin shortly after 3:00 A.M., watched the president as he slept "quietly" for seven hours, and, as Eisenhower began to awaken, arranged for an EKG, taken at 1:00 P.M. The key portion of his letter read as follows:

> It was difficult for me to assume the responsibility of refraining from making public immediately the diagnosis of coronary thrombosis. I postponed public announcement because I wished the president to benefit from the rest and quiet induced by the sedation incident to combating the initial manifestations. This decision also spared him, his wife, and mother-in-law emotional upset attendant upon too precipitate announcement of such serious import. The end result was that all who were intimately concerned were much better able to accept this information, delivered by suggestion during the intermediate hours of rest which were afforded the president. This action, I believe, limited the heart damage to a minimum and enabled us to confirm the diagnosis by cardiogram and make an unhurried transference from home to hospital.[94]

On 5 October Dr. Snyder mailed an even longer letter of explanation to twenty-seven people, fourteen of them previous recipients (whom he asked to "please destroy my former letter on this subject") and thirteen new ones, including Robert Anderson, Leonard Hall, Bill Robinson, James Mitchell, and a number of distinguished physicians. In this final version, he made still another addition; for the first time in any of his correspondence, he wrote that he had administered amyl nitrite, which was first introduced to the medical profession in 1871 for relief of anginal pain. Amyl nitrite excited wonder upon its discovery, but because inhalation from the small, broken glass container caused an immediate flushing of the face, a pounding of the pulse, a throbbing of the temples, a fullness of the head, and other disagreeable symptoms, physicians preferred nitroglycerine. By the 1950s they rarely used it for coronary thrombosis, although Snyder claimed that he did:

> At the time of my arrival at the president's bedside at 3:00 A.M., Saturday, September 24th, I noted that he was suffering with pain in the chest in an area approximately the size of a large hand centered along the intermammillary line. I broke a pearl of amyl nitrite and gave it to the president to sniff while I prepared a hypodermic of one grain of papaverine, and immediately thereafter, one-fourth grain of morphine sulphate; following that, the usual initial intramuscular dose of heparin.[95]

In a period of less than a month, the doctor sent out one hundred letters, counting revisions, to seventy citizens. Many of them went to family and friends of the president, who were understandably eager to learn everything they could or perhaps disturbed about the early reports. "In addition to the information I have given you over the telephone," Snyder wrote to Ellis Slater, "I think this summary of actions taken since the incipiency of the attack will be of interest to you." Others went to members of the medical profession, military and civilian, including officers of the AMA, because Snyder said that "as representatives of the entire medical fraternity of our country, [they] were entitled to know the facts in the case, including quite detailed disclosure of the medical treatment from the early moments of the attack." To a Denver physician, William B. Condon, he explained, "Some early reports in the press in Denver and elsewhere might have left very erroneous impressions on the early treatment in this case." When Condon made the assumption that his letter was sent "primarily because of my position on the publicity committee of the Medical Society," Snyder replied: "My primary reason was because of the pleasure I had in meeting you and Mrs. Condon at your home and at other places, and I felt I would like you, personally, to know the medical facts in this situation."[96]

Dr. Snyder's letter-writing campaign constituted a covert, nationwide apologia. In divulging information about his patient without his permission, it went far beyond the bounds of professional behavior, but it was enormously successful, serving to exonerate him from any criticism and, even more, to elicit praise for his exceptional performance under fire. "How very fortunate he and all the rest of us are," replied Milton Eisenhower, "that you, who know every tendency and every previous illness of the president, should have been on hand to take care of him when this happened." Bill Robinson, who had led the move to obtain the services of an outside consultant, praised Snyder for the burden he had carried, for the poise, confidence, and good nature he had shown in "those first frightful hours of the crisis." He added, "You have guided and preserved the most important and valuable figure in our history and now you have literally snatched him from death's door. You are too modest to be proud of this but I hope you can realize the gratitude of so many as a recompense for your own fatigue and weariness." Most pleasing, perhaps, were the words of Leonard Scheele, the surgeon general of the United States Public Health Service: "Tragic as the coronary itself was, the president and the country are indeed fortunate that you were on the job and that the diagnosis was made so promptly and treatment begun immediately. I am sure that had you not been so prompt the outcome would have been far different. We are grateful to you."[97]

It is understandable that outside observers would have sympathized with Howard Snyder for having postponed a *public* announcement in order for the president to "benefit from the rest and the quiet," but it is shocking that they did not question his failure to seek the *private* assistance of a cardiologist. Dr. Pollock could have traveled to the Doud home early in the morning (as Snyder himself had done) without in any way having excited the household or bothered the patient. Moreover, for Dr. Snyder to have refused to call in an expert lest it might cause emotional upset to the family was utterly irresponsible. The president was his patient, let alone the most important man in the world, and he should not have increased his risk in any way.

But Howard Snyder had the field of explanation to himself, and his letters were convincing, marked as they were by esoteric medical data and kind consideration for the Eisenhower family. So friends and associates were not about to quibble. In a telling letter, Dr. Eli Ginzberg, an economist and good friend at Columbia University, commended the doctor for his control of both the physical and psychological aspects of the case, and continued, "My only regret is that the newspapers, with their somewhat limited understanding of the many intricacies, jumped to all sorts of foolish conclusions. However, I feel reasonably certain that by now the more correct picture has gotten across."[98]

Howard Snyder was able to sell his description of events through the confidential letters to the medical profession and to the president's family, friends, and advisers, and in doing so he became their hero. But he did more than rationalize in private; two months later he had an opportunity to present his case to the American people through a long article in *Look* magazine by journalist Fletcher Knebel—an article with details that could have come only from the doctor. In that early morning, Knebel reported, the president felt a demanding pain, "as though a stream of molten metal had gushed across his chest," and flowed through it "with brutal intensity"; he grimaced as the "mighty muscle" suffered its "blood famine," while at the same time "perspiration oozed from his pores." When Dr. Snyder arrived, he realized "within three minutes" that he was "witnessing what no other medical man in history had observed—acute coronary thrombosis in the body of a president of the United States." He decided quickly that he would sit by the president's side in a "lonely vigil" while the patient rested. When Eisenhower began to awake and Snyder noticed a sudden change in his blood pressure, he called Dr. Pollock, whose EKG "confirmed" his diagnosis.

In addition to adornment by way of the purple prose, Knebel provided a rationalization for the doctor's deception—that to have told the truth might have excited the household to such an extent as to "kill" the president and endanger the health of Mamie, because of her valvular heart disease, and Mrs. Doud, who "was hovering about, her soul wrung with anxiety." In fact, the truth need not have affected the household in any way; the doctor could have told Mamie that he merely wanted to be certain and safe, and thus had decided to take an EKG. Indeed, when Dr. Mattingly read Knebel's story, he questioned that his friend would have made such a decision on the basis of fear that it might upset Mrs. Eisenhower and Mrs. Doud. He noted that "it was not like his usual sound judgment to assume the great risk of permitting a president to die of a severe heart attack there in the private home when expert help was only a phone call away. I will never believe that portion of the story."[99]

Snyder's story went out as more acceptable history in the summer of 1956, by way of the first thorough study of the administration, Robert Donovan's *Eisenhower: The Inside Story.* Donovan, a journalist with the *New York Herald Tribune,* had gained privileged access to a collection of historical materials, including one of Dr. Snyder's long 5 October letters, through Sherman Adams, who wanted to combat the growing image of Ike as a do-nothing president. Donovan's chapter on the heart attack was the first extended discussion of the issue, and he accepted the Snyder version without question. The doctor took "only two or three minutes" to reach the "grave conclusion," then broke an ampule of amyl nitrite, gave an injection of papaverine hydrochloride to dilate the arteries, administered the shots of morphine to ease the pain and shock, and later prepared a hypodermic of heparin to prevent clotting. He sent Mamie back to bed without telling her the true condition, and he put aside the idea of telling the press "because he feared that it would cause great excitement which inevitably would permeate the Doud house and might possibly kill the president."[100]

The story Donovan put forth has prevailed in all subsequent narratives, but it was still not acceptable to Dr. Snyder, who in the early 1960s was still working on the drafts of various chapters of a "health history" of Dwight Eisenhower. In his final narration of the heart attack story, Snyder embellished his role even further. He had been summoned on many occasions in the middle of the night to minister to the president's gastrointestinal problems, he wrote, but this time he detected a note of alarm in Mamie's voice. En route to the Doud home there was "something spooky in the dark stillness of the night," and an "ominous foreboding" ran through his mind. As soon as he arrived he knew he was facing a serious heart injury. The president's "pulse was very rapid, when it could be counted. In fact, at first I could get no blood pressure because of the disordered rhythm. However, I once caught 180/120." He administered the four drugs and then tried to give oxygen, but the president "would not tolerate wearing an oxygen mask." After a second shot of morphine at 3:45 A.M., the patient's blood pressure was dropping, the pulse becoming more rapid, and the skin showing early signs of cool perspiration. He had Sergeant Moaney rub Eisenhower with pure alcohol that had been heated, and piled all of the hot water bottles in the house about his body. But still "the president went into a state of shock. His blood pressure collapsed and his pulse rate climbed alarmingly and again became quite irregular."

At 4:04 A.M., Dr. Snyder wrote, he asked Mamie "to slip into bed and wrap herself around the president to see if this would quiet him and assist in warming his body. This had the desired effect almost immediately. The president settled down and went to sleep quietly." The doctor then had an opportunity to review his actions and question his judgment in the face of this great responsibility. "I was really shaken and was contemplating calling the cardiologist whose telephone number I carried in my pocket, but at that moment the president, though apparently unconscious, responded to the soothing and warming effect of his wife's embrace. After that I was able to fix the compass and chart my course."[101]

Howard Snyder's final account, never published, goes far beyond his "bedside memorandum" or his one hundred letters, and directly challenges the official medical records. His assertion about disordered rhythm and a blood pressure reading of 180/120 upon his arrival specifically contradicts his own notes made at the time and the data he gave to Drs. Pollock, White, and Mattingly. His mention of oxygen takes issue with the precise Secret Service report, which describes an agent picking up the doctor's two bags at the Doud house but says nothing about oxygen equipment; it also challenges the memory of the president, who, if he could recall having received two shots of morphine, surely would have recalled fighting off an oxygen mask or undergoing the immense discomfort of amyl nitrite. In fact, when Eisenhower described in his memoirs the help provided throughout the years by the Secret Service he wrote: "*After* my 1955 heart attack the Secret Service carried along a supply of oxygen and special medicines" (italics mine).[102]

Most astonishing is the doctor's assertion that after the second shot of morphine the president's blood pressure collapsed, his pulse climbed alarmingly, his pulse became quite irregular, and he "went into a state of shock." Dr. Snyder never mentioned this extremely important medical information to any of the cardiologists, and Dr. Mattingly, who was meticulous about details, wrote to the contrary in his official "interval history," recorded at 1:00 P.M. on 25 September: "Chest pain has never been absent since early A.M. at times when awake. There has been no period of shock even during movement to hospital, pulse and blood pressure have remained stable with no arrhythmias. There has been no respiratory distress, no vomiting."[103]

Further evidence of the falsity of this final "historical" account appears on a half-page note in Snyder's handwriting, tucked among his papers, which, as is clearly evident from its contents, he wrote several hours after the hospitalization. It contains a query, "Massive infarct?" Below that is a comment, "No shock—much restless—some pain," followed by a record of the president's blood pressure and pulse at approximately 3:00 A.M. (160/120, 90); at about 4:00 A.M. (130/90, 84); at about 5:00 A.M. (124/82, 76); at about 11:00 A.M. (124/82, 68); "in hosp." (130/84, 76); and "14 hr. later after 2 hrs. in hosp." (134-140/74-84). The first and last readings correspond exactly with those in Pollock's "admission note" and his "doctor's progress reports," which gives credence to their validity. If one presumes that Snyder recorded the others correctly, they belie his claim about the president going into shock.[104]

What one finds in Dr. Snyder's successive accounts over time about the morning of 24 September is both an escalation of the president's symptoms of coronary thrombosis (from pain to perspiration to arrhythmia and shock) and an expansion of the attending physician's treatment (from morphine and papaverine, to heparin, to amyl nitrite, and to oxygen). The accounts likewise present a progressive elaboration of the reasons for his delay in calling a cardiologist, from a desire not to panic the world in the middle of the night, to a wish to have the president rest, to a consideration to spare Mamie and Mrs. Doud any emotional upset, to a determination not to allow excitement to permeate the household and threaten the life of the patient. Along the way he creates a portrait of a physician who, in Richard Nixon's words, deserved "the commendation of his medical colleagues in the country."[105]

One who was skeptical, more than thirty years later in 1987, was cardiologist Oglesby Paul, the biographer of Paul Dudley White. Dr. Paul, a graduate of Harvard Medical School, a president of the AHA in 1960-1961, and one of White's former students, asked in print for the first time since the attack some of the tough questions about the diagnosis and about Snyder's behavior. Why did he not seek a consultation from one or more colleagues at once? Why did he not take an EKG at the very onset of the illness rather than waiting for ten hours? Why was the press twice informed that this was only a digestive upset if Snyder knew right away that it was a heart attack? What was the justification for not telling the family of the probable diagnosis right away instead of making John Eisenhower, for example, wait until Saturday afternoon? Would it not have been judicious to have transferred the patient to a hospital at once rather than waiting twelve hours? Dr. Paul praised Snyder for assuring rest for his patient and for staying with him, but he concluded, "It is doubtful if many well trained medical men or women would in 1955 have behaved similarly with any patient with these symptoms."

The cardiologist-biographer also asked the most important question: "Is it not likely that General Snyder did *not* seriously entertain the diagnosis of a heart attack until some hours after it had taken place?" Dr. Paul did not have any specific document or any "smoking gun" to support his interpretation; he relied on reason, common sense, and a knowledge of the disease. But he was almost certainly correct.[106]

It was not out of the ordinary, even in the mid-1950s, for a physician to mistake a heart attack for acute indigestion. James Herrick's classic study had directed his colleagues to be wary of pain in the area of the breastbone, and other experts had warned that coronary thrombosis often wore a disguise, or what one called a "gastroenteric masquerade." The EKG made it possible to distinguish between the two ailments, but lacking that test, misdiagnosis was still commonplace. In 1951 Dr. Levine singled out such conditions as gallstone colic, perforated peptic ulcer, acute pancreatitis, and acute intestinal obstruction as sources of confusion. "All the diagnostic methods available may be required to arrive at the correct diagnosis in such cases," he warned, "and despite care there will be rare instances in which errors will be made. . . . The electrocardiograms may be the turning point on which a diagnosis will rest."[107]

In that same year, Dr. White considered the confusion so important that he went out of his way in his famous textbook to instruct physicians on how to find the differences and "make the distinction fairly certain." White proposed a number of relevant points in the differential diagnosis between acute coronary occlusion with cardiac infarction and acute abdominal disease. The most important was the past history, "in the one case a story of angina pectoris or other cardiac symptoms or signs, and in the other a record of indigestion or colic." A second was the cardiac examination, which might show abnormal cardiac characteristics such as dilation, poor sounds, or a pericardial friction rub. Third, an abdominal examination might show tenderness or spasm. Fourth, the pain in a heart attack would be more often high under the sternum or both substernal and epigastric, rarely epigastric alone; very frequently it would be referred to both arms, especially the left. Finally, an EKG would show changes in the T wave or other meaningful signs.[108]

White's checklist suggests that any student of his, in the early morning of 24 September, could have leaned toward a diagnosis of acute indigestion. The past history pointed entirely one way—Ike had a long and troublesome record of abdominal pain and distress, and not a single indication of cardiac problems. The initial examination did not show any cardiac abnormalities or any particular abdominal problem, thus giving no guidance. The pain could have foretold either condition, although as White stressed in his defense of Snyder, the diagnosis is especially difficult or impossible at the onset if the pain is low under the breastbone, as it was with the president. The fact that the pain did not radiate to the arms, or down the left arm, also made it appear not to be cardiovascular. Only an EKG—or some further clarifying symptom—could have confidently led to a diagnosis of an Eisenhower heart attack. A prudent physician might have suspected a coronary and arranged at once for an EKG to check it out, but only an experienced cardiologist might have decided within minutes that there likely was an attack.

If two of America's most famous cardiologists considered it difficult under such circumstances to diagnose a coronary thrombosis, how much more so it had to have been for Howard Snyder, who had virtually no experience with the disease. It would have been perfectly understandable, indeed expectable, for him to suspect another bout of indigestion, to treat for the pain, and to wait for improvement or some further sign. That is almost certainly what happened. That is why he told Murray Snyder twice that it was a twenty-four-hour flu, that it was not serious, and that he would not be staying with the president at all times. That is why Ann Whitman, after speaking with Dr. Snyder at about noon, told the Secret Service they would not be needed for the rest of the day. That is why Mamie did not call her son about the attack until the middle of the afternoon, twelve hours after it had occurred and after the physicians had taken his father to the hospital.

Much of the doctor's story, such as his asking Mamie to get into the bed and comfort her husband, may well be true, but it was for his stomach and not for his heart. Clearly something took place to change the situation at about 12:15. It was almost certainly because, as Dr. Pollock reported in his official "narrative summary" of the attack, the president's feeling of heaviness and constriction persisted and when he awoke "he still had squeezing substernal pain, and remained weak." Suddenly it struck Dr. Snyder that this was not the pattern he had seen

❖ 110 ❖

so often with the digestive upsets, and that it was the pattern of coronary heart disease. So he sought help.[109]

To believe otherwise is to believe that Dr. Snyder was negligent to assume that he alone could provide the best possible care in a life-threatening cardiac emergency; that he was stupid to imagine that if he chose to consult a cardiologist he also would have to inform the world in the middle of the night; that he was arrogant to believe he need not inform any public official that the president of the United States was incapacitated; that he was reckless for not having the Secret Service standing by; that he was incompetent for not continuing the administration of heparin and papaverine and for not getting EKG equipment to the house forthwith; that he was unprofessional for not telling Dr. Pollock the truth about the patient's condition or his treatment; that he was callous and insensitive in failing to inform the family of the dire situation; that he was irresponsible for giving primary attention to the problematic emotional responses of Mamie and her mother when such a misplaced priority could adversely affect his patient; and that he was willing to lie to the press for no compelling reason.

Howard Snyder was none of these. He was a decent man and an average medical practitioner, although with limited experience. He was foremost a surgeon and an administrator, and he may never have treated a patient with a heart attack—certainly not for many years. He was also human, and he became the victim of a disease that had confused thousands of others before him. It is a great irony that apart from his failure to seek the assistance of a cardiologist, he acted reasonably. But who else would see it in that light? Under the glare of publicity, in a period of emotion and crisis, to a press and a public ignorant of the finer points of cardiology and clinical care, his actions would stand out as errors, perhaps even as the incapacities of an old man.

Dr. Snyder's deception did not come when he told the press about the indigestion but when, for the most basic of human reasons, he created a new version of the events, a gigantic rationalization. He progressively sought to refashion the early morning of 24 September in such a way that all of the classic warning signs of a coronary were there—pain, perspiration, vital signs, and shock—so as to assure the world, and himself, that *no one* could have missed them. The newsmen found it easy to believe that such a gentleman would lie to serve the president, but it did not occur to them that he would deceive to save himself—his pride, his reputation, his position, and his career.

The extent of his need was apparent in the length of his effort; he rationalized for nearly a decade until his own health would not allow him to do so any longer. Early in 1965, in a poignant response to Eisenhower's remembrance of his eighty-fourth birthday, Snyder wrote, "I am living on borrowed time," and he nostalgically referred back to the years when he had "accepted the responsibility of making your health the entire purpose of my life." He still was agonizing about his reaction during what he considered the worst experience of his life, and he still was claiming a decisive competence. "Actually, it is my opinion that your life was saved on the night of the infarction," he wrote, "that the crisis was met and passed that early morning—and that this was brought about by Mamie's getting into bed with you and folding you in her arms." He then offered another explanation for his failure to seek help, one that was utterly at odds with the real situation in 1955: "It is also my opinion that, except that you were president of the United States, we could have treated you successfully at 750 Lafayette Street after this sudden change for the better which was occasioned by Mamie's act."[110]

Dr. Snyder's rationalizations and opinions did prevail. He wrote the history and he saved his job. That, too, was important, for although it was the consulting cardiologists who were the heroes during the early weeks of the president's misfortune, he was the one who thereafter managed the day-to-day care and who finally had the ear of his patient. His program of treatment went beyond medicine, exercise, and diet to the mind and personality of Dwight Eisenhower. Through it he made history again, and again covertly and although he may not have saved a life, he most certainly shaped a career.

4

Treatment and Recovery

❖ ❖ ❖ ❖ ❖ ❖ ❖ ❖ ❖ ❖ ❖ ❖ ❖ ❖ ❖

To a sick man his doctor's visit is the chief event of the day. Cardiac patients react quickly to the atmosphere surrounding them; they must be helped to keep or gather courage. Cardiac cases are naturally sanguine; depression, when it comes, usually derives from others. It is the doctor's plain duty to enter the sick-room with cheerfulness, to give counsel thoughtfully but confidently, and to leave behind as he goes an appropriate word of encouragement, to comfort the patient in his waiting, to help his suffering, or to allay his fears. A countenance of gloom is as out of place in a sick-room as is a coffin.
    —Sir Thomas Lewis, Diseases of the Heart

The realm of treatment for the heart embraces every organ in the body in the search for some cause of heart aberrancy. The pursuit must extend even beyond the confines of the patient's body, scanning his environment and penetrating into the domain of his thoughts, hopes and ambitions.
    —S. Calvin Smith, Heart Patients: Their Study and Care

There was nothing arcane in midcentury America about how to manage a heart attack. During the early acute period, the doctors could do little more than take therapeutic measures to control pain and forestall potential complications, as through the administration of morphine, papaverine, oxygen, and anticoagulants. Once the initial crisis had passed, rest was paramount —physical, mental, and prolonged. The consensus among cardiologists was for approximately two to four weeks of complete bed rest, during which "the patient should remain recumbent on his back or his side and should be waited on hand and foot for at least two weeks. He should be fed and bathed; he should be lifted on the bedpan and should be spared every physical effort." If recovery proceeded without incident, the physician would devote another four weeks to mobilizing the patient, with a gradual increase of activity from getting out of bed, to sitting in a chair, to climbing stairs, to short walks, and finally to a return to normal activities. If circumstances permitted, the ideal regimen would include a third month to consolidate the recovery.[1]

The technical management was only one part of the medical treatment, however, for complete recovery often was dependent not only upon what the doctor did but upon what he said. The AMA's first code of ethics in 1847 had mentioned that the "life of a sick person can be shortened not only by the acts, but also by the words or the manner of a physician," and described it as a physician's "sacred duty" to guard himself carefully in this respect. A century of experience had taught every good physician the importance of communicating with sufficient effectiveness to allay fear and offer reassurance. A seminal article in 1938, "The Doctor Himself as a Therapeutic Agent," went so far as to propose that a physician was effective in direct proportion to the faith he was able to inspire in his patients.[2]

Attention to the patient's psychological health—especially his perception of his disease—was especially important with an illness as heavily laden with symbolism as a heart attack. Since classical times the heart has represented the vital center of the body not only as a seat of such emotions as love, joy, sorrow, and courage but as the arbiter of life and death as well. "The heart is the beginning of life," wrote William Harvey, who in the seventeenth century discovered the circulation of the blood, "even as the sun may be called the heart of the world: the heart is the foundation of life, the source of all action." Whether a patient saw his heart in mechanical terms as a pump, an engine, a machine, or a clock, he knew that it could cease to function. The "old ticker" could stop, and no doctor could forswear such a possibility, for of all the conditions in medicine, this was the most difficult to predict. "Furthermore, when a patient has an attack of coronary thrombosis there is no satisfactory method of foretelling which individual patient will survive and which will succumb," wrote Samuel Levine. "I have seen patients who were most seriously ill recover and others, who apparently were doing extremely well, suddenly die."[3]

Even though no physician could still completely the fears of sudden death, he could stress the likelihood of recovery from a heart attack and suggest that it need not mean an end to a way of life. It was therefore incumbent upon every cardiologist to tend to the reality of "heart consciousness," lest, as one of them put it, "with a heedless word he may condemn a patient to a life of tortured invalidism." For seven weeks in Denver and six weeks in Gettysburg, the doctors attending Dwight Eisenhower tried to help him understand the meaning of his heart attack. They were wise to the ways of this disease and alert to the feelings of their patient, and they were successful in dispelling most, though not all, of his fears. But they were as confused as he was, and often in disagreement, about what his illness meant for his future, especially regarding the presidency.[4]

For the typical heart attack patient, illness, hospitalization, and the treatment process entail a series of shocks. For a month or more his new world is not a home but a hospital, a strange bed in a small room with its different sounds, unusual-looking equipment, and air of tension. His new family is an unfamiliar staff of doctors, nurses, and technicians who handle, manipulate, and regulate his body. They relate to him in an intimate way, sometimes to the point of indignity, but with an aura of detachment. And while he is trying to adapt to his new physical surroundings, he is susceptible to an array of new emotions. He feels helpless because of his dependence on others and his demotion to the status of a thing, besieged by wires, shots, bedpans, and drugs. He feels powerless because he lacks any precise knowledge of his illness and cannot even comprehend the significance of his vital signs or interpret the data collected with precision every day. He resents the insult the disease has meant to his body and fears its implications—physical, psychological, and economic—for himself, his family, and his future. He wonders if he might become a cardiac cripple, unable to function as a husband or father, or to provide support for his loved ones. He is aware of a loss of self-esteem, sorrowful about his fate, unduly alert to the slightest pain, and anxious about another attack. He will likely experience grief, despair, frustration, or rage and will surely come to know an existential loneliness, uncertain as to whether he will live or die.[5]

What was striking about Eisenhower's experience, however, was how *untypical* it was. The physical facilities themselves differed from the usual hospital quarters. The president's room was small, about ten by twenty feet in size, but it was part of a VIP suite that included an antechamber, an annex for hospital personnel, office space for aides, and a huge, sixty-by-forty-foot sunporch. Across the hall was another suite with a large bedroom, a sitting room, and another large sunporch looking out at Pikes Peak, into which Mamie Eisenhower moved at 7:30 P.M. on the first day of the attack and where she resided until the return to Gettysburg. There was also a room for Dr. Snyder, a reception room where attending physicians stood by, a large assembly room that became the command post for the Secret Service, and a movie theater, a small kitchen, and a dining room. The eighth floor became, in a way, the nation's first coronary care unit (although without the technical equipment that distinguished the CCUs in the 1960s), where shifts of cardiologists, nurses, technicians, medical corpsmen, dieticians, cooks, and security staff were present on a twenty-four-hour basis to serve the patient and his family.

This unique arrangement made it possible for the president to avoid some of the usual sense of aloneness that follows a patient's necessary separation from the "significant others" in his life. Above all, the First Lady's proximity and daily presence allowed her to spend an exceptional amount of time with her husband, whether it was holding his hand when he was in the oxygen tent, reading him the newspapers, or sitting on the sundeck. Indeed, when he returned to the White House, Ike expressed his gratitude by presenting Mamie with a "military medal," a jeweled medallion, for her long vigil and tireless devotion. The carefully controlled treatment process also allowed for the timely arrival of others who were close to the president—his son, his brother, Dr. Snyder, and, beginning with Vice President Nixon on 8 October, the members of his staff and his personal friends. Unlike the typical patient, who out of boredom or loneliness often waits wistfully for a visitor to drop by, Ike had familiar faces present during most of his waking hours. His isolation was broken, as well, by the thousands of "get well" letters from which Mamie read excerpts nearly every day.[6]

Mamie, his friends, and people everywhere let the president know how much he mattered, that he was the most important patient in the world. So, too, did his nurses. In the ordinary hospital environment, the nurses try to make every patient feel that he is their special responsibility, but often they appear as transient figures, hurrying to meet the needs of too many others. In this instance, Ike was their only responsibility, and they tended to him twenty-four hours a day. Their "nursing notes" recorded every development, event, movement, and mood, and typically with thirty to fifty daily notations. The notes are a meticulous record of his blood pressure, pulse, urine specimens, and blood chemistry; of every drug he took and the dosage; of every bodily function—when he ate and how much, when he voided, bathed, and shaved, when he slept, what time he awoke, when he was awake "for a fleeting moment to ask the time of day"; whether he moved and shifted positions in his sleep or turned "on side to sleep—experienced slight twinge of pain"; when he perspired or itched, or his face "flushed more deeply when breathing slowed down"; when he complained ("Appears slightly depressed today and complains of severe muscular pain around right scapula and shoulder"); and how he felt ("Pt. irritable and appears tired and apathetic today").[7]

Even more exceptional than the president's relation with his nurses was that with his doctors. He spent seven weeks at Fitzsimons Hospital under the care of six physicians in a program as intense as any in history. Robert Pollock was the coordinator of the collaborative effort; he kept in almost daily contact with the other cardiologists, with at least one call per day to Paul White. In addition, he and two members of the hospital staff, Drs. Sheedy and Powell, had floor shifts assuring twenty-four-hour attention. Tom Mattingly volunteered for the same duty when he was in town, but he was also the meticulous and studious consultant, poring over every item of available information to ensure there would be no oversights. Howard Snyder had no assigned duties but shared with the others his special knowledge of the patient's personality and preferences. At the outset, however, Paul Dudley White was at center stage, and there could not have been a better choice to ensure a positive interaction between doctor and patient. "He was the best practitioner of medicine I've ever known anywhere," wrote one colleague. "He loved patients as human beings." He was also a superb communicator, as journalist Frances Burns of the *Boston Globe* pointed out: "He used to come to see me in the hospital, and before he was seated in the arm chair he'd start teaching me."[8]

Of equal importance, no one in America was better suited than White to explain coronary heart disease to this particular patient. Through his writing and practice over several decades, he had become singularly famous for his emphasis on optimism, regular physical activity, self-discipline, and the importance of work. All of these, significantly, were the touchstones of Eisenhower's career. Little wonder that Sherman Adams went to Denver convinced that at least for the next few weeks his fellow New Englander would be the "real key figure" in the government, for he was "endowed with much more than the knowledge and skill that had brought him to the top of his profession. Bound together within the confines of a frail physical fortress were a doctor, philosopher, prophet, publicist of the first order, homely country man and avid bicyclist."[9]

When White arrived in Denver his first time, he approved completely of the treatment already accorded the president, and he was in agreement with the other cardiologists as to care during the crucial early days—oxygen for five days, a 1,600-calorie diet, and the use of the long-term anticoagulant Coumadin. In order to emphasize his complete confidence in the military doctors, he chose to leave Denver after only two days, even though some of the president's staff wanted him to remain for several weeks. Before he returned to Boston on 26 September, he consulted with his colleagues about the immediate future, and his notes spell out his program:

> Continue careful nursing and quiet atmosphere. Chest up at 30 degree angle much of the day (a position much easier for the heart than sitting straight up or lying flat). Continue to lift and carry to toilet for bowel movements, and move legs. Oxygen tent to be omitted at intervals today. Medicines symptomatically except for anticoagulant routinely. Light diet. Dr. Mattingly to remain another two days and Dr. Pollock to report to P.D.W. twice daily for a few days. P.D.W. to return to Denver and to see the president in two weeks with Dr. Mattingly and later at his farm at Gettysburg.[10]

Prior to his departure, White also discussed with Snyder, Mattingly, and Pollock the benefits of what was known as the "armchair" method of treating a heart attack. In 1944 researchers discovered that a position of recumbency was not the most restful position for a patient and that under certain circumstances lying flat in bed could actually increase the work of the heart. This finding led some physicians to question the pattern of absolute bed rest that had been the standard treatment for some thirty years—indeed, since the earliest recognition of myocardial infarction as a clinical entity. Dr. Samuel Levine at Harvard Medical School emerged as the pioneer of a radical change, which would have patients spend the greater part of the day out of bed in a chair just as soon as the initial stage of shock and severe pain had passed. He and his coworkers applied the treatment to eighty-one patients with very good physical and psychological results, and subsequent research showed that the "Levine method" could reduce the estimated work of the heart no less than 28 percent.[11]

Paul White was always alert to advances in research, and he began to alter his traditional practice, using his friend's "armchair" treatment "in mild cases with small infarcts." Having had several years of successful clinical experience, he considered it the proper treatment for the president. When he discussed it in Denver, no one objected outrightly, although Tom Mattingly, who was more conservative in his practice, did mention that he saw no reason to rush the out-of-bed activity. Upon his return to Boston, White consulted with Levine, following which he and Pollock decided to have the president moved from his bed to a chair where he would sit for increasing periods of time. Thus on Wednesday, 28 September, the fourth day after the heart attack, at 9:30 A.M. and again at 2:30 P.M., two orderlies lifted the president into a chair where he rested for fifteen minutes. The medical staff continued the treatment two or three times a day, increasing the time in the chair to forty-five minutes.[12]

The decision to try Levine's method was proper, but it turned out to be unfortunate because the doctors vacillated over its use, thereby confusing the patient and his family. On the fifth day of the president's sitting up, Pollock and Mattingly became worried by some clinical and laboratory changes suggesting an inflammation of the pericardium, the fibrous sac surrounding the heart. Mattingly believed the tests showed either slow healing or the more disturbing possibility of an extension of the original area of infarction. In light of the new developments, all of the doctors agreed to temporarily discontinue the procedure until the clinical picture became more definite.[13]

Before they had a chance to tell their patient, an unexpected occurrence caused him undue anxiety. On that Sunday morning, 2 October, after what his nurse considered his "best night" yet, the president sat up again for fifty-five minutes. Around 11:30 A.M., however, while resting in bed, he told his nurse of a twinge of pain in the upper left chest, and although he tried to sleep, she noticed him putting his hand to his chest as if in pain. She called Dr. Pollock, who recorded: "He had two momentary sharp pains separated by a short interval about 1200 hours while moving in bed onto left side." Pollock did everything he could to assure Ike that the pain was transient and likely of no importance, but in this same conversation he went on to explain to him and Mamie (and by telephone to John Eisenhower) the cardiologists' concern over the changes in the EKG and in other tests, and their decision that he stop sitting up in his chair and remain in bed.[14]

The anxiety extended to Washington, where aides to the president feared a serious complication and wanted White to return to Denver earlier than he had planned. The cardiologist wisely chose not to exaggerate the situation with a special trip, but he was concerned enough to have the entire series of EKGS reviewed by a world-recognized authority, Dr. Eugene Lepeschkin of the University of Vermont. Lepeschkin's evaluation was inconclusive, and White thus held to his opinion that the complication was merely a matter of slow healing. So he and Pollock decided to renew the "armchair" regimen after a five-day delay, and on 7 October the president sat up again—but only for two days.[15]

The doctors changed their minds this time while White was on his second consultation trip to Denver on the weekend of 8–9 October because Mattingly still believed in the possibility of an extension of the original infarct, so much so that he had warned in his "consultation note" of the chances for dire complications such as late congestive failure, aneurysmal formation, rupture, or arrhythmias. He sincerely feared that Pollock and White might push the activity program too fast, and he recommended "a slow progress in resumption of activities." White decided to take no chances, so he deferred to his colleague again and then had to deliver some unpleasant Sunday afternoon news. He explained to the president (and separately to Mamie, John, and Vice President Nixon, who had flown to Denver because of concern about a "setback") the decision of the physicians to temporarily cease the "armchair" treatment for a second time. He also spoke of the need to have Ike remain in the hospital for an additional week.[16]

Pollock visited later and noted: "Patient seemed depressed by consideration of Dr. White's information; I talked with him and reassured him that final healing was expected to be complete." White also had sensed his patient's disappointment, and when he arrived in Boston he wrote to assure him that all was going well: "Don't worry about the slowness of the evolution of the electrocardiogram which does, of course, indicate slowness of the healing process, but there is no reason at all why you should not have very satisfactory healing in time."[17]

The practical effect of the cardiologists' controversy about the president's infarction was to slow down the pace of his convalescence, as Pollock and White to a large extent gave in to their worried colleague and adopted a very conservative schedule. They did try to raise their patient's morale by allowing the staff to move him in his bed to the sunporch every day beginning 10 October so he could have thirty minutes to an hour in the sun, but they did not resume the "armchair" treatment until 15 October, the beginning of the fourth week, following a respite this time of six days. Even then Mattingly was recommending a further delay, but his colleagues went ahead, which made it possible for the president to sit in a wheelchair on the sunporch.[18]

The disagreement among the cardiologists about the meaning of the changes in the clinical record persisted throughout the weeks at Denver and eventually became a major issue. Mattingly had come to the conclusion that the president's heart attack actually began when he was playing golf on the afternoon of 23 September, and that Dr. Snyder had misdiagnosed it as indigestion. He considered all of the president's continued activity following this initial myocardial insult—playing golf and working at home on Friday, the trips to the bathroom in the early morning on Saturday, walking down the steps of the Doud home and to the car on Saturday afternoon, and finally sitting up in the armchair—to have been harmful. In his experience such early activity for patients with extensive myocardial damage had a high correlation with myocardial rupture and aneurysms, and he believed strongly that there had been an extension of the original infarction or the development of a new inferior wall infarction.[19]

White and Pollock did not agree. To the contrary, White went out of his way in his news conference on 22 October to emphasize that the slowness of the healing process had been "wrongly called, or sometimes misinterpreted as a complication, when actually it is part of the original injury. It is all part of the original disease, not a complication." Indeed, White was exceedingly upbeat about the president's progress. He told the reporters that the healing process had "speeded up" during the past two weeks and had caught up to normal. The recovery was completely on schedule, and the patient "week by week is on the road back to good health."[20]

Several days later, back in Boston, White was somewhat less doctrinaire about Ike's condition in a private and personal letter to Dr. Cowles Andrus of Johns Hopkins Hospital, whom he hoped to recruit to help look after the president while he was residing at Gettysburg. "He did have a right smart attack and has undoubtedly (and confidentially) had a larger area of infarction than might be interpreted from some of the earlier reports at least," White explained. "Happily we never went into any great detail about the size of the muscle damage. . . . It is barely possible that there may have been an extension of the infarction, not of the thrombosis, in that first week. Some of the fringe of ischemic muscle may have become knocked out as we sometimes see it. That may be the possible explanation for the so-called slowness of the evolution of the electrocardiogram during the first ten days aside from the effect of the pericardial involvement as a part of the process." The difference between White's public and private evaluations was due, as he admitted, to political necessity: "Nationally and even more internationally it has been important for us to present to the country and the world at large as favorable a view as possible. We think we haven't overdone it because his clinical evidence has been so good that we felt we could balance it at least somewhat against the electrocardiogram which has been disappointing."[21]

As a result of Mattingly's continuing reservations, the cardiologists agreed to perform some careful fluoroscopic, kymographic, and X-ray tests as soon as the president was ambulatory enough to go to the radiological laboratory. These tests, which took place between 28 October and 4 November, depicted a bulge along the left ventricular border of the heart over which there were absent pulsations; the radiologist, and later Pollock and White, believed this was a residual of the pericarditis observed in early October, and therefore not of any special importance. Mattingly interpreted the films differently; he diagnosed the existence of a ventricular aneurysm, resulting from the loss of heart muscle, which caused him considerable concern because it could portend future dangerous, even fatal, complications. At his suggestion the radiologist, Colonel Allan Ramsay, repeated the fluoroscopic studies on 10 November, with the same results. Mattingly was alone in his minority opinion, but he was able to convince his colleagues of the need to include a program of long-term anticoagulant therapy in the future management of the patient.[22]

Apart from the disagreement on this single issue, the doctors worked well together, and the convalescence proceeded without incident. Near the beginning of the fifth week, on 21 October, the president sat up on the edge of his bed and dangled his feet; two days later he stood up for the first time; and three days after that he took his first unaided steps. By 4 November he was walking at will on the eighth floor, visiting Mamie in her room, having his meals in the small dining room, and viewing movies in the conference room. On 5 November he began climbing over a two-step platform, the next day up four steps, and by 9 November, two days before he would leave the hospital, he was walking up a full flight of twenty stairs.[23]

During these weeks the physicians also saw to the patient's psychological health or, in White's words, "tried to treat not simply the heart but especially

On the sundeck at Fitzsimons Army Hospital in October 1955 wearing the message "MUCH BETTER THANKS." (Courtesy Dwight D. Eisenhower Library)

the whole man." The most obvious requirement was to prevent him from becoming irritated, toward which end they kept troubling news away by prohibiting newspapers or magazines for five weeks. In another instance Snyder decided to keep from Ike some data Milton had received from the director of Giesenger Hospital concerning the percentage of recurrence in heart attack cases. "Your unusually mentally alert brother, as you well know," he explained, "seizes upon information that appears to bear the stamp of authenticity. He would ponder what liability classification he represents in the several statistical reports. . . . " The president made it easy by assuming some of the responsibility for maintaining his self-control, and remembered that he and Mamie "conversed daily on a wide range of subjects, but on none that might encourage emotional outbursts."[24]

The doctors also tried to keep the president busy—with puzzles, books, games, Autobridge, music, and painting—and sought to give him a sense of accomplishment by allowing him to do small but increasing amounts of work. "We feel quite sure," White explained to the press, "that when a person worries and thinks over what he ought to be doing, it may do his nervous system, and thereby his circulation and heart, more harm than to have a little mental activity which is not going to be strenuous. . . . It is important for a person during his convalescence to feel that he plays a little role."[25]

The schedule for the president's "little role" began as early as 1 October with a brief session with Sherman Adams, who had moved to Denver to be at his side. It would remain a "little" one, primarily because there was nothing at home or abroad that required his attention. Congress was not in session, so there was no legislation to push or to veto, and the spirit of Geneva seemed to quiet the Russians and the rest of the world. "If there ever was a time when the United States in the cold war could get by without a functioning president for a few weeks," wrote one historian, "it was the fall of 1955."[26]

Eisenhower had tried to establish a structure within his administration whereby cabinet members would work togther as a team in his absence. His heart attack challenged that approach because of competition within the party between moderates and conservatives, which meant that in a worst-case analysis the control of the party could be at stake. The president, remembering some confusion in the Wilson years, immediately issued an order through Hagerty that all regular meetings of the cabinet and National Security Council should be held, with the conservative vice president in the chair. Nixon had to be careful about even the appearance of seeking power, however, and the moderates arranged for Adams, over the vice president's objections, to go to Denver, where he could guard access to the president. The power struggle was softened by Ike's eagerness to get back to work; he boasted later that "within five days of my initial attack, staff officers were in my room asking for decisions."[27]

The recovery was not that rapid, but the doctors did consider it good therapy for the patient to sign routine papers and noncontroversial bills, and to discuss his work. On 9 October Vice President Nixon visited and brought Eisenhower up-to-date on various items; two days later John Foster Dulles briefed him on foreign affairs; and throughout that week Governor Adams continued to bring matters to him while Ann Whitman sat in the room taking notes. "He is much more active," she observed, "though still quiet — he moves his arms and legs in bed considerably. His mind is active all the time, and so right, as always. . . . The doctors do not think (and perhaps this is partial guesswork on my part) that any serious decision would upset him;

but the little minor crises do upset him and worry me so terribly. On 16 October, the beginning of the fourth week since the attack, Ike began appointments with government officials and cabinet members, and from then until 10 November he met with sixty-five of them. He also met with personal friends, had a special visit with Field Marshal Bernard Montgomery, and held a reception for the president of Guatemala.[28]

The medical team was pleased with what it considered its conservative program of treatment, and by early November the physicians could rejoice in their accomplishment. During his last news conference at Denver on 7 November, Paul White reported on the patient's "favorable" condition: all of his tests were normal with no evidence of complications, and he would not need a follow-up consultation for about a month. The Bostonian was equally sanguine a few days later when he sat down to write his summary report of the hospitalization: "Clinically the course of the illness has been very favorable despite the electrocardiographic and X-ray evidence of a considerable scar. Convalescence has been steadily and uneventfully progressing without complications. There has been no evidence of either myocardial or coronary insufficiency, or indeed of any other related or unrelated complications." The doctor was euphoric about the president's steady increase in physical and mental activity, his good appetite, his optimal weight. "His mental acuity is sharp and his morale has been excellent throughout," he concluded. "He has been an ideal patient." Howard Snyder shared the sense of "a job well done." Early in October he had predicted that the doctors "should have him in shape to walk onto the plane and make an excellent appearance before the press and photographers on or about 5 November." They had missed by only six days.[29]

The doctors had good reason to be elated; they had tended their patient with their utmost skill and devotion, both physiologically and psychologically. Even with their best intentions, however, and despite their efforts to explain carefully what they were about, they left what one observer has called a "silent world" between doctor and patient. Most physicians throughout history, in the view of Dr. Jay Katz, have confused and estranged their patients by failing to make them part of the decision-making process: "Doctors were rarely heard to invite patients to share the burdens of decision with them," he explained. "Instead, the voices heard were those of doctors' hopeful and reassuring promises, however truthfully, evasively or deceptively made, of doctors' orders, however gently or harshly uttered, and of patients' compliant assent, however cheerfully or resentfully given."

So it was with the six physicians and Dwight Eisenhower; they were with him every day, but they left him with a private world, albeit a small one, of misunderstanding, doubt, and fear.[30]

"It hurt like hell, Dick," Ike told his first official visitor, the vice president, on 8 October. "I never let Mamie know how much it hurt." In similar manner, the president never let the American people know much about his heart attack and hospitalization. His memoirs offer a self-portrait shadowed with bravado: he never felt any pain after the first night, left the oxygen tent after a few days "ready to work," insisted on being informed of important developments and activities, became more eager each day to talk with friends and associates, met with sixty-six official visitors, had to exercise self-restraint because he was feeling fine and ready for a full workload, and was cautious only because his doctors insisted that he must be in order to achieve a full recovery. There was considerable truth in the president's recollections, but there was also a forgetfulness in his claim, "My convalescence proceeded smoothly."[31]

Eisenhower was not the typical coronary thrombosis patient. Far more than most Americans, he was knowledgeable about the disease, not only of its extensiveness but also of the suddenness with which it could strike and kill, as it had during his presidency with Chief Justice Fred Vinson and General Carroll. Even though he was alert to the danger, however, he seemingly never experienced any meaningful fear of sudden death. He surely understood the gravity of the situation, for the heart meant life itself, but he was not a man who worried about things he could not control. He was a man of courage who, in the words of one of his aides, "saw life steadily, saw it whole, and saw it unafraid," a man who could fatalistically advise a nervous Secret Service: "If they're going to shoot me, they're going to shoot me—so what." He was even more direct in a letter to a close friend: "I recognize that men are mortal. Moreover, during the war there were sometimes situations involving decisions compelling temporary and occasionally fairly acute personal danger. I had to become sufficiently objective to realize that great causes, movements and programs not only outlive, but are far more important than the individuals who may be their respective leaders."[32]

The president's recovery was similarly enhanced by his attitude toward his convalescence. He was a man who liked to be in control, and he recognized the irony that his only way to maintain even a semblance of control in this unprecedented circumstance was to defer completely to the experts. "When I once understood what I was up against," he explained, "I decided to put myself in the hands of the doctors unreservedly and to follow their instructions meticulously." His decision was easy because, like most Americans, he looked upon physicians as a professional priesthood, and he looked upon his specialists as the best in their profession. "The cardiologists and even the other doctors in the hospital who so frequently imposed their attentions upon him were new, strange, and entrancing to him," Dr. Snyder noticed, "and the cardiologists in particular seemed to be entrancing for the time being." At the outset, the president appeared to be especially impressed by the Bostonian, and he "hung on every word that Dr. White spoke to him," but he also had immense respect for and "utmost confidence" in the skill of Tom Mattingly. Both sentiments increased markedly as the weeks passed.[33]

The president's trusting relationship with his physicians and his determination to follow their orders "exactly" did not preclude occasional puzzlement and disbelief on his part. One morning four doctors gathered in his room to advise about the routines he should follow in order to minimize the chances of another heart attack. They brought up the issue of smoking. "They earnestly counseled me to avoid tobacco in all its forms," he remembered. "I listened to them politely and attentively. Then noting that all four of them were smoking, I remarked pointedly that I had used no tobacco for more than six years, and wondered why I should be in bed with a heart attack while they were up and working, apparently hale and hearty."[34]

Nor did the intent and skill of the president's physicians prevent one very serious breakdown in communications—concerning the "armchair" treatment—which led the patient to harbor a deep-seated apprehension and long-lasting anger. The doctors had failed to prepare Ike for the surprise of 28 September, only four days after his attack, when, as he described it, "two husky orderlies came to the bed, picked me up, and placed me in a chair. This was for only a short time." His layman's understanding was that heart patients had to be confined to bed for weeks with virtually no movement, but he did not take issue with the new and surprising activity, and even appeared to embrace it enthusiastically. He was understandably taken aback four days later with the sudden reversal in treatment: "I was sitting in my chair when a doctor came in and, finding me looking a bit white about the nose and mouth, ordered me back to bed without delay—

instantly!" Dr. Pollock explained the change as necessary because the heart muscle had shown some enlargement, but no matter how diplomatically he spelled it out, Ike and the family associated the decision with the sudden reappearance of pain earlier in the morning, and they feared the worst. Pollock noted in his record: "I am a trifle worried this evening, since he had his first bad day today. I am hoping, however, that this is but a minor and a temporary setback."[35]

The discontinuation of the "armchair" treatment had other adverse effects for the patient. One was the revelation that his experts were not in agreement or, even worse, were confused. "Now I learned that there were different schools of thought among heart specialists," he recalled. "One group believed in a considerable period of immobility; others thought that slight exercise—sitting in a chair by the bedside, as a beginning—should be undertaken within a few days of the accident to the heart and thereafter gradually increased until a normal level of physical activity was achieved. I suspect that among my own doctors there was a difference of opinion (these doctors are a secretive lot and a patient at times has to form some of his own conclusions as to their beliefs . . .")[36]

The actions of the "secretive lot" with regard to the "armchair" treatment also caused a quiet anger. The president's detached and generous description of the episode in his memoirs belied the emotions that actually simmered within him for more than two and one-half years and erupted unexpectedly on a spring afternoon in May 1958. Sitting in the West Hall of the White House conversing with General Gruenther and Dr. Snyder, he suddenly exploded, charging that the cardiologists had gambled with his life by having him sit up too early. He was more specific; he blamed Dr. White and Dr. Pollock for their lack of good judgment and implied that he hoped he would never see either of them again. He did not stop there; he further apprised Snyder that as presidential physician he should have intervened to stop them. His only kind words were for Dr. Mattingly for having opposed the treatment. In any event, he insisted, no one should have made the president of the United States a subject of experimentation; to the contrary, his doctors should have endorsed the most conservative of doctrines.[37]

In this belated review of his case the president revealed another grievance. Inasmuch as there was a difference of opinion among the doctors, he complained, they should have brought the issue to his attention so as to allow him to make the decision. When General Gruenther gently took issue by suggesting it might have been unwise or inappropriate to present a patient with a critical decision at that point in time, Ike insisted it would have been entirely reasonable. Snyder was perturbed by the Monday morning quarterbacking; he knew there had never been any serious disagreements among the cardiologists about the "Levine method," and he wanted to tell his chief the truth. But the old doctor remained silent, fearing any such challenge might cause an explosion in his patient's blood pressure. Better to let him get rid of some of his anger, bottled up for so long. Thus the president continued to believe that he was carrying a larger scar in his heart because his cardiologists had failed to consult him about a crucial and experimental issue, and because they should have been more "conservative." Not until seven years later did Snyder raise the issue again, at which time, old and sick, he tried to excuse himself and place the blame: "I am sure you hold resentment against me for not protesting more vigorously than I did. I was in no position to put up a fight with two eminent cardiologists, White and Mattingly—and also Pollock."[38]

The physicians' inconsistency as to the "armchair" treatment and their failure to explain it adequately combined with the slowness of the healing process to send their patient into a brief period of depression. On 10 October, the day after White and Pollock ordered the second delay in his sitting up and spelled out the need for him to spend a longer time at Fitzsimons, the president had a lengthy meeting with Sherman Adams. When the governor tried to terminate the conversation, Ike continued talking, saying he had been "pretty depressed" over the weekend when the doctors had told him they wanted him to stay in the hospital at least six weeks. First they had told him that the infarct was about the dimension of a dime, he related, then that it was considerably larger, and then that he had a smallish heart and could stand some enlargement. Again the next day he mentioned to Adams his discouragement that the doctors had told him the heart was more badly damaged than he had thought.[39]

The president's depression was connected to an associated, but even deeper, fear that haunted him for many months—a fear that heart disease would force him into "a rocking chair existence." He had told his friends when he visited Abilene at the end of the war that "no man is really a man who has left out of himself all of the boy," and it seemed that at least one part of the boy was still very much a part of him—the part that fifty years before had made him willing to die rather than lose his leg and become an invalid. His body image was at stake again, not from some external impairment but from an invisible change that he could not fully understand. The damaged part, the infarct, was still there, and there was no escape from his body capsule.[40]

It was in this sense that he complained to Robert Cutler early in November that he would not even know until January whether he would be "OK or a crippled man," that being confined to a chair "would be just as good as being dead," and that it "would probably be a cataclysmic situation to get me to run." In part he was expressing a normal reaction after a heart attack, when self-image takes on exaggerated importance and a sense of diminished worth leads to lower expectations. But he also had an unforgettable reference point in personal experience, for a "coronary" had tragically restricted the life and destroyed the career of Swede Hazlett, one of his longest and closest friends, as well as his foremost and constant correspondent during these dark months.[41]

Ike and Swede met during their first year of high school in Abilene, where, after graduation, the boy from the "right" side of the tracks gained acceptance to Annapolis and was instrumental in inducing his friend to go to West Point. They graduated in 1915 and had little contact until 1923, when Swede's submarine docked in Panama, where he took Ike for a dive. Their careers advanced through the 1920s and 1930s, but Swede's came to an abrupt end in 1939. "As for myself," he explained in a letter congratulating his friend for promotion to brigadier general, "you undoubtedly know that I'm out of the picture. The medicos tripped me up three years ago with a bad heart, just as I was about to join you in Manila. . . . I managed to persuade them that I was at least fit for light duties, such as teaching, and could relieve a better man for sea. . . . It's damned heartbreaking not to be able to get to sea and carry my weight in such stirring times but at the same time I'm plenty grateful that I'm at least able to contribute a little bit."[42]

The two officers stepped up their correspondence during the war, and there was no escape from the terrible reality. In 1943 Swede complained that "it gripes hell out of me not to be *doing* something. Every night in my dreams I find myself diving a pigback, or taking a cruiser into action. To spend one's life working for something, and then find oneself out of action before it starts is bitter medicine." Both men did their best to rationalize. Hazlett insisted that "the old pump could still take a bit of a beating"; argued that he was not completely "on the shelf" because he could hold down a job teaching English at Annapolis; and heralded the pleasures of gardening, fishing, "a perfect and lovely wife, two fine girls and two faithful dogs." Eisenhower, a generous and caring friend, stressed the "vital" importance of a "bang-up prof" and waxed eloquently about the special responsibility of inculcating the young with the obligations of citizenship, the virtue of old-fashioned patriotism, and an earnest devotion to duty.[43]

From Hazlett's letters, with their references to the "heartbreak" of not being able to serve and the constant fear of "sinking into oblivion," Ike came to know what a heart attack could do to a proud man and a promising future. Now he had to weigh the potentially debilitating effect of coronary disease on his own life and worry about the prospect of becoming a "has-been." By late November he found that each day brought "a little less of the feeling of being an 'invalid,'" but the feeling would not go away. "Jim," he said to Hagerty soon thereafter, "the one thing that worries me is that if I am president for four more years, people will think they will have to take care of me—I would hate that. I could not live with myself as an invalid or a semi-invalid."[44]

In the meantime, he had no choice but to reconcile himself to being one of the "invalid class," a phrase he used with a friend, and he vowed he would be "good" and would do everything he was told to do. He did make a valiant effort to be "good" and to overcome the "big problem," which Mamie had predicted early in his convalescence would be "to try to keep his activities to the minimum decreed by the doctors." When Cutler visited for a half hour he found the patient comfortable and completely at ease. "Otherwise, he kept very still—body, hands, and facial expression. . . . Obviously he had trained himself to keep quiet. It seemed odd to me, who knew so well his vigor and vitality, to see this enforced placidity. He complained a little that the inactivity had made the muscles of his arms and legs very flabby, but he was determined to obey orders so as to speed a recovery."[45]

But even as the president was an obedient soldier, he was also restive and a man of action. He chafed at the "enforced inactivity," the "more or less secure curtain that surrounds me," the "stern edicts," and his "jailors." He was impatient, as when he said to Adams, "Well, I walked over to the wall and sat down and came back. I am getting to be a big boy now." He still had an occasional blowup, as when Mamie was trying to turn off a tape recorder and turned it on high instead. He also took advantage of the slightest opportunity to be physical, as one Sunday when the doctors placed a balance scale at his bedside with the intention of lifting him out of bed to weigh him for the first time. "While the cardiologist was standing behind the scales adjusting them," Howard Snyder described, "he told the president he was going to get him out of bed to ascertain his weight. The president swung his legs over the side of the bed and was on the scales before anyone could lay a hand on him. There was apparently no resultant harm."[46]

Apart from the occasional anger, depression, and restiveness, the patient was determined and optimistic. He was pleased about passing each milestone, the first of which he saw as "just getting out from under that oxygen tent." He was confident about his recovery and as early as 7 October told Colonel Powell, "I feel like someone else had this heart attack." He was always looking to the future, especially about playing golf, and on 6 November he wrote down a list of questions he wanted to ask Dr. White about the game—how intensive at first, how much at a time, how much each day, and on what schedule. And he was sensitive about how others saw him, using a sunlamp to improve his complexion and insisting that he not leave Fitzsimons until he was able to walk to the plane. He would leave like a whole man. He did not intend to enter the White House as a disabled president.[47]

As with most patients, the president was especially excited about the biggest milestone of all, going home. He had spent seven weeks in Denver, much longer than normal, and he wanted to get back to his farm. On the day before his planned departure, he dressed for the first time, visited with the doctors and their wives, retired at 10:00 P.M. and slept for seven hours. He awoke rested on the cool and cloudy morning of 11 November, Veterans Day, and found everyone in a holiday mood. After breakfast he took pictures of his nurses, said good-bye to Secret Service agents and hospital personnel, waved to the cheering crowd outside Fitzsimons, and drove to Lowry Field. He spoke briefly with the commanding general, the governor of Colorado, and the mayor of Denver, and then briskly ascended six steps up the ramp to the *Columbine*, where he made a brief farewell address. "Misfortune, and especially the misfortune of illness," he said, "brings to all of us an understanding of how good people are." It was an emotional moment, for as he remembered later, "Experiences such as I had gone through cause a man to develop an unusual gratitude and affection for all those who do so much to help him back to health." He also let it be known that he was not going to another hospital but to the White House and then on to Gettysburg.[48]

Returning to Washington, D.C., on Veterans Day, after seven weeks in the hospital. (Courtesy Dwight D. Eisenhower Library)

Flying home on the *Columbine*, the president had occasional visits with his physicians, including Paul White, who had invited himself for the trip to Washington. At the National Airport he greeted a crowd of some five thousand, among them Barbara and John Eisenhower and Richard Nixon, and told them, "I am happy the doctors have given me at least a parole, if not a pardon, and I expect to be back to my accustomed duties, although they say I must ease my way into them and not bulldoze my way into them." He then drove to the White House in a bubble-top Chrysler followed by an NBC vehicle with so many cameras protruding that it looked like a tank with turret guns. He waved to the tremendous crowd along the way, enjoyed seeing the servicemen on duty every ten feet along Constitution Avenue, and passed under a large banner stretched across the street proclaiming, "WELCOME HOME, IKE." In the White House he visited briefly with the domestic staff, joined in refreshments and the welcome-home ceremony, and then went immediately to his room on the second floor, where the doctors examined him and proclaimed everything "in fine shape."[49]

Howard Snyder was not pleased, however, with a brief outburst. "Damn it, Howard," the president complained following the examination, "why did you not let me stand in the car? It would have been far less exhausting for me had I been able to do so. I attempted to wave greetings, but was forced many times to kneel on the floor of the car in order to make myself seen and show appreciation for those who turned out to greet me." The president was referring to his specific request to have an open car for the trip through Washington, so he would be able to stand up and wave to the crowds. The doctors had decided the day was too cold, so he had to "squeegee" around from window to window in the closed limousine at considerable physical strain. To Snyder, it was understandable for the president to be tired after the experience but worrisome for him to be so annoyed by the inconvenience. Despite all the weeks of relaxation, the old personality was back, quickly irritated by small and meaningless events.[50]

The Eisenhowers' 496-acre farm in Gettysburg, spreading below Seminary Ridge, was to serve as a quiet refuge for the president's convalescence. It was the couple's first permanent home, a place where, in Ike's words, "I have just let Mamie go hog-wild," with fourteen rooms, including a large study, a small office, a workshop, and a painting studio looking out toward Blue Ridge. The most lived-in area was a delightful glassed-in porch opening upon a terrace, which Mamie, looking forward to the convalescence, had arranged to have enclosed. The house afforded Ike and Mamie almost complete privacy, with only the Secret Service agents and his valet, John Moaney, and his wife living there, and the spacious grounds made it possible for the patient to take long walks and to practice on the new putting green.[51]

The farm was attractive for another reason. It was far enough away from Washington (eighty-one miles) to prevent visitors from stopping by but close enough to allow the president to carry on his necessary duties. To that end, four miles to the northeast in the sleepy town of Gettysburg, Signal Corps technicians had turned the local post office into a vital center of government, with a presidential office on the first floor and facilities for Sherman Adams and his staff upstairs. Twenty miles away, at the Camp David retreat on Maryland's Catoctin Mountain, space was available for sessions with the cabinet and the National Security Council.

Once the president was out of Fitzsimons Hospital, the major medical responsibility for his health devolved to Howard Snyder. Like the Eisenhowers, the old doctor was home again—home to what he considered his proper place as physician to the president, and he was supremely confident that for this period of recovery he could tend to the patient better than anyone else in the world. He had done what was necessary in Denver by deferring to the consultants, and he would do so in the future when he considered it appropriate. Indeed, he quickly arranged for Tom Mattingly to examine the patient every week or so, and he was amenable to Paul White's plan to examine him in about a month. But now he had the leading role among the physicians, and he moved boldly to center stage.

During the stopover in Washington, Snyder conferred with White and Mattingly about general goals—to have the president drive to Gettysburg on 14 November, Mamie's birthday, remain there for about six weeks, perhaps go to the White House for Christmas, go south to Key West for a vacation during the first week of January, and then return to Washington for a final test of his ability to meet the full demands of his office. They agreed on a medical program involving a low-fat and low-cholesterol diet, a thirty to forty-five minute rest period before lunch, and the continued administration of the anticoagulant Coumadin. They also established a regimen for the president that involved a gradually increasing routine of exercise and work. The exercise was limited primarily to walking, beginning with about ten minutes and eventually reaching an hour, and to some practice putting—always with a stern edict against excessive fatigue. His other activities involved correspondence, bridge, visits with close friends, regular sessions with his staff, and eventually meetings with the cabinet, the National Security Council, and political leaders.[52]

The president's weeks of recovery at the farm were successful, but he was so conscious of his heart that he worried about small occurrences to the point that he sometimes took it upon himself to restrict his activities. During the first two weeks he was anxious about one higher than normal blood pressure reading, a feeling of soreness in his chest, and one of Mattingly's EKG reports that he found by accident on his desk, which read, "Extensive anterior wall and lateral wall infarction." Snyder had considerable difficulty assuring him that the statement did not indicate a more serious condition than had been recognized by all of the doctors since the second week after his attack.

During the third and fourth weeks, both doctor and patient went through a period of concern. Snyder for the first time detected some arrythmia (in the form of several skipped beats) while he was taking Ike's pulse, decided that he had "cardiac fatigue," and argued with him about his "excessive office commitments." Eisenhower was concerned about an episode of chest pain he experienced one evening at 11:00, which Snyder decided was a gastrointestinal problem, likely caused by a lunch of wieners and kraut. Snyder checked by telephone with Mattingly, who agreed with his diagnosis of epigastric distress and offered to rush to Gettysburg, but the doctor decided against it because he did not want to arouse the suspicions of the press. He chose, instead, to remain at the house overnight. The following day Ike was feeling much better, but he was worried enough that he stayed inside the house all day.[53]

Everyone therefore was looking forward to the first major physical examination since leaving Denver, scheduled for 10 December at Walter Reed. The examination was supposed to bring together the old team, but Paul White could not be present and made arrangements to see his patient the following week. The examination turned out to be uneventful. Mattingly questioned Eisenhower about his various complaints and concluded with a positive report: the cardiovascular status was "good," the EKG stable, the "small aneurysmal bulge" the same size as before, and the progress that of a "normal recovery." Snyder met with the press immediately after the examination (having been warned by the president that he should focus on medicine and avoid politics) and assured the American people that there was nothing worrisome in the day's examination, that everything was perfect except for "a little fatigue," and that there were still two months to watch his patient carefully before it would be time for a decision about a second term.[54]

From Snyder's viewpoint, after a month of convalescence in Gettysburg, all was well with his patient. What he could not reveal to the public—and what greatly perturbed him—was that Tom Mattingly did not agree. Instead, Mattingly held unswervingly to his interpretation expressed so forcefully at Fitzsimons that the president had an aneurysm on his heart; he was so worried that he scheduled the chief radiologist, Colonel Elmer A. Lodmell, to take a new series of fluoroscopic examinations and kymographic studies as part of the Walter Reed examination. The result was the same as before, as Colonel Lodmell explained to Mattingly, Snyder, and Heaton immediately after the examinations. He, like Colonel Ramsay in Denver, had detected a small abnormal area along the anterior wall of the left ventricle that did not contract as did the remainder of the ventricular wall; and he, like his predecessor, determined it to be a fibrous healed scar of the old myocardial infarction, not an aneurysm.[55]

Once again Mattingly disagreed with the interpretation of the tests, and this time Snyder became overtly angry at his colleague's persistent diagnosis of an aneurysm. Mattingly was scheduled to accompany Snyder and Heaton to the White House press conference immediately following the 10 December examination, but he was so perturbed that he asked to withdraw. The generals insisted he attend because even though Snyder would answer most of the questions, the press would expect a cardiologist to be on hand. Mattingly took note of the continued displeasure not only of Snyder but also of Heaton, his commanding officer, and finally agreed. He would simply concur in Snyder's report, he told them, and he did so, but he was ill at ease responding to the occasional question directed to him. He consequently asked to be excused from future press conferences because he found it difficult not to express his honest opinion. He told his superiors that if they did not have confidence in his diagnosis and opinions, they should have another consultant. He also promised Snyder that he would not perform or participate in any subsequent fluoroscopic examinations of the president; henceforth he would simply include the radiologist's reports in his own evaluation, thus avoiding any conflict—a promise he kept for ten years.[56]

When Mattingly arrived back at his office at Walter Reed that Saturday evening, he found a note from Snyder apologizing for his "explosion of temper." The cardiologist felt the need to respond, and he wrote out a confidential report to Snyder explaining his position. From long experience he was convinced that the bulge on the heart was an aneurysm and not just a myocardial scar. He readily acknowledged the right of Drs. White, Pollock, Ramsay, and Lodmell to make their own interpretations, but he believed they were lacking in experience and knowledge of this special area. He would accept Snyder's judgment that the diagnosis of an aneurysm should not be added to the official clinical record or announced to the press, but he wanted the possibility of such a complication to be considered in the postinfarction management because of the possible danger—it could increase the potentiality of subsequent heart failure, aneurysmal rupture, arrhythmias, and thromboembolism. More specifically, he made a strong recommendation for the continuation of anticoagulant therapy and, as he had several times before at Fitzsimons, for a slowly increasing program of physical activities. He also remained testy. "I really desire not to be a part of subsequent press conferences," he concluded. "I find it very difficult not to 'speak my mind' and you and general Heaton (our new conference member) may not like my opinions."

In addition to his medical opinions, Mattingly suspected that Snyder was already "grooming" the president for the political contest the following November, as if certain that his chief would seek reelection unless some serious complication occurred in the meantime. Now, he decided, Snyder had the two radiologists, Ramsay and Lodmell (who had told him there could be an aneurysm but that this was too "hot" a subject for them to "stick out their necks" unless and until they were completely convinced of such a diagnosis), as well as the two cardiologists, White and Pollock, seemingly more interested in protecting the president's political life than his survival. Clearly the odds against Mattingly were imposing, and he chose to withdraw from the conflict. He decided the best he could do was to provide advice that might help prevent the dire complications he had come to expect, and to monitor the president closely for any early and threatening signs.[57]

With Mattingly in retreat, Howard Snyder could rest more easily. He was confident he could trust his colleague to remain a true professional, both as a physician and as a military officer. There would be no unwanted opinions, no public disclosure about the possible "complication," and therefore no threat to the possibility of a second term. But Snyder could not be as certain about Paul White, who was seldom silent and who had the potential to become a loose and very dangerous cannon. The Bostonian had been unable to attend the examination at Walter Reed, but he was scheduled to visit the president and hold his own conference with the press on 17 December.

White had every reason to be proud of his role as a consultant at Fitzsimons Hospital. He had entered a sensitive situation as a supposedly superior civilian whose judgment was required to assist, or even supersede, that of the military, and he had responded with thoughtfulness and tact. In his first comments before leaving Boston, he went out of his way to praise Dr. Mattingly as "among the very best" and to assure the American people that calling in a civilian "is more a morale factor." And in an attempt to forestall any continuing deprecation of Dr. Snyder, and to preserve the latter's close relationship with the patient, he stepped forward with his spirited public defense. He also could relish the "tremendous job," as Mattingly described it later, of treating "the disturbed and panicky nation and world that became sick and anxious with the news of a heart attack in a very popular president and leader."[58]

In addition, White felt very good about the entire experience at Fitzsimons and especially about his relationship with Eisenhower. At his third news conference he was almost ecstatic as he thanked the doctors, the nurses, the press, and the American people, announcing: "It has really been a wonderful experience." He thoroughly enjoyed the president, as was evident in the episode of the good-conduct medal. After the press had presented Ike with some bright red pajamas for his birthday, embroidered with a circle of five stars and the words "MUCH BETTER THANK YOU," White had a Boston jeweler make a large gold star pin. On "a day of bright October sunshine, when the president was seated in a wheelchair on the hospital roof outside his suite," he explained, "I pinned a new star in the center of the circle of the other five, and made him a six-star general for good behavior." The doctor had every reason to believe that his warm feelings were shared by his patient, who soon thereafter sent him an inscribed copy of his book and wrote: "Sometime I shall try to tell you, however inadequately, of my profound appreciation for all you have done. I know, as my doctor, you would not *now* approve of the effort. But permit me at least to thank you from the bottom of this scarred heart for my 'good conduct star.'"[59]

These were heady days for the cardiologist; he had gone to Denver as a mere consultant, albeit a distinguished one, and in the period of a few weeks he had become a national celebrity. He had been able to use the historic opportunity provided by the president's illness to educate the American public about coronary disease, to make the entire nation his classroom. As he put it, "I talked to the country during those next few weeks as I had talked to families of many private patients." His campaign against invalidism was so important as to inspire Tom Mattingly to write later in an encomium, "Every surviving victim of coronary disease today is indebted to him for this help."

For the long term, White's service had enhanced his usefulness as an educator and heightened his visibility as a promoter and fund-raiser for medical research. But more important for the immediate future, it had cast him in the public mind, and in his own perception, as "Ike's doctor." He had entered the case in order to ensure credibility for the American people, and it was perfectly natural, in his thinking, to remain on the case until it was resolved. No one had explicitly asked him to do so, but when the army's surgeon general appointed him as a consultant on 4 October, he mentioned that his professional care would be required for an indefinite period of time; in White's judgment that meant until the president was well. Nor had anyone told him that his services were no longer needed; to the contrary, Eisenhower and his military doctors continued to be receptive to his advice.[60]

During the stopover at the White House after leaving Fitzsimons, White made clear his intention to remain a part of the action. He not only participated in the examination of the president, but he also told Mamie he would like to review the cardiac status with her, Milton, and the patient. So after the other physicians had left, he remained behind for dinner and discussion. He summarized the status quo as favorable and wholly without complications; advised of the need to go slowly rather than rush the convalescence; explained how it was natural to expect a little depression and impatience; and expressed delight at leaving his patient in the "very capable" hands of the military doctors, but mentioned that he would be on call as needed, as would Dr. Cowles Andrus of Baltimore.[61]

At Mamie's request, White put everything important from the conversation into a letter to Ike the following day, 12 November, and he also sent copies to Snyder and Mattingly. To the president's copy alone he added a postscript, apparently referring to the pace of activities and certainly assuming an intimacy with his patient: "Confidentially, I believe that my own attitude is midway between the slightly divergent views of General Snyder and Tom Mattingly. The general's attitude is, I believe, a little more liberal than mine and Tom's a little more conservative. A middle course is, I think, about right." Five days later the president sent White a signed copy of his book, thanked him for the "splendid" arrangements he had made for his medical supervision, assured him that he had conquered his "impatience" about his recovery, and suggested that "it is possible that I have tried to work too hard for too many years—maybe now I will be more selective in my operations."[62]

White was not directly involved in the president's care at Gettysburg, but during the following month there was some communication between him and his military colleagues, though it was occasional and always by letter. Mattingly and Snyder did keep him informed of the president's progress; the former sent copies of all his consultation reports, together with EKGs and

X-rays, and the latter corresponded on several occasions with medical information and with plans for White's visit in December. For his part, White provided Snyder with data he had received concerning long-term anticoagulant therapy and offered one suggestion designed to prepare the president psychologically in the event that something dire might befall Lyndon Johnson. Having heard that the senator might be visiting the president, and having learned that Johnson had been hit much harder by his own heart attack—indeed, that he was more or less in a state of shock for days—White wanted to ease any undue fear that Ike might have in the event the majority leader did not fully recover or if he had a recurrence during the next several years. Snyder considered the suggestion "very thoughtful" and followed through on it; he mentioned to the president in a casual manner that the senator's attack had been much worse than his own.[63]

Although the physicians appeared to be cooperating, in private Snyder, Mattingly, and Heaton, for several reasons, were becoming increasingly disenchanted with White. They felt he was pushy, inviting himself for the trip home from Denver and for dinner with the first family, and generally trying to take over the case. They also believed he was unprofessional, as when he asked Dr. Andrus to assist on the case without clearing it with anyone else, when he continued to ask Dr. Lepeschkin to evaluate the president's EKGs, and when he gave medical advice directly to the president, as he had in his letter of 12 November. "Perhaps it would have been better to have sent such a letter to General Snyder, his physician," Mattingly remonstrated, "rather than direct to the president, the patient." Eisenhower was sensitive to White's activities as well. He jokingly mentioned to his military doctors, "I guess I have a new personal physician now"; but he disapproved of White's failure to go through the proper channels, and he expected Snyder to straighten it out.

Mattingly tried to explain White's behavior as the result of exuberance, but even he was concerned about his friend's propensity to discuss the president's health with physicians around the country without the permission of the patient or his family doctor. When he learned that White was attending a course in Boston, he decided to intervene. He wrote White on 29 November to express his hope that the participants would not ask too many questions, lest something appear in print to bother the president. "He reads all comments now rather closely with definite anxiety," Mattingly advised, "and I believe there is some sensitiveness about his personal illness being one of general medical conversation." Then he went on to chide his friend: "The world has been well informed that the president had a myocardial infarction and that the world's outstanding cardiologist, Dr. White, was his consultant. It seems that our president, as well as our gardener or chauffeur, is entitled to a private illness without it being the subject of discussion in every medical or drawing room discussion."[64]

For the most part, the military doctors were overreacting to White as they circled their wagons. He did assume an intimacy with the president, but it was because of his friendliness and enthusiasm and not part of some plot to displace them. And too, *every* indication he received from his patient suggested that the intimacy was reciprocal. White did intrude on Howard Snyder's turf, but he was not trying to take over the case; he merely wanted to stay in the game and meet what he sincerely considered his "obligation" to the American people to have a say in the final outcome. He did insult Tom Mattingly when he invited another cardiologist, Dr. Andrus, to become part of the team, but the slight was in no way intentional. Nor was White likely aware of one rumor that enflamed his colleagues, especially General Heaton—that some of the New Englanders in the White House wanted a cardiologist near the president and were conspiring to have him replace Snyder. The one area in which the two doctors did have legitimate reason for concern was White's seeming ineptitude regarding politics. From the beginning, in their judgment, he had been too forthcoming with the press in discussing the future, and they wondered whether he could be trusted to remain silent and leave the political decision to the president.[65]

Against this background White journeyed to Gettysburg for his delayed examination of the president on 17 December, a day that took on the air of a doctors' reunion. He arrived at the farm at 10:30 A.M. and joined Snyder and Mattingly for a physical examination, after which they discussed the favorable results with their patient. At noon they retired to the Gettysburg office for a news conference, which began with a ceremony in which they presented a diploma signed by all of them—doctor of journalistic dietetics—to Jim Hagerty for his exceptional service during the autumn crisis. The conference, with White as the keynote speaker, continued in a festive mood. The president was "out of danger" and in "excellent spirits," ready for more exercise toward the end of the month, perhaps some putting and chipping in the South, and for the "final test" in January. The scar on his heart was healed, and the only uncertainty involved the adjustment of the rest of the heart to the scar through exposure to a full load of work. There was no need for unusual treatment—no special surgery, no special medicines, and no wonder drugs. As for the future, "With average luck and commonsense care, it is possible for the president to live for years and be fully active."[66]

After the press conference Snyder and Mattingly left for Washington. Unbeknownst to them, White returned to the farm, stayed for lunch, and took a long walk with the president, which he viewed as an "excellent functional test." The following day White informed his colleagues of his private examination and made a series of medical recommendations to Howard Snyder, advising that he might take them up with the president "without any unnecessary alarm or special bother just to play safe." Specifically he wanted some simple tests (pulse rate, blood pressure, and heart sounds) taken when the president exercised more vigorously than usual; a five- or ten-minute pause at intervals of not over one hour when he was attending conferences; and a "real analysis" by "some dietitian or other expert" so as to prevent the unintentional intake of too many calories or too much fat. With these measures in place, the Bostonian would "feel a little more content."[67]

Upon receiving the unsolicited advice, General Snyder was miffed because he already was doing everything White wanted, including watching his patient's fat intake carefully. His insistence that he had everything under control was correct; the president was active, feeling well, and gaining confidence, so much so that he even denied his doctor's talk of fatigue. "It isn't that I feel tired," he told his legislative leaders. "It's what the machines show up." In the weeks before Christmas he was meeting regularly with legislative leaders and members of his staff, and by the third week in December, as he prepared for a series of National Security Council and cabinet meetings to be held in Washington, he told associates, "Don't give me mush. I want the hard ones now."[68]

Years later it became doctrine that Ike had been bored and depressed during his recovery at Gettysburg. Robert Donovan described him as suffering from slumping morale, low spirits, bad weather, and confinement. "Sometimes he could not get out at all," he wrote, "and when he did, the putting green on the farm as likely as not was frozen stiff. Unable to walk a great deal, he was sometimes forced to ride in a Jeep for something to do. Indoors he was tense and nervous and stalked about the house with a golf club for a cane." Nixon wrote of his "debilitating bouts of depression," noting that he "would sit immobile for long periods of time, brooding silently about the future." The president denied the charge of boredom as early as January 1956, when a reporter asked if he had missed the "bustle of the presidency." He admitted that "anybody who has been busy, when he doesn't have immediately something at hand, has a little bit of a strange feeling," but he was hardly "bored to death." He had "piled up stacks of books I never had a chance to read," had his painting, and added: "I like the actual roaming around on a farm. I love animals. I like to go out and see them. I have got a thousand things to do in this world, so I don't think I would be bored, no matter what it was."[69]

The truth is likely somewhere in between. The president did keep busy and was often in good spirits, but he also had moments of depression, especially as the weeks passed and the uncertainty about his health persisted. After he returned to the White House for Christmas, he worried because he had a "little spell" at his office party and became very tired, and because his blood pressure was sometimes high. Beyond such immediate complaints, he felt that he had no control of what was happening to him. He told Nixon that his doctors probably would never be able to give him any assurance about what his future would hold because he did not have any of the "explicable symptoms" of the disease.[70]

Eisenhower was in an unusual—and frustrating—medical situation. Heart attack victims ordinarily search their individual biographies and discover causal factors that make their coronaries intelligible. By reconstructing their past in such a way as to perceive of their episode as the obvious outcome of a previous lifestyle, they normalize the attack and thus make it less threatening. The president, with the full and eager assistance of his physicians, did a retrospective reconstruction of his biography, but it failed to yield an easy answer. Indeed, after the 10 December examination Snyder, Mattingly, and Heaton talked to him about cholesterol but admitted that otherwise they were perplexed and mentioned the attack as an "act of God." There was good reason for their uncertainty. Eisenhower's parents had lived into their eighties with no discernible symptoms of coronary disease; his cholesterol level was below the normal level for Americans; he exercised regularly and was not overweight; his blood pressure was only mildly and occasionally high; and he had stopped smoking in 1949. Thus, as he saw it, his fate was more problematic than that of the typical heart patient, who could change his lifestyle in some specific way and thereby enhance his prospects of avoiding another attack.[71]

His future was in limbo, he felt, and the situation made him increasingly impatient because it impinged so directly upon his political considerations.

And the greatest indication of his recovery during his weeks at Gettysburg was his growing inclination to run for a second term.

We likely will never know what Dwight Eisenhower really thought about a second term prior to his heart attack. For years he vacillated between his wish for a "onetime performance" and his urge to fight for his program of moderate conservatism. By the summer of 1955 he was insisting that he had fulfilled his "special duty" as president and that only an emergency should override his personal desires. He also was conscious of his age, fearful that older men tended to "hang on too long," that his reflexes were slowing down, and that increased tensions at home and abroad would cause an even greater erosion of his mental and physical abilities. "A man who is getting to be seventy in the job may be slowing up like the devil," he decided, and he was aware of the fact that "no man has ever reached his seventieth year in the White House." At the center of his protestations was his sense of honor, that "no one has the faintest right to consider acceptance of a nomination unless he honestly believes that his physical and mental reserves will stand the strain of four years of intensive work."[72]

In some ways the Eisenhower position resembled that of 1952—a seemingly reluctant candidate fighting off the entreaties of a dedicated group of friends and bemoaning his fate, while at the same time careful not to do anything that would take him out of the running. Surely he yearned on occasions for what Hazlett described to him as the "long twilight honeymoon"; he told Lucius Clay that if "anyone wanted to work for me in a personal sense, they would work for my opportunity to go golfing, shooting, fishing, and loafing, until there overcomes me the urge once more to go to work." He also dreaded the thought of another campaign like 1952, when he had only two days of rest during sixty-three days of speeches; it was a "bitter, hard job," he complained, "and I just have not quite that much remaining energy." But just as surely he could not take himself out of the picture. Much of his talk about retirement seemed like an angling for reassurance, praise, and sympathy for the sacrifices he had made. He was very much like a senator whom he described with insight following a White House visit in 1956: "All in all, he talked like a man who was ready to quit but who would really like to be urged to stay."[73]

On the afternoon of 24 September, all of the considerations became superfluous because, for a time after the heart attack, the second term disappeared as a viable concern. "I have no doubt that he will regain his vigor," Milton Eisenhower wrote to Howard Snyder, "and that the nation and world will have the benefit of his steady, sane leadership for the remainder of the present term. After that, he and Mamie no doubt will have many, many happy years at Gettysburg." Arthur Wilson, an army friend from the chief of staff days who had suffered a heart attack five years earlier, advised Snyder that the "boss" can "live to be an old, old man just as I intend to do *if* he doesn't let the politicians and friendly friends who have much to gain or lose maneuver him into running for office again." As soon as he heard the news, Hazlett tried to cheer the president with a letter of welcome to the Cardiac Club. "Except for the initial wrench, the smothering of ambition, and the adjustment to a decelerated mode of living, I have found much happiness in the Club," he consoled. "There are much worse things than bad hearts, Ike. More annoying, I mean, and more confining. Ulcers, for instance—and second terms. I hope that this attack will settle the latter matter for once and for all. In some ways, I can't help but feel that it is a God-given warning to be quit of that awful responsibility of yours—despite the fact that the world needs you."[74]

One friend who saw God's hand at work was the Reverend Billy Graham, who wrote on 8 October to commiserate about the "terrible dilemma" the president faced. "I want to withdraw my urgent request of a few weeks ago that you run again," he wrote. "I think you have given enough to your country, and you deserve some peace and quiet." The famous minister then engaged in a bit of advice: "None of us can understand why God allows these things to come into our lives and change our plans, programs, and ambitions—but he does! We must accept it as from God and realize that he knows better than we what is best for us as individuals and as a nation." Graham also tried to make the patient feel better. He had talked to a great heart specialist only the day before, who said there was no reason why the president shouldn't live a normal life to a ripe old age. And he told of an old doctor in Minneapolis who had suffered a heart attack at the age of sixty-two and who, twenty-nine years later, was still alive because he had learned to think slowly, walk slowly, eat slowly—and play golf twice a week. If Ike decided not to run again, Graham advised, he would go down in history in the same category as Washington and Lincoln, and would have a position unprecedented in American history: "You will be the most respected elder statesman that America ever had. Your influence and contribution in world affairs can be from the highest level without political taint. Your every suggestion will be carefully listened to by the entire world. You have a tremendous responsibility and a great future."[75]

Political commentators echoed these private reservations about a second term. *Business Week* reported in its "Washington Outlook" on 1 October that when "the shock hit, the GOP gave up and the Democrats put 1956 in their bag." In mid-October *Look* featured an article by Leonard Finder, a friend of the president's who had predicted correctly that he would not run in 1948, that he would run in 1952, and who now believed that Ike had achieved his objectives and had a "definite intention" to retire. Two weeks later *U.S. News and World Report* claimed that Ike was "firm" in a decision not to accept renomination. The conventional wisdom eventually found expression in the statistics. In a 12 November poll of Washington newspaper correspondents, 88 percent thought Ike would not run; a week later the managing editors of the Associated Press forecast the same by a ratio of four to one.[76]

But many Republicans would not accept such an outcome. Only two days after the attack the party's national chairman, Leonard Hall, made what seemed to be an incredible statement: "The ticket still will be Eisenhower and Nixon." The newsmen snickered and laughed, but he persisted: "As far as I'm concerned, the ticket will be Ike and Dick, and thank you very much." In the weeks to come Hall and his cohorts succeeded in keeping alive the "he will run" arguments—that many cardiacs live long, normal lives, that Ike could win without campaigning, that he could take things easy in a second term, and that he could provide better leadership on a part-time basis than any probable successor working full-time. By the end of the year a poll of Republican state chairmen found an overwhelming majority who believed the president would run. "He has a program he's devoted to," explained an Alabama chairman. "He isn't a quitter." By that time the most important politician of them all agreed; he was not giving up. His thinking had undergone the same metamorphosis as that of his supporters, and he had every intention of waiting until the doctors were ready with their advice.[77]

"When I first rallied from my attack of September twenty-fourth," the president recalled, "almost my first conscious thought was, 'Well, at least this settles one problem for me for good and all.'" His response was understandable, for his experience had taught him that heart disease ended careers. A year after V-E Day, in a case similar to that of Hazlett, an old compatriot from the Philippines who had served as his adjutant during most of the war, Brigadier General T. J. Davis, was out of the picture. "You'd be interested in knowing," Ike wrote to a mutual friend, "that T. J. Davis had to retire; bad heart." And there was Pete Carroll, his staff secretary. After Dr. Mattingly diagnosed his dire condition, the president wrote in his diary: "Now he is in the hospital with a heart attack and will probably be away from duty for a matter of several months. But no matter how long I have to wait, I shall still have a place for him." General Carroll returned to the place Ike kept for him but died soon thereafter.[78]

During his first five weeks in the hospital the president was not concerned with the matter of the second term, and, having been denied newspapers and radio, he was unaware of much of the interest of others. As he emerged from this "hiatus" in early November, he claimed to be astonished to find some people already saying that he should run again. "I had a let-down feeling that approached a sense of frustration," he remembered, and in that vein he told former aide Robert Cutler at Fitzsimons on 2 November that he probably would not be physically able to run again. But Cutler learned from Sherman Adams after the meeting that Ike was giving others a different impression and that prospects still existed for a second term. "Adams pointed out that whereas three weeks ago the president was talking of a 'new team,'" Cutler recorded, "the latter now seemed to be thinking more of a possibility that he might himself be able to do it. It seemed to me that Adams himself hopes and almost believes it can be done."[79]

If the president really did intend to drop out of the race, there was no more perfect time than the weeks following the heart attack. No friend would have faulted him, and no politician would have called him to some higher duty. But he chose to follow his previous course—he would keep his options open. It was especially easy to do because the doctors had postponed the need for any decision, explaining to him and the American people that not until early February—after he had returned to the total physical and mental strain of his office—could they make a medical judgment about his ultimate condition. The president accepted their prescription and acknowledged that he "had no recourse but patiently to wait the outcome of all the tests" and "gradually come to a decision myself as to whether or not I could stand the pace."[80]

In fact, Eisenhower was moving more and more toward becoming a candidate. Throughout October and November, as the pollsters and politicians continued their work, and as various groups speculated about his prospects and indicated their preference for a successor, he suffered a psychological wound of displacement. Whereas in the summer he had resented being looked upon as the indispensable man, he suddenly realized it was much worse to be considered expendable. Even his dearest friends, intending to be kind, were willing to write him off. "I am now fully convinced that there is no such animal as the 'indispensable man,'" Hazlett wrote in October. "In fact, that has always been one of my pet theories—except in your own case. . . . But now I accept it even in your case."

A further sense of rejection came from a Gallup poll on 23 October, in which 51 percent of the respondents thought he should not run again, with only 39 percent saying he should. Ike's depression at Gettysburg was probably less a result of boredom, as some thought, than of the prospect of losing his position to others. As the press focused more and more upon the qualifications of one person or another to do his job, his frustration simmered. He was especially upset when Adlai Stevenson announced his candidacy for the Democratic nomination in mid-November and when Senator William Knowland, the California conservative, threatened several weeks later that he would throw his hat into the Republican ring by 31 January if Ike had not revealed his plans by then.[81]

The president was also displeased with the political lists that were forming—Stevenson was one of the "crackpot Democrats" and Knowland was "impossible"—so when he was at Walter Reed for his physical check-up on 10 December, he initiated a series of private and confidential conversations with Jim Hagerty, with whom he had become especially close during his illness. In those four days of discussions, Hagerty found the president excited, "throwing ideas out fast," pacing the floor, "getting off his chest something he has had on his mind for a long time." Ike was intent on one theme—that he could not tolerate turning the country back into the hands of the incompetent Democrats; and he was sensitive to the one abiding reality that had plagued him during the summer—that the Republicans had failed to develop anyone within their political ranks who could take his place. Together the two went over the list of possibilities—Knowland, Dewey, Nixon, Humphrey, Warren, Brownell, Adams, and Milton Eisenhower—and found each of them wanting in one way or another. Faced with that reality, and reaffirming his own sense of worth, the president told Hagerty as they were riding to the airport on 13 December, "I don't want to run, but I am not sure I will not do it. We have developed no one on our side within our political ranks who can be elected or run this country. . . . I don't want to, but I may have to."[82]

The president was still concerned about his medical prospects, but Hagerty concluded in his own mind that his boss was moving toward a decision to place duty above health. So the following day he showed him a column by David Lawrence, the conservative editor of *U.S. News and World Report,* who predicted that Ike would tell the American people something like, "I had no desire to come to public office in the first place. I think there are able men to be found to succeed me. But if the people want me to serve, I shall obey their wish and serve if elected." Ike read it, laughed, and said: "Well, I'll be Goddamned." Then he continued, "Jim, you would think he was sitting in that car. That's almost exactly the words that are forming in my own mind should I make up my mind to run again."[83]

The president also was sensitive in his discussions with Hagerty about maintaining control of the press. He suggested that he should be on television more as his health improved, and he turned down a suggestion by columnist Roscoe Drummond that journalists submit written questions to him during his illness and receive written answers. "No, I don't think so," Ike explained. "If we answer written questions then they are official documents which could rise to haunt us in the future. In a press conference you are answering extemporaneously and you could, if you had to, change the emphasis from time to time."[84]

The president was worried even more lest the doctors say something about politics. As he was leaving his Walter Reed hospital room after the physical examination on 10 December, he learned that General Snyder was giving a press conference. "What the hell are you having a press conference for?" he asked. "Can't you just tell them I am still living?" Then he added, for the benefit of all the other physicians: "I want you fellows to understand that such press conferences will be merely a medical report and not a political one." Riding down the elevator with Hagerty, he repeated his query laughingly, "Can't you just tell them that I'm not dead and let it go at that?" But he turned serious during the ride to the White House. He would have preferred to have Hagerty read a statement prepared by the doctors rather than to have Dr. Snyder conduct the conference. "He doesn't know how to handle the press," he explained. "He is liable to talk too much, and he certainly can't handle the political questions that will be asked. I don't want him to give any indication of my plans at all, and I want you to give him a good talking to on this point before he has the conference." Hagerty did talk to Snyder and also reminded the reporters as he opened the conference that they would be getting "only a medical report."[85]

By Christmas the president was frustrated. He told Nixon that his doctors' inability to explain his disease was a "sword of Damocles" hanging over his head, and he did not see how he could rationally and responsibly consider running again. But he was unable to let political matters await the healing process, and he informed Hazlett that the topic of the second term "swirls daily around my mind and keeps me awake at night," though he admitted he did not want to mar the holiday season by delving into the matter too deeply in a letter. (Ironically, it was during his vacation at Key West, and in its immediate aftermath, that his thoughts came together.[86])

The doctors were sensitive to Eisenhower's depression and uneasiness, and they wanted him to get away from Gettysburg for a holiday in the sun. He felt a responsibility to spend Christmas with his family at the White House, but he finally agreed to leave on 28 December for Key West. During the first week he took walks around the base, pitched and chipped golf balls on the baseball field, played poker twice, watched movies, and worked on his state of the union message. On 4 January his friends Gruenther, Slater, Roberts, and Allen arrived, and from then on he gave most of his time to playing bridge, with occasional respites for walking, chipping, working, and reminiscing.[87]

Ike was concerned early in his vacation about occasional skipped heartbeats, which reached a high point of three per minute, sometimes in sequence, on the day his friends arrived. But Snyder administered quinidine and thereafter the skips went away, so that Eisenhower was able to function in every respect with no adverse repercussions. He even climbed the twenty-two steps to his bedroom and felt well. Snyder was worried enough about the arrhythmia to call Mattingly, who had been anxious about the trip out of fear that Snyder would not be able to recognize the signs of heart failure, and who preferred to accompany his patient. But Snyder did not want a cardiologist at Key West lest his presence there draw attention to the heart problem. Mattingly accepted the situation after medication suppressed the skipped beats, and Snyder wrote in his diary that Ike looked better than he had in years, and that all of his friends had concluded that he would run again.[88]

On Sunday, 8 January, the day of departure from Key West, Eisenhower held a brief press conference at the bachelor officers' quarters and gave a different impression. He told the newsmen that his mind at the moment was not fixed, that he was not hiding anything or trying to be coy, and that he had all the factors for his decision "marshaled in the proper order" in his mind. He acknowledged that the presidency was probably the most taxing job there could be, "as far as tiring of the mind and spirit"; that he was uncertain where the "path of duty" was pointing; that unlike in the past, he now had a "sense of fatigue" and a feeling that he had to take care of himself; and that his future health had a national as well as a personal meaning: "It is a very critical thing to change governments in this country at a time that it is unexpected. We accustom ourselves, and so do foreign countries, [to] changing our government every four years. But always something happens that is untoward when a government is changed at other times. As it happened, he mentioned so many negative factors that twelve out of the fourteen reporters predicted he would retire.[89]

The vacation period at Key West went very well, except for a totally unexpected and troublesome development bearing on the president's future. On the day before Christmas, a group calling itself the American Research Foundation mailed a questionnaire to 444 physicians who were formally certified as heart experts in the *Directory of Medical Specialists*. The Foundation asked two questions:

> Do you think a man who has suffered a heart attack can be regarded as physically able to serve a term as president?

> Based on what you have read about the nature of the president's illness, and assuming a normal convalescence in the next few months, do you think Mr. Eisenhower can be regarded as physically able to serve a second term?

Promising anonymity, the pollsters provided space for comments on the questionnaire and sought to ensure a large and quick response by enclosing a self-addressed envelope with a special delivery stamp.[90]

Howard Snyder learned of the poll on 28 December in a personal note from Paul Dudley White, who was not overly concerned. "I'll bet the majority will say no," he wrote. "What's your vote?" Snyder and Mattingly suspected (unfairly) that White may have personally endorsed the questionnaire, or at least that a letter he had written to the AMA in November had given rise to it. On New Year's Day, by telephone, White read copies of the questionnaire to Snyder, together with a response to the foundation written by the distinguished New York cardiologist Robert Levy, who denounced the project as absurd, ridiculous, and possibly harmful if the results were publicized. "Sound medical advice will be given and expressed in due course by the president's physicians who alone are qualified to speak in this matter," Levy had written. "In my judgment, your meddlesome project should be abandoned." The following day Snyder presented the material to the president, along with his opinion: "I will be surprised if anything comes of this, as I believe all well-informed and ethical cardiologists will reply to the questionnaire as did Dr. Levy." The president was nonetheless very indignant, and he felt that any findings would be "unscientific and mischievous."[91]

In light of the president's annoyance, White drafted a letter to the American Research Foundation for the medical team to sign. Since Levy had already "taken the bull by the horns in a vigorous way," White sought to be more diplomatic, asking simply that the organization respect the wishes of the president. But he also made the fundamental point that the "problem for us all is great enough without having further difficulties put in our way," as would undoubtedly result from such a poll. After a conversation with Mattingly, however, White decided not to issue an official or even semiofficial reply because it would simply stir up more trouble. Besides, as he wrote to Ike, there was hope that prudent colleagues would "come to our rescue."[92]

What the doctors and the president did not know was that the foundation was merely a front, commissioned to conduct its blind poll for the popular *U.S. News and World Report*. The editors considered the second term a "big question" in everyone's mind and wanted to perform a public service by providing medical information that would give "a size-up of the outlook for heart-attack victims in general as well as Mr. Eisenhower specifically." To the dismay of those around the president, the nation's heart experts seemed to agree with their reasoning; 275 of them sent in replies, a phenomenal 62 percent response for a mail poll.[93]

The results of the poll were striking enough to make the cover page of the magazine's 13 January issue (which actually appeared on 9 January), which read: "Could Ike Serve a Second Term? 3 out of 5 HEART SPECIALISTS SAY YES in Answer to Poll." In a ten-page article the editors boasted, "Never before have so many expert opinions been assembled on this important subject." They presented not only their statistics (152 "yes" to 84 "no" on question 1, and 141 "yes" to 93 "no" on question 2) but also the full text of every comment they received. Those who believed unreservedly that President Eisenhower could serve another term made numerous arguments: that "many people serve long useful lives after one or even several coronary episodes"; that "many executives and prominent men have returned and continued a productive life"; that "no one knows whether there will be more such attacks or what time interval will elapse between them"; that "most men who have recovered are better off and know more about preventing another"; that "any man over sixty shares the possibility of coronary thrombosis or some other cardiovascular accident"; that "over 80 percent of my patients return to work"; and that Ike "should be able to serve—much better than the charlatan FDR was."[94]

When Paul White learned the results of the poll, he described it as "entertaining" but "silly." It was much more than that. In their outpouring of long-distance medicine, the American cardiologists had sent a powerful message to the American people and to Dwight Eisenhower—that a heart attack did not disqualify a man from service, even in such a demanding office as that of the presidency of the United States. Although they explained and qualified, most of them were willing to say that, on medical grounds, Ike could run again. Of importance, too, their message appeared in a friendly forum; the *U.S. News and World Report* had impeccable conservative credentials, and its editor, David Lawrence, had the president's highest respect. So no one denounced the poll after the results appeared. As a secret and unknown quantity, it had seemed disturbing and mischievous; out in the open, with words the White House wanted to hear, it took on a very different meaning. Now those around the president could appreciate the advice of one respondent: "Let the doctors, plus President Eisenhower's feelings, decide."[95]

The president was ready for his "final test" on the job, but the doctors who really counted were still waiting in the wings, debating among themselves.

5

"When the Going Gets Tough,

the Tough Get Going"

❖ ❖ ❖ ❖ ❖ ❖ ❖ ❖ ❖ ❖ ❖ ❖ ❖ ❖ ❖

So Eisenhower's palace guard had its work cut out for it. The president must be brought along slowly but surely. It had to be done nice and easy. The thing could not be pushed too hard or rushed, because if it was, Ike might decide not to run after all. The door had to be kept open for Eisenhower and quietly but firmly closed on the other Republican hopefuls.
   —James Deakin, Straight Stuff

And no caricature of the man seemed more frivolous than the image—fearfully held by some and zealously propagated by many—of a spent and sickly president, prodded and goaded by heartless "politicians" to forego the retirement that he needed and coveted. Eisenhower's decision to run for re-election had been completely personal, scrupulously pondered, and, at thoughtful last, utterly unreserved.
   —Emmet John Hughes, The Ordeal of Power

No one in America followed the twists and turns of President Eisenhower's political fortunes with more wonderment, perceptiveness, and dismay than James Reston, liberal journalist for the *New York Times*. In the summer of 1955 he marveled at Ike's popularity, "a kind of national love affair," in which anything Ike did was "automatically wonderful." He perceived the president as a "national phenomenon," a "symbol" of America itself, with an awesome presence for both political parties. Republicans supported him overwhelmingly, loved him as well, and refused even to consider that he would not be their candidate again. Democrats worried and wanted to carp but had to give credence to a pundit's words, "You can't kick a man when he's up."[1]

Reston concluded after the heart attack, as did most Americans, that Ike would not run again. He held to his position throughout October and November, but early in December he noticed a change. The principal advisers to the president were creating an impression that their boss's recovery was complete, that he was as good as new, and that he could run and win without undue physical strain. The journalist was uncertain whether the patient was a party to this "distortion," but by saying nothing he had become "the central figure in a vast drama that affects the whole world." On 19 December, in the wake of Paul White's optimistic medical report and offhand comment about voting for Ike again, Reston deduced that the president was now cooperating with those in his official family who were "planning to run him again," and that well-informed opinion in the capital was gradually accepting that he would do so.[2]

Reston was concerned about the new developments. Over the Christmas vacation he received a letter from a Democratic partisan, the editor of *Holiday Magazine,* complaining that the press "ought to tell the people the truth about Eisenhower's physical condition, that no respectable physician would advise Eisenhower to run again, that Eisenhower would surely die in office if reelected, and that a standard medical textbook supported his view despite recent published statements by a doctor attending Eisenhower, Paul Dudley White." Reston agreed. "This is a very serious question," he replied, "one that has disturbed me, I think, as much as anything since I have been in Washington." He privately criticized the newspapers for having led the president and the people to believe there really was no "big issue" at stake and admitted having felt for some time that Dr. White was "going beyond his proper bounds as a doctor getting into the political realm."[3]

In his 8 January column Reston lashed out at the press for its failure to seek the truth. He denounced the "conscious effort" on the part of many powerful and widely circulated publications to minimize the seriousness of the heart attack and the inescapable burdens of the presidency. He singled out *Time* for its December article "Heart Attack Victims—They Can and Do Come Back," with its illustrated, heartwarming stories of such prominent men as Lyndon Johnson, Sinclair Weeks, and Eddie Cantor, all of whom successfully renewed their careers; and *Reader's Digest* for its January article "Run Again Ike," which challenged the belief that heart trouble incapacitates a man and cited the conclusion of a distinguished cardiologist, Dr. Arthur Master, that "patients who resumed work fared as well as those who retired." The journalist denounced the magazines for the "sin" of omitting the "dark side of the picture" and for ignoring the "controversial medical aspects" of the situation. "It is not a good or fair argument," he remonstrated, "that a sixty-five-year-old man who has had a heart attack in his first three years in the White House is just as good as he was before or that the conditions of the job will get better, or that he is likely to be able to avoid the tensions and worry that are precisely what every heart specialist warns a heart patient to avoid."[4]

Reston's call for inquiry and balance did not take hold, and shortly after the president's decision to seek reelection, Reston again expressed his frustration about the "silence of the press and the medical profession on the merits and implication of a second term" and tried again to piece together the "human drama" that led Eisenhower to change his mind and take the risk. He mused in his 2 March column that the president might have made the decision on his own, because men of action "never like to quit at any age, especially if they can retain power." But he quickly jumped to a different conclusion—that Paul Dudley White and James Hagerty were most responsible because they had created a political situation between November and March from which the president could not escape without serious injury to the Republican party.

The cardiologist, he argued, had issued reports stating that it was important for a heart attack patient to feel he was carrying on in his accustomed work, and the press secretary had dramatized the reports in "one of the most brilliant public-relations jobs in history." Reston was anything but dogmatic about his alleged conspiracy. His scenario was not complete; the Eisenhower story was still a "great novel with an unfinished plot," and the "novelists and the historians will have to take it from here." And perhaps even they might never get at the "whole truth," for it lies "where truth can scarcely be pursued with assurance—in the innermost thoughts of the president's mind, in the reactions of his dutiful wife, and in the actions of his doctors and associates."[5]

Reston was overly optimistic to believe that others might show a persistent interest in the Eisenhower decision. No novelist ever seized upon the subject for a "great novel," and no historian saw any reason to finish the "plot." Ironically, it was a fellow journalist, Robert Donovan, who in the summer of 1956 made the first determined inquest, and his scenario in *Eisenhower: The Inside Story,* was simple and straightforward. It portrayed a president who had a "deep desire" to serve only one term; who was still grappling with the problem before his heart attack; who took it for granted in the hospital that he could not run again; who went home to Gettysburg and suffered "five weeks of torment" —of depression, of low spirits and morale, of frustration over government affairs, of nervousness, tension, and bad weather; who went to Key West over the Christmas and New Year's holiday and returned feeling more vigorous and confident; who sought out the positive views of his close advisers at a famous meeting in January; and who finally made his decision on the basis of the same considerations that "would have influenced him whether he had had a coronary thrombosis or whether he had not." He wanted to use his unique position to preserve peace in the world; he wanted to hasten the trend away from the centralization of the New Deal toward fiscal stability and free enterprise; he wanted to continue the reform of the Republican party and make it more progressive; and he realized that he alone within his party could win.[6]

Donovan's book provided the basic outline for all subsequent historical accounts, and Eisenhower deviated from it only slightly when he wrote his memoirs in 1963—by placing more stress on his disinclination to run again; by insisting that he was not bored during his recuperation at Gettysburg; and in clarifying his options, as he had perceived them, as between duty (to preserve peace and prosperity, continue the reform of the party, and ensure a Republican victory) and self-interest (to protect his own health and live longer). Neither of them viewed the heart attack as a significant factor in the president's decision. Donovan described it as merely an "intervening event," because its consequences served to cancel one another. It was true that a person who had suffered a coronary was more likely than others to have a second attack; but it was also true, as the doctors had acknowledged, that the frustration of retirement could be a greater strain on the heart than the burdens of the presidency. The heart attack was therefore "neutralized" as an element in the decision. "So far as his health was concerned," the journalist concluded, "it was six of one or half a dozen of another." The president gave even less attention to his illness; it was simply an event that "prolonged and intensified" the speculation about what he would do.[7]

James Reston, who had sensed some "human drama" involved in the second-term decision, who was suspicious of the doctors and sensitive to the "innermost thoughts of the president's mind," was close to the "larger truth." New evidence shows that the doctors did play a crucial role in the outcome, although not in the way Reston imagined. And a different perspective, one that looks at Eisenhower as a man coping with a disease, suggests that his decision was as much personal as it was political, based upon medico-psychological reasons as well as a desire to preserve peace, prosperity, and the Republican party.[8]

In his memoirs Eisenhower ignored the role of his physicians in his deliberations about a second term, except for their positive "verdict" given to the American people on 14 February. But within weeks of his heart attack he was concerned about the doctors because he knew they had influence with the public, which could mean the power to dictate his future. And they were intimately involved. All of them wanted first of all to ensure the continued good health of their patient, but they had their own special considerations about how a second term might bear upon that goal. During the five months of speculation and prediction, each of them, in public and private, and for reasons both medical and personal, tried to affect the political decision.

Their influence was great because of the ambiguities surrounding the disease. The possible causes of a heart attack—family background, diet, lack of exercise, obesity, body build, tobacco, alcohol, stress and strain, personality, hypertension, or some unknown "X" factors—were lined up cafeteria-style, out of which every doctor could select those he considered most applicable to his particular case. His choice would ordinarily reflect his own intellectual predilections and his patient's history, and his prognosis would depend upon the prospects for change and control. With Eisenhower the process was exceptionally wide open simply because there were no obvious factors to explain his attack. In medical terms, as a consequence, his case created special problems for his physicians; in a political sense, it afforded them unusual flexibility.

Paul Dudley White was the first to intervene in the political process by virtue of his typically positive statements about recovered heart patients. Even before leaving Boston, he said it was "conceivable" the president could run for a second term. After examining his patient, he conceded in his first Denver news conference that "many people can not only live out this condition but can be normally active for many years after"; that the president would be "physically able" to run again; and that the choice would be "up to him." His statements were not meant to be political; nor were they meant as a medical prognosis in Eisenhower's specific case, because for a scientist like himself there could be no decision until all of the evidence was in. They were simply off-the-cuff comments reflecting his general view about the value of optimism in the treatment of coronary patients, something he wanted to share with the American people, and especially with his patient. But others took note of the political implications, and he had to retreat. "I was sorry about the mix-up in the headlines that occurred after a casual remark of mine last week," he wrote to Hagerty, "but I am sure it has straightened out now and that there will be little or no fuss and furor in the future."[9]

He was wrong. On 30 September he told television host Dave Garroway that "many things are possible that may not be advisable. . . . If I were in his shoes I wouldn't want to run again, having seen the strain." The fuss was so great that White had to explain later the same day that if the president had a "good recovery" he would have "no objection whatsoever to his running again." He repeated that message in his 9 October press conference, but he further confused the American people at his final conference in Denver on 7 November in which he made a speculative comment that could be construed as a preference against a second term. When a reporter asked what he would do if he were in the president's shoes, he answered, "I haven't enough information yet. I would want to know how I might face these problems in the next few months before making a decision. Of course, I might have made up my mind long ago, anyway." The only decision the president could have made "long ago," and which White was intimating would be perfectly reasonable, was to forsake a second term.[10]

The military doctors, accustomed to leaving sensitive political issues to Jim Hagerty, were dismayed at what they considered White's careless statements. Yet in private Howard Snyder was propounding an even more sanguine opinion, and one that had far more powerful political implications. It is unlikely that Snyder *ever* entertained the possibility of Eisenhower retiring; as a partisan Republican philosophically committed to keep the cause going, he certainly wanted Ike to continue. He also could believe on medical grounds that a second term was possible, for as White had pointed out so persuasively, "The notion that you are finished after a heart attack is obsolete." Others reasoned the same way; a few days after the attack the president of the AMA wrote to Snyder, "Personally, should he recover, . . . which I feel sure he will, I can see no reason why he cannot safely, with the help of us, run again. . . . I just have the feeling that under your wise care he cannot be counted out simply because he had this one serious setback."[11]

Snyder also was alone among the doctors in arriving at an immediate medical determination as to the cause of the president's heart attack. He was sure it had to do primarily with his emotions, and especially with his expressions of tension, impatience, irritation, and anger. He was drawing in large part upon the general conception so prevalent in his lifetime that hard-driving executives were coronary-prone; echoing both Osler and White, he announced that Eisenhower was the "type" to suffer a heart attack—"controlled, driving force, muscular, heavy boned." But he went beyond that to locate the source of coronary disease in personal behavior. He arrived at his conclusion because of ten years of experience with Eisenhower's red face, hostile voice, protruding veins on the forehead, and sudden explosions of temper—a conclusion that seemed too obvious and too simple. In fact, it was strikingly prescient. It foreshadowed the widespread interest during the following decades in what came to be known as the type A personality.[12]

Snyder's medical assumption led him quickly to two equally farsighted conclusions. The first was that it would be possible to check the progression of the disease by changing the president's environment through the control of his workplace, ensuring fewer demands and less tension; and by changing his behavior through a program of self-control, focusing on his anger and his temper. This was a sophisticated approach, looking forward to research developments thirty years later, when refinements concerning the type A personality identified anger, hostility, and cynicism as the expressions most likely to lead to heart disease, and when experts proposed strategies to alter patient behavior. Snyder's second conclusion, based upon his personal judgment, was stunning—the president could best improve both his environment and his behavior, and thereby increase his life expectancy, if he chose to run for a second term rather than withdraw into a life of inactivity. Four more years in the White House would serve the interests not only of the country but of the patient as well.

As for Ike's behavioral problem, Milton Eisenhower addressed it a week after the attack in a "personal and confidential" letter to Snyder, mentioning that he was sure he could help keep "controversial issues from causing him to lose his temper, as he sometimes does with others." The brothers had "a sort of healing, soothing" effect on one another, he believed, and had never had a disagreement or quarrel in twenty-five years of close association. "So I am keeping my work in such shape that I can, at a moment's notice, take off for Denver, for Gettysburg, or for Washington," he volunteered, "and I'll devote as much time to helping Ike as the situation requires. Perhaps you, better than any other, will understand what I am saying." The doctor understood. A month later Snyder replied that it would be necessary to get the president to adopt a "more passive philosophy," which would be difficult because of "certain characteristics" and would "necessitate deliberate and continuous effort on his part." By that time, however, his thinking had gone far beyond that of Milton, who merely wanted to ensure his brother a more relaxed life until retirement. "If certain of the recognized hazards can be eliminated," the doctor proposed, "I believe the president could assume the responsibilities of a second term with less probability of accident to his health than has been applicable in the past."[13]

Snyder made his case for reelection to Mamie and John Eisenhower while Ike was still in the hospital, and the former became a convert. John was surprised because his mother for some time had favored retirement, but he acknowledged that "knowing Dad as she did, [she] agreed with Doc Snyder that inactivity would be fatal." The doctor likewise educated members of the staff. Sherman Adams recalled that he "told us all that for a man of the president's restless and energetic temperament, retirement from public service might be far more injurious than four more years in the White House."[14]

Dr. Snyder's missionary work with Mamie, Milton, John, members of the official family, and friends of the president was of decisive importance, for it fostered the belief that it was perfectly natural, indeed beneficial, for a recovered heart attack patient to serve in the most difficult office in the world. Indeed, his months of quiet and persistent preaching brought about an evolution of thinking among virtually all of those close to the president—an evolution starkly portrayed in the diary of family friend Ellis Slater. When Slater first learned of the heart attack, he was certain that, "Beyond any question, I think it means he will not be a candidate." After a visit to Fitzsimons in November, however, during which he talked with Snyder, he reasoned that if Ike were able "to avoid inward tension" he could very well go along as president even beyond his present term. Several weeks later, after spending the Thanksgiving holiday at Gettysburg, Slater saw the issue as open, imagined that his friend's sense of duty would urge him to continue, and decided that the presidency would be less exacting than some new position. During the New Year's vacation with the Eisenhowers at Key West, he found agreement among all of the gang that Ike "could as easily worry and fret and have a heart attack upon seeing things go to hell and not be able to do anything about it as he could from putting into a new administration the effort necessary to make it work." He listened to Snyder's explanation that he thought the president would be happier in office, and that Mamie agreed. Slater came to the conclusion, as the result of "mere logic," that Ike would run again.[15]

In effect, Snyder planted the seed that would eventually blossom into a second term by selling his prescription that it was necessary for the president to serve again in order to better avoid another heart attack. There is no evidence to suggest that he shared his theory about the relationship of personality and heart disease with the president prior to January 1956, but he certainly gave his patient an optimistic prognosis, and one that did not exclude reelection. Very early in the game he went far beyond his compatriots, for neither White nor Mattingly was ready to support a second term.

Despite Paul White's strong feelings about the need for most coronary patients to return to a normal life, including to their work, he had reservations about Eisenhower continuing as president. There was a personal basis for his uneasiness, for to a striking degree this one patient could put White's credibility at stake. As his biographer explained, he had reason to approach the issue with "powerful, worrisome" considerations in mind: "It would indeed be a blow to the role of the medical expert in prediction if Eisenhower were approved by his doctors for reelection and should die in the campaign or in office. Such a happening would surely affect adversely the aura of optimism toward heart attacks engendered by the president's illness and by Paul White's remarks." For decades White had waged his campaign against invalidism, and suddenly he realized that his efforts of a lifetime depended on the future health of a solitary patient. It was a large risk.[16]

White, unlike Snyder, also was not confident about singling out a cause for heart attacks. He kept up with all of the literature in his field and had written several weeks before Eisenhower's misfortune, "The extraordinarily slow recognition of coronary heart disease through the ages is matched only by our ignorance of its etiology today, in September 1955." In Denver he admitted that the experts knew very little, and after his examination of the president at Gettysburg, a reporter wondered if he had any clearer idea of what was responsible. "No," White admitted. "That is the sixty-four-thousand-dollar—hundred-thousand-dollar question." Since he was so indecisive about causation, he certainly could not find a theoretical basis to support Snyder's incredible proposition that a heart patient could benefit in a position with a very high level of stress.[17]

White

Paul White was a dedicated professional compelled to give attention to whatever specific medical evidence might bear upon a decision for a second term, in this instance evidence relating to longevity following a myocardial infarction. That data were limited and ambiguous. In White's own important and pioneering study published in 1941 (a 10-year follow-up of 162 patients with an average age of 56.7 years who had survived the acute attack by one month) there was a five-year survival of 49 percent, with 31 percent surviving for 10 years. Several other studies between 1949 and 1953 reported survival rates ranging from 45 to 66 percent for 5 years, and from 20 to 44 percent for 10 years.[18]

White was so insecure about the existing data that he decided to ask "all the physicians of the country" about their experience regarding the total longevity of coronary thrombosis patients and the time interval between attacks. In mid-November, in preparation for the press conference to follow his scheduled examination of the president on 17 December, he made an appeal through the *Journal of the American Medical Association* (further publicized in *Time*'s issue of 21 November) for information on patients who had had heart attacks ninety days before the president's, and asked whether they were back at work, retired, or invalids. A few weeks later he asked Mattingly in a personal letter and "on the spur of the moment" to send the results of his own research: "How many of your cases have had only the one attack in a survival period of *five years* and how many two or more?"[19]

White's public request for information rested upon his assumption that his responsibilities continued even after the president left Denver, and that he, as well as the other doctors, had "the obligation to present an objective nonpolitical assessment of his fitness to accept the heavy burden of presidential office for a second term." His quest for data, however, evoked an angry response through a stern letter from Mattingly on 15 December. The colonel considered his own research material incomplete, and he preferred to present it in a medical paper rather than in a press conference, "where it will become a political football" and at the same time probably give "our patient" increased anxiety. Statistical data on a five-year survival period, he pointed out, would be "meat" for every editorial writer. "Those desiring the survival of the Republican party would use the good side of it to encourage the president to run again and disregard any hazard it offers to his health, while those desiring his withdrawal would merely emphasize the hazards and poor prognosis." He resented using the president "as a medium of public education."[20]

Acutely aware of the political implications, and wishing to keep White out of political turmoil, Mattingly preferred to have the consultants present prognostic data only to the attending physician and the patient, "and leave it to the president the choice of what he decides rather than let newspaper reporters philosophize for him." In the meantime, the cardiologists should "forget our egotism" and state with "humility and honesty" that it is impossible to accurately predict on any individual case. In a masterful blend of medicine and politics, the colonel counseled the consultant:

> If we desire the president to continue to have confidence in us and have respect for our advice, then we must respect his wishes, give him the same courtesy and confidence that we would give to any patient, and not make his ills a matter of medical and political debate, and a public exhibit for a world clinic on the treatment of heart disease. I feel that when the proper time comes we should give the president our advice as to his future as we would to any other patient and give him the free choice of decision as to his future activities according to his own philosophy, sense of duty, etc. If the Republican party should not desire to renominate him or the country decides not to reelect him because of his heart, that is their choice and duty.[21]

Mattingly's scolding was not occasioned by any preference for a second term. To the contrary, he personally was more averse than White to such a prospect because his concern about an aneurysm made him afraid the president would not survive another four years. But because of his long collegial and friendly relationship with White, because he had strongly supported White's appointment to the case, and because he had explained away some of White's earlier gaffes as the result of excessive enthusiasm, Mattingly was under pressure from Snyder and Heaton to keep his colleague from interfering in Eisenhower's business. Indeed, he felt especially responsible for, and certainly embarrassed by, the Bostonian's actions, fearing even that the president might fire him as a consultant, which was not likely because any such action would make it appear that the patient was unwilling to accept an unbiased, civilian opinion about his health. But the colonel did have reasons enough to assume the role of intermediary between the private wishes of Eisenhower and Snyder and the private agenda of White, hoping to prevent any hard feelings.[22]

Mattingly was too late with his advice to his friend, however, because White had already secretly initiated what he later described as "my vain effort to persuade the president not to run for reelection." It began in November, when Conrad Hobbs, a friend of White's and "one of the class of Harvard 1900," joined with some others in an "open letter" asking the president to appoint a commission to study the vast and complex problem of world peace. Nearly a hundred years before, the petitioners argued, an obscure Swiss businessman, Henri Durant, had crossed the bloody battlefield of Solferino and, upon viewing the abandoned wounded, dying, and dead, vowed that such inhumanity must no longer be endured. Out of Durant's passion came the far-flung, humanitarian Red Cross. Now another inspired leader, aware that a "major war would inflict on all mankind—on victors as well as vanquished, on civilians as well as combatants, on children and women—the most cruel calamity in history," could seize a similar opportunity for a great organized movement. If the president would muster a commission from among the industrial and financial leaders, clergymen, scientists, lawyers, farmers, labor leaders, educators, statesmen, philanthropists, historians, publicists, and others, it could lead the way "to a spiritual and moral resurgence, and propose a definite, feasible plan for peace."[23]

White was fearful, as was Hobbs, that the open letter would be lost in a mass of White House mail, so he offered to raise the issue directly with the president. He also decided to go much further; he would advise Eisenhower to forsake a second term for a new vocation—to fulfill his "major aim in life," promoting world peace. Hobbs was ecstatic, but he was also sensitive to a political danger. The politicians would be angry, even vituperative, if they were to learn that White had counseled the president to interest himself in other fields as an outlet for his energies, the more so if Ike decided not to run again. "The 'pols' might say that you had exceeded the proper limits of a doctor," he wrote. "They might charge that you had set yourself up as a political adviser. . . . They probably believe that they are more competent than you to prescribe avocations for him." Hobbs wrote that he would rather have his dream remain an idle one than to have his friend attacked as one who had led the president astray.[24]

White was eager to take the risk, and his chance came on 17 December during his postponed trip to Gettysburg to see his patient—exactly one week after Eisenhower had his excited discussions with Hagerty. At the press conference following the physical examination, White insisted that he knew "nothing about politics"; said that the future "rests in the lap of the gods"; repeated what he had said before—that with "average luck and commonsense care, it is possible for the president to live for years and be fully active"; and announced that if the president decided to run again, he would vote for him. He had a starkly different message an hour later during his unscheduled and unannounced luncheon meeting with Eisenhower. It is unclear who initiated the meeting. White said he was invited, but the military doctors said later that he had forced himself upon the president—an unlikely prospect in that Ike easily could have declined to discuss politics. Perhaps both wanted to talk. White had a mission to perform, and Eisenhower had his future to decide. He knew that if his health continued to improve, the political issue would rest not in the lap of the gods but in his own.[25]

So on the sunporch of the Gettysburg farm, over a light picnic lunch on a clear winter day, attention turned to the second term. Ike shared some of the reservations he had mentioned to Hazlett on earlier occasions, especially about his age and the stress of the office. White agreed and seized the opportunity to press his case and that of his friends— since the president had said in previous conversations that his major aim in life was to promote world peace, he should give up seeking reelection and lead a practical crusade to that end. It was not a matter of medicine, the cardiologist admitted, but of peace; his patient's heart could stand the strain, but the maneuvering of a political campaign might endanger the crusade. The president mentioned that one of his own friends had made a similar suggestion (Hazlett had written that in terms of serving the world, "Perhaps you can do even more good *outside* the White House than in it"), but he expressed skepticism about the effectiveness of any individual in promoting world peace apart from high office. Nevertheless, he would think about it. In addition, he emphasized to White that he did not want to be dependent on the doctors' medical advice unless it should be distinctly unfavorable.[26]

After less than an hour the conversation ended, and the two men took a long walk in a cold wind around the farm—down to the duck pond, through the cornfields, up the gentle slopes, and around the barns. The doctor was pleased with his patient; he was not short of breath, and he had no discomfort, leg weariness, or fatigue. But he was even more excited about his own proposal. He could not get it off his mind, and in Boston the next day he sat down to write a personal letter, in longhand, to the president. "Ever since our conversation on your porch yesterday afternoon I have been wanting to tell you again of my own strong approval of the advice given you by that friend of yours and also urged by one of my many recent correspondents who has at heart the welfare both of the world and of yourself," he wrote. "Your own reflections and comments about age, constant tensions and the major role that you very well could assume . . . agree with my own."[27]

On that same Sunday White sent his medical recommendations to Snyder and Mattingly, upsetting both of them. The former resented the implied criticism of his careful medical regimen, and the latter resented the very fact of the secret meeting. Clearly his old friend had gone "solo," Mattingly deduced; he had gone out of bounds, off the reservation. And although White made no mention in the letter of his shocking proposal, Mattingly was perturbed about his postscript: "Confidentially in my conversation with President Eisenhower, it became quite evident that he agreed with us that he does not want to be dependent on our advice for his decision unless it should be, of course, distinctly unfavorable. I hope, and I am sure you both do, that he will make his own decision and it would be nice if he could make it even before our next major conference in February." Since Ike could not realistically announce for renomination without the doctors' final physical examination and advice, White was actually suggesting that he should withdraw from the race. "This would relieve everyone concerned," he told his colleagues. "Don't you think?"[28]

It was time again to remind his friend of his proper role as a physician, Mattingly decided, and he did so in what he described as a "brutally frank" response. "I am glad that you have learned firsthand from the president that he does not desire his physicians to make decisions about his future," he wrote. "He will make his own decisions. He has much experience in the past in making decisions on important and vital problems in both war and peace. What he likes from his staff and advisers, medical or otherwise, is accurate and usable information, regardless of whether it is optimistic or pessimistic. What he wants is facts, and not our philosophy or wishful thinking. He has long learned and taught that you cannot win battles that way. Either you have the ammunition or you do not." Mattingly continued with a powerful statement of his own position:

> His question from us is likely to be—"Have I or have I not a good heart?"—and he would like a yes or no. We know it is not normal and he knows it also. He likewise knows what has happened to many of his officers and staff in the past. He knows, for instance, how soon General Carroll died (nine months after first attack), and less than a week after Vice President Nixon foolishly dissertated on the marvelous "cure" and "recovery he had made from a heart attack." He now hears the same dissertations and press reports from people like Martin, Adams, McKann [*sic*], etc., who are quoting medical opinions and saying that they are sure that "he will receive a certificate of health from his doctors."[29]

Mattingly's efforts reflected a growing fear in the White House—a fear shared by Eisenhower, Snyder, and Hagerty—that White, because of his enthusiasm and his carelessness with the press, might blurt out his personal feelings in some public forum. But however much they wanted to constrain him, they had to be accommodating because in the real world his was still the voice the American people wanted to hear. As a result, Eisenhower and Snyder concealed their true feelings. The president complained to his military physicians that White was becoming too "publicity-minded," but outwardly he remained very friendly to him. Shortly after Christmas Eisenhower sent a note to thank him for the "Paul Dudley White" golf ball and for his "interest in the question that is, quite naturally, paramount in my mind"; and to express his "best wishes" and "warm personal regard" with the gift of a colored, signed photograph taken on the roof of Fitzsimons Hospital. Snyder likewise remained silent; perhaps he was not inclined to criticize face-to-face the one person who had done so much to bail him out in Denver, and certainly he knew that for professional and political reasons it would be dangerous to remove White as a consultant.[30]

Thus it was left to Mattingly to persuade his friend to hold back, and even over the Christmas holidays there was no respite from his task. White had gone to the West Coast to study whales, but in the beautiful waters off Baja California he still could not escape his dilemma. On 28 December he wrote to Mattingly, mentioning again his wish that the president would make his decision "long before" the next press conference. "It will certainly be a relief when all of us, including DDE, get off the hook," he opined. "Personally and confidentially I hope that he has other plans than to run again." In an end-of-the-year, handwritten response Mattingly restated his disappointment about 17 December, for as he put it, "You were playing for Dr. White and the stands and not for the team." Hoping that his friend could agree that "one can say too much as well as too little," and that "the novelty of the press and publicity has worn a bit," he explained how "distinctly unhappy" the president was about magazine articles and polls relating to his heart attack. "I believe that we can accomplish more as a team and through General Snyder," he volunteered, "than by any personal and confidential visits with the president, appeals to the press, etc."[31]

But White was a man with a mission, and he returned to it shortly after New Year's Day. On 4 January he wrote directly to Eisenhower regarding their sunporch discussion at Gettysburg. He was pleased to report that a small trust of which he was chairman could make funds available to support the president as the leader in a practical crusade for world peace. He also enclosed a copy of a letter written by one of his colleagues in the venture (written "at the risk of appearing to be a starry-eyed dreamer of empty dreams"), and for the first time Ike could read the grandiose expectations that others held about his future: "The foremost soldier of modern times acting as the commander in chief of an unarmed host of millions," the optimist wrote, "would rivet the attention of the world on the great crusade of which the president has so often spoken. I am convinced that he would give it an irresistible impact, such as no other man could give. I doubt that even the Iron Curtain nations would be impenetrable to his appeal. I can even foresee, in my most ardent periods, a crusade which would spread like Christianity throughout the world." Moreover, out of office and searching for peace, the president could avoid the stresses and strains, and the "roughness and rudeness" of politics. He would be his own master, make his own schedule, enjoy a placid home life and work between rounds of golf. "He would be in many ways the foremost figure in the world," the idealist intoned. "Success would make his achievements as a soldier and as president seem trivial and would place him high among the immortals. . . . The people of the world are crying for peace more prayerfully than ever before, as well they should, with hydrogen bombs hanging over their heads. They would hail as a sort of second Christ—I do not say this irreverently—the man who could lead them to a durable armistice and perhaps to a permanent peace."[32]

The president took ten days to send a personal reply to White, and it was decisive. He disavowed the enterprise with such subtlety that the doctor was never aware of his own illusions. Ike reported that he had tried to test the idea on his friends as frequently and thoroughly as he could, and he had discussed it with his close associates only the evening before. They had dismissed it, unanimously. "It is astonishing," he wrote, "how universally they have rejected the idea that an individual, no matter how well known in the world, could be reasonably effective in the promotion of a peace based on understanding, unless operating from an official position of great power." Dwight Eisenhower was hardly astonished. Only eight months before, when Sherman Adams had suggested that for the rest of his life he could donate his energies to peace, he pointed out that "his ability to direct those energies toward that goal could only be accomplished from the desk at which he was now sitting." This was surely no sudden insight for one of the most perceptive politicians of his time, but having led White along for some weeks, Ike let him down gently by adding: "Nevertheless, I am not completely convinced." That was the last word on the subject, except for White's comment in his autobiography fifteen years later: "I have always felt that it would have been worth the trial!"[33]

When the president returned to Washington, with only five weeks left before he would have to undergo the most important medical examination of his life, he had good feelings about his health. The first day back, 9 January, he had a physical, and the following morning Snyder, Mattingly, and Pollock gave him a favorable report on his medical tests and handed him a memorandum stating in detail the regimen he must follow. He was to continue a low-fat diet, with fat not exceeding 25 percent of total calories, maintain his weight at 170 to 172 pounds, walk at will on level ground, climb one flight of stairs at least once a day, and exercise from ten to twenty minutes in the swimming pool. He also was to have a midday rest of one-half hour recumbent before lunch and one quiet hour in a chair after lunch (for which carpenters had built a small sunroom where he could sit quietly), take a ten-minute rest break during long conferences, and cut back his daytime work if he had any kind of social engagement at night.

There was some good news in the doctors' directive—Ike could begin playing golf on the course at the soldiers' home, which was flat and readily available, slowly building up to nine holes. There was also a challenging dictate: "Cultivate an attitude of equanimity toward personal and ever-present official problems. Emotional states are to be avoided to the greatest extent possible, that is, annoyance, anger, perturbation, anxiety, and apprehension. Avoid where possible situations conducive to emotional tension."[34]

The doctors' list of instructions was part of their standard operating procedure, but it was much more than that for the president. It served as a watershed because it provided him with the prescriptions requisite to a longer life. Throughout his recovery he had felt uncertain about what his future might hold, especially because the physicians had been unable to give an answer to the question that comes so quickly to a patient with a chronic illness: "Why me?" The new regimen in the memorandum of 10 January gave him at least a partial understanding; it implied that his own behavior was the likely source of his problem, and it was explicit about how to change it to avoid another attack. It was a road map to security in health. By adhering to it, he could lift the sword of Damocles from above his head and finally regain some control over his life.

He also felt well because he was gaining back his energy. On his first day back at the office after the Key West vacation, he told Bernard Shanley, "You know, Bern, the last couple of days I have just gotten my strength back," and he complained that his schedule was too light and that he intended to do the job "100 percent and not halfway." His appointments secretary started him on a heavier schedule the next morning and added to it the following Monday when he arranged for the resumption of weekly sessions with legislative leaders, the cabinet, the National Security Council, and the press. "Starting this week we really moved into a very hard and tough schedule," he recalled, "and I really feel the president had never run a tougher schedule than he ran in the ensuing three weeks, which was a test period in which the doctors wanted to see how he stood the load." In meetings, in letters to friends, and in the largest number of diary entries of any month of his career, Ike surveyed the broad range of foreign and domestic problems that would confront him in a second term. And he did so without any serious repercussions to his health.[35]

His new sense of well-being had a noticeable influence on his thoughts about the future. He became immersed in politics and began looking for the brighter side of the situation. He jumped into the fray with a positive turn of thought on 10 January—after receiving his memorandum of instructions—when he had a long discussion with Secretary of State John Foster Dulles, who reviewed their successful efforts for peace, argued that no man had the standing throughout the world of Dwight Eisenhower, and claimed it would be "calamitous" if he should withdraw. In the privacy of his diary Ike agreed with his secretary's assessment of his personal influence. What would happen, he wondered, if individuals of lesser experience, prestige, and familiarity with other world leaders were to succeed him and Dulles. He did bemoan the unhappy suggestion that an individual who "so earnestly wants to lay aside the cares of public office" might not be able to do so, but he accepted the implication that he must try to "carry on" regardless of any other factor. "The soup thickens," he concluded.[36]

Eisenhower had arranged to have a top secret dinner meeting on that same day specifically to discuss the issue of a second term with a group of friends, but someone leaked news of the meeting to the press. So he rescheduled it for three days later and invited Dulles, Hagerty, Adams, Lodge, Hall, Persons, Summerfield, Humphrey, Brownell, Stephens, Howard Pyle, and his brother Milton. They all agreed that he had earned the right to "lay down the burden" free of criticism, acknowledging that it would be calamitous if he had a setback during the campaign and difficult for the country if the same happened during a second term. But each of the men at the table, with the exception of his brother, took his turn to make the case that the president should run again, restating all of the previous arguments about peace, prosperity, the reform of the party, and the inability to win without him. Milton, who had already told Ike of his personal opposition, summarized both the positive and negative sides, stressing for his brother his right to think of his own health and the possibility that he might lose the election when the Democrats raised that issue. "I know what loneliness you must experience in working toward a decision which only you can make," he concluded. "I wish I could help."[37]

Historical accounts have focused on this Friday night dinner meeting, but it was anything but an impartial inquiry. "If Eisenhower was looking for cogent reasons for leaving his office," wrote participant Sherman Adams, "he would have hardly sought them from his own appointees, who were working with him in the government and who believed in him and what he was trying to do." John Eisenhower was equally skeptical. He wondered what his father could have expected from this fine group of subordinates and concluded, "His colleagues were telling him what by that time, he wanted to hear." Six days later, John sent his father a long memorandum with his own views, which ended with a recommendation not to run, and suggested "playing it cool" rather than following an "unselfish course of action." The decision should be close only if Dr. Snyder, "the best judge in the world," could estimate that the office would not have an adverse affect upon his life expectancy; otherwise he should tell all of his well-meaning advisers to "go to hell."[38]

By mid-January Ike had listened to all of the arguments and had lined up the sides in his mind. On the negative side were Milton, John, and his good friend George Allen. On the positive were all of his administration, his political advisers, the rest of his personal friends, and Mamie, who felt by then that idleness would be "fatal" for one of Ike's temperament and that he should do whatever semed to engage his "deepest interest."[39]

The president was in especially good spirits at this time because of a letter from one of his cardiologists. Colonel Pollock had written to Snyder on 16 January that data from the most recent physical examination showed an excellent recovery; he further advised that Eisenhower was in a favored position to avoid another attack and hoped that he would "see fit to accept the presidency and all that it entails for another four years." In a most unusual action, Pollock also wrote directly to the president and told him that he had sent his advice to Snyder. Not surprisingly, Ike asked to see the letter, and he was effusively grateful after reading it. It "does clear up a number of points in my mind," he wrote to the colonel, "and I have no doubt that it will aid me immeasurably when I do have finally to make any public announcement concerning my political intentions." He thanked the Fitzsimons cardiologist for "the most encouraging diagnosis—or prognosis—that I have had"; he added, "I think it was very fortunate you were here in town when it was time for my last checkup." Indeed, he was so excited that he mentioned Pollock's "most optimistic" report in letters to two of his nurses at Fitzsimons.[40]

Eisenhower felt increasingly stronger as the weeks passed—he was in remarkably fine health throughout January and early February—but he never tried to deny that he was still a man with a heart condition. "It would be idle to pretend that my health can be wholly restored to the excellent state in which the doctors believed it to be in mid-September," he stated at the opening of his 19 January news conference. "My future life must be carefully regulated to avoid excessive fatigue." At times he worried about his heart condition to intimate friends. "When he wasn't perky," as Shanley put it, "he would blame his heart."[41]

And he continued to fret about his doctors' foremost stricture—the one about controlling his emotions. He could accept their verdict that it was the "silly little annoyances" rather than the "big problems" that upset him, but he grumbled to his secretary on 11 January, "The doctors can tell you 'this is best for you'—but the individual himself has got to decide how long he can go along with their suggestions. . . . it looks to me more and more that if a fellow has a job he has to do it in his own way." For the next month he expressed annoyance about their advice. He told his former nurse, Colonel Edythe Turner, "I have to smile every time I hear anyone advising me to avoid situations that tend to produce annoyance, irritation, frustration or any kind of tension. The entire official life of a president is made up of this kind of thing—if subjects are not those that will produce some of these reactions, they are not brought to this office." He put it in slightly different words to a British general and old friend Bill Stirling: "The one rule the doctors try to insist upon is that I avoid tension; the one thing that is impossible in this job, at any hour of the day, is just that." The underlying reason for his concern, as he explained in his diary, "is that I have always worked one way all my life. Now that is the way the doctors tell me I really must not work, and to switch over at my time of life is very difficult."[42]

Even though he complained over and over again about having to change his ways, he did so. Shanley, who had recorded the previous summer that "he was constantly going through the roof and it was taking its toll," was amazed at this "tremendous effort to avoid blowing up when something aggravated him" and at Ike's success in controlling his emotions for an entire month. "Never once did he blow, as he did so often, prior to his illness. He realized that he had done himself considerable harm in the past and that explosions of temper were serious for him because of his condition."[43]

Considerations about his responsibility to the American people also were very much on the president's mind throughout his waiting period, and during the week of 22 January he expressed them both publicly and privately. "You can yourself, without any long dissertation here, just lay out all of the factors of the energy, the intensity with which you can attack your problems, the zip and the zest that you can take into conferences when you have to get something done for the good of the United States," he pointed out at his news conference. In letters to friends he was more explicit. A gradually failing health or merely a constant and increasing loss of energy could slow up the operations of the president's office, impede the work of all of his subordinates, "and by doing so, actually damage the cause for which he may even think he is giving some years of his life." Thus it was necessary to make the best calculations possible as to what those effects might be. "I do want you to know that I am not giving any concern as to what, under the changed conditions, this job might do to me," he assured Tex and Jinx McCrary. "The great and grave question is, 'Over a five-year stretch what might I do to the job?'"[44]

He had to ponder an even larger question — whether he would survive over that five-year stretch — but he could not resolve it. "Right now, still only four months after the first heart attack that ever hit the Eisenhower family," he complained to Hazlett, "I have soon to decide what is my answer with respect to the *next five years*." In looking forward there was no way to know what might happen. The doctors had been of little help in terms of specific data on longevity; indeed, they had taught him no more than what any informed citizen might know. Bill Robinson had summed it up when he reflected on the heart attack that only recently had struck their mutual friend, Clifford Roberts. "Cliff's care reminds us again that there is no pattern of life which foretells a heart condition, one way or the other," he wrote. "Certainly the doctors have no way of assuring the public that this or that man, as president, will or will not have a heart attack." Eisenhower thought that if he could only have an entire year to evaluate how full a load of work he could assume, his decision would have more validity. Instead, as he saw it, "I have no real index by which I can sit here and say what I can do in the next five years." His only consolation was his understanding that if he were to have another heart attack, it would be more apt to come during this first year, especially because during a campaign "the tirades of demagogues and the newspaper quarrels tend to reach a venomous level." In that event, he still would have time to withdraw.[45]

In the final analysis, Eisenhower's strong desire for a second term overshadowed his concerns about emotions, responsibility, and survival. He apparently arrived at a firm decision sometime during the first part of February. Dr. Snyder presumed that until that time he had not been convinced in his own mind that he would be physically able to carry on, but that there had been "a real change in attitude on his part." Ann Whitman settled on 6 February, a day when her boss was apprehensive about several episodes of skipped beats but was also in "radiant spirits"—a day when he gave the chairman of the Republican National Committee a "definite understanding" that he would run if his health continued to be good, after getting a promise that there would be no pressure on him to campaign as he had in 1952. That was probably too early, because the next day Ike told a friend that the "arguments, pro and con, descend around me in bewildering and overwhelming fashion." He cited something he had read about Lincoln waiting earnestly for God to reveal his will, and wrote, "I, too, desire to know wherein my duty lies."[46]

One sign that helped him discern his ultimate duty arrived when the American people officially and overwhelmingly revealed *their* will. Eisenhower seemed especially sensitive about what his fellow citizens might think of a chief executive who could not assume the full load and who had to be more remote than formerly, in the sense of hosting fewer receptions and meeting fewer people. Richard Nixon, who viewed Ike as a "very complex, subtle figure, not the simple-minded boob so often advertised," believed that after the heart attack he "spent a lot of time batting out fungoes to see what reaction he would get. He was no fool." Whether consciously seeking a reaction or not, the president got one. In thousands of letters his countrymen "almost prayerfully hoped that I would consider the matter favorably," as he put it, and on 9 February they registered a more precise judgment through a Gallup poll in which 61 percent said they would like to see him run again and only 25 percent said he should retire. That news was so pleasing that he told Hagerty he *thought* the answer would be yes. Two days later, another Gallup poll gave him a 61–35 edge if Adlai Stevenson were to be his opponent again. Eisenhower claimed to be "absolutely dumbfounded" with such results and said to an aide, "This decided me." Two days later he told his cabinet members, "Don't any of you fellows come to me January first, saying you have something else you've got to do."[47]

The president had promised during a news conference that he would announce his decision before the end of February and at the same time explained, "I think I will probably trust my own feelings more than I will the doctors' reports." He had to be pleased when he learned from his physicians on 14 February that he would not have to show a preference because his feelings and their reports were synonymous. What he did not know was that they had been agonizing about his future almost as much as he.[48]

Journalist Russell Baker predicted just before Christmas that the "power to chart the nation's future political course" had been summarily transferred "from the politicians to the physicians, from the smoke-filled room to the clinic." Even more important, Paul Dudley White had become "a central figure in this political-medical drama. What he says about the president's health will have a profound effect on the fortunes of both political parties." The pundit was surprised and pleased that fate had chosen this "bizarre figure" (who had seemingly stepped out of the pages of James Thurber, who gave the impression of the "absent-minded professor," who was the "innocent man in a hostile world," who refused to obscure his meaning in the argot of the medical cult, and who was utterly ignorant of political duplicity) to hold center stage in the political arena—indeed, to "carry history about in his pocket."[49]

The journalist was partially correct. White had become the star of the medical profession, he was Ike's doctor in the view of the American people, and he was famous. His recommendation also would be crucial to the president, though probably not as crucial as John Eisenhower described it at a later time. "There's no doubt that without White's endorsement, Dad could never have run a second time. . . . In other words, he almost had a veto power over Dad's political career." The New Englander was also the foremost subject of rumor and speculation in the press, and he certainly felt at home with that attention. But Baker and his fellow journalists failed to understand what was happening because they accorded too much influence to the hero of Fitzsimons Hospital. They were correct that one of the physicians would play a central role in the president's decision, but it was Snyder and not White who truly carried history about in his pocket.[50]

Howard Snyder did more than proselytize for his particular point of view among the president's friends and family. He did everything possible to checkmate the contrary views of others. He was in a unique position to do so; he served, in effect, as Eisenhower's medical chief of staff, and ten years of total dedication, together with the intimate sharing of ideas and hopes, had won him the complete trust of his boss. As such he had an almost unlimited opportunity for persuasion; he was in a position to speak his mind to Ike every day, and he could choose what information to present to Ike, in whatever fashion he believed would best serve his welfare, medical and otherwise.

As if intent on laying claim to his rightful place, or at least to counteract White's influence with the press, Snyder leaked a tendentious account of his role to *U.S. News and World Report.* On 20 January, as it had done in the past, the magazine published an inside story about the president's physician. The two-page revelation, "The Decision Depends on Word from Old Friend," reviewed Snyder's medical career, focused on his long association with Eisenhower, and philosophized: "Few men have been in a position to form judgments that will affect the history of the United States and of the world so profoundly." He, rather than the medical specialists, would most strongly influence the president, the writer predicted: "Now, unperturbed, Dr. Snyder stands close to a great moment in history. Mr. Eisenhower's big decision is a tough one for the doctor, too. In reaching it, he may be subjected to some pressures from those who are eager that the president run again. But his old friend, Mr. Eisenhower, is counting on him for straight facts upon which to base his answer to the great question of 1956. And straight facts, says Dr. Snyder's friends, are what the president will get."[51]

With that responsibility and with the final examination planned for mid-February, Snyder began collecting the long-term prognoses of the medical team. He was already aware of White's bizarre proposal, having learned about it from the president, which made him even more intent upon soliciting other points of view. He received a "special delivery" verdict from Mattingly during the first week of the new year. The cardiologist had already expressed his thinking in several telephone conversations, but he took the opportunity "to restate them and make them a matter of record for future reference," as he explained to Snyder, "should you desire to take them [into] consideration." Mattingly remained generally opposed to a second term, but he toned down his opposition. He was ready to be a team player.[52]

As to the patient's present condition, Mattingly could not say that Eisenhower was physically fit to perform the usual full duties of the presidency, but with reasonable restrictions he could function in the job without harm to his health. As to a second term, neither he nor any other physician could obtain the accurate, infallible medical data necessary for a "definite finding." He could only give an opinion, which he admitted, was probably a poor one:

From my present knowledge of his recent cardiac insult, my general observations and knowledge of the mental, physical, and emotional strains, political harangues of the presidency, and my past observations and experiences of a somewhat comparable nature, I am of the opinion that a second term would offer definite hazards to the president's health and life. Since I am a physician concerned with his health, I cannot strongly endorse a future activity which would, in my humble opinion, offer definite hazards. If asked, I feel that I should honestly and sincerely give such advice.[53]

Despite his concerns, Mattingly posed no threat to Snyder. He held to his earlier promise not to put his reservations about the president's heart on record, so in his recommendation he made no mention whatever about his long-standing fears of an aneurysm. He also agreed to limit his participation to the traditional, narrow role of a consultant and deferred completely to the primacy of the family physician. "I will stand by you in whatever recommendation you make," he assured Snyder, "as I believe you know what is better for him than the rest of us." He likewise offered to keep his different findings to himself, unless the patient asked specifically for his personal advice. In these various ways Mattingly backed away from the forceful stance he had taken earlier with White, to the effect that the consultants should remain silent until the time came when they would fulfill their responsibility by giving their data and prognoses to the president. Now they would present their case only to Snyder, without knowing whether, or how, he passed it on to his patient. Indeed, thirty years later Mattingly was still wondering if his reservations had ever reached Ike; the latter never asked him for his views, and neither he nor Snyder ever gave a hint as to whether he knew about them.[54]

Mattingly was more deferential to Snyder because, as a true professional, he sincerely believed that a consultant had no right to advise a patient directly. He may have been less aggressive for two other reasons. For one, he was on weak ground in his diagnosis of an aneurysm, simply because all of the other experts had disagreed with him, at least for the record. He may also have restrained himself for a very personal and human reason—if he spoke out he had nothing to gain and much to lose. He once explained to Paul White that Snyder was more than the president's personal physician; he was his closest friend, confidant, and adviser on many issues. "I should not mention this again," he added with a wisp of warning to his fellow cardiologist, "but in the past four years I have seen many individuals at the White House attempt to ignore this and see them fail." Mattingly probably took his own admonition to heart; he knew of Snyder's planning for a second term, and he must have recognized that there was no promising future in military medicine for anyone who threw his monkey wrench into that well-oiled campaign.[55]

Snyder received another opinion from Colonel Pollock, who had flown from Denver to Washington on 10 January to join him and Mattingly for the physical examination of the president. Pollock believed Ike had made a "fine recovery" and argued that the president would suffer frustrations of "a rather devastating kind" if an unsympathetic group took over in the White House and deviated from his goals and objectives. He wanted the president to run again, and he told Snyder that he was submitting his thoughts for the purpose of long-range planning, "and for whatever use you may wish to make of them."[56]

By mid-January Snyder had received three very different recommendations from the cardiologists, with Mattingly leaning against a second term, Pollock strongly for it, and White wishing the president would choose another vocation. The doctors seemed to be agonizing even more than their patient, and Snyder, aware of the need to reach some kind of consensus, acceded to White's request for a "very quiet dinner" to discuss their number one problem. He invited the latter, together with Mattingly and General Heaton, to meet at his apartment on Wednesday evening, 18 January, where they could review the president's case in a relaxed atmosphere, discuss the forthcoming problems, and clear the air. That did not happen, as White described in his notes:

> Much debate—prolonged and from all angles concerning the hazards and wisdom re: continuing in the presidency after this term is completed. It was obvious that all believed that the president would be active no matter what he decides about the presidency and that the hazards to him might not be very different but he is concerned deeply about the possibility of recurrent illness or death while in office after this term is finished. . . . Dr. Snyder stated that he was giving the president all information he thought necessary about the risk of the next five years. The president realizes this. Mattingly and P.D.W. insisted that he must make it clear that the risk is great. Dr. Mattingly thinks it is even—P.D.W. inclined to think it is less than even but also

agreed that no adequate statistics are available even though they may be referred to and quoted ad nauseam. Dr. Mattingly's experience has obviously been far more unfavorable than that of P.D.W. He has seen too many patients who, while apparently in good health, within a year or two of their attack, had sudden illness or death. It was thought wise at the conference that we cannot prophesy, that the hazard is great but that it is impossible to present any adequate statistics. The impressions of some are unfavorable, of others favorable, but everyone acknowledges the unpredictability in the face of coronary disease and furthermore that it is impossible to predict for anybody, especially a middle-aged or older man for the next four or five years even in good health.[57]

[handwritten margin note: they can't predict!]

Mattingly, in particular, was upset during the discussion and at one point referred to White as a Jekyll and a Hyde. He chose not to embarrass him in front of the others by telling him what he meant, but a week later he explained his anxiety in a typically candid letter. On the one hand, he averred, White had gone out of his way in press conferences to present the president's recovery as excellent and had downplayed adverse symptoms such as fatigue. By doing so, he had presented the Republican party with a "flat endorsement" of the view that Ike could run again, and cabinet members had taken such for granted. On the other hand, he had advised the patient at private lunch and dinner meetings and in personal letters that he should not seek reelection, the exact reasons for which, whether medical or otherwise, Mattingly still did not know. In whatever case, White had confused his colleagues as well as his patient with his conflicting liberal and conservative views. "You speak of working as a team yet you send advice and instructions direct and ignore the team," the colonel complained. "All this confuses me greatly and causes me to have anxiety as to what your next recommendations and advice will be or what you might give in a press conference."[58]

White took the criticism well. After all, he knew better than anyone about having taken some risk in approaching his patient about political affairs, and he remembered the warning of Conrad Hobbs. The criticism was unfair to some extent, however, because he had not tried to exclude his colleagues completely; in fact, he had mentioned to the president early in January that he might want to share the "world peace" plan with Snyder. He also was sincere in his conviction that there had been a mutual appreciation of the opportunity, that both he and the president were considering it seriously; he had good reason to feel that way, because Ike had played along with him in a friendly manner. Nonetheless, on 9 February White spelled out to Mattingly for the first time the details of his discussions at Gettysburg and suggested that he explain the situation to General Snyder. He admitted to some lack of candor. "I do believe that we can still act as a team . . . now that I have made this confession to you," he wrote. "My motives have been of the best (actually probably too idealistic for this rough-and-tumble world) and I hope that you and General Snyder (and the president too) will accept my explanation and apology for any confusion."[59]

Candor and apology may have improved personal relationships, but they did not ease Paul White's anxieties about his patient. In the week following the "consensus" meeting, he wrote three letters to Snyder. In one he asked for information about Ike's family history, hoping to determine the cause of death of his parents and grandparents. In another he expressed his worry that some of the recent newspaper photographs suggested the president was fatigued. "Does he often appear as haggard as in the New Haven paper?" he asked Snyder. "If so, we (you) must watch him more closely, I suppose, and may need to shade our ? neutral opinion about his health." He mentioned that if the patient's appearance worsened or anything else developed, he might become as apprehensive as Mattingly. Finally, White sent Snyder the draft of a confidential statement, with copies to Mattingly and Pollock, that he wanted to use at the forthcoming conference, asking for a vote of *Yes, No, or Uncertain* as to what they thought of "Ike's physical ability to carry on an additional four years."[60]

In his draft proposal, White set a negative tone by suggesting two potential problems. One was the damaged heart musculature itself; it had carried on well thus far, but it was "still possible though not probable that during the arduous months ahead the heart muscle may not be able to continue to stand up as well. . . . One must recognize that the strain of the presidency is great and that no precedent exists." The second problem, a "greater risk," was the possibility of new trouble with the coronary circulation. This might come even without a second term, "although it would seem probable that the strain of the presidency itself might be an aggravating factor even though my own belief is that hard work alone, such as the presidency, is not responsible per se for the underlying disease."

After positing the risks, White became speculative, noting that no two persons are alike and that one could find "mass statistics favoring either optimism or pessimism." For him and his colleagues it might be best to follow "a middle course between the optimists and pessimists in the president's case by stating that there may or may not be (perhaps an even chance) of further coronary trouble within the next five (to ten) years," and by insisting that no one else could justify "any dogmatic prophecies." A few days later, White sent Snyder two additional paragraphs for the press statement, both discussing the effect the president's decision could have on "an important need now in the limelight," namely, "our development of rehabilitation of cardiac patients."[61]

White's colleagues were quick to respond. Pollock argued they would do well to tell the president of his physical condition "as it is and avoid introducing conjecture as to trouble which might or might not develop in the future." He felt the "slant" of White's statement could raise serious doubts that might not be justified. "Personally, I should be happy to see the president accept renomination," he wrote to White, and he enclosed a revised draft that included the positive factors in the president's case. Mattingly's "humble opinion" was even less congenial to White. He wanted a shorter, more simple factual statement of the medical realities, without ambiguity, without double meanings, without quotations of statistics, and without individual opinions. It would not be ethical to divulge anything without the patient's consent, he insisted, least of all material that could be twisted by the opposition. He would release the brief statement to the press and dispense with the press conference, which, after the first one or two in Denver, he had felt were unnecessary anyway.[62]

During the weeks before their final gathering, White continued to agonize about what to tell the president and the American people. He wrote numerous drafts of what he might say; he thought about giving a special interview to the newsmen; and he wondered whether he should present a detailed analysis of the research on longevity, including his own, in order to counter speculation by columnists Reston, Pearson, and the Alsop brothers. He had spent a career preaching optimism about heart attacks and about the benefits to some patients of returning to work, and he wondered now whether the proper focus should be solely on the safety of the president himself or upon "the importance of the president's case in our development of rehabilitation of cardiac patients." His honest estimate of Ike's age and condition was that a second term would pose many risks and hazards; he simply could not accept Snyder's thesis that four more years of presidential stress and strain would actually enhance longevity. So White persisted in his reservations; he revised the draft of his proposed press release with some deference to his military colleagues, but he would not appease them completely. He still insisted that "the strain of the presidency is great and that no precedence exists; that there was "risk" and possible "new trouble" for the future; and that "it would seem probable that the strain of the presidency itself might be an aggravating secondary factor."[63]

By this time White was standing alone in his desire for a public discussion of the pros and cons of the complex issue. Mattingly wanted no public airing and wanted to say virtually nothing. Snyder had favored a second term for months and wanted nothing to jeopardize it. He was afraid the forthcoming press conference was taking on too much importance, primarily because of White, and considered it no more definitive than others in the past. Pollock was foursquare behind Snyder, though inclined to be more outspoken, and he offered to fly to Washington to make his case. Although Snyder had not meant to have him attend the conference, lest his presence add to its significance, he finally changed his mind. "I know the president would be happy to have you here at any and all times," he told Pollock, "and you may be sure that we doctors feel the same."[64]

The pressure was on White to join the team, and he could honestly sympathize with the reasoning. He, too, sometimes felt the tug of politics and the Eisenhower magic. On the front and back of an envelope dated 6 February, he jotted out his rambling thoughts:

I personally am so impressed by his value in the world today that if he believes that he can be of greater service to the greater number in office than out of office I would actually consider his taking the risk not only medically acceptable but also in his case desirable—favor his accepting the risk and the rest of us too, even though we recognize the strain of the presidency and even though he could have another heart attack tomorrow which, however, we believe quite unlikely. The hazard continues uniformly except for some increase with age. To a lesser extent it does for all of us here.

Then, grasping at straws, he added a few explanatory facts to the problem at hand—that earlier statistics did not take account of anticoagulants; that a second term in the presidency would be easier than the first; and that many of the world's leading statesmen were over seventy years of age. Clearly it was becoming more and more difficult to remain an objective professional.[65]

The time for a decision arrived on Tuesday, 14 February, Valentine's Day. Eisenhower had an early morning meeting with Senator William Knowland, who was angry and bitter about an expected veto of a national gas bill, but the president gave little attention to a mere confrontation at a time when his entire future was at stake. The doctors gathered later in the morning to look over the reports of the cardiovascular examination taken at Walter Reed three days before. There were no symptoms indicating cardiovascular weakness or enlargement of the heart. The patient's blood pressure, pulse, circulation, blood count, serum cholesterol, blood-clotting time, and weight were all normal, and he had made "a good recovery." Everyone agreed that his health was "satisfactory," but White accompanied Snyder to the president's living quarters to make his own hour-long examination, after which he concurred in his colleagues' findings. Still undecided was what the team should say at the press conference. Snyder, Mattingly, Pollock, and Heaton had already decided to ignore the statement White had worked on for so long, and to replace it with a brief, straightforward medical report. After discussing the issue at lunch (attended also by Adams and Hagerty) and for about an hour thereafter, they agreed to add a scant, three-paragraph summary, which White wrote in longhand on a small library card.[66]

At about 2:00 P.M. the five doctors, together with Hagerty and Adams, went to tell Ike of their encouraging findings. One of them, Colonel Mattingly, was in for a surprise. The president quickly turned to him and said, "Tom, all the people are wanting to make you a general." The cardiologist was flabbergasted, so much so that he could not come up with a response. Even after some moments to think about it, he decided to say nothing; he was not even within the zone of consideration for promotion, and he knew there were many others with greater seniority who deserved such consideration before he did. He also knew that General Heaton would not be happy about recommending him when it would require pushing him ahead of others. He was embarrassed, and he suspected the others were as well.[67]

In the days to come Mattingly pondered why the president would choose such a time to raise an issue so incongruous with the tenor and purpose of the meeting. The two men saw each other every few weeks, which provided ample opportunity for mention of a matter that had no pressing timetable and seemed more appropriate for a private setting. He wondered, too, whether "all the people" really did favor his promotion, when neither Heaton nor Snyder came forth to discuss it with him, or even to offer congratulations. He was more at sea when he learned that Eisenhower, on the day before the doctors gathered, actually had sent a recommendation to the secretary of the army. Like any officer trying to send five children to college, he could use the additional money, and he reasoned that the impetus for the action was coming from the wives of retired officers whom he was treating with skill and success. He understandably did not imagine, or at least did not record, that the president's recommendation and surprise greeting were possibly no mere improvisations, and that Ike may have been playing his own hand.[68]

Mattingly was one of only two people in the world who had the medical knowledge and authority to threaten the option for a second term, and although Eisenhower and Snyder, in the ordinary course of events, trusted his earlier assurances to remain silent and leave the decision to them, there was a new and troublesome ingredient. On 22 January, in a column about Ike's "future great decision" and the "grim question" of survival over another term, the popular columnists Joseph and Stewart Alsop had discussed a "most authoritative study" that reported a less than 50 percent survival rate for heart attack cases over a five-year period. The journalists were bothered, they declared, because the positive-minded Paul Dudley White apparently did not accept this "cold statistical" assessment, and they added in bold type: "But it can be stated on positive authority that the eminent army heart specialist, Dr. Thomas E. Mattingly, does not make so light of the permanent impairment caused by a heart attack as Dr. White has recently done in public."[69]

The president had to be concerned about the source of this story, and even more that it might come up at the press conference. Would Mattingly, a man of unquestionable honor, deny the statement, try to expound upon it, or in any way reveal that he had on several occasions expressed reservations about a second term? It would be only prudent for Ike to do everything he could—including to bestow the highest praise possible, a promotion to general officer—in an attempt to protect against any discouraging word from his cardiologist, however unlikely that would seem to be. The timing of his action supports such a likelihood, as does the tone of his letter of recommendation. It was very brief, in no way effusive, and notably understated for such an exceptional request.[70]

There was another surprise at the Valentine's Day meeting, one that surely pleased the president. Paul White sidled off the fence and joined the chorus for a second term. Mattingly thought his colleague seemed relieved and relaxed following his decision but suspected that White was neither enthusiastic nor confident about it, hoping only that Ike would survive and thereby save his reputation. The president's appointment secretary saw it differently, noting that "old Doctor White is getting to be quite a politician which caused us more difficulty than any six people. He said there was no reason why the president couldn't carry on for ten years the similar duties he had been carrying on for the past three." Whatever his deepest feelings, White's choice was predictable. He saw the president's chance to survive another term as a toss-up, and having spent a lifetime preaching optimism about cardiac patients returning to work, he could not opt for caution now. He would have preferred to have Ike work as a crusader for peace, but when the choice was solely between his serving as president or retiring, White remained true to his philosophy and looked upon the brighter side. And, too, as he wrote years later, he "was heavily outnumbered."[71]

After the meeting Ike went off to take a plunge in the White House pool, while Hagerty escorted the doctors to the Executive Office Building for a 3:28 P.M. conference the reporters had been awaiting eagerly for months. He had his secretaries pass out mimeographed copies of the medical statement, signed by the physicians, and he asked to say a few words. The gentlemen sitting with him were doctors and not politicians, he emphasized, and he very deliberately set out the parameters of the conference (and implicitly conveyed a warning to the participants): "They are here to report medically on their findings, and only that." Dr. Snyder read the relatively brief medical report, after which he pointed out that it was more complete than usual because the president wished the people of the country to have the facts.[72]

When Edward Folliard of the *Washington Post and Times Herald* asked the obvious question—"Is it the judgment of the doctors that he could serve another four years in the White House without any damage to himself?"—Snyder replied: "We believe that he can serve four or five years or longer in a very active position of great responsibility." Then he quickly turned the conference over to White, whom the team had designated earlier as the spokesman for the cardiologists, and who drew from his pocket the library card and read: "Now, as to the future, after weighing very carefully all available evidence, including our own experience, and fully aware of the hazards and uncertainties that lie ahead, we believe that medically the chances are that the president should be able to carry on an active life satisfactorily for another five to ten years." In his qualification about "hazards and uncertainties," White was providing himself with an insurance policy, albeit a tiny one, in case he needed one in the future; and with his comment about "five to ten years," he was raising the ante from what Snyder had already mentioned. The reporters asked for a definition of "active life," and after some sparring, feigning, dodging, and laughter about the precise wording, White admitted that it would include serving as president. At the end of the conference he forthrightly proved his fealty to the team decision. When a reporter asked, "Would you vote for him now?" he replied, "If he runs."[73]

For a meeting with such potentially important implications, there was no elaboration by the experts. None of them cited a single scientific study to support their claim that the president could serve safely for another five to ten years. There was no mention that the two cardiologists who knew the most about the patient believed his chances were in the neighborhood of fifty-fifty to survive a second term, and that they had seriously questioned such an undertaking. Instead, the message for the American people was that their president was in "very good health." When a reporter asked if Ike was as well as he had been prior to his heart attack, Dr. Snyder finessed by admitting that during the summer of 1955 he had enjoyed better health than he had for the previous ten years, yet he had a cardiac accident. "We don't know that he won't have another cardiac accident," he answered philosophically. "We don't know that I won't have one tomorrow, although I am feeling fit today; and so it goes." In the final analysis, he implied, heart attacks were part of the human condition, and the president was just like everybody else.[74]

The doctors took the position that they were being "neutral," and perhaps they even believed it. Following his comment that the president should be able to carry on for another five to ten years, White was asked if that was the end of his statement. "Oh, no," he replied. "I should have said, but the choice is his, not ours." The newsmen laughed, well aware that the doctors, by giving a positive prognosis, had put immense pressure on their patient. The nation had been waiting earnestly for months to learn what they would say, and once they said that Ike could go, it would be virtually impossible for him to do otherwise. "Dr. Paul Dudley White did not exactly push President Eisenhower into another campaign for the presidency today," the *New York Times* explained, "but he certainly opened the door and invited him in. The least that can be said . . . is that he made it much more difficult for the president to refuse to run on the ground of health."[75]

The choice finally ended up in the lap of the president because of several realities. The doctors were unable to oppose a second term because the scientific evidence to support such a position simply did not exist. Coronary heart disease was so complicated that even Mattingly and White, in spite of their fears, would quickly acknowledge the possibility of long-term survival for any particular individual. The press likewise contributed to the sense that no one really knew what to do, even though certain members tried to inform the public. Reston and the Alsop brothers wrote columns looking into the data on longevity, but the scientific studies they examined were inconclusive. And, too, the journalists were exceedingly timid in questioning the president's doctors. At the final news conference no one asked Mattingly about the Alsops' claim that he really did have reservations about the "permanent impairment" of his patient's health. Nor did anyone ask White the scientific basis for his assertion that Eisenhower could survive another five to ten years in a position of immense pressure.[76]

Only one journalist, Drew Pearson, did any meaningful research into the medical aspects of the decision, and his views were suspect because of his unfounded charges about the president's "heart condition" back in 1953 and his silly comment shortly after the heart attack in 1955 that the patient "was so sick he was blinded in both eyes." Immediately after the president's attack, Pearson hired an investigator, who found no evidence and left him with only his suspicions. Nonetheless, he claimed in his column on 27 February that men around the president had "hushed up" some unpleasant facts and were "pushing him to run" so they could remain in office.[77]

Pearson centered in on Dr. White, whom he believed was now "singing a different tune" because he had allowed his professional standing to be exploited by a partisan political conspiracy; and he charged that many Republican doctors were aghast that the doctor would make a report to the nation so obviously contrary to "known medical knowledge" and to his own previous medical advice. He went on to quote specifically in his column from an article by White in the *Annals of Internal Medicine* of December 1951, where the cardiologist had depicted fear, great pleasure, anger, and the excitement of an athletic contest as the causes of "innumerable deaths" among coronary patients, and where he had advised that such persons "avoid nervous strain." The columnist made some telling points that, had they appeared prior to the 14 February meeting, might have attracted some attention; but nearly two weeks after the event they seemed more like troublemaking.[78]

In any event, it was Dwight Eisenhower who was most responsible for preserving his own right to choose. In January, when a friend wrote to him of the duty of keeping the public fully informed about all aspects of his health, he replied, "In the past we have seen unfortunate results of attempts to keep such things secret when they apply to a president. I have no intention of being any party of a cabal to confuse the American people." He was not, in truth, the leader of a cabal, consciously plotting with subordinates to mislead the public. But from early December, when the first glint of probability about a second term entered his mind, he carefully controlled the situation. To attain his fundamental goal—to keep open the option to run again—he faced two problems: he had to prevent confusing medical news from reaching the public, and he had to keep the doctors out of politics. Further, he had to achieve these political ends without letting the public know he was politically engaged. To do so he maneuvered behind the scenes, shrewdly making use of intermediaries and indirection.[79]

To some extent those close to the president acted without any prompting; they simply assumed what he would want them to do. Although Hagerty released a flood of information about the heart attack, he never practiced full disclosure; he was careful, for example—even before Ike hinted at his expectations—not to reveal the occasional small medical setbacks, such as the transient pains during the "armchair" treatment or the worries about arrhythmia at Gettysburg. In like manner Dr. Snyder recognized how devastating it would be if the public learned of Mattingly's concern about an aneurysm, and he took strong measures, including an explosion of temper, to keep his colleague quiet. In early December the president telegraphed his desires; he shared privately with Hagerty his thoughts concerning a second term, he mentioned to Snyder his concern about White's publicity seeking, and he warned all of his doctors to stick to the medical facts of his case. Thereafter Hagerty and Snyder became his eager associates, the former dictating the content of every news conference, the latter directing a hard-pressed campaign, primarily through the willing efforts of Tom Mattingly, to put the muzzle on Paul White.

For his part, the president had two targets—the press and Dr. White. As for the newsmen, he had to convince them that a second term was a distant possibility but not a likelihood. As long as they understood that he could

not do anything until well into the future, and the more often they perceived him to be leaning toward a negative decision—both of which he
fostered in his press conferences—the more likely they were to postpone
any attempt to marshal medical data against him. Thus, by concealing his
growing inclination to run again, he was able to forestall any careful investigation of the medical literature bearing upon his condition. With
White he had a more difficult challenge; he had to keep him silent lest his
personal preference for a presidential retirement—which he had hinted at
during his final news conference in Denver—become apparent to the public. In addition to prompting Snyder and Mattingly to restrain their friend,
Ike massaged White with friendly words and privileged treatment. He let
him believe he was his cardiological confidant, in which intimate role he
would naturally keep his thoughts for their private consideration. His
artful display of kindness and respect toward White, in contrast to
Mattingly's forceful candor, furthered the sense of intimacy between doctor
and patient. And intimates, Eisenhower knew well, seldom turned against
their leader. When the time came, Paul White did not.

The president persisted in his stratagem even after the doctors had given
their Valentine's Day report to the nation. The following day he was scheduled to leave for a vacation, and he had an exceptionally busy morning,
including a visit from the famous physicist John von Neumann, who was
dying of cancer. The occasion was so upsetting that he was not sure he
could go through with the ceremony, but he still found time before departing the White House to use his guile once again. He jotted a note to White
thanking him for the valentine he had sent and for his coming to Washington. "It is seemingly quite useless," he continued, "for me to attempt to
tell you how much your professional opinion means to me, and what a
great service you have done to the American people in giving them your
honest estimates of my condition. And, of course, as always it was a great
pleasure to see you." Soon thereafter he instructed Snyder and Hagerty to
exclude White from any news conferences in the future. They did so.[80]

The vacation trip to George Humphrey's plantation in Thomasville, Georgia, entailed ten days of quail hunting, golf, and bridge, during which time
the president went out of his way to extend himself in the fields and on
the golf course as a final test of his physical strength. On the eighth day
he played eighteen holes—for the first time since before his attack—with

no adverse effects. He did not give any indication of his future plans, but Dr. Snyder could not avoid speculation. At an impromptu news conference under the pine trees on the day before departure, Snyder said that a second term might be safer because his patient had received a warning and had consequently learned to regulate and pace his activities. "Even young men die, have a heart attack without any warning," he explained. "All he can do is trust in God if he goes ahead."[81]

Eisenhower returned to Washington on 25 February, a day during which Adlai Stevenson ridiculed him as the "head coach" who "seems to have missed the plays and not to be too sure of the score." Ike was irate at the insult, but by then he knew that soon he would have his revenge. Three days later he met individually with Adams, Hagerty, Hall, Nixon, and Persons and told them he had decided to run again. He waited until the last moment to tell Mamie, who had called Ann Whitman that afternoon to ask if the secretary knew what he had decided. At dinner Ike mentioned to Lucius Clay that tonight was the night, and Mamie said, "It's your decision, not mine. I'm not going to have anything to do with it." The president replied, "I've made up my mind, I'm going to run again."[82]

Hagerty had convinced the president that he was obligated to give the first break of the news to the White House reporters at his regular Wednesday press conference. Thus it was that at 10:30 A.M. on 29 February, a crisp, clear Leap Year Day, he strode across the street to the Old State Department Building, where 311 reporters were waiting. "I told Mamie this morning that I felt exactly like Charles I when he mounted the steps to the guillotine," he mentioned to Shanley just before he left. He teased the newsmen with comments about the Red Cross campaign, the farm bill, and the Upper Colorado Basin before he mentioned his decision, about which he then refused to elaborate. He waited until 10:00 P.M. to go into the homes of the American people on television and radio with a full exposition. He had been guided by the favorable reports of the doctors and by consultations with multitudes of friends and associates, he explained, and had decided to follow "the path of personal responsibility" and of "duty to the immense body of citizens" who had supported his administration.[83]

He took special care to reassure his listeners about his health. As a "recovered heart patient" he was possibly at greater risk than others his age, and as such he would not wage the customary political campaign; but the doctors had told him the risk was not great and that hard work did not injure any "recovered coronary case." Indeed, some of his medical advisers had suggested that any adverse effects on his health from the presidency would be less than in any other position, he reported, and that because they could maintain their watchful care over him, he was in less danger of physical difficulty than other citizens. He also could cut back on certain public speeches, meetings, ceremonial activities, and travel. He admittedly would have to follow a prescribed medical regimen of exercise, rest, and recreation for the rest of his life, but he was prepared to obey the doctors and do so out of respect for his duties and responsibilities. He wanted to make one thing clear: "As of this moment, there is not the slightest doubt that I can perform as well as I ever have, all of the important duties of the presidency."[84]

Ike did not explain in greater detail the reasons why he had crossed his "personal political Rubicon." To some extent he was uncertain in his own mind, for as he had told the press earlier in the day, "When you come down to comparisons, I am not certain what influences a man most in this world." Two days later, in a five-and-one-half-page, single-spaced personal and confidential letter dealing specifically and solely with the subject, he repeated the theme to Swede Hazlett: "I wish I could tell you just exactly what finally made me decide as I did, but there was such a vast combination of circumstances and factors that seemed to me to have a bearing on the problem—and at times the positive and negative were delicately balanced—that I cannot say for certain which particular one was decisive."[85]

In that remarkable letter and later in his memoirs, Eisenhower revealed as much as he probably understood of his motives. On the positive side, he clearly wanted to preserve the accomplishments and continue the policies that marked his presidency. "We had converted the United States of America from a nation at war to a nation at peace, productive and happy," he boasted in stark simplicity about his first three years, and he expected he could still do something "in promoting mutual confidence, and therefore peace, among the nations," and "help our people understand that they must avoid extremes in reaching solutions to the social, economic and political problems that are constantly with us." The arguments of many around him played to that sentiment, for, as Richard Nixon put it, "We knew that Eisenhower was not a quitter—that he liked to finish a job which he had started." In that light, Ike wanted to keep together the extremely able group of civilians in the executive branch who had worked with him in his cause and to respond favorably to the millions of others who had supported his purposes. He did not want to let them down, as he explained to two of his "faithful friends," and have them "believe at this time of my life I would begin to give more attention to my own personal convenience and possibility of a long existence, than I do to the great issues that inspired the crusade."[86]

Eisenhower also acknowledged that only he among the Republicans could win the election and admitted "a guilty feeling on my own part that I had failed to bring forward and establish a logical successor for myself." His insistence that he had tried hard to "acquaint the public with the qualities of a very able group of young men," an echo from the summer of 1955, was true, but his sense of failure about it was either naive or dissimulating. As long as he was available for the nomination, he had to know that no other Republican could possibly approach him in stature, and that no image-building campaign could make a difference. Indeed, his protestations merely placed the spotlight on a truth that everyone understood—there was only one Eisenhower. He was indispensable; he knew it, he generally savored it, and he finally accepted its implications.[87]

ONLY ONE IKE ←

Finally, as he had done so repetitively in 1952, Eisenhower explained his decision primarily in terms of duty and responsibility. His friend Swede Hazlett agreed and wrote, "I suspect that I appreciate more than anyone outside your immediate family just what a sacrifice you have made, and how your inherent conception of duty (bred nowhere as it is at West Point and Annapolis) played its part." There is no doubt that Ike was a "sucker for duty," as one political scientist has described him, but there was in 1956, as there had been four years earlier, another major factor at work: he wanted to be president. His coin of duty always had a flip side—ambition—but in his mind the markings were so alike that he never saw the difference. His failure to claim retirement after the heart attack was not a mistake but a choice, and it had less to do with duty than with desire. He could not visualize a replacement for himself in the most powerful position in the world, and he would rather accept all of the frustrations and demands than to forsake the opportunities and privileges. That desire for office and his sincere belief that he could serve his countrymen better than anyone else were enough to account for a second term. But there was something more in the scales, having less to do with what he wanted than what he had to have. His heart condition had created some powerful and

He WANTED IT!

compelling needs, and they could be fulfilled only by his remaining in the White House.[88]

Supportive Letters During his recovery at Gettysburg Ike discovered that a pleasant by-product of his thrombosis was a flood of letters from old friends. To one of them, retired general Bill Gruber, he responded, "When such a message comes from one who, like yourself, has been through a similar experience, I gain renewed conviction that I shall win another battle." For Eisenhower, surviving the heart attack—merely staying alive—became a battle of a very personal nature, and to that end he listened carefully to his medical advisers, adhered scrupulously to a long and boring regimen, and strove even to change his attitudes. By January he was confident enough to claim a battlefield victory by virtue of his recovery from the disease, but he had to face the new reality—he had not won the war. Heart disease conveyed not only the possibility of dying, which he had faced forthrightly and without fear, but also the possibility of turning into an invalid or semi-invalid. This proud athlete and soldier could not conceive of such a future; he told *Importance of Self-Image* Sherman Adams that "if he gave up and went into retirement after such an illness, it would seem like accepting a personal defeat." The only way he could reconstruct his self-image was to return his life to the way it had been before. That meant serving as president.[89]

The doctors, for their part, had put forth an understanding of the disease that allowed Ike little room for retirement. White had told him that work is beneficial for "cardiacs," and Snyder had advised him that work as president might even lengthen his life. Their teaching, in its most stark terms, deprived him of any medical excuse to withdraw from the race; they had, in effect, neutered the enemy disease. The same message was implicit in many of the get well letters from cardiacs who gave personal testimony to the president about their recoveries. The working president of the Bank of America welcomed him to the Coronary Club, noting that "there are various kinds of heart troubles, but . . . I know that yours and mine were identical." And a former West Point classmate from Texas advised him "to get well—and don't ever let a little thing like 'ticker trouble' get you down. We know you *can* and will lick it. *We* did!" The press was explicit about the increasing number of Americans who were choosing to carry on with their normal lives after heart attacks. *U.S. News and World Report* offered some examples of leaders who "scored comebacks" and returned to high-pressure jobs—the governor of Colorado, Edwin Johnson; a supreme court justice, Sherman Minton; Major General John T. Sprague, the commanding officer of Lowry Air Force Base; and eight congressmen, including the eighty-year-old Republican Daniel Reed.[90]

The success of others in continuing their careers brought the emotional issue of competition into the president's decision-making process. The boy from Abilene hardly needed a lesson about fighting long and hard, but he received one unintentionally through a kind and well-meaning letter from the master of competitiveness, Frank Leahy. "There is a saying with which I have long been familiar and which I have used many, many times in speaking to my football squads at the University of Notre Dame," wrote the famous coach. "It is a simple statement, stating merely, 'When the going gets tough, the tough get going.' I don't know of any one person in America today giving better proof to this saying than yourself." There was simply no way Ike could ignore the implication of Leahy's well-known homily, least of all when the extent of his toughness would be evident to everyone in comparison to that of two of his fellow cardiacs—one a close friend, the other an important politician.[91]

The friend was Cliff Roberts, who went out for a walk in Manhattan on the cold and windy night of 25 January and felt a little out of breath, with constriction in his chest. He returned to his hotel lobby, and although he felt no pain whatever, he suffered a little "wooziness," which persisted and prompted him to call the hotel doctor. The doctor sent him to Lenox Hospital, where the experts diagnosed a "mild attack" with minimal damage to the anterior wall of the heart. Within days his outlook was "very, very good," and in less than a month he was well enough to go home. The president kept very close tabs on his friend's condition, and although he could jest with him that his attack was of the "juvenile variety," he could not miss the point that Cliff was returning quickly to his usual affairs.[92]

There was another recovered heart patient—Lyndon Johnson—with whom the president had commiserated in polite correspondence after Johnson's heart attack in July, and whose activities were particularly relevant. The majority leader had informed Ike in mid-September that his doctors thought the chances were good that he would come out of his situation without any damage having been done to his heart, and *Newsweek* predicted two months later that he would be able soon to return to the Senate, that he would play a decisive role in the Democratic National Convention, and that he even had an outside chance to be the nominee. "My heart attack saved my life," the senator proclaimed in bold headlines as he set about making his plans for the future; and in a January story about the "Nation's No. 2 Heart Case," *Life* began to define what that future would be. It pictured the senator taking command of his life, resuming arduous tasks in Congress, and even leading the partisan attack against the president's state of the union message. "Pronounced fit by his doctors," the story went, "Senator Lyndon Johnson, who last summer had been brushed by death, was back on the job in Washington." Ike might rationalize that Johnson was a much younger man at forty-six, but he was also aware (thanks to Dr. Snyder) that the senator's attack had been much more severe than his own. He may even have remembered LBJ's telegram to him: "Have just heard the report of your heart attack and am reassured to be told that it is only mild. No matter how mild take care of yourself."[93]

Lyndon Johnson and many others had taken care of themselves and eventually claimed a complete victory over their heart attacks, and Dwight Eisenhower could do nothing less. When he was contemplating the travails of a campaign, he told Hazlett that he might have to be more active than he wished because "I am a competitor, a fighter, so . . . my own reluctance ever to accept defeat might tempt me into activity that should be completely eliminated from my life." These exact words should be applied to his larger decision for a second term. He did not like to lose, or settle for a halfhearted effort, whether in golf, bridge, politics, or life. He was a courageous man who did not worry about personal risks; he was an avid competitor who could not falter before a disease; and he was confident he would prevail. God had always given him a good hand, and he could not fold on this one. From the very center of his being, he was compelled to run again.[94]

Thus in arriving at his ultimate decision, Dwight Eisenhower was both a politician responding to pressure and a man responding to his disease. It is likely that he would have arrived at that same positive decision if he had not suffered a heart attack. For many different reasons he wanted to continue as president. But his illness was central to his decision. The only way to master his own doubts and silence the suspicions of others, the only way to prove that he was not an invalid, was to serve another term. To do otherwise was to opt for semi-invalidism, to step back down the ladder he had climbed all his life, to forsake a lifetime of courage and give way to fear. Unlike Hazlett, he simply could not accept a role where he would have to serve in relief for a "better man." For him there was no better man, in either the competence to serve as president or the courage to fight another battle.

Eisenhower was not a man of introspection, and he seems never consciously to have sorted out his motivations, to have separated duty and ambition, or balanced his sincere desire for a peaceful retirement with his driving need to struggle, to win, and to be whole again. He did sense that something was different because of his illness. "You know if it hadn't been for that heart attack," he told Sherman Adams, "I doubt if I would have been a candidate again." And he *was* aware that his single momentous decision on Leap Year Day to leave behind his illness and his invalidism and look to the future had something to do with history—not only his nation's but his own. On a piece of White House stationery, dated February 1956, he wrote in longhand: "As I embark on the last of life's adventures my final thoughts will be for those I've loved: family, friends, and country."[95]

6

The Politics of Illness

❖ ❖ ❖ ❖ ❖ ❖ ❖ ❖ ❖ ❖ ❖ ❖ ❖ ❖ ❖

We cannot expect a president's physician to tell us any more of the truth than the president or his political advisers want us to have. The doctor's lips are sealed. Worse yet, if the president or his party's leaders desire it, the doctor must lie manfully, and maintain that a very sick president is wonderfully fit. If consultants are called they also must remain silent, unless they are given permission to speak.
　—Walter C. Alvarez, private correspondence

The president opened his eyes, thought for a moment, and then said three words, and went to sleep again. Those three words were: "Tell them everything." This wise order was greatly appreciated and fully followed by the physicians and others involved and was the key to all our news gatherings. A breath of fresh air had blown through the old policy!
　—Paul Dudley White, My Life and Medicine

Four days after Eisenhower's heart attack, Lyndon Johnson hosted Adlai Stevenson and Sam Rayburn at his Texas hill country ranch, where he was recuperating from his own heart attack. He greeted his guests late at night with a warning: "Adlai, there's a hell of a lot of newspapermen around here—they've been here all day like vultures—they think Ike is dying and the three big Democrats are sitting here plotting to take over the country. We can't let them think that because we're not going to do that. So we'll be up and out early and tour the farm and they can come with us and interview us so there won't be any secrets." For the next two months, however, when virtually everyone believed the president would retire, there was a secret of sorts within the Democratic ranks—that the nomination was now a prize worth seeking, not a burden to bear. "I guess Eisenhower is not going to run," said one politician. "If he doesn't there'll be a chance for the Democrats, and everybody and his brother will be in it."[1]

By the end of 1955, serene expectations had given way to quiet fears. As early as November, a Stevenson aide heard that his Eisenhower counterparts, "abetted knowingly or otherwise by Doctors Snyder and White," were developing a strategy to induce their patient to run again. As press reports and editorials gave increasing support to such a prospect, the Democrats remained silent, fearful of making an issue of the heart attack. Then came Eisenhower's announcement, the effect of which was to turn the political world topsy-turvy. "As the anxiety and tension declines I cannot help but smile at the way you have unwittingly, albeit painfully, kept all the Democrats as well as a lot of the Republican politicians off balance," Bill Robinson reviewed the situation for the president. "Just as the Democrats were hoping and praying and guessing that you would not run again, you had the heart attack, and then they were sure of it. Correspondingly, most of the Republicans up for election in 1956 walked around with worried looks on the same score. Then your wonderful recovery and your announcement that you would run again upset the Democratic applecart and renewed hopes in the breasts of the Republican candidates."[2]

The Democrats never found an effective response to Eisenhower's recovery. Soon after the heart attack, Adlai Stevenson assured the American people that party lines could not affect the "anxiety and sympathy" for the "shadow of the sad misfortune that has befallen our president," and when he announced his candidacy in November he promised that health would not be an issue but only a "consideration." Thereafter he tried to be clever, arguing that "a "new and compelling issue" was the "manner and mode in which the duties of our highest office are to be discharged." Since Eisenhower would have to place limits on the time and energy he could give to the office, he would alter the structure and fundamentally revise the role of the presidency. "I think the important thing is not the condition of his health," the Democrat explained on *Meet the Press* in April; "what is very important, in my judgment, is the office of the presidency, and what happens to it."[3]

Stevenson held to his decision to ignore the illness and focus on the office even after Eisenhower underwent surgery in June for a second chronic disease, ileitis. His advisers did whisper and argue among themselves, and one member of the reelection staff proposed facing the issue head-on—Democrats should urge voters to ask their family doctors whether a man of sixty-five who had suffered a heart attack and a serious abdominal operation was qualified to serve. But Stevenson was sensitive to the political danger inherent in the health issue, and he would not waver. Instead, he tried to enlist his party's help in espousing his thesis. "It seems to me that, given the difficulties of attacking his deficiency directly," he wrote to Harry Truman in July, "it should be possible to make vital and appealing a proper concept of the presidency, and no one can talk about it with range and depth like yourself." After Stevenson became his party's candidate in August, he tried a variation on his theme, insinuating that Richard Nixon would have much more power in a second term, but until the last moment in the campaign he was unwilling to exploit the president's condition forthrightly.[4]

Stevenson's failure to launch a frontal assault against his opponent haunted the campaign. In the view of his biographer, "It may have been one of his worst political mistakes." Perhaps, but not likely, for any persistent mention of health almost certainly would have incited a backlash. As one of the candidate's aides, historian Arthur Schlesinger Jr., explained, "People who had recognized no limits to taste or truth in their attacks on Franklin Roosevelt and Harry Truman began to act in 1956 as if statements about Eisenhower—e.g., 'He spends a lot of time on the golf course,' or 'He has had a heart attack'—are almost blasphemous." In fact, Stevenson had both reason and emotion against him. He could not challenge the judgment and integrity of the medical experts, especially a distinguished outside consultant like Paul Dudley White, without appearing arrogant and unreasonable. He could not accuse Eisenhower of deceiving the American people about his victory over a heart attack, at the very time he was still struggling with the dread disease, without seeming to be cruel and insensitive. Most important, Stevenson could not hawk the supposition that Ike might die in office without entering treacherous ground. Americans were loath, in general, to contemplate their great fear of death, and they would resent, in particular, anyone who forced them to confront the prospective death of their most beloved hero.[5]

The Democrats' inability to use the issue of health therefore was inherent to some extent in the public's deep affection for Eisenhower. "Ike was a hero again," wrote journalist Marquis Childs after the long drama of the heart attack. "He had won out over an illness increasingly common in

America with an aging population." The Alsop brothers likewise saw the illness as a political asset. "A good many people apparently intended to vote for the president rather as one might send flowers to a sick friend, and cheer him up," they noticed. "And the heart attack has clearly made a real human being of the president in a way that no other political personality is real and human."[6]

The Democrats' dilemma rested, as well, on the fact that medicine did become the handmaiden of politics. Eisenhower determined in early December 1955 that substantial openness about the everyday details of his heart attack or his general health could lead to political disaster, and from then until the end of his second term his governing dictum was to prevent the disclosure of any data that might be susceptible to misinterpretation, and thus exploitation, by his political opponents. Snyder took charge of restricting disclosure during the recovery from the heart attack, and immediately after the president announced his decision to run again, he and Hagerty instituted a policy of silence and secrecy. They would not allow their patient's health to provide the slightest advantage for an opposition they considered eager to exaggerate and distort every item of medical information, and they worked closely to keep the secrets through two other politically threatening illnesses—the ileitis surgery of June 1956 and the small stroke of November 1957. The Democrats complained about the "Hagerty curtain," charging that it kept them in the dark about the true nature of the president's physical condition. But they could not break through that curtain, drawn even tighter, as it were, by the willing collaboration of Dwight Eisenhower. Rather than being the hapless stooge of this palace guard, the president was calling the shots. He wanted to be reelected, and he was willing to make the necessary compromises to achieve his goal. He knew what his staff was doing, and he took no issue with them. His staff knew what he wanted, and they served him well.

In the relatively quiet springtime months following his decision, Eisenhower concerned himself with issues of agricultural subsidies, civil rights, the Middle East, and the first charges of a missile gap. Most of all, he ruminated about a running mate. His damaged heart had changed the chemistry of politics not only for the Democrats but for his own party as well. His attempts to induce Richard Nixon to leave the ticket are well known, and Stephen Ambrose has wisely noted that in finally judging

Nixon suitable as a running mate at a time when his five-year prognosis was problematic, Ike actually gave him the "highest possible compliment" he could give. From his personal point of view, however, the president was not putting his people at much of a risk. His gut instinct was that he would last out his term, and his doctors were confident about assuring that end.[7]

During this period the medical team underwent a reshuffling. The primary responsibility for the president's medical care remained with Howard Snyder, who continued to call upon Dr. Mattingly every two or three weeks for a cardiovascular consultation, and who relied increasingly upon the advice of Dr. Leonard Heaton, the commanding general of Walter Reed General Hospital. Heaton had become interested in medicine while working as a young man at a drugstore soda fountain; chose the rigors of military medicine for economic reasons and remained out of a love for the service; first made his mark as chief surgeon at Schofield Barracks in Hawaii at the time of the Pearl Harbor attack; developed a friendship with Howard Snyder during World War II when the latter was caught in a freak snowstorm at his hospital headquarters in England; and in 1953 assumed command of Walter Reed, which he succeeded in building into a world-renowned institution. Heaton and Snyder were proud of their kind of military medicine, and once the crisis of the heart attack had passed, they were intent on claiming their proprietary right to look after the president.[8]

Their foremost objective was to forestall another heart attack, and their only available approach was to institute a program of preventive medicine. At the forceful urging of Mattingly, who wanted protection against a possible aneurysm, they continued the anticoagulation therapy initiated shortly after the attack. On the strong recommendation of Paul White, they put the patient on a stringent low-fat diet, getting rid of egg yolks, all glandular organs, very fat meats, milk and cheese products, concentrated fats in salad dressings and vegetable oils, most desserts, rich gravies, olives, nuts, and avocados. In accordance with the insights of Howard Snyder, they tried to regulate the president's emotional life by minimizing his stress and anger. And they all agreed to let him indulge in his hobby with the use of a golf cart, for, as Snyder explained, "He has to have an objective pursuit such as golf or other pleasure to get him away from his desk."[9]

Snyder and Heaton had another important priority—they wanted to exclude White as much as possible as a consultant, and to control him otherwise. They had no lack of respect and liking for him, but they saw him as a publicity seeker at a time when publicity could be dangerous.

They had to go about their purpose, however, with a full measure of friendliness and tact. They had no wish to insult White, and they dared not alienate him, because any indiscretion on his part could still harm the president's political fortunes. Thus when Snyder learned of the Bostonian's planned trip to Washington early in May for a Senate hearing, he invited him to meet with him and Mattingly to review the one new cardiogram they had taken and to discuss the general aspects of the case. Along with his invitation, Snyder told White he thought it would be best "to make a simple statement to the press that you had called upon the president for an informal chat. . . . It might be advisable to include a statement that you find the president's condition satisfactory. We believe it better not to hold a press conference at this time."[10]

White did have a short visit with his old colleagues. Unbeknownst to him, at the same time the president was telling 214 reporters at a news conference that he would soon have a "head-to-toe" checkup. When asked if Dr. White had been dismissed from his case, he replied, "No. As a matter of fact, I think he is in town today." When a reporter wanted to know if White would examine him before the Republican convention, Ike said, "Ask the doctor. I don't know. He hasn't told his plans yet." The truth was that Dr. White was not making such decisions; indeed, he was surprised upon his return to Boston to learn about the general physical examination, scheduled between 10 and 12 May, at a time when he had to be in Italy. The evaluation, "from the scalp to the soles of the feet," as Snyder described it in a letter, would take place much earlier than expected because at the very last moment the president had asked for it to be at that time. "I had anticipated that you and Pollock would be here when an examination of this scope would be made," he explained. "It would have been preferable that way; however, when the president gets an idea in his head, I don't like to interpose objections." In fact, Eisenhower's political advisers had made the decision to prevent White's participation; they did not want him in attendance at the news conference following the event, the more so because this might be Eisenhower's final evaluation prior to the election.[11]

White did not accept his exclusion in complete silence. He asked Mattingly to send reports of the examination and then returned to him and Snyder his own proposed comment for the press. "We may not need to use it at all," he admitted, "but there is some ammunition in it which may be helpful to the country at large." His three-page draft gave a general review of the factors presumed to aggravate coronary disease and stressed that the president's job was not responsible for his heart attack. He believed his health to be "better, even on this kind of work, than if he sat in retirement the rest of his years fretting because of his enforced idleness."

But White included one slightly troublesome sentence that mentioned the need for anyone facing a serious disease to place a limit on his job. That was enough to incite Mattingly. He wanted no rehashing of what had already been said, and such an emphasis, he warned White, "would only be construed by many people throughout the country [to mean] that the president's physical state of health was such that he could not carry on the job of the presidency." Assuming again the responsibility of putting his old friend on a leash, Mattingly insisted that he divorce all of his articles entirely from the health of the president; he added: "In spite of the spark that it might give, as you know I have never felt that we should use the misfortune of the president's illness to gain importance and publicity for other purposes." Snyder, who was also worried, advised White on the same day that all comments "in this connection are worthy of being coordinated" through James Hagerty.[12]

This time White took the message to heart. He was chastened. "I agree with you entirely and certainly shall not voluntarily do anything about the matter of the comments that I sent you," he assured Mattingly on 7 June. "I have been delighted to have gotten into the background lately with respect to the president's health and examinations and I hope to continue to do so. Once in a while I refer in passing to his good health but not for publication." Little did he know that by the time his letter reached Washington, he himself would be back there as well, at the bedside of the president.[13]

His special trip was not the result of any problem with the heart. Indeed, after several consultation visits in March and April and a full-scale examination in May, Mattingly was exultant about his patient's cardiovascular health. He found the myocardial infarction to be well healed. There was still a small area of decreased contractions over the anterolateral wall (front side) of the left ventricle, but there was no evidence of an aneurysm, and the total size of the left ventricle was within normal limits. Otherwise there was no enlargement of the silhouette of the heart, no signs of coronary insufficiency, no complications with anticoagulant therapy except for a tendency for the gums to bleed during brushing, no difficulties with a low-fat diet, no fatigue or distress during a daily swim in the White House pool or after playing eighteen holes of golf twice a week, and no worry about a blood pressure that remained normal and stable. The patient's only complaint was a consciousness of occasional cardiac arrhythmias, which seemed to occur more frequently with emotion than with physical activity; otherwise, as he told a group of supporters, the only way he knew he had been ill was because the doctors kept reminding him of it. The cardiologist's only concern was to ensure the proper management of the anticoagulant therapy.[14]

The doctors were not able to derive a similar satisfaction during their two-day examination of the president's gastrointestinal tract. The X-rays showed the esophagus, stomach, duodenum, and colon to be normal, but the radiologist, Colonel Elmer Lodmell, had obtained some startling pictures of several constricted areas in the terminal ileum. Surprise gave way to enlightenment. This one barium gastrointestinal series suddenly made sense of all the troublesome abdominal symptoms going back to the 1920s. The president had chronic ileitis, an inflammation of the lowest portion of the small intestine, also known as Crohn's disease after Dr. Burrill B. Crohn, who first described it in 1932. It was a little-known disease, considered mild rather than severe, and it primarily affected the young. It usually had a slow onset, but once established its symptoms tended to recur over months or years, nearly always ending in surgery.[15]

Since the president was free of any active symptoms, the diagnosis did not pose any immediate medical problem. The doctors found no indication of a need for surgery and were content to rely on continued observation and possible dietary changes. They did face a critical problem, however, as to whether they should share their diagnostic discovery with the world. The political implications were apparent, and after lengthy deliberation among Snyder, Heaton, Mattingly, Pruitt, and Lodmell, the two generals decided upon a policy of deliberate concealment. They told the press that the X-rays "showed a normally functioning digestive tract," and they rationalized their deception on the grounds that the examination did not demonstrate an actual obstruction. They also agreed to make no mention of the constriction to the president. Such knowledge, they deemed, together with the fact that there was no treatment available to alter the progress of the disease, would cause him unnecessary anxiety. They did not record, but might well have considered, that it would also provide him with "plausible deniability"—the ability to maintain that he was unaware of his disease and unconnected with any activities to hide it from the public.[16]

Soon thereafter, lying on his back in Walter Reed Hospital awaiting surgery because of a complete intestinal obstruction, the president learned of his doctors' deceit. He "took great exception to our decision in this matter," Snyder recalled. Perhaps so, but he was almost certainly challenging them for having deceived *him*, more so than the press. He was definitely not concerned enough to hold his doctors to the standard of full and complete disclosure in the future.[17]

Shortly after midnight on Friday, 8 June, the First Lady called Dr. Snyder to report another abdominal attack. Snyder recommended a tablespoon of milk of magnesia, which she gave him. She called again twenty minutes later because there was no improvement and informed the physician that a White House car would pick him up. Snyder arrived and found the president's blood pressure at 140/100, pulse 94 to 100, and considerable arrhythmias, together with the persisting abdominal discomfort. He administered quinidine sulfate for the abnormal heartbeats (for only the third time since the stay at Fitzsimons), after which the patient slept intermittently. The discomfort continued, together with soreness over the lower right abdomen, and at 6:00 A.M. Snyder administered an enema. At 7:40 A.M. he called Ann Whitman, telling her that the president had a headache and a digestive upset; he asked her to cancel the president's morning appointments but to schedule the cabinet meeting for 2:00 P.M. He followed with a call to Jim Hagerty to suggest that he announce the problem as a "stomach upset."[18]

Snyder was worried. In the many previous attacks he had been able to unblock the gas in the intestinal tract and bring relief by early morning. Having failed to do that, he thought of the fearful possibility of an intestinal obstruction—a much greater likelihood since the diagnosis of chronic ileitis in May. His concern heightened when he learned about a presidential indiscretion in diet. The previous noon, ignoring the prohibition against raw vegetables, Ike had specifically requested Charles, the butler, to prepare a Waldorf salad. Suddenly Snyder had visions of pieces of undigested celery lodging in one of the constricted sections of the terminal ileum. Fully conscious of the president's apprehension about the "many battles" they had fought against this kind of condition in the past, and especially his fear of a recurrence of the disabling illness of 1949, he now had good reason to share that apprehension.[19]

Snyder realized that he might be facing a crisis, for in the worst-case analysis, surgery would be necessary. So at 8:45 A.M. he decided to call General Heaton, only to learn that he was away on vacation at Gloucester Point, Virginia. But as the president's abdominal distention increased and his hands and feet became cool and moist, Snyder called again to inform Heaton that he would arrange for an airplane to pick him up. Then he phoned Mattingly's home, only to discover that the cardiologist had left very early that morning for South Carolina. He was disappointed because the two Walter Reed experts most acquainted with the president's care were not immediately available. In the meantime, he and his assistant physician, Dr. Walter Tkach, tended to the patient with a cup of tea, heating pads to the abdomen and feet, and a small enema. The abdominal distention continued nonetheless, and at 10:00 A.M. the patient had cramps in the calves of his legs, which prompted Snyder to contact Walter Reed and ask Colonel Francis Pruitt, the chief of medicine, to bring intravenous apparatus with a glucose and water solution, to arrange for an ambulance to be on call, and to think about civilian consultants.[20]

During the next two hours the excitement accelerated. The president vomited three pints of dark green fluid, slept fitfully, had a cramp in the calf of his right leg, complained of generalized abdominal discomfort, and perspired noticeably about the hands and forehead. At about noon Colonel Pruitt arrived and found the president listless, apathetic, sweating freely, and with a blood pressure of 105/70, which made him worry about shock. He began the intravenous treatment to control vomiting and replace electrolytes, and Snyder asked the Secret Service to intercept Dr. Mattingly. At 1:25 P.M. the doctors decided to remove the president by ambulance to Walter Reed Hospital, where they carried him in on a stretcher. Upon arrival they learned that General Heaton would be there within the hour, having been picked up by a tiny plane in an open field and with a police escort waiting for him at National Airport; and that the state police had found Colonel Mattingly in a small town in the countryside of North Carolina and would soon have him aboard a jet plane for return to Washington.[21]

Snyder was relieved when he saw the president comfortably in bed in the hospital, but he was not complacent because he knew how deceptive this man's exceptional reserve capacities could be. And, too, Ike had never before suffered a bout of abdominal cramping and distention of this severity, accompanied as it was by recurrent vomiting and unrelenting pain. So the doctor went about obtaining X-rays and an EKG, and passed a tube with a suction attachment through the patient's nose to the stomach. When Heaton arrived at 2:15 P.M., the two generals studied the X-rays and detected a partial obstruction of the small intestine at the upper portion of the ileum, with increasing dilatation of the jejunum, the middle section of the small intestine.[22]

They easily diagnosed ileitis and decided to call in some surgical consultants. The first to come to Heaton's mind was Dr. Isador Ravdin, the world-renowned head of surgery at the University of Pennsylvania and a longtime associate of the armed services. He had joined the Indiana National Guard in 1916, operated the best field hospital in the army during World War II, became the first physician selected for the rank of major general in the army reserve, and enjoyed the friendship and respect of the military medical hierarchy. Remembering the hurt feelings of some of the practitioners in Denver who were never consulted about the heart attack, Heaton decided to invite two local physicians—Dr. Bryan Blades, professor of surgery at George Washington University Medical School, and Dr. John Lyons, a highly esteemed friend who was in private practice. One other physician was soon on his way to the hospital. Paul White, upon hearing news reports of the president's hospitalization, called Snyder and offered his services. The general told him that Mattingly would be present, but if White wished to "stop in," they would be "glad" to have him there.[23]

By 6:00 P.M. all of the surgeons had assembled, including Ravdin, who had rushed in from Chicago. A second set of abdominal X-rays confirmed a partial obstruction, and Snyder argued strongly for immediate surgery. He was certain that some improperly masticated celery was the source of the problem, believed that there was no likelihood that suction could remove the obstruction, and was aware of the old adage from medical school, "Never let the sun set on a case of intestinal obstruction." But as he described it, "no surgeon present felt like putting a scalpel into the president's abdomen. Procrastination was, therefore, the method utilized by the surgeons to avoid attacking the problem directly." The discussions continued for two hours and the signs persisted, accompanied by increasing distention and a lessening of the bowel sounds of the abdomen, which carried the threat of gangrene. At 9:00 P.M., after a break for dinner, the consultations resumed and the surgeons asked for another set of X-rays, which indicated a larger area of distention.[24]

The stalemate dragged on until midnight, with Mattingly and White circling around the huddling surgeons urging them for the sake of their patient's heart to make up their minds. ~~But Dr. Lyons held out stubbornly against surgery;~~ he thought nature would eventually push the food through the restricted portion of the ileum. The surgeons then resolved to obtain another picture and, at Snyder's insistence, agreed to have the litter ready in the hallway to rush the president to the operating room. The X-rays revealed a further increase in the distention; this finding, together with the absence of bowel sounds, moved Lyons. "I give up," he said. "I agree with all of you now." Heaton felt somewhat shaky about operating on a president of the United States. "Judas Priest! That's pretty serious business," he thought. "Very serious." But he informed his patient of the unanimous decision in favor of surgical intervention, and Ike replied with almost the same words he had used to send Allied forces across the English channel for D-Day, "Well, let's go." As he was taking the anesthetic he said, "You know, Leonard, I have a lot of bills to sign and I am going to have to be able to sign them within three or four days."[25]

The procedure began at 2:20 A.M. on 9 June, with Heaton performing the operation and Ravdin assisting, and with Blades and Lyons standing at the table but not as participants. Mattingly and White, who had examined the president and declared him fit for surgery, and who had some concern about the possibility of bleeding because of the anticoagulant therapy, monitored the cardiovascular status during and immediately after the operation. Snyder served as a liaison with Mamie and her mother, who were in a suite next to the president's. Snyder would complain later, in private, about the delay caused by the "recalcitrant" consultant, noting that this "case would have been operated upon early in the afternoon of 8 June if the patient had been plain Mrs. Murphey."[26]

Once in the abdomen, Heaton had to make a decision about the surgical technique he would use—a decision about which he felt insecure. At the time there were two preferred procedures for regional ileitis. One was resection, a relatively long and radical procedure that involved removing the diseased section of the ileum and tying together the remaining ends. Heaton rejected resection because he found the president's ileitis to be in a dry or burned-out stage with a very small likelihood of recurrence, because the emergency did not allow sufficient time to clean out the bowel for major resectional therapy, and because he was afraid that resection might take too much time for a patient who relatively recently had suffered a heart attack. As he expressed to Blades, who fully agreed: "I mean, we've got to get this patient off the operating table. And we've got to do it damn fast." The other most desirable procedure was "bypass in discontinuity," which involved cutting loose the diseased area, stitching shut its open end, which was left dangling, and bypassing it. Heaton rejected this technique because it would take considerable time, because it involved the risk of a blowout of the diseased section, and because it would require a subsequent operation to remove that section. He chose instead a procedure that he and other authorities considered inferior, "bypass in continuity," whereby the diseased section of ileum was left in place and a bypass made parallel to it. It was a faster procedure that would not require surgery at a later date. But it also involved a greater chance of the problem recurring.[27]

The operation continued until 4:51 A.M. on Saturday without complications, after which the physicians went home, cleaned up, had brunch, and then appeared before a news conference at the hospital arranged by Jim Hagerty, who was hoping to recreate the friendly relations with the press that had existed in Denver. The hour-long conference took place in a jammed, sweltering room where newsmen, photographers, broadcasters, and newsreel cameras filled nearly every inch of space. Reporters sat and stood around a long table, and Hagerty and the doctors (excluding Paul White, who was not invited) occupied another table placed like a crossbar of a "T" at the head of it. Photographers were festooned on two tall stepladders positioned against one wall, and cameramen were packed along another. The doors were closed to prevent anyone from leaving with an early news break, which made it all the more uncomfortable for the eighty-five or ninety persons present. The newsmen were expectant, nonetheless, because they knew so little about what had taken place. The previous morning Hagerty had told them on two occasions that the president was suffering from a stomachache, and shortly after noon he changed the condition to "an attack of ileitis," which he related to the "acute case of gastroenteritis" in 1949 and the "case of blood poisoning" in 1953. Throughout the night the press had stood on the lawn in front of the hospital, sometimes climbing the concrete fountain or standing on automobiles to gaze with their binoculars at the amphitheater on the third floor, but at best they could only discern the shadowy figures moving around the room.[28]

That night, as Ann Whitman put it, "was in the truest sense of the word, a nightmare." The following morning, as General Heaton saw it, was bright. He was the star of this conference, and he had good news. The president was in excellent condition; he should have a complete and rapid recovery and be able to resume his full duties in four to six weeks and play golf by mid-August; his cardiac condition had no relation whatever to the ileitis; and "there was no reason why his illness or surgery should prevent him from running again." Using a blackboard, the general sketched a diagram of the diseased ileum, which he had found upon entry into the abdomen was "markedly contrasted, inflamed, and had the consistency of a hard rubber hose," and which left an opening only the size of a lead pencil. Then he drew in the bypass, which involved about ten inches of the terminal ileum as it entered the large intestine, and which he believed would improve the patient's life expectancy. The surgeons had removed nothing, he explained, they were confident they would never have to remove the diseased section, and there was no need for a biopsy. When asked if the president had ever had an attack of ileitis before, Heaton deferred to Snyder, who mentioned that it "probably carries back many years." To a follow-up question as to why the ileitis did not show up in the examination in May, Snyder answered with artful deception: "Because in the recent head-to-toe examination there was no inflammation of the ileum."[29]

Hagerty continued his education of the press by releasing an hour-by-hour chronology of the illness together with photographs and diagrams of the surgery, and by holding several meetings with reporters in order to elaborate upon the physicians' comments. As he had done at Fitzsimons, he emphasized the president's increasing work schedule. On 11 June, only two days after surgery, he revealed that the patient had conferred with staff members, signed an executive order and an international wheat agreement, and walked eighty feet in his hospital room. The next day, he reported, the patient was still on intravenous feeding but was able to confer with aides, sign eight bills, and dictate to his secretary for thirty minutes. The following day was even better, and Hagerty informed the world that the president had signed twenty-seven bills, conferred with aides, and met for a half hour with Chancellor Konrad Adenauer of West Germany, who subsequently expressed his own amazement. "I was very happy to . . . have seen him in such excellent shape," the visitor told the press. "I have asked the doctor to explain this miracle, and he has told me that it is a healthy organism which offers the best foundation to overcome any obstacle of this kind. I must say that I would not have thought it possible that a person, so few days after an operation, could look that way, could talk that way and could participate so vividly in the discussions."[30]

Once again Hagerty earned plaudits for his openness. *Editor and Pub-*

lisher praised his "forthright and tireless" efforts and offered its "hearty congratulations for being honest and fair with the press and the American people." The Associated Press was even more generous: "You couldn't find a newsman around the hospital who wasn't grateful all over again to Jim Hagerty. He was living up to the wonderful standards of frankness which he set last year in Denver." This time, however, the acclaim was not unanimous, as some reporters began to demand additional information and to raise questions about both the medical facts and the political implications concerning the president's health. Hagerty reacted aggressively. He refused to arrange any further news conferences with the physicians, and he announced on 19 June that the doctors, for their part, would refuse to engage in controversy with those who had no personal knowledge of the case. "Each case is a law unto itself and cannot be answered in terms of generalities," the press secretary philosophized as he raised the stone wall. "Every thoughtful physician realizes that there are biological variations in all disease processes."[31]

Hagerty's blackout did not put an end to the "bee-buzz conversations over cigarettes and coffee in many a hospital or medical-center common room since the president's operation," as *Time* described it. Nor could it prevent a public debate, which was all the more intense because it took place in a partisan political atmosphere.[32]

The Democrats looked upon the ileitis surgery as a political blessing. By their simple arithmetic, the president now had two chronic diseases with which to contend, instead of one. Thus they were angry and suspicious from the moment General Heaton claimed in his press conference that Ike could serve a second term. They became angrier when a contender for the head of the AMA declared that the president's recovery would leave him in better physical condition than any of his opponents had been at any time in their lives. The Democrats' newfound opportunity seemed about to vanish almost as quickly as it had appeared, and they struck back. Paul Butler, their national chairman, assailed Hagerty for having "propagandized" the president in a "new science of politico-medicine." Senator Pat McNamara of Michigan accused the press secretary of arranging "one of the most masterful suppressions of facts ever put across by the advertising techniques of Madison Avenue" and warned of a one-party press unwilling to challenge his handouts and medical interpretations. The *Detroit Free*

Press, a newspaper friendly to the Democrats, quoted Hagerty's admission that his main interest was to get Eisenhower elected and editorialized: "That underscores heavily the truth in much of what Ike's real well-wishers have been saying in recent weeks. To the men around the president he has ceased to be an individual to whom the nation owes great consideration. To them he's become just the biggest, bluest chip in the 1956 political game."[33]

Journalists friendly to the Democrats also suspected a cover-up. Robert Allen, who at one time in his career had coauthored the popular "Washington Merry-Go-Round" column with Drew Pearson, the longtime critic of the president, expressed such sentiment in a private letter to his former colleague. Allen had heard from one of his Republican sources that the precipitating factor in the president's stomach ailment was his consumption of a number of greasy appetizers at a cocktail party. He gleefully related to Pearson the story of "Dopey's" (Eisenhower's) immoderate consumption of the "hot and greasy tidbits," and of his "quack" (Snyder) expressing concern about it. Having set the tone, he attacked the Walter Reed crew for saying it would not be necessary to remove the diseased portion of "Ike's innards." Not only had his own doctor said flatly that the inflamed section would have to be removed eventually, but so too had Dr. George Calver, the physician to Congress. "Now Calver is corroborating that to the hilt," Allen advised Pearson, "despite all that Walter Reed crap about Ike being better than ever before, and that they were going to leave this infected intestine in him and blooey, blooey, blooey. I don't often agree with Butler, but he sure as hell hit the target with his remark about Hagerty running a propaganda hoopla and not a news-disseminating agency."[34]

Pearson was so certain of a Republican deception that when he first heard reports of the ileitis operation he believed the doctors were really "scraping for possible cancer." He quickly dispatched an investigator to find out what those in the White House were saying in private. His source reported that every Republican he had talked to expected Ike to stay in the race, and that presidential aides were giving out the line that since the operation would cure an ailment he knew he had, he would be more inclined than ever to run. He informed Pearson:

What they are saying, in other words, is that Ike is really healthier for having had the operation. I tried to find out whether this line was

cooked up by the publicity boys and dished out ready to serve. I could
find no evidence of it. For example I checked through reliable friends
to find out whether any of the Madison Avenue crowd were master-
minding the public relations. . . . I couldn't pick up a clue that Madison Avenue was so much as being consulted. The impression I get is
that the Ike-is-really-healthier line was picked up by the White House
crowd as the best explanation. I don't think there was any deliberate
decision to spread this line.

Pearson remained skeptical, nonetheless; he denounced the "suppression of
any word about ileitis" in the May report and described it as "part of the
news suppression picture" being drawn by those around the president.[35]
In contrast to their behavior in Denver, newsmen began to seek out the
opinions of experts within the medical community about several key issues. One query had to do with the sudden announcement of a diagnosis
of ileitis at 12:25 P.M. on 8 June, just before the president went to the
hospital. The *Reporter* argued that Ike's doctors must have known before-
hand that he had the condition. "To diagnose this particular disease that
way de novo at the bedside," one of the journal's medical authorities
pointed out, "is almost a medical miracle. It just doesn't happen. They must
have known he had the condition long before." Dr. Samuel Standard, an
associate professor of clinical surgery at New York University, agreed that
such a diagnosis would be "brilliant," and added that it would be
"illuminating" if the White House made public the X-ray plates of 10–12
May. "It is my guess," he said, "that these might show the typical picture
of regional ileitis at that time." The *Washington Post* hassled Hagerty about
the truth, but he insisted that the doctors had reported what they had
found in May and referred the newspaper back to Dr. Snyder's assurance
that there had been no inflammation of the ileum at that time. Since there
was no way to prove conclusively that Snyder had lied, there was no way
to keep the issue alive.[36]

Reporters were somewhat more successful in investigating another matter—the likelihood of a recurrence of the ileitis—because they found considerable published medical evidence to support their misgivings. They were
able, for example, to cite the bible of insurance underwriters, *Risk Appraisal*,
which described ileitis as "serious. Always serious," and continued: "Short-
circuiting operations offer hope, but not much more. Prognosis always dubious. . . . Disability coverage no. Positively no." Fortuitously for the critics,

as well, an article by Dr. Louis Zetzel of Boston in the May issue of the *New England Journal of Medicine,* published prior to the president's operation, had described the high recurrence rate of the disease, had defined surgery "as palliative rather than curative," and had concluded: "There is pessimism and disillusionment about the effectiveness of any regimen of providing more than palliation and control of symptoms. . . . They all suffer from the disappointing sequel of recurrence and persistence of the disease." Likewise Dr. Burrill B. Crohn, the foremost authority on ileitis, reported that the recurrence rate after surgery had risen to about 35 percent, and even *Time,* friendly to the president, decided that "in 50 percent of cases like his there are relapses within five years." An anonymous "specialist" made the point the Democrats wanted to hear: "I wouldn't recommend the strenuous life for an elderly man who had just overcome an operation for ileitis—let alone on top of a coronary thrombosis."[37]

The press struck out completely, however, when it raised questions about Heaton's choice of a surgical technique. Shortly after the operation, Dr. Crohn precluded any extensive criticism by defending the army surgeons. "I really shouldn't discuss the president's case because I have no personal knowledge of it," he offered. "But I should say in general that they exercised splendid judgment in not attempting to do anything more than they did." Other surgeons also refused to second-guess their colleagues, and reporters could not break through their solid front. Heaton, however, was so sensitive about even the limited criticism that some eight years later, with the patient's permission, he wrote a description and defense of his decision in the *Annals of Surgery.* Eleven years after that, in an oral history for the Eisenhower Library, he restated his case and proudly revealed for the first time another of his motives, which was clearly political. Prior to the surgery, he recalled, the president had related his intention to seek reelection despite this latest problem, and thereby made a "bypass in discontinuity" unacceptable because it would have required another operation in about a month. "Now I was the only one around that operating table that morning that knew this gentleman was going to run again," Heaton explained. "And that would have been a very, very sobering experience for him to awaken and find out that . . . this . . . necessitated further operation. . . . That would have taken four to six weeks to recover from that. You're talking about three to four months, there's no question. . . . And I think that would have influenced him in his decision to run again." The whole truth was finally out—the surgeon's political assumption had shaded his medical judgment—but it was nineteen years too late to have any effect upon the campaign.[38]

Despite the spate of "expert" opinions, it was impossible for any debate in the newspapers and magazines to make an authoritative case against a second term. Ileitis was a "weird disease," as one specialist described it, "Prognosis can never be made with certainty. You can't always even tell the different types of the disease apart." Because it was relatively new, the scientific studies were often suggestive rather than conclusive, and the facts about it were changing every year. The very essence of ileitis, whether of its cause or its cure, seemed to inspire disagreement and dispute. Crohn suspected a mystery virus, but Heaton and others suspected nervous tension or a similar psychosomatic explanation. Nearly everyone agreed there was no cure. "There's great positiveness in the profession about only one thing," explained an authority from the East Coast, "and that is about there being uncertainty about the disease." Members of the press could interview their own experts, but they could not ensure the certainty or relevance of their answers.[39]

Even when they suggested a cover-up, the critics did not focus their blame on the president. Instead, they put forth the view that he was somehow a passive spectator or, as some saw it, a victim of those around him who were hiding the truth not only from the public but also from the patient. Drew Pearson argued that the "men around Ike are doing what Democrats around Woodrow Wilson and Franklin Roosevelt did when these two presidents were ill." Doris Fleeson noted that the "psychological warfare over the president's new illness was begun by his army doctors almost before he was out of ether. His aides are continuing it." Senator McNamara was "quite sure the president has not been party to the shotgun medical bulletins and the huckster barrage from Madison Avenue that has been fired at the American public from his bedside." And Hal Burton of *Newsday* went so far as to warn the president to be on guard against pressure from the selfish individuals around him: "You are surrounded by people who are there only because you are there. If you go, they go—painful thought. These people have sat, at least now and then, in the seats of the mighty. They like that sort of sitting."[40]

Even Adlai Stevenson saw the White House staff and the doctors as the culprits, espousing a self-serving attitude that "if he can walk he can run," and "propping the poor man up as a facade for vote bait." In one of his many misreadings (or wishful thoughts) during the campaign, the Democratic candidate decided that aides would not be able to prop up the president well enough or long enough and that he would step down. "I doubt if he will submit to it in the long run, although I could be unhappily mistaken," he reflected. Stevenson's mistake was to misunderstand Dwight Eisenhower. The president was more determined than anyone around him that he should have a second term, and, unlike his opponent, he did not view the ileitis surgery as a complication. Indeed, once the doctors had spelled out for him the larger picture of his illness—ileitis was a young man's condition, and in his age group there was virtually no chance of a recurrence—he was ready for the battle. His simple arithmetic added up differently from that of the Democrats; he now had only one chronic problem, not two. For him the surgery was a temporary inconvenience with a permanent payoff—after a lifetime of suffering, he was now rid of his stomach ailments, once and for all. His only worry was the time required for recovery.[41]

The Democrats were reduced to speculation—and frustration—because they really knew nothing about the president's recovery beyond the soothing assurances of Hagerty that his muscle tone was improving and that he was in generally good health. Their only hope of breaking through the "Hagerty curtain," indeed, their one brief moment of opportunity, came on 1 August. That morning columnists Joseph and Stewart Alsop, Eisenhower supporters, wrote that the problem of the president's health had reached "the stage of rumor and innuendo and worried or malicious private gossip, like the gossip about Franklin Roosevelt's health in 1944." They asked Hagerty to convene a "full and frank" press conference by the president's doctors without "further delay or equivocation." Even more heartening for the opposition was the August issue of the *Atlantic Monthly*, which appeared that day on newsstands, in which a distinguished professor at the Harvard Medical School charged that the American people did not know the truth about their president's health.[42]

Dr. David Rutstein, head of Harvard's Department of Preventive Medicine and vice president of the AHA, began by taking issue with the handling of the Eisenhower heart attack. The fault, as he saw it, was not with the patient but with his doctors. The president had been the friend of truth; he wanted to avoid the secrecy that still shrouded the illnesses of Wilson and Roosevelt, and thus approved a series of press conferences to discuss his condition. But his physicians had given only the "appearance" of full disclosure; they had put forth an optimistic prognosis of his life expectancy at variance with several scientific studies—all of which reported that only 50 percent of the patients who recovered from a heart attack lived more than five years. They compounded their folly with their public assurance in February that President Eisenhower "should be able to carry on an active life satisfactorily for another five to ten years," a statement that denied the incumbent any choice on medical grounds to forgo a second term. "This episode," he concluded, "demonstrates the powerful influence a medical decision may have on our national history."[43]

Rutstein then focused in on his subject, "Doctors and Politics," by criticizing the president's physicians for having failed to report his true condition prior to the 8 June attack, because "ileitis is a chronic disease which very rarely has obstruction as its first symptom." He found fault with their news conference: "At no time did they give any indication that ileitis is a chronic disease with a rate of recurrence varying between one-third and two-thirds of those on whom the operation is performed." He questioned their optimistic prognosis because "the emergence of a second chronic illness cannot by any stretch of the imagination improve the total health status of the patient." He belittled their credibility on the grounds that "political judgments by physicians have as little merit as medical judgments by politicians on the ability of a candidate to run for office." And he accused the White House, in the face of controversy, with having changed its policy of open and free discussion of the health issue and with insulating the president's physicians from the legitimate queries of their medical colleagues.[44]

The White House quickly instituted a program of damage control. At a press conference that same day, the president addressed some of the rumors and answered some questions about his health. He told the pesky reporters that he was not suffering from a dysentery-like condition; that he did not feel as well as he had a year before but that he had improved every day since the operation; that he had no problems sufficient to prevent him from doing his work; that he had never considered leaving the race; that he had no fear of a recurrence of ileitis because the doctors had assured him that of the four known cases in men his age, none had suffered such a fate; and that he had no doubts about his ability to serve for another four years. He admitted having to rely completely upon what his doctors told him about his condition, but when reporters asked him to approve a conference for Heaton and Ravdin to meet with them, he refused, arguing that he could not make a commitment without checking with them first.[45]

The president never arranged such a conference. Instead, at his press conference the following week he announced that he would not discuss the topic of his health again. He did reveal that he would have another complete physical examination before the election, and he promised that "if at any time I have any reason to believe that I am not fit as I believe myself to be now, I will come before the American public and tell them." He held to his position of silence during the subsequent eight news conferences prior to election day, departing on occasions only to deny a rumor that he would require surgery after the election, to emphasize that his health had placed no limitations on his campaign, and to reiterate strongly that he would not go before the American people with an explanation of his current condition. "I said I would go for a full-scale examination and the doctors could put out what they chose," he said in a flash of testiness on 31 August. "All I am discussing is when I am here. If you people think I am healthy, you can say so. If you think I am not healthy, o.k."[46]

The White House also moved immediately to minimize the impact of the *Atlantic Monthly* article. "All of us here are in accord that this article should be ignored," Howard Snyder wrote, and "are in agreement that we should not engage in discussion through the press, with Rutstein or any others, the problems in connection with the president's current illness." To accomplish that end, they had to restrain Paul White and Isador Ravdin, for both of whom the article was a special irritation. White was upset that Rutstein, whom he described as one of his "old friends," had "out of the blue" and in public not only impugned his motives and ethics but misrepresented and misquoted the facts of his 1941 study on survival after coronary thrombosis. White was inclined to overlook the article, but he also prepared a statement to correct the "politically slanted" and misleading charges, just in case the White House thought it would be useful. Howard Snyder immediately disabused him of any such thoughts. Snyder went on to spell out the administration's policy: "We have no wish to withhold from the people of this country any facts concerning this latest illness, which we hope was thoroughly presented on June 9th, but we believe that no good could be served by repeating those facts. It may be proper at a later date to present again a report of the president's then condition and prognosis."[47]

White assured Snyder that he would not publish his statement and that in all instances he would be "as everlasting careful" about his comments as possible. Dr. Ravdin, who considered Rutstein a "scoundrel of the first order," was less amenable to the policy of silence. He agreed that there should be no discussion of health or illness with newspaper reporters, but he suggested to Ike in mid-August that he be allowed to write a case report for the prestigious *Journal of the American Medical Association,* which would reach a circulation of 175,000 and could "squelch a good many things that might be said in the future." Eisenhower expressed appreciation for his proposal, but it ran into trouble at a White House meeting, as described by Snyder in his notes: "Ravdin strongly in favor, endorsed by Hagerty, questioned by Heaton, and not approved by me." By the end of the month, nevertheless, Ravdin had sent his report to the White House for review, where it fell into the now unfriendly hands of Snyder and Heaton. They revised it to the extent that "one would not recognize the original," and when the surgeon declined to make further revisions, they informed him of the decision not to publish it. "I shall of course drop the matter," Ravdin wrote to the president, "even though I do not agree with them. The publication of the case history would have provided the means of getting a tremendous amount of coverage regarding the present state of your health, and would have given an immeasurable amount of confidence to people who wish to be reassured that you are well."[48]

In his letter of response, the president thanked his friend for his expression of "unselfish interest," apologized for having put him to "a lot of work only to have it all go for naught," and conceded having given in to the arguments of his close advisers. Both Snyder and Heaton were strongly averse to publication, and Hagerty had come to believe that the case report would probably confuse the layman more than it would inform him. Politics had taken precedence over medicine. As Ike admitted, "It would seem to me that the minute the election was over, there would be no objection to the report coming out." In the meantime, there would be an absolute ban on any discussion of health, even if it were to be made by friends and even if its message appeared to be favorable. It was better to deprive the issue of any importance whatever, and to bury it if possible.[49]

By proscribing any public discussion of the president's illness, the administration succeeded in stifling most of the potential criticism. The Democrats were left fuming, for the most part relegated to passing around the joke that if one operation could improve Ike's health, he ought to have another before November so as to be in really top shape. But Snyder, Heaton, Hagerty, and Eisenhower also had created a potentially dangerous situation. They had placed the burden of proof squarely with the patient, or, as the latter explained to Ravdin, "The feeling now seems to be that the results of the operation are evident in my obvious state of good health." It was crucial thereafter that his good health remain obvious.[50]

The first five days of Eisenhower's postoperative convalescence at Walter Reed were especially "rough," certainly at odds with the bulletins of cheer Hagerty was dispensing to the public. The doctors had him walking on the second day and eating on the fifth, but they could not get rid of a troublesome infection around the incision. Thereafter the recovery was uneventful, although the president never escaped from depression about what he perceived to be the slowness of his improvement. His impatience at the end of the first week prompted Mamie to write, "I am going to put the 'slow me down Lord' prayer in the president's mirror when he gets home as a daily reminder, and I think it is most apropos." He was uneasy about leaving the hospital on 30 June, after only three weeks, but he deferred to Heaton and Snyder, who believed a change in environment would expedite his recovery. Gettysburg did seem to have a positive influence. His first night there he said he felt better than on any preceding night, despite the drive from Washington. Snyder was delighted after a week because Eisenhower's appearance was improving, his anxiety was rapidly disappearing, his appetite and digestion were good, his elimination was all it should be, he was walking around the farm, and he was enjoying his putting green.[51]

Above all, the patient remained unreservedly committed about his long-term future. He, and not his doctors or his aides, was writing the script, as he indicated at a morning legislative meeting at Gettysburg on 10 July. "To refer to myself for a minute," he said, "I have had a rough ride. But if I was right on February 29th, I am now in much better condition. I think it is fortunate that the operation took place, but unfortunate that it came at such a time and when I was in such condition that a slow recovery is noticeable—when I should like to be out fighting. The thing that was wrong with me, that flared up so many times, has been corrected. This operation was the sternest test that my heart could have. I am not going to say anything more about it."[52]

The recovery, both physical and psychological, was unquestionably slow. The infection in the upper third of his incision required a dressing

Leaving Walter Reed, thin and weak, after surgery for ileitis.
(Courtesy Dwight D. Eisenhower Library)

every day, and it was so bothersome as to require General Heaton and his wife to be at the farm with the president and to reside in the guest cottage for more than two weeks. During the second week Ike developed some pains in the right side of his abdomen, which the doctors believed were due to an accumulation of gases in the large intestine, but he worried anyway because, as Snyder recorded, "Any pain in that area causes the president great apprehension and is so psychologically disturbing that it is quite depressing to him."[53]

Equally depressing was the president's inability to regain his strength. Nixon noticed that Ike "hobbled about, bent over, during his post-operation convalescence," and he suffered more pain and looked worse than after the heart attack; John Eisenhower never saw his father look worse until the last days of his life. Heaton eventually instituted a walking program whereby every day the two of them would hike an increasing distance to one of the trees along the driveway, each of which was named for one of the states. The patient was utterly determined because he had a target date; as he repeatedly told Heaton, "Got to get me ready to go to Panama." He was referring to a trip to Panama originally scheduled for June, which had been rescheduled for 20 July because of the surgery. He considered his ability to make the trip a test, and he was so anxious to go that Snyder realized it would be "very upsetting" if he could not. There was a good sign on 9 July when he was able to walk a mile to the main gate and back without fatigue, but Snyder was still concerned that the trip would place a greater demand upon him than he even wished to contemplate. He decided to have Ike return to Washington a few days before leaving, and if he were still suffering from fatigue, he would call it off.[54]

Eisenhower went home to Washington on Sunday, 15 July, and during the next three days he was "terribly depressed" because he could not seem to get rid of gas and soreness in his lower abdomen. Snyder instituted an old treatment of ground carrots and yogurt, and whether because of that or some other reason, by departure day on Friday Eisenhower was much improved, showing the first real change for the better in the abdominal condition since his transfer from the hospital to the farm at Gettysburg. He slept well on the plane, "put in three strenuous days in Panama, the likes of which you have never seen," in Snyder's words, and gained "a new lease on life" through his ability to handle the heavy physical and emotional demands, forgot his "belly" troubles, and seemed relieved of the anxiety that had depressed him for many weeks. Jerry Persons, a presidential aide, described even more dramatically the impact of the trip: "The old man was to go to Panama July 21, and that Friday before he left, he was a sorry sight. And he said to me privately, 'If I don't feel better than this pretty soon, I'm going to pull out of this whole thing.' So he goes down to Panama, almost gets crushed by the mobs, meets God-knows-how-many

Latin American diplomats, suffers through all the damn receptions—and Tuesday, *Tuesday,* mind you, three days later, he comes waltzing back looking like a new man."[55]

The Panama trip represented a turning point for the president. He had met his physical test and seemed ready for the campaign. Snyder found him cheerful, in contrast to "the real depression that marked his convalescence up to that point." When Emmet Hughes visited with Eisenhower in early August, having not seen him in nearly a year, he took note of the "undiminished" vitality, "the eyes as brightly alert and intense as ever, the excited stride around the office still as brisk and assured. Every gesture, every response, seemed to speak for a man astonishingly strong. . . . Wherever he conversationally turned, he showed sheer zest for a second term."[56]

Despite his confident demeanor, Eisenhower remained seriously attentive to his health. After returning from Panama, he was somewhat fatigued and had a little more gas in his abdomen, but it was his heart that concerned him more than his stomach. Even during his recovery he was uneasy about his rapid (and irregular) pulse, which had averaged about 65 beats per minute prior to the operation but 80 afterward. On 28 July Ann Whitman noted that he "admitted he was gaining a little weight, was worried about his pulse and took it himself—but it was fairly low and not skipping." On 6 August Snyder found him to be "hyperconcerned" because of a fast pulse and four skipped beats per minute, and he recruited Mattingly and Heaton to help him relieve their patient's increasing apprehension by explaining that there was some reasonable cause for the increase. Snyder also used a "beefing-up" program of steroids, endocrine products, and his favorite liver extract injections until the November election.[57]

On 21 August the president left for the Republican National Convention, which served as an additional tonic for him, with thousands of people proudly wearing their "I LIKE IKE" buttons and speaking confidently of peace, prosperity, and victory. But he could not stop worrying, and throughout the campaign, in the judgment of Emmet Hughes, "the question of his unknowable physical resources haunted all weeks and most days."[58]

The Democratic and Republican nominating conventions met in back-to-back weekends in mid-August. Following his nomination, Adlai Stevenson was still unwilling to speak directly about the president's illnesses, so he continued to imply that an Eisenhower victory would weaken the office of the presidency. Most of all, he focused on Richard Nixon: "The American people have the solemn obligation to consider with utmost care who will be their president if the elected president is prevented by a higher will from serving his full term," he advised. "It is a sober reminder that seven out of thirty-four presidents have served as the result of such indirect selection. . . . The choice for that office has become almost as important as the choice for the presidency." With his unprecedented action Stevenson was trying to shock the American people into thinking carefully about the Republican party, both the problematic health of its leader and the questionable competence of its second-in-command.[59]

Stevenson's suggestions that an Eisenhower victory would mean a diminished presidency did not ring true because by election day most Americans considered the president the more healthy of the two candidates. Indeed, the prominent irony of the campaign was that the fifty-six-year-old challenger ended weary and hassled, while his sixty-five-year-old rival appeared vigorous and relaxed. The Democrat had not planned it that way. From the time of his announcement a year before, it had been part of Stevenson's strategy to travel and speak in all parts of the country in order to accentuate his good health and vitality, in contrast to the poor health and weakness of his opponent. But the primary campaign proved to be so demanding—fifty-five thousand miles and three hundred appearances—that Stevenson ended up "absolutely exhausted," as one friend put it, or in the words of another, "just an animated shell of the *real* Adlai."[60]

In contrast, Eisenhower's strategy was to husband his energy. He accepted the nomination and then went off with his friends for a vacation on the Monterey Peninsula, where he played golf and bridge for four days. Ellis Slater found him more relaxed than in years and deduced that the job was not troubling him too much. The president decided to wait until well into September to open his campaign, as a precaution against becoming exhausted, and to forsake whistle-stopping except for one quick trip to the West Coast and one brief incursion into the South. He gave only seven major speeches before political rallies and concentrated instead on television appearances produced with the assistance of the Hollywood actor Robert Montgomery and the advice of the famous advertising agency Batten, Barton, Durstine and Osborn. Appearances were important, and Ike always was alert to the political requirements so aptly expressed by his brother: "It doesn't even matter what you *say*—just get out and around and show the people how healthy you really are."[61]

He did travel more than he had planned initially, in part to ensure a substantial margin of victory and in part to "prove to the American people that I am a rather healthy individual." He went out of his way to look hearty. "I just can't afford to *look* tired," he explained to Emmet Hughes. "I haven't had the slightest suggestion, you know, of any trouble whatsoever since the heart attack. But the doctors have warned me: If I feel the slightest bit weak and tired, I sit down—*right away.* Well, if I do that in the middle of a speech we're *through,* that's all." He even fretted about the consequences of failing to meet a schedule, make an appearance, or take a trip: "There'd be political yapping all around that the doctors yesterday *really* found I was terribly sick and ready to keel over dead."[62]

Everyone in the White House was sensitive to the possibility that "the merest cold or stomachache, sending the president to bed for as little as a day or two, could cause instant political chaos," especially in light of a whispering campaign, ostensibly fostered by the opposition, about a "slight relapse." Jim Hagerty was prepared even for that. "If it happens, we'll call in only independent doctors, beginning with the head of AMA, if need be—*no* personal doctors, *no* Army doctors, *no* one who's politically suspect for having attended him before. We'll meet it head-on." The abiding reality of the 1956 campaign was that they never had to. Eisenhower awed those around him with his resilience and his vitality. It may have helped that the staff did everything possible to protect him from stress; as one aide put it, they added "a new dimension to the old deference: an acutely conscious solicitude for the president's health of body and peace of mind. So fond a concern often seemed to threaten to insulate Eisenhower against the impact of critical or unwelcome facts." Howard Snyder had prescribed such insulation as a necessary part of the treatment for a heart patient, especially one inclined to outbursts of anger, and staff members merely became good doctors. But so, too, did the patient. He disciplined his anger, and during the months of campaigning he never exploded "with the raging impatience so familiar in the past."[63]

It was also important that Snyder prevent any potentially damaging medical information from reaching the public, and the American people might have had second thoughts had they known about some developments. During September Ike was bothered by high blood pressure, and at the end of the month Snyder noted, "I seldom tell him his exact blood pressure and never mention the skips unless he brings it to my attention." In October he had some worrisome days because of arrhythmia. On 4 October he had a considerable number of skipped beats, and Snyder cautioned him to curtail his golf practice. On 9 October he had a premature contraction every four or five beats, with as many as twenty per minute, apparently the result, as Snyder deduced, of the stress and strain of speech-writing together with the responsibilities of his job. His worst day was 18 October, when he was campaigning in Portland. After a cold, rainy morning, a speech at the College of Puget Sound, and a tiring experience in a motorcade, his pulse was 100 and irregular. By late afternoon the doctor noted that Eisenhower "was emotionally upset because of exhaustion of these three days, and at the prospect of the requirements of the days to come." He was further irritated because of an accident to his secretary's typewriters, and he ended up "screaming" at her to finish his speech. That evening he arrived at the civic auditorium with his pulse still 100 and irregular, and he made the extraordinary request for a nitroglycerine tablet, which he took with no untoward results except a little dizziness, and which seemed to relieve the apprehension of the afternoon.[64]

As late as mid-September a survey of political reporters claimed in a *Newsweek* article that "the overriding issue of the 1956 presidential campaign is the state of Dwight Eisenhower's health." The facts were otherwise. Stevenson was unwilling to exploit the issue of health, Snyder refused to discuss the details of his patient's daily condition, and Eisenhower quite simply looked well enough to govern the country. But there was more.[65]

One reason the electorate ignored the issue was that Eisenhower, Hagerty, and Snyder worked assiduously to prevent even the slightest discussion about health to enter the campaign. To do so, they had to deal firmly with one old friend, Paul White, and harshly with one longtime antagonist, Drew Pearson.

Although White professed to Snyder in May that he was delighted to be in the background, he really wanted to be part of the action again. He had enjoyed immensely his personal relationship with the president, and he had never received the slightest intimation that the feelings were not reciprocal. Thus he continued to correspond with his former patient. Two weeks after the ileitis operation, for example, he wrote to advise him about exercise. Two weeks later he sent Eisenhower an 1887 magazine article entitled "Cadet Life at West Point" and an account of his own Scammon Lagoon expedition to record the heartbeat of the gray whale. The president's reply was touching and exaggerated; he not only thanked White graciously for the material and for standing by during the surgery but also reiterated his "profound gratitude" for "looking after me *for these last nine months*" (italics mine).[66]

White also still felt a close kinship with the medical team and, more strongly than ever before, shared its confidence about a second term. After the ileitis operation, even though he was excluded from the official press conference, he made his own comment and gave unqualified support to Heaton and Snyder. The president's heart was as good as ever, he assured reporters, and with his abdominal problems cured he would now "be better than ever." The Bostonian was expressing his honest convictions. To a greater extent than in February, he was optimistic about the president's prospects because of his new thoughts about the promise of preventive medicine.[67]

In late May and early June, White had presented a paper, "The Ways of Life and Heart Disease: A Plea for Positive Health," to university medical groups at Harvard, Syracuse, and Wake Forest, in which he argued that commonsense health measures could not only neutralize but actually transcend the hazards that might be inherent in such basic factors as race, heredity, age, and sex. In addition to his long-standing beliefs that exercise could counteract a "soft push-button way of life," that hard work, "physical or mental, never killed a healthy man," and that a low-cholesterol and low-fat diet could serve as a deterrent to heart disease, he mentioned the influence of the "psyche." "In some way," he argued, "I believe, that bad effects of the alarm reaction, of grief, of fear, of anger, and of pessimism can be neutralized and even superseded by inculcation of the positive virtues of courage, patience, and optimism."

White's focus on personal habits, especially "equanimity," as a pathway to better health seemed to have sharpened as a result of his experience with Eisenhower. As he explained to a colleague, proper attention to these habits could actually retard the progression of coronary atherosclerosis. It had done so for hundreds of his patients, making them healthier than they had been before their heart attacks; and it could have the same benefit for the president. Preventive measures were particularly important, he noted, because "we may all be dead before the researches are finished."[68]

White wanted to be of help, and he sent his paper to Snyder to pass along to Eisenhower. Apart from such gratuitous counsel, however, there was no opportunity for him to play a larger role, as Snyder made clear in August when he told White to remain silent about the Rutstein article. White did remain silent, even though he was itching for a chance to speak out; but at the end of September, while addressing a group of medical students in Iowa City, he inadvertently caused a stir. At the end of his address, a student asked how he was going to vote. White innocently remarked that he was not sure because he had been out of the country for five weeks and would need to learn what was going on. The local press centered in on his response and inferred that he might have some privileged and unfavorable information about the president's condition. White knew immediately that he had goofed, and he fired off an airmail, special delivery letter to Hagerty in which he explained the situation. Apprehensive that his miscue might be used politically, he enclosed a two-page statement of clarification for the American people.[69]

For some months he had felt it desirable to respond to the many questions directed at him, the doctor explained, despite "the fact that I am merely a specialist consultant in his case, and have not been needed during the past few months and have had constantly only favorable reports about his health." In his statement White stressed that the president had shown no evidence of heart weakness and that "the ease with which his heart withstood the strain of his operation was further proof of his complete recovery from the coronary attack of a year ago." He included some favorable statistical evidence he had compiled about survival after heart attacks, averred that he would doubtless vote for the president, "especially since seeing the need of his services in our international relations overseas," and added a final comment: "Were I asked the question: 'If not 100 percent sure, how sure are you?' I would answer 99.44 percent with the expectation that the remaining 0.56 percent would evaporate by election day."[70]

The next day, 2 October, brought a hurried exchange. White sent another letter to Hagerty, apologizing for having caused so much bother with a seemingly innocent remark. He also had remembered the ban on discussions of health and decided that "it may be best not to try to make any explanation right away." Instead, after an interval of two or three weeks, he could return to his original statement of a year ago and make a positive declaration about the election itself. Hagerty replied with a telegram: "Agree nothing needed now. Will talk to you later." White responded with a promise to "act accordingly" but presented another statement for future use: "Having now had an opportunity, after an absence overseas, to become acquainted with the political campaign issues at home, I welcome this occasion to declare my full support of the president's policies and the Republican cause in the coming election. Medically, I have always been and continue to be confident of his capacity to serve again. The odds are heavily in his favor although no one can guarantee the future health of anyone. I shall do all I can to support the president, medically and politically, for his reelection."[71]

The president tried gently to close the case by writing White that the press had often misquoted him, and that he should pay no attention to such things. But the doctor chose to keep it open. Between 11 and 16 October he made several proposals to Hagerty designed to counteract the "absurd publicity" occasioned by his casual remark—publicity that, in reality, was virtually nonexistent. Perhaps he could add a statement to some forthcoming speech, for example, his scheduled address before the AHA, a nostalgic reminiscence about the heart attack, which he enclosed for the press secretary to review. Or he could belatedly join the Committee of Artists and Scientists for Eisenhower (CASE), as an opportunity to give a speech. Or "a neat way to do it" would be to arrange a press interview with Frances Burns of the *Boston Globe* on some other topic, with an appropriate divergence. Or perhaps it was better to say nothing at all. His vacillation ended when he sent Hagerty a paper, "A Note on the Prognosis of Coronary Heart Disease," written specifically for release to the Associated Press and United Press, in which he noted: "I would like your O.K. for this article."[72]

White had actually prepared an abbreviated version of a paper he had just published in the October issue of the *Journal of Chronic Diseases*, "A Completed Twenty-five-Year Follow-up Study of 200 Patients with Myocardial Infarction." He had seen these patients in consultation between 1920 and 1930, and had presented an initial follow-up study in 1941, which showed a five-year survival rate of 49 percent and a ten-year survival rate of 31 percent for the 162 patients who survived their attack beyond the first month. At the press conferences following Eisenhower's heart attack, he had omitted any mention of his 1941 study and had been reluctant to discuss prognosis because of insufficient evidence. But he had promised to bring his material up-to-date, and by campaign time he was ready to declare the results surprisingly good and encouraging. Of the subgroup of

55 patients who had shown a complete clinical recovery after their coronary thrombosis, he reported, and were therefore in the same category as the president, 45 (82 percent) were alive after five years, and 31 (56 percent) were alive after ten years. "Thus I have given you at last a more detailed statistical basis for our attitude about the president's recovery which a year ago seemed so dubious," he explained to the press secretary.[73]

Hagerty and Snyder were not elated about White's prospective news release. They could see no benefit, just before the election, in reviving an issue long since resolved in the public's mind. They also could see a potential danger in the cardiologist's statistics. A scientist could be comfortable starting with 200 patients and reporting on a subgroup of 55, but troublemaking journalists or unsophisticated laymen might read the results differently. They might argue that of the original 200 patients, 38 died within a month; and that of the remaining 162, 63 were limited with angina, 44 were crippled by shortness of breath (myocardial weakness), and only 55 recovered completely. Of those 55, 10 died within five years, leaving only 45 healthy people (capable of serving as president) out of the original 200. Quite understandably, Hagerty informed Snyder, "I can't see any reason why he should put out something like this," and he refused to give White the "green light" he had expected.[74]

Snyder delivered a final blow to his former compatriot through his scheduling of the president's preelection physical. White had originally asked for the examination to be held in mid-October, but Snyder opted for the end of the month. Then White submitted a detailed itinerary, pointing out that he would be able to adjust or postpone any dates except for 28 October, when he had to be in Cincinnati to receive an award, and 29 October, when he had to be in Iowa for a convention. Snyder scheduled the physical for 27 October and a press conference for 28 October, which would allow White to be part of the medical team but exclude him from speaking to the press. Snyder had never been able to accept the famous New England specialist into the inner circle, and he would not change now. White was a civilian and unpredictable, and the risk was much too high for any kind of indiscretion.[75]

Thus on Saturday, 27 October, Paul Dudley White's role as "Ike's doctor," which for a few historic weeks had captured the attention of the nation but for nearly a year had existed primarily in the eyes of the public, came to an end. He attended the president's physical examination and then left for Ohio to accept the Blakeslee Award from the AHA. He was nostalgic but in no way bitter. In his prepared comments he expressed his great appreciation for the privilege to serve "a patient whose family included the whole United States and much of the rest of the world." He reveled in the unprecedented opportunities his experience had brought, and rightfully so—to educate the lay public and the medical profession about the scourge of heart disease; to gain support, both moral and material, for essential medical research; and to stimulate international cooperation as a potent force for world peace. And he reflected, with pride, on the "appalling but inevitable" publicity surrounding the case: "We were obliged to tell the most intimate details of the progress of his illness. The president quite rightly, insisted upon it. Not once did we knowingly make a misstatement." He admitted regret, in this election year, about the inability to defend himself against those who saw a political significance in his medical observations, for "silence may be most suspect of all," but he remained silent. He was a good trooper at the end.[76]

The White House was able to stifle its erstwhile consultant, but it could not control its foremost journalistic nemesis, Drew Pearson. The staff was not surprised at the source of the attack, for it was only another in a series over the years in which this particular columnist seemed intent upon embarrassing the president, including his charge right after the ileitis surgery that Republican leaders had compelled the president to stay in the race against his own wishes. Pearson had left the country for the Middle East shortly after the nomination but not before expressing his cynicism about the president: "Even if he had died en route to San Francisco, Len Hall would have stuffed him and run him anyway." Pearson was absent during most of the campaign, but upon his return in early October he resumed his search for what he believed was the fire behind the smoke. His suspicion grew stronger as the result of a letter from a professor of medicine at the University of Washington School of Dentistry, who wrote, "I have been reliably informed by one of my medical colleagues that President Eisenhower has suffered not one, but *two* heart attacks." The informant gave the name of his source, a distinguished physician and dean of the School of Medicine at Washington University in St. Louis. "If this information is true and has been suppressed by the president's physicians," he continued, "I believe the silence to be grossly unfair to the American people. Possibly careful investigation on your part may confirm or deny this story."[77]

Pearson was unable to verify the lead and arrived at a dead end on the issue of a previous heart attack. But he considered it a possibility and reasoned that if there might have been a cover-up about heart disease, and since there definitely had been a continuing deception about the ileitis, it was impossible to believe anything the administration said about the president's health. Then he learned from a friend in the White House that some members of the staff, supported by Mrs. Eisenhower, were deeply concerned about the politicians pushing Ike too hard after his surgery, and that they did not want him to win at the expense of a drastic setback in his health or possibly his death. Other informants gave him enough information about the candidate's trip to the West in mid-October to inspire a provocative column on 27 October, on the eve of the candidate's scheduled physical examination at Walter Reed and only ten days before the election, reporting that Ike had "apparently suffered a mild relapse" because of "campaign exhaustion or something more serious." He asked for an impartial bipartisan checkup of both candidates, because the doctors were playing politics by timing their tests on election eve and "wouldn't dare find Ike in anything but the best of health a week before the election."[78]

Jim Hagerty did not need instruction about political timing. When he received a leaked copy of Pearson's column on 26 October, the day before it was to appear in newspapers across the country, he saw it as a last-minute attempt to exploit the issue of health. Alert to the danger, he struck back angrily, describing the column as "the most amazing document of falsehoods that I have ever seen," and gave examples of ten misstatements of fact on one page alone, and three in one sentence. Pearson retorted that he believed his story was true, reviewed what he considered the White House denials and deceptions of the past, and argued, "Mr. Hagerty has been operating an iron curtain on information for a long time. His technique is to deny and clobber over the head any newspaperman who disagrees with him." He denounced Snyder for having the same attitude and noted that on one occasion the doctor had gone so far as to threaten a member of his staff in an attempt to prevent a story about Ike having a portable oxygen inhalator in his car. The journalist charged: "The fact is that the politicians are overworking the president. . . . to overwork a sixty-six-year-old man who has had two major illnesses in nine months is nothing short of criminal." Recognizing that there was "hell to pay" but refusing to back down, Pearson issued his column on Saturday, 27 October.[79]

The impact was short-lived. On that same Saturday the papers carried a story about the president's physical examination, and the following day Hagerty quickly issued the promising results, including even the laboratory findings. But Pearson would not accept defeat. On the day before the election he issued a long response with new "evidence"—the statement of a woman who had watched the president's motorcade and "saw death drive by in a big black Cadillac. . . . Don't ever let anyone tell you Ike looks good. . . . It'll be a miracle if he lives six months." By relying on an anecdotal opinion of one person, Pearson was clearly reaching to make his point, but he did make a stronger case when he stressed the problem of getting the truth because of secrecy and the practices of the press secretary. "Life with a hostile Hagerty can be difficult," he complained, and he recalled an "amazing" incident in the winter of 1956 when only one of the White House press corps had dared report that the president, given the wrong golf club by his caddy, threw it in a burst of anger across the side of his golf cart.[80]

Not for a long time had a newspaper story created such a sensation as "Mr. Pearson vs. Mr. Hagerty," wrote the editor of the *Oceanside (California) Blade-Tribune.* Two upright, honest newsmen, committed to publishing the facts, were dramatically at odds with one another. The editor had a balanced explanation for the discrepancy: "Pearson's desire for a good story sometimes, it seems to us, leads him to exaggerate, and Hagerty's desire to protect the president sometimes, as in the case of the president's gastric condition, leads him to minimize the president's occasional illnesses." He was close to the truth. A year later Pearson would refer in his diary to the "boo-boo" on Eisenhower's health, and Hagerty was continuing his policy of secrecy.[81]

The California editor also had no doubt as to who prevailed in the controversy. He concluded that the president was not really ill and that his "vigorous campaign of the last few weeks would in itself be the best denial." It was.[82]

The final weeks of the campaign provided a more intense version of the various elements that had prevailed for months—the president's success with his image, his ability to hide some real concerns about his health, and his opponent's enduring frustration. As to image, for the second time in the wake of an illness Eisenhower was exceedingly lucky in regard to the state of national and foreign affairs. After the heart attack, when he needed a substantial period of calm in order for his heart to mend, Congress was not in session and there were no problems or crises requiring his attention. Thus he was grateful for the "fact that I could not have selected a better time, so to speak . . . even if I had been able to pick the date." After the ileitis surgery, when he needed to prove that he was vigorous enough to conduct the affairs of state, he had a very different reason to be grateful, for as he explained, "October 20, 1956 was the start of the most crowded and demanding three weeks of my entire presidency."[83]

The simultaneous upheavals in Eastern Europe, where Hungarian free-dom fighters were in revolt against Russian tanks, and in the Middle East, where the British, French, and Israelis were in collusion against Egypt and the Suez Canal, provided a luminous stage for the display of Eisenhower's ability—physical and otherwise—to be president. There was nothing the Democrats could say that could blur the picture of the commander in chief handling these crises. Through the endless hours of meetings, telephone calls, and messages, he revealed a full range of emotions but was invariably cool, poised, relaxed, and confident. Indeed, in those two weeks prior to the election, he erased ten months of Stevenson's attempt to craft a portrait of a part-time president.

Ike's doctors provided additional timely support to the image of a healthy, working president. On 27 October he entered Walter Reed for the "complete physical examination" he had promised to the American people for their enlightenment prior to the election. Even as he walked through the hospital corridors, he was at work preparing a note to David Ben-Gurion, which led him to quip, "Israel and barium make quite a combination." Immediately after the examination his seven physicians— Snyder, Heaton, Mattingly, White, Ravdin, Lyons, and Blades—reported that he "gives every appearance of being in excellent health." Indeed, every system was in perfect order. As for his cardiovascular health, there had been no symptoms whatever of coronary insufficiency (angina pec-toris) or of myocardial insufficiency (heart muscle weakness); the heart size was unchanged; the heart sounds were normal and without mur-murs; the rhythm was normal at a rate of 75; and there was no evidence of aneurysm. As for the abdomen, there was no indication of any exten-sion of the old disease process; there was a well-functioning ileocolos-tomy for the relief of the obstruction due to ileitis; and the bowel function was absolutely normal.[84]

The "perfect" medical report was not, in truth, an accurate reflection of the president's anxieties, which persisted through the election, seemingly in tandem with the awesome pressures he faced. On 5 November, the day before the election, French and British paratroopers landed at the Suez Canal, and the Russian premier proposed that the Americans join with the Russians and march into Egypt to restore peace. Ike told Snyder that if he were a dictator, he would tell Russia "If they moved a finger he would drop our entire stock of atomic weapons upon them." The stress was such that he had his blood pressure and pulse taken on *seven* occasions during that afternoon and evening, more than on any day for which there is a record. At times he averaged as many as eight skips per minute; his pulse was in the 80s and reached a high of 90 just before he retired; he complained of abdominal distress and gas; and he had a headache. That night Ike was restless, and on election day he called Snyder because of a swelling and tenderness on his abdominal scar, which he mistakenly thought would need lancing. His blood pressure and pulse, taken on three occasions during that day, were pleasantly lower.[85]

The president's healthy appearance and his doctors' optimistic report were politically and personally devastating for Adlai Stevenson, and his frustration found an unfortunate outlet on election eve. In a nationwide broadcast from Boston, he slashed at Eisenhower for failing to "run the store" while the world was aflame in Hungary and the Middle East. Then he forsook propriety and stunned his audience with mention of the hitherto unmentionable. "And distasteful as this matter is," he said, "I must say bluntly that every piece of scientific evidence we have, every lesson of history and experience indicates that a Republican victory tomorrow would mean that Richard Nixon would probably be president of this country within the next four years." He decried such a prospect and continued, "Distasteful as it is, this is the truth, the central truth, about the most fateful decision the American people have to make tomorrow." There was shock and anger in the Eisenhower headquarters. "Four years ago," Ann Whitman explained to a friend, "I had a considerable respect for Mr. Stevenson; this time none at all—and my liking for him turned to something akin to hatred for his attacks on the president's health, in such a sanctimonious manner, too."[86]

Stevenson's unseemly outburst shamed many of his own supporters and surely cost him more votes than it won. He never understood the true relevance of Eisenhower's illnesses to the campaign—that the American people, in the most human sense, wanted their president to get better. They were rooting for him and would register their empathy at the polls. As for Ike, on election eve his competitive spirit was still running high. He told Anthony Eden in a telephone conversation that he did not "give a damn" how the election went, but he was more honest with Emmet Hughes: "When I get in a battle, I just want to win the whole thing. . . . Six or seven states we can't help. But I don't want to lose any more. . . . That's the way I feel." A year of agony about his health found its outlet in that single ambitious wish, and by midnight the next day, 6 November, the American people fulfilled it by giving him a landslide victory. At 4:00 A.M. he went to bed in good health and feeling well. He was ready to be president for another four years.[87]

Snyder, Heaton, and Hagerty served Eisenhower faithfully throughout the ileitis episode. Snyder dissembled about the initial diagnosis of ileitis in May; Heaton did not reveal the truth about his choice of surgical techniques; Hagerty kept White and Ravdin away from the press; and all of them played down the president's actual problems with his heart and blood pressure, as well as his constant concern about them. With the tacit approval of the president, they put in place a policy that would govern throughout the second term—tell the press nothing, preferably, and as little as possible, if necessary. They were well prepared when a third potentially dangerous illness struck the president on 25 November 1957.

On that Tuesday afternoon the president was hosting King Muhammad V of Morocco at a ceremony that included a parade through Washington. At 3:10 P.M. he returned to the White House and went to bed immediately because he felt chilled. The doctor put him under two blankets, with a hot-water bottle at his feet, and took his blood pressure and pulse. He rested for an hour, had lunch, and returned to his office at 4:23 P.M. When he sat down at his desk, he experienced a sense of dizziness and found it impossible to pick up a piece of paper. He dropped a pen and failed after three attempts to retrieve it. Mrs. Whitman had noticed that he was walking rapidly when he passed her window and was inclining a little to one side. She went into the president's office and found that he was unable to express himself clearly; he sensed that he was speaking "nothing but gibberish" and began to feel "truly helpless." She quickly sent a note to General Goodpaster to come to be with the president, and went to her phone to call Howard Snyder.[88]

The doctor appeared within minutes, just as the president was attempting to dictate to Goodpaster and was so aphasic that he could not make himself understood. He also was having difficulty coordinating the movements of his hands, as he dropped his spectacles and was unable to find them to pick them up. He was very irritated when Snyder appeared, apparently because it disrupted his concentration in dictating to Goodpaster.[89]

Snyder quietly removed himself, had Ann Whitman tell Goodpaster to accompany the president to his room, and met them there. The president had no difficulty throwing off his overcoat and coat, and he walked from the elevator to his dressing room without support, although his locomotion was somewhat uncoordinated. The two generals put him into bed, at which time he continued trying to formulate a letter, unable to get out the words. He kept repeating the name "Jones," and Goodpaster would say, "W. Alton Jones?" The president would say with difficulty, "No, Jones" and try to explain but with disconnected words. Realizing that anxiety plays an important role in determining the functional deficiency of individuals with organic brain disease, Dr. Snyder immediately gave him a sedative.[90]

Snyder then called Colonel Pruitt at the office of the surgeon general and asked him to come immediately. He gave the colonel his estimate of the situation—that the president either had a small thrombus or a vasal spasm in a terminal branch of the middle meningeal artery of the left side of the cerebrum. Colonel Pruitt examined the president and found no neurological changes, although he did find the blood pressure to be 160/90, the highest systolic pressure since the heart attack. He recommended bringing in Colonel Clausen, the neurologist from Walter Reed, and Snyder made the call at 5:30 P.M. He then informed Mamie of the situation, but he could not allow her to remain in her husband's room because Ike became irritated at his inability to express his thoughts to her.[91]

Colonel Clausen arrived at 6:10 P.M. Shortly thereafter, the president awakened from an hour's rest, arose, walked to the bathroom, and returned to bed. Clausen determined that Eisenhower's general health over the past several weeks had been good, though he had exhibited evidence of tension and strain, particularly during his recent stay at Augusta. But there was no history of unconsciousness, convulsions, headaches, neck stiffness, or weakness of the extremities either before or after the episode. Clausen examined the president carefully, checking all reflexes and sensory areas. The president spoke reasonably clearly to him. He repeated "Methodist Episcopal" when requested but failed to repeat accurately "round the rock the ragged rascal ran." He identified accurately the colonel's ring, the button on his coat, his trousers, his wristband, and other objects presented to him. The movements of his hands and fingers were well coordinated, and his responses were normal except for repetition of the alliterative quotation. Clausen gave his diagnosis: "Occlusive phenomenon involving the speech area in the distribution of the left middle cerebral artery, probably in one of the smaller terminal branches in the temporoparietal area, due either to thrombosis or cerebral vasospasm."[92]

The indications were that after only an hour's rest the president had improved markedly, so much so that while Snyder was discussing the case with Heaton and Mattingly, who had just arrived, his valet called to report that the patient had risen from his bed, put on his dressing robe, and walked through the hallway and into Mamie's room. Snyder hurried to the room and found the president discussing with his wife and Sherman Adams the question of his appearance at the state dinner to be held that evening in honor of King Muhammad. The doctor told him there was no possibility of his attending the dinner, and that he should be back in bed and not worrying about anything. The president rose and walked to his room with Mamie and Snyder; he remarked, "If I can't go to that dinner, this spells the end of it for me. We'll be farmers from this time on." Snyder got him back in bed and told him that his concern was for him to rest quietly during the night and not bother about his official problems. The president said, "Did I have a small . . . small . . . ," but could not utter the next word he wanted to say. Snyder asked if he meant "a small stroke," and he replied, "Yes." The doctor told him that he could not at that time state whether he had had a stroke, but that at least he had a vascular spasm of the small artery in the brain. For the time being, rest was the prescription; they could continue the discussion in the morning.[93]

Snyder, Sherman Adams, John Eisenhower, and Mamie reached an agreement with the president that Mrs. Eisenhower would carry on with the dinner; she would announce for the time being that he was recovering from a chill induced by his noontime exposure. The president slept until 8:00 P.M., but then he tried to explain to Snyder that he expected to see Mamie and some of the guests assembled for dinner. When Snyder gave him some pills to help him sleep, the president asked, "My God, Howard, look at the time. How long will these last?" The doctor replied, "It doesn't make any difference. I am going to keep you doped tonight." The president then propped up in bed with a Western novel and by 10:00

P.M. had fallen asleep. Snyder and John Eisenhower kept watch throughout the night.[94]

When the president awoke the next morning he pointed in the dim light to his favorite watercolor, *The Smugglers,* and tried to name it. He could not, and the more he tried, the more frustrated he became, finally thrashing around in his bed, beating the bedclothes with his fists. Even after Mamie named the painting for him, he could not say it, but he was able to relax, and when the specialists arrived to make their examination at 7:30 A.M., he was talking quietly to John. Colonel Clausen's examination revealed no abnormalities other than slight aphasia (an impairment of the ability to use or understand language), which had improved considerably during the night. Mattingly concluded that the heart revealed no changes since his last examination. But the cardiologist held to an opinion he had offered the previous evening—that the probable cause of the event was a small cerebral embolism from the ventricular aneurysm that he alone believed the president had suffered during his heart attack. Since Snyder and Heaton had never allowed Mattingly's earlier complicating diagnosis to appear in the medical records or the press, and had expected him to "forget it," they resented his raising the issue now; they stated in their press report that "the present symptoms have no relationship to the previous heart attack."[95]

Dr. Snyder also arranged for outside consultants to see the patient—Dr. Houston Merritt and Dr. James F. Hammill, respectively, professor and assistant professor of neurology at Columbia University Medical School in New York City; and Dr. Francis M. Forster, professor of neurology and dean of the Georgetown University Medical School in Washington, D.C. The consultants arrived at 3:45 P.M. on 26 November and remained for an hour. The president seemed to enjoy them, particularly Dr. Merritt, who found his patient to be "well oriented, cooperative, and . . . not acutely or chronically ill. The flow of spontaneous speech appeared to be greater than that of the average individual but might not be unusual for the patient. At times there was hesitancy in the use of a word and there were occasional circumlocutions." The specialist's summary was optimistic:

On testing speech function, patient was able to name most of the common objects in the room without difficulty. Occasionally he would grope for the word or perhaps describe the article before being able to name it. His comprehension of conversation and commands was immediate and his response appropriate. He complained of slight difficulty in reading but could read a sentence without difficulty. . . . His handwriting was good. Sample sentences were written readily on command. Mental status appeared to be perfectly normal. The patient was sometimes irritated by inability to think of the correct word promptly. He was also somewhat depressed because he felt that the present episode was an indication that he would not be able to function as well as formerly or withstand the pressures placed upon him."[96]

Dr. Merritt made an attempt to assure the president that he would recover, and stated his diagnosis: "The history and findings would indicate that the patient has had an occlusion of the small branch of the middle cerebral artery on the left which nourishes the brain adjacent to Broca's area [which controls the speech effort]. It is difficult to predict whether there will be any residual defect. The degree of improvement in the past twenty-four hours is a good prognostic sign." He thought it would "seem wise to allow him limited activity in his own home, but further activities should be restricted until we can determine the extent of the lesion and the further course." The outside consultants favored occlusion or spasm as the likely cause, as opposed to a cerebral hemorrhage, and agreed only that Mattingly's theory was a possibility.[97]

Thereafter the president improved rapidly. At 6:00 P.M. Dr. Snyder visited him and noted: "The president was really cheerful and conducted a lively conversation with Mamie and me. He really seemed reluctant to let me go." At 9:40 P.M. the president was in a "pleasant mood" and "cheerfully reported that he had learned a number [of] more words during my absence." After retiring, the president awoke at 3:10 A.M., and speaking of his sleeping pills, he realized he couldn't think or say the words he wished to, so he said, "Oh, nuts, I will go to sleep." And he did.[98]

The White House bungled the press coverage of the illness at first. As one reporter put it, "Everything went to hell entirely." Jim Hagerty was in Europe, and his deputy press secretary, Anne Wheaton, initially reported that the president had developed a chill and that it was not serious. The next day she was two hours late for the usual 4:00 P.M. briefing in the lobby of the West Wing. In a voice breaking with emotion, she told the more than two hundred reporters, frantically restive in the wake of rumors about another coronary, that Eisenhower had endured a "cerebral aphasia." Hounded by questions, she became confused, and at one point said that it was some kind of heart attack. Most of the press deciphered her comments to mean that the president had suffered a stroke, but the initial report of the United Press described a "heart attack of the brain."[99]

Hagerty, after a hurried return from Paris, took charge brilliantly. In four press conferences on 27 November, the day before Thanksgiving, he described the president's condition in optimistic terms; he was shaving, eating, walking, painting, meeting with aides about important issues, and laughing at his own inability to pronounce a few words. Hagerty read a terse comment from Dr. Snyder about the "excellent" progress, but he would not allow reporters to meet with the specialists and would not answer "theoretical" questions about the meaning of this "very transitory" episode. He also refused adamantly to countenance the use of the word "stroke." He tried to explain that the doctors would not call it a stroke because the latter was not a medical term, but rather a layman's word, and that it had a popular connotation of paralysis and hemorrhage, neither of which specifically applied to the president's case. He went round and round with the reporters over the issue, holding to the statement that the specialists were uncertain whether the occlusion in the brain derived from a clot, which might denote a stroke, or merely a spasm, which might not. The White House never officially acknowledged that the president had suffered a stroke, although it became generally accepted that such was the case.[100]

During the next two weeks Eisenhower made a significant recovery from the aphasia. He was able to read fluently and speak with very little impairment. He still showed a slight tendency to supply synonyms for certain words, but the substitutions were appropriate and close to the meaning he wished to convey. Snyder arranged for a follow-up neurological examination on 10 December, and Clausen, Merritt, and Forster expected no further difficulty; indeed, they regarded his progress as so encouraging that they decided to allow him to attend the upcoming NATO conference in Paris (scheduled for 13-20 December) provided he would maintain a reasonable restriction of his activities while there.[101]

Although Snyder had not scheduled a cardiovascular examination for that day, he did include Mattingly in the conference following the evaluation. Once again the cardiologist privately took issue; he feared a repeat embolization and opposed the Paris trip as an unnecessary hazard. Even more, he suspected Snyder of excluding him from the formal examination lest the president should ask his advice directly and get an honest answer. Mattingly did not go beyond stating his opinion to Snyder, however, even when the latter's press release deceitfully placed Mattingly's name among those approving the trip, but he considered himself an outsider from then until his retirement in August 1958.[102]

The president was somewhat aware of the "argument" over his health and his trip. "Doctors, friends, family, and associates protested now," he wrote in his memoirs, "but I was determined to have my way—and for a good reason." He felt that he had to undergo this therapeutic "test" to determine whether he was physically and mentally capable of serving as president; he was intent on avoiding, at any cost, the kind of situation that had occurred during the Wilson administration. He told John Foster Dulles—who had heard Drew Pearson's radio broadcast asking the president to resign, and who privately talked with Nixon about what they could do if Eisenhower became incompetent but was unable to realize it—that if he was not able to go to Europe, "it would in his opinion raise a serious question as to whether he should not then 'abdicate.'" He did go to Paris and returned without incident, but his sensitivity to the problem of succession led him to make a remarkable grant of power to his vice president.[103]

Eisenhower recognized that in each of his illnesses "there was some gap that could have been significant—in which I was a disabled individual from the standpoint of carrying out the emergency duties pertaining to the office." After his heart attack he asked his attorney general to work on a constitutional amendment, but Congress was slow to act. After the stroke he was frightened about something "that might incapacitate you mentally and you wouldn't know it, and the people around you, wanting to protect you, would probably keep this away from the public." So on 5 February 1958 he wrote Nixon a letter naming him "the individual explicitly and exclusively responsible" to make the decision to take over in the event he ever became so disabled as to be unable to recognize it. His letter became the basis for similar arrangements by Presidents Kennedy and Johnson, and the inspiration for the Twenty-fifth Amendment, ratified in 1967.[104]

Apart from this single political development, the "small stroke" seemingly had no lasting effects. There were some occasional reminders when the president "flubbed" a particular word, as in a conversation in August 1958 when he was unable to say the word "flyswatter" and had to rephrase his sentence, or in the summer of 1959 when he mentioned to Mamie that the brain damage resulting from the vascular occlusion still bothered him considerably when he tried to verbalize his thoughts. As late as 1965 he would admit to a difficulty in uttering the words he chose. "Even today, occasionally," he wrote, "I reverse syllables in a long word and at times am compelled to speak slowly and cautiously if I am to enunciate correctly."[105]

Once the president returned to work, the press did not pursue the issue. "The stroke coverup was like the heart attack coverup and the ileitis coverup," one journalist charged later. "They were just little coverups. Who cared?" The American people did not care because they trusted Eisenhower more than they believed his occasional, and usually partisan, critics. And Ike consoled them with his humor. When he first met with the press after the stroke, he flashed his famous grin and remarked that the doctors had assured him that no damage had been done to whatever intellectual powers he had. In the people's mind, he was still a courageous man struggling to stay well in the service of his country.[106]

At his press conference on Leap Year Day announcing his decision to seek reelection, a reporter asked Eisenhower how he expected the health issue to be handled in the campaign. The president replied, "Well, I haven't given it any thought, but as for my part, I am going to try to be just as truthful as I can be. I believe this: I think even people who would classify themselves probably as my political enemies do believe I am honest. They may call me stupid, but I think they think I am honest."[107]

In fact, he was not "just as truthful" as he could have been. His policy throughout the campaign and for his remaining years in office was to prevent anyone from exploiting his health as a political issue. He was especially sensitive about the medical details of his daily life—the rapid pulse, skipped beats, elevated blood pressure, exhaustion, and, most of all, his occasional use of nitroglycerine—which he considered a strictly personal affair and nobody's business but his own. Above all, he considered such details unimportant within the larger truth as he saw it—that his health was good enough to enable him to do his job. He believed he owed that assurance to the American people, but nothing more.

However successful he was with the public, the president could not dispel his personal anxieties about his health. After the November illness he had to worry about occlusions in his brain as well as in his heart, knowing that either could take his life or, more likely than ever before, turn him into an invalid.

7

The Life Apart

❖ ❖ ❖ ❖ ❖ ❖ ❖ ❖ ❖ ❖ ❖ ❖ ❖ ❖ ❖

Much depends on the patient himself—on the life he has led—the life he is willing to lead. The ordinary high-pressure business or professional man may find relief, or even cure, in the simple process of slowing the engines, reducing the speed from the twenty-five knots an hour of a Lusitania *to the ten knots of a Bilbao tramp.*
   —William Osler, "The Lumleian Lectures on Angina Pectoris: Lecture III"

In human beings the heart is inseparable from the whole individual. If the whole individual is kept well, the broken heart can be left to the poets.
   —Helen Flanders Dunbar, Mind and Body: Psychosomatic Medicine

A little after 10:00 P.M. on election night 1956, Dwight Eisenhower arrived at his suite on the third floor of Washington's Sheraton Park Hotel. The mood was already buoyant and gregarious, as his friends and supporters sensed the verdict at the polls. He moved among them, down the corridor, into the small rooms, grinning, jesting, sharing sentiments, playing out the last, exhilarating moments of a long campaign. Shortly before midnight he slumped down on a hard bench beside his speechwriter, Emmet John Hughes, and for a moment reflected on a reality far away from victory or its celebration:

> Boy, I've got to sit down. I had my rest this afternoon, but, you know, the thing is for me to take it a bit easy so I *don't* have trouble. It's funny, you know, *emotions* are the things you got to watch out for. So all the doctors say. The worst is anger. . . . You notice I don't get *angry* any

more—like I used to? . . . Just don't *let* myself. Can't afford to. . . . And after anger, any great emotional strain or worry is bad. . . . Very curious. . . . But these *are* the things that do affect the heart. . . . Haven't had a twinge since the first one, but. . . . Just got to be careful, I guess.[1]

Hughes found the president "so softly reflective" that he felt the two of them were "isolated behind an invisible shield, locked inside a little bubble of a life apart." For an instant the barriers of position and power were down, and he came to know one of the "little recesses" of the man. "The world—just a few feet away—is counting votes. He is counting the beat of his pulse."[2]

As the president struggled throughout the second term with the troublesome problems of civil rights, balancing budgets, *Sputnik*, and recession at home, and with every threatening movement of communism abroad, he continued to worry about his health. Unbeknownst to the American people, the politicians, and even his friends, he went through a continuous and arduous ritual of preventive medicine. Dr. Snyder was on duty every day, and Mamie was on the alert day and night for the slightest sign of threat to his well-being. But the president himself was the most vigilant sentry. He strained to find every hint of danger in the beat of his heart; he sought to avoid any tensions that might elevate his blood pressure; he restricted his diet so as to manage his weight and cholesterol; he kept a watchful eye on his Coumadin count; he exercised to condition his muscles and reduce his stress; he studied his emotions in order to keep his temper in check; and sometimes, out of frustration with his doctors and familiarity with his disease, he became his own physician. At one and the same time he had to struggle with the momentous challenge of serving his country and also cope with the mundane demands of staying alive.

Eisenhower claimed to have run for a second term to achieve certain goals —a Republican victory, the reform of his party, prosperity without the stifling centralization and reckless spending of the New Deal, and peace in the world—but they remained for the most part elusive. He was not able to bring his party to the middle of the road, and by 1960 he had so little support among the Old Guard that he told Mrs. Whitman he was "disgusted" with their congressional leadership; he added: "I don't know why anyone should be a member of the Republican party." His political problems extended to Democrats as well, who screamed of "bomber gaps" and "missile gaps," complained about his golf, his vacations, and his part-time presidency, and rallied around the cry "to get the country moving again." He could not convince politicians to accept his apprehensions about the future, and sometimes it seemed as if he were standing virtually alone as an advocate of foreign aid, as a conservative on domestic appropriations, as a skeptic about defense spending, and as a crusader for peace.[3]

Year after year, developments the president could not have foreseen weighed heavily upon him. Civil rights simmered as an issue throughout 1957, exploded at Little Rock, and remained, as he put it, "troublesome beyond imagination." Even before that crisis had disappeared from the front pages, *Sputnik* sent shock waves across the body politic, with accusations that Eisenhower had lost the race for space and jeopardized the nation's security. Then came his stroke, attendant with rumors of an old man too tired and too sick to run the country. His popularity declined steadily; his approval rating fell from a high of 79 percent early in the year to 57 percent in December; three months later it reached the nadir for his entire presidency, 52 percent. In 1958 there was no surcease from his troubles—another battle over military spending, the "Eisenhower" recession (the worst since the Great Depression), an armed intervention in Lebanon, a crisis in the Taiwan Strait, an embarrassing uproar over the ethics of Sherman Adams, and the election, which was at one and the same time disastrous for the Republican party and disheartening for him.[4]

There was no hiding the extent of the president's disappointment during his final year in office. When the Russians shot down a U-2 plane on 1 May 1960, they shattered his dream of bringing peace to the world. "I would like to resign," he told Ann Whitman. Some time later, as if to search out the reasons for his depression, he told his science adviser, George Kistiakowsky, that he "saw nothing worthwhile left for him to do now until the end of his presidency." Howard Snyder noted in his diary in mid-July that "the president has lost his sparkle. His facial expressions at most times seem grim and determined. This, I think, is because his 'empire of glory' seems to be crumbling about his head, due to the press reaction to his management of the Cuban situation, the Russian PB-47 incident, the Congo situation, the slippage of our OAS program, etc." But the worst moment came in November, when the American people elected his young antagonist, repudiating, he thought, four years of his efforts and hopes.[5]

The president left office still disappointed. Despite all the trials and tribulations, he had not found many sources of satisfaction. He had stayed the course, however, by virtue of which he was able to relish one truly satisfying accomplishment—he avoided another heart attack, maintained good health, and thereby met his obligation to the American people. His achievement had an even deeper meaning. By fulfilling the prediction of his doctors about the likelihood of living for five years, he won a very personal victory. But in his mind it was no casual victory, registered statistically by the mere luck of the draw. He had to work for it during virtually every one of the 1,461 days of his second term.

During a weekend visit to Gettysburg in July 1956, Ellis Slater arose one morning at seven o'clock for an early walk, only to find Howard Snyder already out on the porch. The doctor's schedule inspired some kind words in the businessman's diary that evening. "These are long days for Howard, and have been ever since Ike's heart attack," he wrote. "He waits each night to check over the patient before he goes to bed—and then is around in the morning before he gets up. There is no more devoted a man alive than Howard who for a man of seventy-six is putting in strenuous and anxious weeks and months. During the next four and one-half years, even after he reached the age of eighty, Dr. Snyder continued tending to the health of his friend with care, caution, and extraordinary commitment.[6]

After the election of 1956, Snyder remained the choreographer of the president's health, but he presided over a noticeably different medical team. Paul Dudley White no longer had any responsibility, either official or unofficial; there was no need for his special competence, and no fear of letting him go. Henceforth his association was limited essentially to a friendly correspondence with his former patient. General Leonard Heaton became a major team player by virtue of his roles as surgeon general of the army in command of Walter Reed General Hospital, as the respected surgical expert on gastrointestinal problems (and the "personal surgeon" to the White House), and as an "old army" man whom the president liked and trusted. Tom Mattingly, still a favorite of Ike's (and after October 1957 a brigadier general as a direct result of the president's earlier intervention), remained as chief cardiologist at Walter Reed and the cardiologist of choice at the White House until his voluntary retirement from the Army Medical Corps at the end of August 1958. At that time he turned over his responsibilities to colleagues at Walter Reed, but from his new position at the

Washington Hospital Center he could still serve as a consultant on those few occasions when Snyder considered it necessary.[7]

Unlike the months at Fitzsimons and Gettysburg and the period after the ileitis operation, when Snyder had to concern himself with civilian consultants, the press, and the public, he now was free to establish his own program of care. But his challenge during the second term was greater, and far more threatening, than the first. Because of the heart attack and ileitis (and later the stroke), his patient was at risk, and so was he. Despite having come through the various crises looking like a hero, Synder knew he could expect very little sympathy if he were to make any kind of mistake. It was therefore imperative, for his benefit as well as his patient's, to ensure exceptional medical care. So he was scrupulously thorough. He arranged for Mattingly to make short visits to the White House or Gettysburg about every two weeks to take EKGs and blood specimens; he had the president enter Walter Reed General Hospital for annual physical examinations; and he was quick to talk by telephone with the specialists at Walter Reed when any kind of problem arose and, in several instances, to have them examine the patient at home.

Snyder worked very closely with Heaton, and the two of them were jealous of their prerogatives in managing the president's health, even with respect to cardiovascular matters. Mattingly, sensitive to their feelings, was careful not to intrude. He kept his examinations brief, usually less than half an hour, and businesslike, with no extraneous conversation and no personal advice. Despite his circumspect professionalism, incidents occurred to strain the relationship. In May 1957 the president suddenly turned to his cardiologist and asked if he thought he could fly to Denver to join his friends for golf at Cherry Hills. Mattingly answered with an emphatic "No," and the president seemed displeased. Then he said, "Tom, I will not go. You are the only one around here who has the guts to tell me something which you know I will not like but which you know is not good for me." These were not pleasant words to the two generals, who made it a point always to be present during the examinations, and Heaton later told Mattingly that he had been too emphatic. In any event, Ike did make an occasional visit to Denver in subsequent years, but he never played golf there and never went to his favorite fishing camp in the Rockies.[8]

Mattingly angered both Snyder and Heaton again in November 1957 when he reached back to the past and mentioned as a possible cause of the president's stroke an embolism from the "ventricular aneurysm"—a possible complication the two generals had never acknowledged, had banned from the official medical records, and had told the cardiologist to "forget." A month later, concerned about a further embolization, Mattingly expressed a minority opinion (together with Colonel Pruitt) against the president's trip to Paris for a NATO conference. When Snyder and Heaton issued a press release falsely stating his concurrence with the trip, he decided that he was no longer a member of their team and that it was time for him to retire.[9]

Although relations sometimes were strained, Snyder had to work closely with Mattingly on the one medical treatment that seemed likely to protect against another heart attack—the administration of long-term anticoagulation therapy. Mattingly wanted to use Coumadin to lower the coagulation time to about 50 percent of normal, fearful as he was that if the blood were too thick, a lethal clot might break loose from the aneurysm which he continued to believe was on the wall of the heart. Snyder was skeptical about any substantial lowering of the coagulation time, mindful as he was that if the blood were too thin, some gastrointestinal problem or unforeseen accident could cause the president to bleed to death.[10]

The Walter Reed staff agreed to Mattingly's regimen and left it to Snyder to maintain the daily therapy. But in November 1957, at the time of the "small stroke," it appeared that Synder had been remiss in his day-to-day care because the prothrombin time was 80 percent. Mattingly argued strongly to his colleagues, including the neurologists, for a more precise administration of the anticoagulant, which then held the promise of protecting against further strokes as well as heart attacks. Thereafter Snyder was more careful and tried to achieve Mattingly's ideal therapeutic level of 50 percent, but his administration of the drug remained erratic, susceptible to his judgment and sometimes even to the whims of the patient.[11]

Ike was knowledgeable about the use of Coumadin, but he sometimes worried when he found a pink stain in the mucous when he coughed, or when he detected an unusual amount of bleeding after brushing his teeth or shaving. He believed the doctors were too casual about the side effects, and on occasion he would refuse to take the full dosage or try to convince Snyder to cut back for a day or two. In order to mollify him, Snyder would sometimes tell him his prothrombin time was actually higher than it was. But Ike's concern persisted, as the doctor noted in his diary in June 1959:

> The president spoke to me about the bleeding of his ear last night and the fact that he knew "God damn well" his blood was thin by the fact

that he was getting frequent episodes of bleeding during shaving in the morning. I told him that Leonard Heaton, Francis Pruitt, and I believed in keeping his coagulation time at approximately 40, and that he was very little below that. He said he thought we wanted it at 50. I then made the comment that during this period of exceeding stress, in order to prevent possible cerebral arterial occlusions, we all agreed we should keep it below 50. He said, "Doesn't this render me liable to hemorrhages such as General Marshall has?" I said no, that he wasn't in the pipe stem artery condition of General Marshall; that what we were worried about was a vascular spasm with occlusion which might result if his coagulation time was too short.[12]

The president also sparred with the doctor over the medications he was taking in addition to Coumadin. At a conference at the beginning of the second term, Snyder and the Walter Reed doctors decided that every day their patient should also take two doses of Metamucil, one teaspoonful of liquid vitamin mixture, and one capsule of vitamin B_{12} and folic acid. But Snyder was quick to add to the list, and by the end of 1960 his patient was taking a thyroid hormone, a multivitamin, vitamin E, a tablet to aid digestion (twice a day), and a steroid (three times a day). The president was constantly griping about all his medication, and after one "hell of a night" in 1958, he jumped all over Snyder. "You see, Howard, I did not lose anything with your God damn pill," he said. "I don't see why you keep experimenting with me and give me medicine all the time. The urine examinations I have at Walter Reed indicate there is nothing wrong with my urinary tract, so why do you give me a pill at night?" When the doctor explained his intent to determine whether there was any buildup of liquid storage in his body, Ike retorted, "Why don't the physical examinations determine this fact so you don't have to give me medicine?" And sometimes the president stubbornly tended to health affairs himself. He regulated his use of oxygen, often taking it twice a day because he thought it was responsible for keeping his blood pressure and pulse in good order; and he took nitroglycerine tablets whenever he became sensitive to some feeling in the chest.[13]

Despite the genial give-and-take reflected in Snyder's daily management, the president—apart from the small stroke—was by any measurement exceptionally healthy. The official records present a surprisingly favorable picture of his gastrointestinal health. During the five years following the emergency of 1956, he did not go to the hospital for the treatment of any illness or for any complication of the ileitis or the surgery. On only one occasion—after he ate a hearty meal of roast goose and blueberry pie—did Snyder consider it necessary to seek outside advice or assistance. The records do not tell the full story, however, because the doctor did have to deal with recurring and troublesome "tummy" problems in which the predominant symptoms were of two types. One, marked by intestinal hyperactivity with some crampy pain, was usually associated with nervous tension or stress. The other, accompanied by abdominal pain and obvious abdominal gaseous distention, seemed to occur under a variety of conditions such as hurried meals, tension, or fatigue.[14]

Most happily, Eisenhower's cardiovascular status remained virtually unchanged during his entire second term. At no time did he mention chest pain such as might suggest the presence of angina pectoris. And at no time during all of the repeated examinations did the consulting cardiologists or internists find evidence or symptoms of congestive heart failure, of murmurs, gallops, or other abnormal auscultatory findings, or of any major arrhythmia or conduction abnormality, although there were occasional premature ventricular contractions (skipped beats). The numerous twelve-lead EKGs gave a record of marked stability of the abnormalities from the heart attack and indicated no transient myocardial ischemia or new area of infarction; and the radiological studies showed no increase in the size of the heart. Indeed, the final evaluation in December 1960 showed results essentially the same as those in 1956, and Dr. Mattingly, reviewing all of the evidence years later, found "little to indicate that his performance of a second term in the presidency had, in any manner, provided additional damage to or a progression of the coronary heart disease beyond that which would have been expected under the most ideal situations."[15]

Given Eisenhower's age and his background of cardiovascular and gastrointestinal problems, his official medical history displays a dispassionate record of success. He was convinced he was healthy because he had strengthened his resolve to hold to a program of preventive medicine, even though the experts were not always sure as to what he could do.

Throughout the 1950s a revolution was taking place in the cultural perception of coronary disease. As one expression of the change, the dread disease was much less dreadful, as the sense of terror so rife in previous decades gave way to confidence about the future. Unlike cancer, the other great scourge of the time, which was still so overwhelmingly about the likelihood of death, heart disease was now about the possibility of life. Unlike cancer, too, where only the doctor could enter the field of battle, here the victims could participate in their own recovery and even hope to stem the progression of their disease.

The problem was that most Americans, even the educated elite, were ignorant about coronary heart disease. More to the point, most *physicians* in America felt insecure about their knowledge, and the preventive measures they suggested to their patients seemed ill defined and problematic. Both doctors and patients had good reason to be confused. Despite the high expectations at the beginning of the decade and the rapid escalation in funding for research, medical scientists in the 1950s did not achieve any startling breakthroughs in their search for a cure for heart disease.

It was understandable that research experts could not find a magic bullet for coronary disease, but it was frustrating when they were not able to provide a definitive answer with regard to even one of its alleged causes. Newspapers and magazines were filled with dozens of scientific reports on the possible effects of smoking, diet, cholesterol, triglycerides, fats, exercise, and stress, but readers were left with tentative results, cautious suggestions, promising evidence, and endless controversy. There was no official voice to guide the layman; the conservative AMA was not ready to take a stand on any of the relevant causal factors, and even the American Heart Association was unable to make up its mind. The AHA was torn between those who wanted to wait for absolute scientific proof, a position usually favored by the leadership, and those who felt a responsibility to inform the public of the most up-to-date evidence, a position usually inspired by the affiliate associations and the medical community. The association dithered with regard to smoking and diet until 1960, when it finally issued committee reports linking both to coronary disease—along with disclaimers that its reports were not official policy and required more research.[16]

The only serious and substantial attempt to educate the public about current research came from the indefatigable health crusader Mary Lasker, through the auspices of her National Health Education Committee. In 1957 she induced four sterling Harvard experts—Paul White, Samuel Levine, Howard Sprague, and Frederick Stare—to issue a statement, "Factors which predispose YOU to arteriosclerosis, heart attack and stroke," citing heredity, overweight, elevated blood cholesterol level, elevated blood pressure, and excessive cigarette smoking. Early in 1959 four other distinguished cardiologists—Louis Katz, Irvine Page, Jeremiah Stamler, and Irving Wright—joined the group to present a similar "statement for guidance," supported with authoritative citations from twenty-eight recent studies, designed to "prolong the life for many at this time":

> If you have a strong hereditary background regarding arteriosclerosis of the heart and brain, it is most important that you minimize the effect of the other factors. You are "stuck" with your heredity, but you can influence the other factors, and hence lessen your chances of being a victim of arteriosclerosis. Consult your doctor, and if desirable, try to reduce to your proper weight, try to reduce your blood pressure, your blood cholesterol level, and your smoking.
>
> Hard work itself is often wrongly blamed for this disease. In fact, regular, moderate, physical activity appears to lessen the hazards of arteriosclerosis.[17]

The eight experts, five of whom the press identified as former presidents of the AHA, had presented the public with the first listing of what later would become widely known as "risk factors." In doing so they created a stir within the leadership of the AHA, which felt they were taking positions at odds with those of the organization. Even those who supported the statement, including the famous epidemiologist Ancel Keys, had their worries. "The main question," he pointed out, "is what are the physicians supposed to do when almost all of the male population of the U.S. come clamoring at their doors for advice?" He suspected that prescriptions for tranquilizers, diuretics, and antihypertensive drugs would make a bonanza for the drug houses.[18]

Dwight Eisenhower was alert to most of the controversy and confusion, certainly to that exhibited in the newspapers, which he read devotedly. But for several reasons he was able to tune out the discordant voices and fears. For one, he was far ahead of the field; he already had settled upon his version of risk factors when he determined to follow the list of directives his doctors had given him in January 1956. For another, his doctors never wavered in their recommendations; Dr. White was absolute in his commitment to a low-fat, low-cholesterol diet, accompanied by exercise; Dr. Snyder was equally convinced of the need to control emotions. And, too, the president had a much stronger motivation than the general public to follow a course of action because he felt a deep sense of responsibility to prevent another disabling illness. Like a poker player intent on improving his odds, he was willing to try anything that might help. What did he have to lose?

As a result, he was aggressive in pursuit of his regimen, sometimes even more so than Dr. Snyder. His assertiveness was particularly evident concerning his diet. In a sense, he was able to build upon past experience. He had spent a lifetime tending to his weight, making sure it conformed to his athletic image, and he had put into place a low-fat diet as early as the late 1940s in order to ease his stomach problems. After the heart attack Dr. White turned Eisenhower's predispositions into a prescription. Even though the Bostonian was uncertain about the scientific evidence, he decided it was prudent for any "coronary" to cut back on his intake of cholesterol and fat. According to General Heaton, White "really impressed upon him the necessity of keeping an eye on his cholesterol and old Ike was very conscious of cholesterol." He "fixed" that in the president's mind, the general added, and it was an "obsession" with him: "'What is my blood cholesterol, Leonard?' after every check. And he held her way down."

Dr. Snyder worked diligently to keep the fat content of his patient's diet below 25 percent of total calories, but he was less concerned about keeping the cholesterol "way down," and with reason. In the eight readings taken between 1946 and September 1955, Eisenhower's cholesterol had averaged only 202.5, scarcely high enough to be considered a causal factor in the heart attack. Nonetheless, the doctor was conscientious about monitoring cholesterol level. Prior to the attack he arranged for only routine cholesterol readings, usually one per year, and never more than two. After the coronary, he obtained an average of ten readings each year.[19]

Ike wanted to lower his cholesterol not because he could rationally blame it for his problem but because it was one of the few things he could do to try to save his life. He had already stopped smoking; he already exercised; he was not overweight; and he did not have high blood pressure. And the only method of dealing with his cholesterol was through diet, because the scientists were no longer confident about producing an appropriate drug. During the first two years of his second term, he was very pleased with his cholesterol level—an average in the 180s—and he was able to maintain it by continuing his low-fat diet and by watching his weight.

Eisenhower's primary focus in these early years was on his weight. Overall during his second term he was able to keep it between 169 and 180 pounds, with an average of 172. But whenever it reached the higher 170s he would take corrective action. His diligence led to disagreement with Dr. Snyder and became the pretext for frequent lectures about his health. When Snyder learned in the summer of 1958 that for some time past Ike had dispensed with a steak for breakfast and was eating only fruit (papaya or melon), melba toast, and decaffeinated coffee, he told him several times it was not a satisfactory breakfast for a man who did not have lunch until 1:30 or 2:00 P.M. and who, in the meantime, was exposed to arduous hours of mental exercise. Snyder concluded:

> The president, however, is so hypnotized by his conviction that he must maintain a weight standard that it is very difficult for me to persuade him that this is a wrong habit in eating. I tell him his blood sugar is so low by 1030 hours that he becomes irritable and cannot satisfactorily meet the requirements of his mornings' obligations. Then, too, he may combine with this a meager lunch and then try to play golf in the afternoon. On occasion, when his game is bad and his muscular reflexes slow I remind him that in my opinion this is due to the fact that he insists on maintaining his weight average at the expense of proper eating habits.[20]

For the most part Ike remained disciplined and stubborn about his diet. Early in November 1958, when his weight hit 176, he began fretting and told Moaney to give him nothing but fruit for breakfast, because even with oatmeal and skim milk he was carrying too much weight. A week later he was still fussing, after having eaten nothing but five prunes for breakfast and a light lunch. "He does not understand," Snyder pondered, "and it is difficult for me to understand why he remains at this weight level inasmuch as he has played golf the last three afternoons, and did a good deal physically on the trip West over the weekend, including going out to shoot ducks on an evening and the following morning." The president was certain that he was gaining weight because of too much food, and several days later he refused to eat breakfast.[21]

On 4 March 1959, Eisenhower's relatively contented attitude changed dramatically. His morning issues of the New York newspapers carried articles about the diet of the "Anti-Coronary Heart Club," a group of seventy-nine middle-aged men who had lowered their cholesterol levels significantly in a period of six months. Dr. Norman Joliffe, director of the Bureau of Nutrition of the New York City Board of Health, released the preliminary findings and instructions for the low-cholesterol diet—high-grade protein with each meal, several servings of fish each week, an ounce of corn oil each day, and a complete ban on butter, margarine, lard, and cream. Ike discussed the articles enthusiastically with Snyder, and thereafter became a fanatic about his cholesterol level. Dr. Heaton quipped to Dr. Michael Debakey that Eisenhower worried more about his cholesterol than about his golf score.[22]

The following month initiated a period during which fifteen out of sixteen cholesterol readings were above 200, and the president worried. And he acted. When Ellis Slater had breakfast with him—wheat cakes and sausage with melted butter—he noticed that the president would not use butter because of his rising cholesterol, so he did not enjoy the meal. He sacrificed even when he cooked for others. At Augusta he used a butter that was low in cholesterol, and he went so far as to cut the fat out of the stewing chickens he prepared. By the end of the year he had developed a theory that when he gained weight, the additional fat in his body somehow increased the cholesterol in his bloodstream. His sense of a relationship between weight, fat intake, and cholesterol levels was incredibly sophisticated, much more akin to the understanding of experts thirty years later, and far ahead of that of his own doctors.[23]

On 20 February 1960, after successive readings of 200, 200, and 214, the president complained to Snyder. Dissatisfied with "the gradually ascending scale in cholesterol," he commented that "the one difference in his physical characteristics that he could note was that he is having a hell of a time losing weight; that a diet on which he had formerly been able to lose when he wanted to no longer served that purpose." Snyder noted cynically to himself that he "probably had a good dinner with his bridge gang last night," but he took seriously Ike's desire over the next two months to lose seven pounds. He resented the repercussions, however. Early in April he noted, "He is in the same irascible mood because of his faulty manner of eating. He eats nothing for breakfast, nothing for lunch, and therefore is irritable during the noon hour. The butler, Charles, and I do not seem to be able to do anything about this. The president does this to maintain his weight, and comes in and gives us hell at noon."[24]

The spring of 1960 was a difficult time because Eisenhower and Snyder continued to argue about weight, as the doctor noted in his diary on 22 April:

I asked him what his weight was when he came back from Augusta, and he said 177. I said that was ideal for this time and purpose, and he said no, that's too much. I countered that his health in the last few months of his presidency was of more importance than his weight for these few months, and that even though he took on more poundage, he should maintain a good sugar level in his blood during his hard-working hours, which I was sure was not the case with the minimal breakfasts and luncheons that he has eaten for the past several months. John was there, and I asked him to help me persuade the president to eat adequate breakfasts and lunch while he is so busy as the chief executive of the United States, especially during these last critical months. I told the president he could adjust his weight very easily when he concluded his term of office. He shook his head and did not seem to agree with me. When he asked how, I said, "I am an old doctor, Mr. President, and I think you should listen to a wise counsel."[25]

The following morning, when Snyder arrived to take a blood pressure reading, Ike discussed with him at length what he thought to be the relationship between weight and blood cholesterol. He weighed 179 and felt that he had to lose at least 7 pounds. Snyder took exception and advised against his curtailing his breakfasts. The president ignored his "wise counsel" and continued to diet, and to worry. "He was fussing like the devil about cholesterol," Snyder noted on 28 April. "I told him it was 217 on yesterday's CBC (actually it was 223). He has eaten only one egg in the last four weeks; only one piece of cheese. For breakfast he has skim milk, fruit, and Sanka. Lunch is practically without cholesterol, unless it would be a piece of cold meat occasionally. He has no fried foods. His foods are cooked in Emdee or soybean oil. His bread is the Vita-Pro Health Bread." The controversy subsided in May, when the president's cholesterol dropped below 200, where it remained until November. But even with the improved readings, he remained anxious. By August he was complaining again that whenever his weight was above 172, his cholesterol would go up. In the last reading before he left the White House, it went up again, and Snyder decided to play it down in a different way. "I told him that the cholesterol was 209," he recorded, "when it actually was 259. The real figure would have shocked him."[26]

In thirty-nine tests during his second term, the president's cholesterol ranged from 174 to 259, with an average of 197. But there was no consensus at the time about what it should be. "What is elevated cholesterol?" asked Dr. Keys. "From our epidemiological studies we would estimate that anything over 220 mg.% for a man of forty carries a considerably increased coronary risk. But this figure includes 90 percent of the forty-year olds in our part of the world." Whether "normal" was 220 or the more widely accepted 240, Ike was below it, in no small part because of his obsession with his diet. Being resolute placed him among a tiny minority of his contemporaries, for as a preventive medicine expert complained as late as 1991, Americans "are typically impervious to even the most obvious need for reforming our ways," and believe that "agents and agencies such as physicians, public health officials, and clinics are the way to protect one's health."[27]

Eisenhower also challenged the customary approach to exercise. At the beginning of the 1950s, cardiologists were generally opposed to such vigorous exercise as running upstairs, pushing a stalled automobile, and, most symbolically, shoveling snow, suspecting such activities as precipitating events for a heart attack. They prohibited these activities for their "coronaries" and even advised their patients against such mild exercise as sexual intercourse. In 1953 a British doctor, J. N. Morris, turned the tables by proposing that exercise might actually protect against heart disease. In his highly acclaimed statistical study of twenty-five thousand drivers and conductors of double-decked buses in London, he found that the former, who sat at the wheel all day, had a greater frequency and severity of disease than the latter, who walked back and forth and climbed stairs.[28]

The British study raised as many questions as it answered, and most physicians continued to recommend against strenuous exercise, especially for those over forty. Even an exercise enthusiast like Paul White, who believed Americans were "soft" because of "lazy ways" and "push-button devices," and who favored an hour of exercise a day, was cautious when it came to his patients. In the summer of 1956 he stated publicly that bicycling on safe paths should be good for the health of middle-aged Americans, but when he learned that someone had sent Eisenhower a bicycle, he quickly advised the president to "please don't think for a minute that I want to get you to use one. Your golf, swimming, and fishing are quite enough exercise for you." Ike was amenable to this particular restriction, but he would not hold back at all when it came to indulging his love of golf.[29]

On a spring day in 1959, John Moaney collected more than five hundred golf balls from assorted storage places in the White House and placed them in Eisenhower's dressing room. The president was surprised that so many had been spread around the house and kept for so long. Indeed, he had received many of them immediately after his heart attack, and they still bore the imprint "GET WELL IKE." He spent fifteen minutes looking over the accumulation—"pawed them over like a miser counting his gold"—and then took several dozen to put in his practice kit. For many years golf had been his addiction, setting forth its prospect for recreation and joy; now it was his doctor's prescription, holding forth a promise of "stay well, Ike."[30]

Eisenhower believed in exercise, and in his mind his heart attack had endowed his golf game with even greater import. It could help control his weight. It was a measure of his rehabilitation, for as long as he could swing the clubs he could maintain his sense of well-being. And it served, in a perverse way, as his consolation prize, a way to repay himself for the sacrifice he believed he was making. So he sought out the game more avidly than ever before. During his first three years in office he teed off 64, 85, and 61 times, respectively. During 1956, despite his health problems, he played 72 times. In his second term, according to Snyder's records, he played even more often; he teed off a total of 430 times, 97 in 1957, 95 in 1958, 122 in 1959, and 116 in 1960—for more than a 50 percent increase. He also practiced on 363 occasions, which meant that he either played or practiced more than once every other day.[31]

Snyder considered golf "a mental and physical tonic" for the president: "It is good for his nerves and for his muscle tone, and it takes his mind off the scores of anxieties that confront him daily." Golf did provide relaxation through its camaraderie or, as a subsequent generation would call it, male bonding. Ellis Slater described the atmosphere at the Augusta National Golf Club, where there "was a great deal of banter and kidding about not minding constructive critics. When the boss made a particularly good shot, we blew our little cart horns." He judged that it was "the levity, the crabbing at each other, the apparent disgust at a partner's poor play or shot that brings the laugh that makes for fun."[32]

For various reasons, however, the game also could serve as an irritant. The president would be disappointed if the weather was bad. He would become upset if he had to play with someone other than his coterie of friends, as when he had to accede to a demand by his publisher, Jim Black, to play with Bob Hope. Above all, he would become extremely frustrated if he did not play well. "It's unfortunate that bad shots annoy him so,"

Slater commented. "Most of us just slough it off, swear a little and recognize these poor shots are really part of our regular game. But in his case I guess he had come to look for something close to perfection, and when it isn't there and he is involved, he blames himself. When I talk to Howard Snyder about it, he in part agrees that this crabbing about his games isn't the best form of relaxation and then goes on to say that it's a way for him to blow off steam, which has to find its way out. Better, in fact, to blow it off here than somewhere else."[33]

Snyder had to use all of his wiles when his patient was perturbed. On one occasion, when Ike was disconsolate because he shot a 92, the doctor decided it was better not to fraternize with him at all. On another he tried to reason with him, pointing out that he played better golf than many men his junior, and that he should not take it so seriously. The president replied that "he wouldn't mind if he were not so God damn stupid at the game at times." Snyder mollified him by insisting that it was overwork and not stupidity that took the snap out of his wrists. For the most part the doctor tried to play the role of psychologist and ease the president's stress with friendly joshing. During one game when he was walking the course with Ike, he praised him: "My God, two pars and a birdie on the first three holes!" The president retorted, "Keep your God damn mouth shut, Howard." When Eisenhower made a bum drive and ended with a double bogey on the next hole, he spoke loudly to his caddie, "Too God damn bad you have to have people around who shoot off their mouths." The doctor was pleased. "This of course was a safety valve for this disappointment for playing a bad fourth hole after three perfect ones," he deduced, "and I think it was a good safety valve; otherwise he would have bottled up his anger. He likes to find some excuse for the things he does not do well."[34]

But Snyder continued to worry because sometimes Ike "got so damned mad at golf that I think he built up an artificial blood pressure." The game could create more frustration than it released, as on a spring morning at Augusta in 1959. "The president's golf was reasonably good on the first nine," Snyder recorded, "but the worst I have ever seen on the second nine. The president was so mad that on the seventeenth green when he made a bad explosion shot out of the trap and I yelled, 'Fine shot!' he got so mad he yelled, 'Fine shot, hell, you son of a bitch,' and threw his wedge at me. The staff of the club wrapped itself around my shins and the heavy iron wedge missed me; otherwise, I would have had a fractured leg. He apologized perfunctorily and said, 'Oh, pardon me.'"[35]

It is doubtful that the exercise Eisenhower obtained through golf deterred the progression of his coronary disease. Even at its most demanding it was not aerobic exercise, the kind a later generation of experts would determine to be essential to cardiovascular health. The game may have contributed to his general sense about feeling well, and it may have served at times as an outlet for pent-up frustrations. Paradoxically, it had its greatest effect on Snyder in strengthening his belief that by far the most important preventive measure he could undertake was to soothe the president's emotions. He was afraid the violent outbursts of temper on the golf course, however rare, might bring on another heart attack, or, after November 1957, might cause another stroke.

Snyder's attention to Eisenhower's emotional health was especially timely because during Ike's second term there was a greater exploration than ever before of the relationship between behavior and coronary disease. The interest was intense enough to prompt the AHA to sponsor a panel in October 1958 to discuss the role of emotions. Dr. Henry Russek of Staten Island reported that in a comparative study he had found the "young coronary patient" commonly possessed "an ambitious driving nature" and often "sets Herculean tasks for himself exceeding his normal capacity and tempo." Dr. Stewart Wolf of the University of Oklahoma Medical Center compared the "coronary-prone individual" to the mythological King Sisyphus, whom the gods had condemned to pass his time in Hades pushing a large rock up a steep hill without ever quite being able to get it to the top. "Just as the alcoholic meets a challenge by taking a drink and the gambler by taking a chance," he argued, "so the coronary-prone person meets it by putting out extra effort." The person with a "Sisyphus complex" could never relax, and even though he was always seeking new worlds to conquer, he could not achieve satisfaction.[36]

Another stimulating report at the conference—but one that was greeted by the audience with utter silence—was that of Drs. Ray Rosenman and Meyer Friedman of San Francisco, who gave a preview of what they would name some years later the "type A personality." Generalizing from impressions gained through a structured interview, they identified a constellation of behavioral characteristics they believed made a person coronary-prone, including impatience, a chronic sense of time urgency, ambition, competitiveness, and sustained aggression. Unlike the practitioners of psychosomatic medicine so popular right after World War II, Rosenman and Friedman did not attempt to identify traits that led to neurotic conflicts and thence to illness. They were less concerned with motivation than with the overt, observable behavior of individuals who were engaged in a persistent struggle to complete an unending number of poorly defined tasks in the shortest time possible.[37]

Snyder and Eisenhower could not have missed the behavioral similarities between the various coronary-prone types described in the press and the president of the United States. The doctor therefore approached with extreme gravity the matter of his personal relationship to his patient. "To arouse the president's anger would seem like committing murder to me," he wrote, and he made it a rule never to take exception to anything Eisenhower said lest he rouse him unnecessarily. He also impressed upon members of the staff and the cabinet—successfully—the need to keep their leader calm. As speechwriter Bryce Harlow said of his boss, "He was still under the doctor's orders to keep cabinet meetings absolutely quiet, so he'd go to meetings with agendas so watered down it was ridiculous. You couldn't so much as hiccup because everybody said you shouldn't upset the president."[38]

The "boss" became a willing participant in the cooperative venture to control his emotions, and his success in managing his temper was most apparent in the fact that there were few, if any, explosions of the magnitude of those during his first term. He was not able to control his anger completely, as George Kistiakowsky, his special assistant for science and technology, discovered while working with him in 1959 and 1960. He became "very angry" about a State Department leak; he "grew heated" about atmospheric tests; he "was intensely angry and just managed to control himself" in a meeting with Khrushchev at Camp David; he was "white with anger" at an "inexcusable" indiscretion by General Maxwell Taylor; and he "lost his temper" at a National Security Council meeting.[39]

Snyder recognized that despite all of his and the staff's efforts, the president sometimes simply had terrible days. He remarked in his diary about one such "blue Monday" in the summer of 1958 when Ike attended a legislative leaders meeting at 8:30 A.M. and "snapped someone's head off"; then returned to the mansion at noon and "batted off Mamie's head in the lower hall"; then went upstairs and "blew off" at Snyder, complaining that he did not have a minute to do anything. He was in a "vile" and "frightful" humor, and he jumped into bed with a scowl. Often he became angry over the "little things," as in early 1958 when he worked himself "into a storm" because John arrived at Gettysburg twenty minutes later than expected. He was so agitated because of the delay that Mamie asked the doctor to go to the second floor and be with him, an invitation the doctor declined. Though more controlled, the anger could appear at the bridge table as well. "He will jump all over a partner for a bad play," Ellis Slater bemoaned, "or even for missing an easy trick—not because the loss itself is important but because the player could have done better."[40]

There seemed to be no way that Snyder could control all of the potential irritants because the president could become incensed even about simple household matters, as he did over an incident early in 1960. Ordinarily the butler, Charles, placed a shaker of vegetable salt and one of regular salt on Eisenhower's tray, but Snyder suggested removing the regular salt in order to learn his wishes. Ike asked for the shaker of regular salt, which was missing, and told the butler to return both shakers the next time. Charles forgot. "When the tray was served without a shaker of regular salt," Snyder recorded, "the president went into a rage. He called me on the telephone, and with much profanity wanted to know what the hell I was doing. We had a very short telephone conversation and that was the end of it." The next morning, however, Mamie mentioned to Snyder that she had thought her husband was going to have a stroke during their conversation the previous evening. The doctor then worried because his failure to check the small details had caused his patient's irritation.[41]

For the most part, nonetheless, Snyder was pleased with his venture in preventive psychotherapy, and later developments show that he should have been. His commonsense conviction about the relationship between emotions and health found sophisticated support during the 1960s, as more and more experts came to recognize the role of psychosocial and behavioral factors in the etiology of coronary disease. They especially studied the type A personality, described by then as a behavioral syndrome or style of living "characterized by *extremes* of competitiveness, striving for achievement, aggressiveness (sometimes stringently repressed), haste, impatience, restlessness, hyperalertness, explosiveness of speech, tenseness of facial musculature and feelings of being under the pressure of time and under the challenge of responsibility." By 1978 a panel meeting under the auspices of the National Heart, Lung and Blood Institute added the type A behavior pattern to its list of "risk factors" for coronary disease, and scientists in the 1980s worked to refine their findings by determining the truly toxic components of the global pattern. They found suppressed anger, hostility, and cynicism (the latter defined as a belief that others are generally mean, selfish, and undependable) to be the fundamental characteristics that could act over a life span to produce pathogenic changes in myocardial tissue, and thus contribute to coronary disease.[42]

The research developments in the 1980s led to the development of "anger management strategies" to help patients cope with their emotions. Had Dr. Snyder been alive to study them, he might well have smiled at the suggestions for a conscious monitoring of a patient's reactions and for positive feedback to help him understand them, or for the need to alter his environment and to change his perception of it, or for the preference for "anger-out" over "anger-in." He had tried these and many other strategies on Eisenhower during the second term, and with success. Bryce Harlow described as "marvelous" the way Ike was able to control his anger after the heart attack, and Ann Whitman recorded in 1960 that since the summit meeting, her boss had been "almost without exception in a bad humor— with me, that is—but on the surface has managed to hold his temper and control emotions far better than I thought even he could."[43]

Snyder had no doubts that his program of secondary prevention had been worthwhile, and on 3 October 1960, the day before Eisenhower would pass Andrew Jackson to become the oldest man in history to serve as president, he gave his final, exclusive interview to the journal that had served him so well, *U.S. News and World Report*. In "Ike's Health Secrets: Six Rules for Long Life," he explained how a man nearly seventy years old could enjoy "health success" in the "world's toughest job." To some extent the old doctor was engaging in some well-deserved self-congratulation, but he also was quick to define the president's remarkable self-discipline as the key to his excellent health. He had faithfully held to the rules— proper diet, avoidance of excessive fatigue, plenty of rest, lots of moderate exercise, frequent physical examinations, and a controlled temper.[44]

Eisenhower's virtually unblemished official medical record during the second term owed much to Snyder's management of the traditional medical care and his attention to his six "rules." But together they did not begin to describe the depth of the doctor's commitment—and concern.

There was another health history that took place apart from the examinations and consultations of the specialists at Walter Reed and apart from the program of preventive medicine, both of which aimed at diagnosing, treating, and controlling a specific disease. The other history centered around the efforts to understand and cope with the experience of chronic illness, as expressed in the habits and rituals of daily life. It was family history, so to speak, lived out in the fears of the president, the worries of his wife, and the reassuring counsel of Dr. Snyder. It was a matter of mind more than body, of speculation as much as science, of emotions along with knowledge, and it touched at times upon obsession and desperation.

This private history revolved around Howard Snyder, who became more than ever before a full-time monitor of facts and feelings. His role was to learn as much as possible about anything and everything that might adversely affect his patient. His first approach was to collect a mass of physical data, in the hope that measurements might foretell potential dangers. In addition to the biweekly EKGs and blood tests by the staff at Walter Reed, which measured primarily prothrombin time and cholesterol, Snyder took the president's blood pressure and pulse nearly every day, usually in the morning or upon his return to his quarters around noon, and sometimes several times a day. In accordance with his belief that anxieties could affect health, Snyder was equally intent upon learning when the president was tired, upset, frustrated, angry, or fearful. In a daily record entitled "progress reports," which he had begun keeping immediately after the heart attack, he made notes not only of the vital statistics but also of particular meetings, events, conversations, and, whenever possible, the president's reaction to them.

The doctor's daily quest for evidence turned him into a detective searching for the slightest hint of anything suspicious. His most obvious source of information was the president, and he quizzed him regularly. But Snyder had to be discreet with his interrogations, lest he do more harm than good. "It would be wrong for me to repeatedly question him about headaches, numbness, or tingling in an extremity. I am sure it would make him apprehensive, and this would increase, rather than delay, the changes about which I am apprehensive."[45]

Even when Snyder asked, he was not sure he would get full cooperation. On one occasion, following an early morning EKG, Ike complained of a pain in the left side of his chest and revealed that he had taken nitroglycerine the night before, which had worried Mamie. Mamie told Snyder Ike also had taken one several days earlier because of this pain in his chest. The doctor tried to determine whether the nitroglycerine had helped the pain, which would indicate angina; when he learned that it had not, he was relieved but not pleased. "The president had never apprised me before the examination this morning of his having pains in his left chest," he noted. "When he came through with that information this morning, he indicated that he had been having the pain for several days and had not mentioned it. This is typical of the president."[46]

Snyder's need for information inspired him to listen carefully to others around the president. One spring morning Mamie informed him that when she had mentioned to Ike that she had been suffering from a headache for several days he retorted, "That's nothing. I have also had a headache for the last several days." Snyder was immediately apprehensive regarding changes in the cerebral vascular supply. So he quickly went on a search for information, hoping first to learn something from John Moaney. He tried to stimulate the valet's sense of responsibility with talk about the two of them being a team in caring for the president's health. He failed, not being able to overcome Moaney's loyal silence. That night he worried. "About 0200 hrs. this morning, while I was lying awake," he wrote, "I was reflecting upon measures to ensure me that I would not miss any indications of ill health on the part of the president. I had determined to call Ann Whitman to ask her whether she had noted any changes in the president's personality over the past several weeks, whether he had ever complained to her of any headaches, or whether he had ever mentioned numbness or tingling in an arm or leg." The next morning he checked again with Moaney, who agreed to be forthcoming only insofar as the president complained of numbness or tingling in his extremities.[47]

The doctor garnered occasional bits of information from Moaney or from John Eisenhower, but Mrs. Eisenhower became his one very willing ally. Mamie had spent her adult life trying to serve her husband, accepting his success as her "career." As she explained, "I never pretended to be anything but Ike's wife," and she rarely deviated from her subservient role. "She did, in short, all that Eisenhower wanted a wife to do, and more," his biographer concluded. "If her share in his life was limited, it was nonetheless satisfying, rewarding, and giving." One of the things she tried to give was psychological support, believing that a "man has to be encouraged. I think I told Ike every day how good I thought he was. Your ego has to be fed." After the heart attack, however, there was much more than ego involved; she had to look after her loved one's life, and she perceived of her function as that described in the February 1956 issue of *Mademoiselle:* "The romantic man of the old-fashioned novels laid his heart at his lady's feet. Today he gives it into her keeping."[48]

In order to protect her husband she became obsessively alert to every conceivable manifestation of his illnesses. "Mamie is constantly worried over every little condition of the president," Ellis Slater deduced from his weekends at Gettysburg, "things that would be only mildly alarming to the average wife." The businessman was on the mark. Mamie worried when Ike had a headache, when he appeared tense, restless, or depressed, when he ate too much or too fast, when he went to bed too early, when he slept too little, when he played too much golf, when he got too much sun, and when he looked like a "dark cloud." Above all, she worried about his irregular heartbeats, as she had worried about her own throughout much of her life, and about the tortuous vessels on his forehead, the veins that looked like "ship cords" and seemed to her the harbingers of another heart attack or stroke. The latter frightened her so much that she wondered if Ike would last until retirement; as she quietly remarked to Slater, "I'm not so sure we're ever going to be able to live in Gettysburg." She worried so much that she attributed some of her own headaches and high blood pressure to concern about her husband. Snyder conceded that she was probably right, and he explained one of her stomach upsets as the kind that "comes about usually when she is nervous and tense because of apprehension about something the president is doing."[49]

Like the doctor, Mamie was always on the lookout for information. She obtained it by taking the president's pulse, by observing his appearance and his moods, by keeping an eye on the kind and amount of medicine he took, and by paying attention to his complaints. Even at night she was on the alert; she would listen to his breathing, observe whether he was restless, and take note of how long he slept. "Mrs. Eisenhower told me this morning," Snyder recorded on a spring day in 1958, "that the president did not get to bed last night until 2400 hrs. She reached over and felt his pulse. It was skipping and she told him about it." Another time she told Snyder that on mornings of late the president was breathing so heavily that she was worried. "She wonders whether this is due to the condition in his chest or because of his heart," he noted. "I have reassured her in each instance when she has commented about it."[50]

Mamie's role was far more wide-ranging, however, than that of an anxious informant. She became a diagnostician, frequently drawing upon her "common sense" and her own health history—the import of which was oftentimes unfortunate for her husband. Throughout much of her life she had been inordinately concerned about her poor health and her ailments. She was suspicious of extremes of cold and heat, afraid of flying, claustrophobic, and, as Ike explained to a friend in 1954, "used to suffer very greatly from indigestion and heart flutter, which would make her extremely nervous and fearful, and the results were sometimes almost alarming." She did have a rheumatic heart, which required a restriction in her physical activity and led her, among other things, to avoid high altitudes. Her mistake was to believe that her husband's "heart condition" was akin to her own, and therefore to complain constantly that he was "overdoing" it.[51]

"Dr. Mamie," as Snyder referred to her in private, was confident enough to make a medical determination in virtually every circumstance. When she detected one night that Ike was short of breath in his sleep, she decided it was because he had "overloaded" at dinner the evening before. When he coughed up a bit of mucus one morning, she concluded he had fluid in his lungs, which she believed was caused by his heart condition. Even when she could not come up with an easy diagnosis, she would hypothesize, as in the spring of 1959, when she noticed on frequent occasions that the president had tortuous vessels on his temples during the evening. "She thinks it is sometimes due to his drinking two or three scotches," Snyder wrote, "and yet he had the [same] temples the night before last when he had had no Scotch, and they showed again last night with a couple of Scotches. She has attempted to ascribe it to the fact that the president practices golf too hard. This is what Moaney believes, and she learned it in discussing the situation with Moaney. But last night, after the president had sat quietly painting with no golf practice, the same thing occurred. So Mamie is in a quandary as to the cause."[52]

Whatever the cause, Mamie wanted to act when she detected a problem, and generally she would go to her doctor to enlist his support. She asked him to direct the president to call off his bridge game when she thought he was tense. She asked him to return to the White House to check Ike when he had a headache. She asked him to give him more or fewer pills depending upon her reading of the situation. And she "raised hell" with Snyder if he did something she considered ill advised, as when he allowed the president to play golf on a cold day or ride in an open car in Denver, and when he let him walk up the front steps of the Doud house in the mile-high altitude. She was willing to take on the entire medical profession, as in 1959 when some consulting cardiologists advised that Ike could safely deliver the commencement address at the Air Force Academy. She believed it would be dangerous because of the elevation, and she gave her husband "hell" for even considering a trip to Colorado Springs.[53]

As in this instance, she usually ended up giving the president advice. If Ike ate a large dinner she would try to keep him up late, in accordance with her opinion about his need to digest his food while awake. If the weather was unusually hot or cold, she would tell him not to play golf. If he seemed tired, she would try to persuade him to lie down. If he went out in the sun without his hat, she would get after him. If he set up too many social obligations, she would lecture him about taking it easy. If she checked and found that he had not taken his medicine, she would remind him. If she found him "puffing and steaming" at night, she would turn him over. If he complained about having "a hell of a morning," she would offer sympathy. And she would "doctor" him with loving care, as she did one day at 4:00 A.M. when he had a severe chill: "Mamie got her hot water bottle and snuggled up against him. She put a heavy coverlet over him. It took about an hour to warm him up. She tried to give him an aspirin . . . but he would not take it."[54]

The president responded in many ways to his wife's attentiveness. Sometimes he did as she asked; sometimes he ignored her; sometimes he stayed up for only a little while, hoping to pacify her; sometimes he was contrary, as when he would go to bed after she asked him to stay up or eat when she wanted him to wait; and sometimes he would leave for another room, as on an afternoon when he was sitting drinking his beer and she turned down his lip and said, "See, Howard, how purple it is." On many more occasions, however, he became irritated and angry about her "dictating" to him. On a winter day in 1958 he was grouching about a cold, condemning all doctors in no uncertain terms, and told Mamie at lunch that he wanted to go to Thomasville. "She immediately took exception to it and tried to persuade him to delay departure until Thursday," Snyder noted. "He agreed; however, he flew off in a rage and went into his dressing room, where he remained all afternoon. He would have no part of Mamie. She was quite alarmed for fear his anger would induce a recurrence of cerebral trouble, but there was nothing she could do to correct the initial reaction."[55]

Some months after the heart attack, Swede Hazlett wrote to Eisenhower: "Tell Mamie I want her to ride herd on you and make you avoid tensions and anger. She'll have a lot to do with your physical fitness—and I speak from experience!" The irony was that despite her good intentions, Mamie became the most frequent and lasting source of her husband's anger. Ike's response was not in any way shocking, because it always had been a part of the marriage. As John pointed out about the early years, "Sure, he's good-natured at home as long as everything goes his way, but if someone musses up the paper, for instance, before he's had a chance to read it he has a fit. Mother makes the house revolve around him, and he just sits back and lets it revolve." At times the marital relationship was tempestuous, especially during and after the war because of the Kay Summersby episode, but by the 1950s it had settled into a pattern. Ike would blow up about trivial things, oftentimes having to do with Mamie's failure to do something right, whether it was incorrectly setting her watch and thus failing to waken him on time, or her inability to balance the checkbook, or her saying something of which he disapproved. He did not change, even in retirement, as Julie Nixon Eisenhower noted, describing a typical scene at the bridge table:

> Ike (making a valiant effort not to yell): "Why did you make that play?"
> Mamie (with a pouting underlip and a shrug of her shoulders): "Oh, I don't know. Just 'cause I wanted to."
> Ike throws his hand down, leaves bridge table in disgust, his face a flame of color.[56]

The heart attack merely provided a new source of irritation. Mamie once offered some words of wisdom to her granddaughter-in-law about living with the Eisenhower men. "There can only be one star in the heaven, Sugar, and there is only one way to live with an Eisenhower. Let him have his own way." But in this circumstance she would not let her husband and his doctor have their own way, so she meddled. In doing so she stepped out of her customary, limited role to an extent unacceptable to Ike. Her "worries" about his health "approached and often went beyond, nagging," one observer noticed. "Added to her childlike insistence of having her way, this would irritate him to the point of explosion. Then the Eisenhower temper, which was almost as famous as the Eisenhower grin, would explode and he would bellow at her in a voice generals had come to fear."[57]

Heart illness affects all members of a family, and it has been said that the patient may recover from his coronary but his wife may not. "The secret that haunts many cardiac marriages," in the words of one clinical psychologist, "is the spouse's unexpressed and unsoothed agony over the current and future struggles that this myocardial invasion has brought into the couple's life." Mamie had many of the same anxieties and fears about the illness as Ike, as well as numerous misconceptions about "heart disease" drawn from her past. In the best of circumstances, she would have received considerably more attention to help her adjust, but her husband was understandably at the center of attention to a greater degree than ever before. Dr. Snyder did try to calm her fears, but her aggressiveness suggests that he was only occasionally successful.[58]

The concern, caring, irritation, and anger were all part of the "family's" attempt to cope with chronic illness, and despite the frustration stemming from the complexities of the disease and of their own interaction, the three old people worked together relatively well to still their individual fears. For the most part, the couple worked as a team. Even though Ike resented Mamie's interventions, he appreciated and needed her; when he told her at night about some ache or pain, or about being unusually tired, he was reaching out for support or relying on her as a conduit to his doctor. In like manner, he tried to keep Snyder around as much as possible, especially when he was away from the White House. And the doctor was always happy to be there, listening, probing, reassuring. But even with the fullest measure of attention and cooperation, there were times when the president wanted to deal with his disease alone—as on an autumn day in 1959 when he told Snyder, "I think I would like to go out to Walter Reed and stay a few days just to get away from people—immediately after the departure of the president of Guinea."[59]

Snyder understood this need at times for "separation from people," the more so because the president had an especially difficult time in coming to grips with his disease.

Eisenhower's heart attack gave rise not only to a spate of articles to educate the public but also to a testimonial literature to console the victims, two of the most widely read of which were those by the respected journalist Dorothy Thompson and a presidential adviser, Clarence Randall. Writing in the *Ladies' Home Journal,* in a piece entitled, "May I Tell You About My Heart Attack?" Thompson sought to make coronaries fashionable. "A certain snobbery exists among people who have recovered from heart attacks," the writer admitted, "probably attributable to an unconscious realization that, in some respects, they belong to an elite.

Recovered victims—and their number is innumerable—have what amounts to an exclusive club; and the president's heart attack made them even more snooty." Randall, who suffered an attack while on government business in Lisbon, crowed about it in "The Happy Cardiac" for *Harper's*. "The most surprising thing I have learned is that cardiacs are a happy lot," he claimed. "We now know where we stand. The thing we feared most has happened, and, glory be, it isn't bad at all." He was "gay as a cricket" and willing to "let the winds of fate whistle" as they would. "Living happily within my new limitations," he boasted, "is turning out to be just one more of life's adventures."[60]

Eisenhower was neither snooty nor happy about his attack. From his perspective it was a sign of weakness, an assault on his ego. The true elite were those who had bodies strong enough to take them to an old age without any physical breakdowns, who never had a heart attack that forced them to change their lives. He accepted the attack, and he fully intended to fight back and avoid another, but he was not a "happy" cardiac. He worried about his condition every day, to the extent that he sometimes went looking for sympathy, as when he appended the "touching little parenthesis" to his comments, "if I live that long." Sometimes he sought understanding in the most unexpected places. Russian foreign minister Andrei Gromyko recalled that during his visit to Camp David in September 1959 a tired-looking president approached him and complained, "My health is playing up," and added: "It's my heart. It's giving me trouble and I've got to be careful."[61]

He had to be so careful that his heart condition stole away forever a beautiful corner of his life, that of fishing in the Rockies and playing golf at his favorite course, Cherry Hills—reasons alone for resentment. So he never felt "at ease" with his coronary, and he was in no way sentimental about it. When he learned in 1959 that Dr. Snyder's secretary was still answering letters from well-wishers, he flared and said, "God damn it, Howard, I told you to throw those letters in the wastebasket." And years later, when Paul White planned to have a ten-year reunion to commemorate the attack, Eisenhower refused to celebrate something that he wanted to forget.[62]

The victim of a heart attack is different from what he was before, and every individual responds in a unique manner to his coronary event. There is a pattern to these reactions, however, and one specialist in cardiac rehabilitation has tried to explain their variety by posing a continuum of four quadrants between two very rare extremes—at one end "absolute denial," a conscious or unconscious refusal to acknowledge a cardiac condition or the need for behavioral change, and at the other end "morbid absorption," a preoccupation so extensive as to compromise functional activities in other areas of life. In the first quadrant is a milder form of denial, "minimization," in which the patient acknowledges but minimizes the seriousness of his condition, and likewise the need to comply with a regimen to control smoking, diet, exercise, and other habits. In the second, or "optimism," quadrant, the patient accepts his status with little anxiety, is very hopeful about his recovery, and responds readily to therapy. In the "pessimism" quadrant, the patient is more open about fears, worries, discouragement, and doubts, more likely to report symptoms, and strongly motivated to seek protection by means of compliance with a rehabilitation program. In the final, or fourth, quadrant, the "preoccupied" patient is more chronically anxious, more apt to exaggerate the seriousness of his condition, more dependent on his doctors, and more in need of reassurance.[63]

Within this theoretical spectrum Eisenhower would fall within the third and fourth quadrants. He responded to his disease with chronic anxiety and intense preoccupation. For such persons, in the words of another expert, "details are all. To cope with chronic illness means to routinely scan bodily processes. Attention is vigilantly focused, sometimes hour by hour, to the specifics of circumstances and events that could be potential sources of worsening. There is the daily quest for control of the known provoking agents." As an athlete who had always been alert to his body, Ike was particularly sensitive; he was like an auto mechanic on duty twenty-four hours a day, straining to hear the slightest knock, rap, or skip, sensing that a failure to detect the malfunction could be fatal. He became a scanner, searching for signs, and the daily presence of a personal physician afforded unending opportunities to find them. Every physiological measurement—altogether thousands of them—carried a potential message of comfort, concern, or, very often, confusion. And by far the most omnipresent and overwhelming were the readings of his pulse and blood pressure.[64]

The pulse, especially, became a monitor, a way of touching Ike's heart. Whether Snyder or Mamie was taking it, or whether he was doing it himself, he listened for its two disturbing revelations—an accelerated rate, which in his mind was anything above 80, and "skipped beats," any number of which he considered troublesome. A rapid pulse caused him the least anxiety because it rarely lasted throughout an entire day and because he usually could explain it as the result of food, drink, exertion, or tension. And the doctor was purposefully creative, attributing it to an endless variety of causes, such as a reaction to a news conference, going seven hours without food, drinking two cans of beer before dinner, or awaiting the consultants' verdict on whether he could attend the NATO conference.[65]

It was not as easy with the skipped beats, which Eisenhower had never consciously experienced before the heart attack, and which never failed to bother him. Only three days after taking the oath of office, he mentioned to Snyder that he had detected four skips per minute, and the latter cautioned him to go more slowly when he climbed the thirty-nine steps to the executive mansion. For the remainder of his term he suffered an undercurrent of anxiety concerning skipped beats and was constantly on the alert for the slightest change. His apprehension reached a high point during a threatening two days in the campaign of 1960, when Snyder detected what he thought (almost certainly mistakenly) to be ventricular fibrillation, treated it with quinidine, and insisted on a quick change of schedule.[66]

According to the data in his medical record, the president had nothing to worry about. Indeed, his EKGs did not register a single threatening abnormality during the five years after his heart attack. By the late 1950s, as well, cardiologists recognized that most of the arrhythmias occurred at times in a fairly large percentage of healthy people, provoked by such factors as physical fatigue, nervous tension, excessive smoking or eating, and infections. They accorded them relatively little importance, and least of all the skipped beats, the very name of which was a misnomer because there was no "skip" but instead a premature ventricular contraction (PVC) of the normal beat.

For laymen, however, the slightest dysfunction could give rise to anxiety and fear. "There is nothing quite so frightening as strange sensations in the vicinity of your heart," explained *Changing Times* in 1953. "It is the kind of fright that stays on and on, like the ghost at a feast, spoiling your fun. And no wonder an acting-up brings fear. The heart is the center of life, its steady pulsing the symbol of survival. When it races or pounds or skips or hurts, most people, no matter how brave, immediately think of the slender thread upon which life hangs." Eisenhower, despite his exceptional knowledge about his heart, had a layman's perspective, and he was always in need of reassurance.[67]

Ordinarily Snyder displayed very little concern about the PVCs, but he had to be ready at all times with some kind of explanation. On one occasion

Ike told him he "unconsciously" put his hand on his pulse and noted the irregular rhythm, after which Snyder noted: "He said this didn't alarm him, but he couldn't understand the cause. He asked me what it might be. I simply remarked to him to pay no attention to it; that he had had arrhythmia to a certain extent for years prior to his heart attack, and that it occasionally appeared since that time. This seemed to reassure him." Snyder generally ascribed the skips to the tension resulting from a particular event, such as a meeting or a press conference, or to some dietary indiscretion, or to Ike's having "pushed" himself too hard at work or golf. If no precipitating event was readily available, he searched around for an answer. "The only cause I can ascribe for this considerable arrhythmia," Synder supposed on a spring day in 1957, "was the fact that when he came home at noon, he went into Mamie's room to make some statement to her but she was on the telephone. This fact frequently occasions an angry reaction on his part."[68]

There were times when the pulse caused such anxiety as to preoccupy Eisenhower completely, as during a two-day period in the spring of 1959. On the afternoon of 24 March, while the president was in bed for his daily relaxation, Snyder found a low pulse with twelve skipped beats per minute. During the next twenty-four hours he and Ike and Mamie checked the pulse repeatedly, and although the PVCs disappeared, the rate was above 80 on more than ten occasions. Snyder was not concerned, attributing the condition to wine and exercise, but the president could not stop worrying because in his mind a rapid pulse—even without skips—was somehow associated with his other great fear, high blood pressure. In fact, during lunch he had told Snyder about occasional headaches he was having in the frontal area, a clear sign of his concern about his blood pressure and the possibility not only of another heart attack but also of a stroke.[69]

By the 1950s cardiologists were certain there was a relationship between hypertension, the medical name for high blood pressure, and two dangerous heart conditions, congestive heart failure and atherosclerosis. They still were very much at sea about the causes of hypertension, however, and were scarcely able to hypothesize about a cause-and-effect relationship to coronary disease. The large majority of Americans, including Eisenhower and Snyder, were not attentive to the complexities of the disease and simply assumed that a "hypertense" person—whom they generally perceived as the prototypical "red-faced, overweight man who is always in a hurry, is intolerant of others, has a violent temper, and is likely to display excessive reactions to relatively trivial disturbances"—would necessarily have high blood pressure and thus would be courting the dangers of a heart attack or a stroke. Their prescription was equally simple—to help such individuals become less "hyper" and less "tense," primarily by controlling the stress in their lives.[70]

As with his arrhythmia, the president had no ostensible medical reason to be concerned about his blood pressure because during most of his second term it remained within the limits of normal for his age (less than 140 systolic and under 90 diastolic). In 1959 and 1960 he was mildly hypertensive, with an increasing frequency of elevations above the normal during times of stress, but there were no significant periods of sustained hypertension. He was almost constantly anxious, nonetheless, because he could make the connection between the "coronary-prone" personality and the "hypertense" individual and himself. As a result, he often overreacted. "According to Mamie," as Snyder noted in a typical instance during the fall of 1958, "the president was so concerned about his blood pressure that he spoke to her and said, 'This is the highest blood pressure I have had in four years.' Mamie repeated this to me. I said that his heart attack was not yet three years past, and that the year and a half before that, his blood pressure was so much higher than it was on that day, there was no comparison."[71]

Despite his attempts to downplay the importance of the blood pressure, Snyder also worried. In part he was concerned about a stroke, understandably so after November 1957, but he was no less fearful of progressive cardiac damage. In the fall of 1959, after noticing Ike "puffing" a little from walking upstairs after lunch, he noted: "His blood pressure was quite irregular, and there were many reinforced beats on the diastolic all the way down. This leads me to believe that he doesn't have too much cardiac reserve or else the walk up the steps should not affect his pulse so much as to rate and rhythm." Several months later he was fretting about the same problem: "His blood pressure shows considerable exhaustion. It is better tonight. I believe it is beginning to show that he does not have cardiac reserve—as he had eight months ago. I believe the toll of the Bonn, Germany, trip and the Europe-Asia-Africa trip is beginning to show. I am going to have to watch his blood pressure carefully."[72]

Snyder was not prepared to institute a program using the new antihypertensive drugs, as Dr. Lynn at Walter Reed proposed, but the records indicate that he periodically administered such medicines on his own without informing the consultants, especially when the president had headaches associated with an elevation of blood pressure. He was committed, on the other hand, to collecting as much information as possible about the blood pressure; his unoffical records show 103 readings prior to the stroke and a far more extensive 942 thereafter. A satisfactory reading was a source of elation for everyone. "Mamie was present when I took the president's blood pressure," Snyder wrote after one lunch hour. "She asked me what it was. I told her 138/80, and she made a wry face. The president remarked, 'If it was any lower than that, I would forget my swear words,' and then he laughed."[73]

More often the process led to an interaction between doctor and patient whereby they sought to find an explanation for any variation from "normal." Eisenhower ideally wanted to keep his systolic pressure below 130 and his diastolic around 80, and he was ill at ease whenever they went higher, or if the "spread" became too large. Snyder was more flexible and forgiving, and he was not averse to cheating a little in order to keep his patient from worrying. "The president has realized for some time that the diastolic pressure is up a little," he mentioned on one occasion, "but I have reassured him each time he has mentioned it. I usually knock off 8 or 10 points on the systolic, if it is more than 132, in commenting to him."[74]

Snyder was adept at explaining away every high reading. He blamed food and drink, exercise and fatigue, defeat at the bridge table or on the golf course, stress within the family, the various pressures of the job, or any general issue of the time or any specific event of the day. Even with the readily available explanations, the president continued to seek reassurance. Following a 1958 meeting of the National Security Council, he stopped by Snyder's office and mentioned that he was very tired. The doctor accompanied him upstairs and took a reading of 144/90. "The president was insistent that I tell him his blood pressure," Snyder noted. "He was concerned because the diastolic pressure was creeping up, and he cussed the doctors who had encouraged him to accept a second term. He said the fact that, in recent months, the diastolic pressure has shown an increase whereas for many months following his heart attack it had remained low, caused him to feel that just as in increases in weight which tend to creep up if not carefully provided for, so his diastolic pressure would be inclined to climb." Snyder had a "philosophic" discussion with the president and returned to the latter's dressing room prior to Ike's scheduled departure for an evening dinner. This time he practiced a small deception: "I told him his diastolic was 80 to reassure him that a moderate period of rest relieved the tendency to an increase in diastolic pressure about which he was apprehensive. I did not want him to go down to dinner with a concern for his blood pressure."[75]

These conversations—comparing notes and calming fears—bespoke a remarkable, even historic, relationship between a physician and a presidential patient. Howard Snyder was only an average medical practitioner, but he was a supreme family doctor. "For what should be the work of the physician of the chronically ill," asked a specialist from a later generation, "if not this: that he is there in the realm of suffering together with his patient and the members of his family. He joins them in that difficult experience to help where feasible with the medical management of the disease process." Snyder was a superb manager of the medical care, but equally important, he became the Eisenhowers' psychotherapist. In that role, too, he excelled, in part because he knew the president so well and had earned his trust but also because Eisenhower insisted on sharing actively in his own care. He could never entrust his life completely to anyone, and he was always a little suspicious of experts, including physicians. As he told Snyder on the last day of 1956, "These experts don't know anything about my heart. It isn't as good as they say."[76]

There was a *busyness* about it all—two old men, and sometimes Mamie, huddling over the daily happenings—in a way that could not help but exaggerate the problems. Clearly Ike's vital signs and symptoms were sometimes too much with them. And even with all of their chatter they could not tend to the full meaning of the illness and its many scratches on the president's mind—of restlessness, anxiety, foreboding, and the lack of ultimate control in the face of an ever present threat to life. For those he had his quiet moments, as when he secretly reached down to take his pulse, wondering what it would measure and what it would mean; or when he felt a twinge of pain, too slight to allow a "he-man" to call his doctor but threatening enough to make him reach for a nitroglycerine tablet to place under his tongue; or when his aloneness led him to reach out to that community of others like himself—numbering in the millions, sometimes even celebrating their distinctiveness in clubs and groups, but likewise at times alone and bereft—as he did on a morning in 1960 after reading in his newspaper about a famous actor:

Dear Mr. Gable:
I learned from the paper this morning that you have suffered a mild

coronary thrombosis. I trust that your recovery will be rapid and complete.

Presuming on our very brief acquaintance, I likewise offer one piece of advice—which is to follow the instructions of your doctors meticulously. I have found this to be fairly easy to do, except for the one item in which they seem to place the greatest stress, which is "don't worry and never get angry." However, I am learning—and in recent weeks I have had lots of opportunities to practice![77]

What did all of the doctoring—professional and personal—mean? There is no exact scientific measurement of how preventive action can affect an individual's health. But in the short term it certainly helped Eisenhower cope with the unaccustomed feelings of precariousness and fright attendant on his disease and to control those risk factors, especially his diet and his emotions, that may have contributed to it. As to the long term, or longevity, it would be difficult to argue with the conclusion of the conservative Dr. Mattingly: "Actually, with the daily care of his physician, the periodic evaluations and consultant advice by cardiologists, and the institution of measures of secondary prevention, he probably added years to his postmyocardial living."[78]

The real question Americans were asking in the late 1950s, however, was not what Eisenhower was doing about his health but what he was doing to the country.

Increasingly throughout the second term, critics complained about inactive leadership and wondered if Eisenhower was too old or too infirm to govern. Most of them focused on golf as the symbol of his passivity, and their endless references created the image of a president who was nothing more than "a nice old gentleman in a golf cart." Even some insiders bemoaned the lethargy inside the government. Gordon Gray, a special assistant for national security affairs, said "he didn't mind the president playing golf and understood he needed it for his health, but he found it unfortunate that the president never had enough time even when in the city to discuss matters thoroughly."[79]

For the most part, this kind of criticism reflected the increasing frustration of politicians after 1957—Democrats primarily, but also a few liberal Republicans—over the unwillingness of Ike to use his immense popularity to promote liberal reform. When a reporter told Lyndon Johnson there was a "new" Eisenhower, for example, the senator complained to Drew Pearson: "I told him there wasn't any new Ike. Here he is up at Gettysburg golfing while we are working. Does he come down like Franklin Roosevelt to read his veto message? Does he take any interest in legislation other than to say, 'No you can't have housing for old folks,' or 'You can't have housing for college classrooms.' . . . I want you to write a story on the new Ike and show that there ain't no such animal."[80]

Partisanship aside, there *was* an overall lack of vigor in the White House. The president did not work as hard or as long after the heart attack, simply because he and those around him worried about his health. One day when Dr. Snyder asked if he would give a speech to commemorate the AMA's hundredth anniversary, Ike "bit off" his head and said that "he knew preparing these speeches required so much work on his part that it ran up his blood pressure." He undoubtedly had such a feeling a thousand times, and he surely was less energetic because of it. Emmet Hughes thought there was a direct association between Ike's health and his inactivity. Within the administration, he decided, there "seemed to prevail the kindly but paralyzing consensus—to avoid 'upsetting the old man' with any too realistic reports of the disarray in his own ranks. Solicitously, but destructively, the president's aides were adjusting themselves to the quietly accepted task of laboring for a man whose *physical* welfare must be their first concern. And the shadow of such concern seemed almost visibly to warn of the settling, upon all the White House, of a time of twilight—a twilight of softened speech, muted feeling, hesitant motion."[81]

Scholars have been very reluctant, however, to draw anything other than vague conclusions about the impact of the president's physical condition on public policy. "What he eventually gained in experience may have been more than countered by the deterioration of his health through a heart attack, a stroke, and a major abdominal operation," a political historian typically and tentatively suggested. "There can be little question that he had lost substantial vigor and capacity for work by the end of his second term." As late as 1995 another historian noted, "What remains unclear at this writing is what effect Eisenhower's cardiovascular condition and physical debility resulting from it had upon such intangibles as levels of energy and clarity of thought." The experts are right to be cautious because of the impossibility of connecting Eisenhower's illnesses to his foreign or domestic policies. Above all, he did not believe in more government activism of the New Deal variety, but when he felt strongly about an issue, such as that of keeping federal expenditures in check, he could be extremely active and dynamic. And his positions on such issues as civil rights, defense spending, *Sputnik,* and the search for peace were the result of personal feelings, politics, and philosophy, not of medicine. In only one instance—the election of 1960—did his health and his feelings about it have a bearing, and they very likely changed the course of history by ensuring that John Kennedy rather than Richard Nixon would become the next president of the United States.[82]

In 1960 John Kennedy would not allow Richard Nixon to use the accomplishments of the Eisenhower presidency for his own benefit. "You've seen those elephants in the circus with the ivory in their heads—you know how they travel around the circus by grabbing the tail of the elephant in front of them," he explained. "That was all right in 1952 and 1956. Mr. Nixon hung on tight. But now Mr. Nixon meets the people." Eisenhower was slow to lend his prestige to Nixon, but in late October he was ready—even eager—to strike hard against Kennedy, the "young whippersnapper" who was impugning his record with his cry to get the country moving again. The campaign was drawing the curtains on his presidency, the highlight of his life, and he wanted to speak to the American people one last time about the quality of his performance.[83]

At a meeting on 31 October with Nixon, Hagerty, Hall, and his speechwriters, Ike said he wanted to expand his speaking schedule. His offer seemed to be a godsend; it would bring his reputation and popularity to bear during the crucial final week, and it might very well ensure victory. But Nixon turned him down and noted, "He was hurt and then he was angry." The vice president stood his ground anyway, noting that Eisenhower "finally acquiesced. His pride prevented him from saying anything, but I knew that he was puzzled and frustrated by my conduct." Ike did say something afterward to Leonard Hall, and it was not flattering: "Goddammit, he looks like a loser to me." And he continued, as he hunched his head and shoulders forward in imitation of a withdrawn Nixon, "When I had an officer like that in World War II, I relieved him."[84]

Neither at that time nor in *Six Crises* did Nixon give the reasons for his refusal of Ike's offer. But in his 1978 memoirs he reported that on the day before the meeting Mamie had called Pat Nixon—with the request that Ike "must never know I called you"—to express her fear that her husband "was not up to the strain campaigning might put on his heart." She had been unable to persuade him, so she "begged" Pat to have her husband convince him to avoid any additional burdens. The next morning Dr. Snyder called to give support to Mamie's plea and told Nixon to "either talk him out of it or just don't let him do it—for the sake of his health."[85]

Two recent biographers of Nixon disagree on the validity of his account. Historian Stephen Ambrose accepts it unreservedly, but journalist Tom Wicker doubts it and argues that Nixon's "failure to bring in a bellicose Eisenhower" was based upon his confidence that he could win the election on his own and upon his bitterness about their relationship in the past. "Nixon surely wanted to be seen as having won the presidency in his own right," Wicker decided, "and not owing to an Eisenhower blitz; he was tired of being obscured by Eisenhower's giant shadow—so tired that he made another mistake in judgment, to limit the president's campaigning."[86]

The historian is surely the wiser, for Ike's caretakers at the time were unquestionably and seriously concerned about his health. By the summer of 1960, Mamie was worrying about nearly everything he did. During a trip to Chicago in late July she asked Snyder to prevent Ike from writing any more speeches; she thought the activity built up such great tension that she feared for his safety. She recounted how the night before he had screamed out loud in a dream and had almost jumped out of bed, after which he took a sedative, which then led her to worry about his becoming addicted to it. That same evening she again "raised hell" with the doctor for letting the president ride in an open car. Two days later, in Colorado Springs, she lectured Ike for attending a luncheon and for taking on too many social obligations; within her general complaint that Ike was overdoing it in the high altitude, she criticized Snyder for allowing him to walk up the front steps of the Doud home. By campaign time, as one aide described it, she "had turned into a tigress protecting Ike. She wasn't about to let politicians destroy her president, so she would scratch and scream every time they tried to put him back on the road."[87]

Dr. Snyder was very disturbed as well, primarily because of an episode that occurred while Eisenhower was in Detroit to address the Automobile Manufacturers' Association. At 2:45 P.M. on 17 October, the doctor measured Ike's pulse rate, which was about 90, and discovered twelve skipped beats; when he took the blood pressure he found the skips to be "all over the map." He decided the "bizarre cardiac action" was caused by Ike's anger at a UAW-CIO-AFL leaflet he had seen, which stated, "A vote for Kennedy is a vote for liberty; a vote for Nixon is a vote for bigotry." Indeed, when the president received the key to the city and had to give a brief comment, "his lips were so tight that he could hardly smile." Snyder gave him one tablet of quinidine for the arrhythmia and told him to rest for two hours.[88]

After sleeping for slightly more than an hour, Ike called for the doctor and reported that he thought his pulse was more irregular than before. It was. The pulse was between 96 and 100, with approximately twenty skipped beats every minute and the same "erratic registration of systoles" evident in the cuff of the sphygmomanometer. Snyder kept him resting in bed and at 5:00 P.M. gave him a second quinidine tablet. Ike related that the same thing had happened to him on another recent occasion in New York when he had eaten a larger lunch than usual and had taken a drink with it. The two decided that he should have no more drinks that evening. The president then finished working on his speech and picked up a Western novel; the arrhythmia calmed down to eight skipped beats per minute. Thirty minutes later he called the doctor in again; in counting his pulse he had noticed that there were occasional runs of half a dozen rapid beats. Snyder found that his pulse, including the skips, was 102. He gave his patient a third quinidine pill to take later that evening, just prior to his speech.

By 6:00 P.M. the president was ready to leave for a banquet, and his pulse had steadied completely. During the next four hours he mingled with guests and gave his thirty-minute televised address. After returning to the Sheraton-Cadillac Hotel, where a large group of friends had gathered in his suite, he went to his bedroom and called for Snyder to take his blood pressure. "There was such irregularity and so little registration of blood pressure that I could not get a decent systolic or diastolic reading," the physician recorded. "It was just a trickle at the wrist, with runs and occasional pronounced emphasized systoles. He was having ventricular fibrillation, which is very dangerous." Snyder had no way of knowing the source of the arrhythmia, and as Mattingly has argued, it was almost certainly an atrial fibrillation, which is far less threatening. But the doctor acted on his assumption. He gave a sedative and administered oxygen for twelve minutes, after which Ike's pulse steadied to 82 with ten skips per minute. The president went to sleep, but the doctor left the door open between their communicating bedrooms.[89]

Snyder was so concerned that he convinced the president to cancel a planned trip to Denver and to leave directly the following morning for Palm Springs, where his friends had gathered for bridge and golf. That afternoon in the resort city, while socializing with the gang, Ike had the doctor take his blood pressure every now and then to see how he was doing. At dinner he checked his pulse himself and found "plenty of skips." At 8:30 P.M. he started playing bridge, and as Snyder prepared to leave, the president asked if he did not want to give him "one of those things." He was referring to the white quinidine tablets, and the doctor, not wishing to mask any symptoms, said he did not need one. Ike seemed quite disappointed, apparently thinking he should have one for prophylactic purposes.[90]

The next day the pulse had returned to normal, and during the several weeks prior to the election there were only occasional skipped beats. But the trip had chastened Snyder. Just before leaving Washington, he had missed the motorcade to the airport and had to follow in another car at speeds between ninety and one hundred miles per hour. Fate was playing the cards, he thought, because if he had missed the plane he would not have gone at all. "Had this been the case," he feared, "the president unquestionably would have been in extreme danger because of the episode he had with his heart action." Snyder's response was to caution Ike during the coming days about his involvement in the campaign, to have him take extra oxygen because of the extra work, and to sympathize with Mamie, who on 28 October, only three days before Nixon's meeting with Eisenhower, was "plugging" at him "to tell the president he had to quit speaking and working for Nixon—that he might pop a cork."[91]

Within this context, the circumstantial evidence overwhelmingly supports Nixon's account of the last-minute intervention by Mamie and the doctor, both of whom were unusually upset about the president's condition. Nixon rejected Ike's offer not because of resentment about the past but out of a sense of decency concerning the present; he would risk his election rather than risk the health of the president. The great irony is that Eisenhower, acting out of a similar sense of propriety, was unwilling a few days later to help Nixon by speaking out about the health of John Kennedy.

Kennedy had been successful for more than a decade in deceiving the American people about his Addison's disease (a malfunction of the adrenal glands that causes a general weakness, weight loss, and an inability to fight infection), but he was not able to keep the issue out of the campaign. Indeed, his own words at a 4 July press conference, where he maintained that the office demanded "the strength and health and vigor" of young men, "for during my lifetime alone four out of our seven presidents have suffered major heart attacks that impaired at least temporarily their exercise of executive leadership," led to a call for a medical examination for every candidate.[92]

Lyndon Johnson, contesting for the nomination, saw the comment as an unfair reference to his own heart attack. Later that afternoon two of his supporters, John Connally and India Edwards, held a press conference in Los Angeles during which Mrs. Edwards said that she objected to Kennedy's "muscle-flexing in boasting about his youth," and added that "several doctors" had told her that he had Addison's disease and that he would not be alive were it not for cortisone. Robert Kennedy responded with a statement that his brother "does not now nor has he ever had an ailment described classically as Addison's disease, which is a tuberculose destruction of the adrenal gland." He bitterly told a Johnson aide that the majority leader had "lied by saying my brother was dying of Addison's disease. You Johnson people are running a stinking damned campaign and you'll get yours when the time comes."[93]

Johnson's staff tried to collect evidence to support its charges, with some success. Shortly after noon on 5 July, Walter Jenkins received a telephone call from a friend who had spent the previous afternoon with the president of a pharmaceuticals company who was in contact with doctors throughout the country. The executive had told him that Kennedy was treated for Addison's disease at the Lahey Clinic in 1948 and 1949. "He tells me that if a patient stays under medication," the informer related, "he is put in a position of an automobile that is able to drive only at one speed and if a patient comes under any stress (physical or emotional) it can produce a complete state of exhaustion. I am told he not only *had* it but *has* it now and is receiving treatment for it." The friend promised to send a detailed memorandum, including names of endocrinologists the senator could approach. And he touched upon the political implication: "Someone who is knowledgeable in the field could make a statement about the disease and the effects of it and then keep needling on the candidates to submit themselves for medical examination and for the reports to be made public."[94]

Johnson decided not to pursue the issue. He probably realized the difficulty —even impossibility—of proving his charge without the public support of some physician who had treated Kennedy. In view of the doctor-patient privilege of secrecy, no such authoritative voice was likely to come forth. He had no choice but to accept the younger senator's claim that it was time to focus on partisan issues rather than personalities, that the "only 'health' issue is the anemic health of the American economy today." With Johnson's selection as the nominee for vice president, and with a press friendly to the Democratic ticket, the talk of Addison's disease disappeared until the end of the campaign, when it became partisan.[95]

On 3 November John Roosevelt, the only Republican son of the late Democratic president, called upon both Nixon and Kennedy to reveal their complete medical histories. Roosevelt wanted Nixon to speak about the residual effects of his knee surgery, and Kennedy about his adrenal deficiency caused by Addison's disease, for which Roosevelt claimed Kennedy was taking drugs. Roosevelt's request had no effect on Kennedy—except to elicit a statement from Pierre Salinger that he had made public his complete medical record at the Democratic National Convention. It may have served as the catalyst, however, that two days later prompted Nixon to approach Ann Whitman and have her ask Eisenhower to put out a statement calling on the candidates to publish the results of a thorough physical examination, just as he had done for the American people prior to his seeking reelection in 1956.[96]

The president very likely was alert to the issue because specific evidence about Kennedy's condition had reached the White House. In August a physician at the Peter Bent Brigham Hospital in Boston approached a colleague in Rhode Island (who knew Howard Snyder) to express his frustration concerning the misinformation the public was receiving about the senator's illness. The friend arranged for the physician to present his information to Snyder, the gist of which was that he had learned from two "clear and authoritative" sources that Kennedy had a severe case of Addison's disease that was difficult to control. His sources, a professor of medicine at Georgetown University Medical School who claimed to have treated the senator within the past three years, and a member of the senator's present medical staff who claimed to have tended him at the Democratic National Convention, gave a "grim picture" of Kennedy's illness. The cortisone left the patient apathetic or euphoric, these doctors said, depending on the dosage, and often affected his critical judgment.[97]

Snyder had the names, addresses, and telephone numbers of the informants, but although he characterized the information as "for possible use in political campaign," it is unlikely that he proceeded further. There is no record to prove that he told Eisenhower of his conversations, but given his habit of discussing every issue with his boss, it is reasonable to assume that he did. In whatever event, the response in the White House was negative. Jim Hagerty called Nixon's desire to exploit the issue a "cheap, lousy, stinking political trick." And when someone tried to explain the rumors about Kennedy's Addison's disease to the president, he replied: "I am not making myself a party to anything that has to do with the health of the candidates."[98]

Eisenhower's decision was consistent with his feelings and his principles. As to the former, he had an old-fashioned modesty and sense of privacy about the human body. When he wrote his memoirs, he recalled the "acute embarrassment" he had felt after his heart attack when he read a news clipping wherein Dr. White described in quite specific terms certain "physiological functions"; he was unable, even then, to use the term "bowel movements," at least in public. He was likewise "hypersensitive," to use Dr. Snyder's characterization, about some prostrate troubles in 1959 and 1960 (the nature and extent of which are not evident from the medical records), so much so that the doctors referred to it as "the problem," and he talked of having surgery on a cruiser or a so-called vacation trip in order to avoid discussion in the press.[99]

He also felt strongly that health was a private, personal matter that constituted privileged information between a patient and his doctor. When John Foster Dulles was dying of cancer and aides suggested the need to release details of his treatment, Ike insisted that the secretary must make the decision. He personally thought "it was a lot of rot giving it to the press," and he resented the Democrats' dramatizing "poor Foster's health." And only a month before Nixon's request, Ike made an infrequent stop at Snyder's office to complain about the article in *U.S. News and World Report* discussing his own condition. He reprimanded the doctor for releasing health information without his prior approval.[100]

As a matter of principle, Eisenhower believed a presidential candidate owed the American people the truth about his health but not the complete truth. He must be fully honest about his ability to fulfill the responsibilities of the office without impairment, as he had been in 1955 and 1956; but he had no obligation to reveal the intimate details about his daily health, as he had not. Ike may well have known from the secondhand sources that Kennedy and his staff had lied repeatedly about Kennedy's Addison's disease, but he had no reliable evidence to prove that Kennedy was so impaired as to be unable to serve as president. In fact, the younger man's vigor during the campaign suggested the opposite.

The issue of health in the 1960 campaign therefore turned out to be a disaster for the Republicans. Nixon's sense of honor precluded his using the president more often and effectively during the crucial last days, which in itself might have changed the outcome of the election. And Eisenhower's sense of honor precluded his asking the Democratic candidate to issue a full statement about his health or to charge him with lying, either of which almost certainly would have been decisive. Their moments of honor had the same effect—the defeat of Richard Nixon—and both of them despaired of the result.

When the president arose on the morning after the election, he told Mamie that there had been only one other occasion when he had felt that life was not worth living, and that was when it was determined that he could never again play football because of his injured knee. Now he was depressed primarily because he felt a sense of rejection, and he feared that the Democrats were trying to do to him what "Roosevelt and his gang" had done to Hoover: "that is, tear down everything that has been done—make everything look sour—create the impression that the administration has failed —all for the purpose of making themselves look better."[101]

During the ten weeks between the election and the inauguration, Eisenhower nonetheless worked hard to ensure that there would be a balanced budget; he held two transitional briefings for the incoming president, gave the most well remembered of his speeches, his farewell address, and made plans for his retirement. As an ex-president he would be able to keep his valet and driver, but he knew there would be a fundamental change because he could not afford a personal physician. Dr. Snyder continued his routine of caring and commitment right up to the end, however. He believed the president had used up all of his cardiac reserve in the last days of the campaign and that the election had been a shock to his "emotional system," so he worried about his occasional bouts of high blood pressure, especially the "spread," even while assuring "Dr. Mamie" there was nothing to worry about. And on the morning of 19 January, he gave his friend a final report of his blood analysis. He told him that the cholesterol was 50 points lower than it actually was; for one last time he would hide the truth because he did not want the real figure to shock him.[102]

Eisenhower's last day as president was 20 January 1961, and his son remembered an "eerie" atmosphere in the White House that morning. There was a strangeness and a touch of sadness in the prospect of departure. As the president had told a friend as he heard the hammers putting up the reviewing stand for the inauguration: "Look, Henry, it's like being in the death cell and watching them put up the scaffold." The ceremony went well, however, and he and Mamie slipped out a side door to a waiting car and on to a retirement luncheon with the cabinet and close friends. Then they headed north by car for the eighty-mile trip to Gettysburg. As they approached Emmitsburg, and Ike saw the students and sisters of St. Joseph College standing in the deep snow in a final salute, his mind returned to the past. "Much had happened since that day, over five years before," he thought, "when the college had paid us a similar compliment as Mamie and I were driving to Gettysburg for convalescence from my heart attack."[103]

John Kennedy ended his magnificent day, marked above all by his stirring inaugural address, at the home of friends in Georgetown. It was well past midnight when he began reminiscing about the campaign and about Eisenhower, and he marveled at something that had struck him so forcibly that morning: "The vitality of the man!" he exclaimed. "It stood out so strongly, there at the inauguration. There was Chris Herter, looking old and ashen. There was Allen Dulles, gray and tired. There was Bob Anderson, with his collar seeming two sizes too large on a shrunken neck. And there was the oldest of them all, Ike—as healthy and ruddy and as vital as ever. Fantastic!"[104]

With that the old man would have agreed.

8

The Struggle to Stay Alive

❖ ❖ ❖ ❖ ❖ ❖ ❖ ❖ ❖ ❖ ❖ ❖ ❖ ❖ ❖ ❖

*You perhaps have never been deeply and chronically sick; you perhaps do not
know from within how sickness humbles—how it clouds and corrodes and
befouls the sense of self. I do not know why this should be so, that physical
disease plays such cruel vanishing tricks upon the ego, even the sturdiest ego,
given time enough. But I have seen it happen . . . , and I have read a bit about
such things and I know that this is classic in long chronic disease; this is what
the failures of the body do unerringly to the soul.*
—Martha Weinman Lear, Heartsounds

*His humor, wit and cooperativeness persist unabated, courageous in living and
dying.*
—Loren Parmley, medical report

Of all the shocking headlines of the 1960s, surely one of the few most
gripping for Eisenhower was that of 15 July 1965 in the *New York Times*:
"ADLAI STEVENSON DIES IN LONDON STREET AT 65." The ambassador to the
United Nations, the account explained, was walking near the United States
embassy with his friend Marietta Tree on a warm, sunny afternoon, when
he suddenly fell to the pavement. "Mrs. Tree ran to the nearest building,
the International Sportsmen's Club," it continued, "and asked for a doctor.
In a moment or two one appeared. As the doctor attempted artificial respiration, Mrs. Tree knelt down and tried to revive Mr. Stevenson by breathing into his mouth. There was no response. An ambulance took Mr. Stevenson
to St. George's Hospital at Hyde Park, and attendants applied oxygen on
the way. But he was pronounced dead on arrival." An unconfirmed med-

ical report said that the ambassador had suffered a "coronary thrombosis, a massive blockage of the arteries near the heart." Friends said that he had no history of "heart defect," and one noted that at a party the previous evening, "He went up the stairs like a bird."[1]

Whatever thoughts were going through Eisenhower's mind when he read the news article had to be jolted by a companion piece about the Stevenson legacy, for among the expressions of appreciation, it quoted the *Times* of London: "Through all the placid confidence of the Eisenhower era and the clumsy crusades of Mr. Dulles, he reminded the world that there was another American—sensitive, self-critical, thoughtful and visionary. At home he kept the light of intellect burning through a period when it was not fashionable to think." Even in death, it seemed, Ike's longtime rival was able to denigrate his presidency. But had the general known the truth about the heart attack, he would have been moved less to anger than to pity, and perhaps even to sorrow. For Adlai Stevenson, in a tragic sense, had failed to cope with his illness.[2]

In January 1962 Stevenson went to a New York physician, Dr. Henry Lax, with questions about his heart. The physician, who told him he was suffering from arteriosclerotic heart disease with hypertension and marked obesity, prescribed a drug to lower the blood pressure and a diet to reduce the weight. For nearly a year, the ambassador followed the regimen, losing thirteen pounds and bringing his blood pressure down to normal. But then he became uncooperative; he missed appointments with the doctor, failed to take his medicine, resumed smoking after a respite of ten years, retreated to his compulsive eating habits, and gained weight. He often worked himself to extreme exhaustion, as on one occasion when his son saw him "literally staggering with fatigue late in the evening, clutching at chairs and walls and tables." Adlai told friends only that he had a "heart problem" and "heart flutters," and that he was having trouble sleeping, but he could not leave his "damned job," which he considered the source of his problem. In May 1965 he went to see Dr. Lax again, admitted that he had ignored his advice, and said that he was going to parties almost every night. The doctor said, "Governor, it cannot go on like this. You have to stop this way of living, even if it means to resign as an ambassador; you are on a suicidal course." Stevenson smiled and replied, "How do you know that I want to live long? My father died at the age of sixty, my mother at sixty-five. I am now sixty-five; that will be enough for me."[3]

Stevenson returned to see Dr. Lax one more time at the end of May, having gained an additional five pounds, and he simply shrugged his shoulders when the doctor complained about his general condition. He was, by then, depressed about his life. A close friend, George Ball, had coffee with him ten days before he died and was saddened by Stevenson's unhealthy lifestyle but tried to put it in perspective: "He was going through the motions, making speeches, yet with a feeling in his heart that it didn't make any difference to the world if he fell over and had a heart attack. . . . Adlai was a terribly unhappy man. History had passed him by. His life had passed him by. He had no place to go."[4]

Dwight Eisenhower never would have understood how anyone could be so reckless about his health. He had described his own feelings in 1956 when he told reporters, "Readiness to obey the doctors, out of respect for my present duties and responsibilities, is mandatory in my case. I am now doing so, and I intend to continue doing so for the remainder of my life, no matter in what capacity I may be living or may be serving." He held to that philosophy for nearly five years out of a professed commitment to his countrymen, and for eight years more out of a concern for himself. He was not a great intellect, nor a visionary. But he would never defect from life and let history pass him by. He would continue to work at living; he still had places to go and things to do.[5]

Several weeks after the Kennedy inauguration, John Eisenhower visited his parents at Gettysburg and was "shocked and worried" at his father's demeanor. "His movements were slower," he noticed, "his tone less sharp, and he had time even during the work day to stop and indulge in what would formerly be considered casual conversation. I feared for his health. Fortunately, I could not have been more in error; the boss had simply relaxed."[6]

After decades of fantasizing about retirement, Ike was finally able to enjoy it. He had enough time and money to do what he wanted, whether it was puttering around the farm, spending hours with Mamie, his son, and his grandchildren, or traveling. Each winter he and Mamie took a train to Palm Desert, where wealthy friends provided a residence at the Eldorado Club, an office, an automobile, and four months of golf and bridge. During the spring and late autumn they went to Mamie's cabin at the Augusta National Golf Club for more happy times with the gang. In 1963 they again boarded the *Queen Elizabeth* for a leisurely trip to France, this time to work with Walter Cronkite on a documentary about the D-day invasion. Less happily, Ike made another trip to London in 1965 to attend the funeral of his longtime friend Winston Churchill.[7]

The nation's foremost senior citizen was not content merely with the pleasures of relaxation and travel. He continued to work hard. In 1961, he informed Churchill that "there seems to be little cessation from the constant stream of demands upon my time and energy," and he noted that Mamie thought retirement was "nothing but a word in the dictionary." He wrote his two-volume memoirs, published in 1963 and 1965, and his more informal reminiscences, *At Ease: Stories I Tell to Friends*, which appeared in 1967. He still received more than two thousand letters a week and tried to answer most of them. He remained active in the Republican party, speaking at countless fund-raisers out of a belief, as he told Ellis Slater, that "when the time comes that a person can't do some good he might as well die." He also served President Johnson as a senior statesman and a supporter of the Vietnam War. Sometimes he resented the deluge of requests for his time, however, and he grumbled after the 1964 convention, "I don't see why they are always dragging out an old retired man."[8]

One symbolic role the retiree happily accepted in 1961—and occupied for the next eight years—was that of honorary chairman of the board of the American Heart Association. The position did provide a small window into the continuing developments concerning heart disease and, together with the information he gleaned from the press, gave credence to the private war he had been waging since 1955. The newspapers were filled with articles about the dangers of smoking, bolstered by the pathbreaking surgeon general's report of 1964, which indicted tobacco as a progenitor of both heart attacks and cancer. The controversy over the benefits of a low-cholesterol, low-fat diet raged on, and despite the absence of definitive scientific proof, the evidence increasingly came down on the side of restriction.

Studies continued to suggest a causal role for emotional stress, defined at various times as aggression, ambition, excessive drive, and time consciousness, and furthered especially by the research of Friedman and Rosenman on the type A personality. Toward the end of the decade, cardiologists were incorporating smoking, high cholesterol, and stress, together with a lack of exercise and high blood pressure, into their list of "risk factors," the control of which would purportedly help prevent a heart attack. Perhaps the most heartening—and shocking—news to Eisenhower was the belated decision by a prestigious AHA conference in 1968 to give top priority in the future to the *prevention* of atherosclerosis, and to acknowledge the need for more behavioral scientists, because "individuals would have to be motivated to help themselves"[9]

During these retirement years, Eisenhower still had access to superb medical care, even without the service of a White House physician. General Heaton, now surgeon general of the army, assumed responsibility for Ike's and Mamie's medical needs, continuing overall direction from Walter Reed and utilizing outside consultants whenever he thought it necessary. He also arranged for care and evaluation through the facilities at March Air Force Base near Palm Desert and at Fort Gordon near the Augusta National Golf Club. Heaton was attentive to Eisenhower's great respect for Tom Mattingly, whom he kept on as a civilian consultant to his office. He likewise took account of the long and close relationship between Ike and Dr. Snyder, who had retired at eighty, by appointing the latter as a consultant and providing him with an office at Walter Reed, where he could work on a medical history of Eisenhower and visit with his former patient when he was in the hospital.[10]

Snyder, who was slow to get to work on the Eisenhower health history, despite the urging of his son and his secretary, remained intently interested in the general's well-being. He collected as much data as possible from the physicians in charge, complimented Ike when his cholesterol, weight, and prothrombin levels were promising, and kept members of the gang informed of his current medical status. Snyder also sent his friend articles that might be helpful—about diet, cholesterol, and emotional stress; and others that he might find interesting—a *Wall Street Journal* editorial about his inspiring influence on others who had suffered heart attacks and a *Washington Star* report that Lyndon Johnson's physical examination on the last day of 1964 gave "no evidence" of cardiac damage from his 1955 attack. "This to me indicates," Snyder boasted, "that President Johnson could never have had a cardiac attack of near the severity of that suffered by you."[11]

Eisenhower's relationship with Paul Dudley White remained occasional and distant. He visited with him briefly in Palm Desert in 1962, at which time the cardiologist chided him for riding in a golf cart rather than walking. In October of the following year, after seeking assurances from Mattingly that he was not being "used," Ike agreed to present the Bostonian with a gold stethoscope at an International Cardiology Foundation banquet honoring White for his pioneering work. But Eisenhower's gesture did not bespeak any sentimental attachment to White—whom he still resented for being what he thought was indiscreet and self-serving in 1955 — or any fond memories about his stay at Fitzsimons. Two years later, when the cardiologist admitted having a "wild idea" and "conspired" with a few others to arrange a ten-year reunion of those who cared for Ike after his heart attack, the general declined to celebrate "a past event that he would like to forget." A disappointed White told Snyder that "perhaps we can get together somehow, someday," because even though Ike preferred to forget his heart attack, "I am sure all of his doctors remember it with interest."[12]

Eisenhower's medical regimen continued as it had during the presidency, with periodical physical examinations and either frequent overnight hospitalizations or outpatient visits to maintain the long-term anticoagulant therapy. He worried about his prothrombin time; on one occasion in 1964 when it was at 80 percent, the "rather strange experience" prompted him to write directly to Leonard Heaton: "The question I should like to ask is, Is it normal for the prothrombin index, which in my case normally stands steady on the dosage that I am used to over the years, to vary so much in such a short time and with no change in the medication?" Otherwise he continued to take Metamucil daily to forestall stomach distress, and carried nitroglycerine with him to administer if chest pains occurred when he was not in the vicinity of a medical facility.

For the most part he held to his program to prevent a recurrence of cardiac problems. In two areas—control of his temper and his opportunity for exercise—there was improvement simply as a result of retirement. In contrast, he had difficulty with his diet because he no longer had a White House chef committed to preparing low-fat meals. At the end of 1961 he was seven pounds heavier than normal, and a physician at March Air Force Base cautioned him about his ingestion of high-calorie foods. He reached a maximum of 186 pounds during his trip to Europe in 1963 but, as he had for many years, took measures to lose weight upon his return.[13]

Eisenhower did persist in his battle against cholesterol, as Ann Whitman reported to Dr. Snyder in February, 1962: "The doctors think he has been fooling with the anti-poly saturated diet, or maybe it is the poly saturated diet, whatever saff flower is. Me I know none of these things. . . . Meantime I noticed DDE, who really seems to be feeling fine, had two sausages this morning for breakfast." Snyder worried about his friend's experimenting with a polyunsaturated diet, which he considered a fad, and sent him the latest AMA recommendation about the use of vegetable oils for cooking and a low cholesterol margarine as a table spread. In any event, his cholesterol level was higher during these years, with an occasional reading above 220, but the physicians were not unduly concerned.[14]

By taking care of himself Eisenhower enjoyed very good health for nearly five years, with no significant complications in his gastrointestinal or cardiovascular systems. He did have recurring symptoms of bronchitis and one seven-day hospitalization in 1964 for an acute respiratory infection. His doctors also discovered in 1965 that he had a late onset of type II diabetes, which required nothing more than dietary regulation. His foremost concern, however, as it had been for many years, had to do with his heart—occasional skipped beats and one instance of arrhythmia that led to a five-day hospital stay in the spring of 1963. At that time he was in Augusta during hot, humid weather, when he became fatigued after two days of "tough golf" and became aware of many skipped beats and a grossly irregular pulse. He mentioned it to Snyder, whom he sometimes invited to Augusta National to allow him to socialize with his old friends. The doctor found some of the symptoms alarming and immediately called Dr. Mattingly. The cardiologist recommended a respite from golf and the administration of quinidine. When the irregularities continued, the general returned to Washington and entered Walter Reed on 11 May.[15]

After careful monitoring, the physicians were certain there had not been another myocardial infarction, and they were not seriously concerned about the arrhythmia. The EKG did detect frequent premature beats and some short runs of tachycardia (rapid heartbeat), but the latter appeared to be from an atrial focus, which was not life-threatening, rather than ventricular, which could be. By the fourth day they were able to restore the heart rhythm to normal through the use of drugs, and they had the patient start walking. The next day, 15 May, he returned to Gettysburg with no restrictions on his activities but with directions to self-administer an antiarrhythmic drug if he detected a rapid heartbeat. But Ike could not get rid of his fears, for stirrings in the chest are forever a compelling alarm for anyone who has had a heart attack. His very first evening at home, after taking his pulse and noticing occasional pauses, he called the hospital for reassurance. His apprehension persisted, and in September he went as an outpatient to Walter Reed, at which time the cardiologist tried again to convince him that the "dropped beats" were innocuous.[16]

As Eisenhower noted to a friend, the doctors used this episode as a pretext to have him curtail his activities. "As I understand the more or less technical terminology of the doctors," he explained, "the crux of the matter is that due to my history of heart damage and my advance in years, I have gradually lessening cardiac reserve (I think this is the term they used). As a consequence my own doctor, who came up to spend the long weekend with me, following upon a recent checkup at the hospital, advised me to 'take it easier.'" Dr. Snyder did advise him to play golf no more than five days a week and to avoid early rising and fatigue; as in the past, he asked Mamie to help keep her husband under control. Ike, fearful that his friend might think of him as "a helpless individual," elaborated upon his doctor's advice: "He makes no dark predictions that I am about to depart this Vale of Tears; rather he insists that if I will be wise enough to listen to doctors there is no reason that I cannot have an expectancy approximately that of any other individual."[17]

Throughout these years the physicians found virtually no clinical evidence of the progression of the underlying coronary heart disease. There was no indication of angina, although the general mentioned on one occasion "a little burning feeling in the upper chest" after a mile walk. He did show a decreasing tolerance to physical activity, including golf, resulting in fatigue or the need to get a second wind, but there was no way to connect these developments with the heart. There was some question of congestive heart failure in 1965 when he had a respiratory infection, accompanied by pulmonary congestion and some dyspnea, but his condition cleared. The episode did move Mattingly to approach General Heaton about using some new diagnostic procedures—a ventriculogram and a coronary artery arteriogram—as a possible first step toward cardiac surgery to repair what the cardiologist still believed was a ventricular aneurysm. Heaton politely told him to "forget it," that Eisenhower "was doing well and why rock the boat." Heaton did respond to Mattingly's request that he appoint Colonel Loren F. "Tex" Parmley, a first-rate cardiologist who had trained under him, as his chief of medicine responsible for Eisenhower's care. But no one was prepared for the new development in the fall of 1965.[18]

During the annual vacation pilgrimage to Augusta in 1965, several of the Eisenhower gang arranged a party to belatedly celebrate "General Ike's" seventy-fifth birthday. Ninety people gathered from around the country, and many of them stayed over for several days of golf and festivities. It was a pleasant time. Ellis Slater noted in his diary that "no one could have appeared in better spirits and good health than the general," and Ike mentioned to his son that he had more than fulfilled the prediction of the doctors that he could live an active life for five to ten years. He had reason to be proud for having reached the outer limit of their prognosis. But coronary disease allows for no abiding respites. Less than two weeks later he suffered his second heart attack.[19]

On the evening of 8 November, the Eisenhowers had an early dinner with friends and then returned to "Mamie's cottage," where the general retired at about 11:00 P.M. Shortly after midnight he experienced chest pains—the first such episode reminiscent of his heart attack in 1955—and during the next hour he self-administered several nitroglycerine tablets sublingually. When the discomfort persisted, Mrs. Eisenhower called the club manager and the Secret Service, and within fifteen minutes a local cardiologist, Dr. Louis Battey, arrived and gave additional nitroglycerine, a painkiller, and oxygen. Soon thereafter an ambulance and physician appeared from nearby Fort Gordon, having been summoned by the Secret Service according to a prearranged plan. They decided to transfer Ike to the army hospital, and as they carried him out on a stretcher, he was reported to have said that "this episode was of his own doing." They arrived at about 2:20 A.M. and placed the general in a small room of a makeshift suite in the VIP quarters. In the meantime, Mamie had called Dr. Mattingly to tell him that her husband wanted him as a consultant. True to the promise he had made at retirement—to always be available if the president needed him—Mattingly took a quick flight and arrived at 8:30 A.M. the following day.[20]

An EKG taken on admission gave no evidence of a new myocardial infarction, but it did show coronary insufficiency accompanied by intermittent ventricular irregularities, a potentially life-threatening complication. The doctors administered antiarrhythmic drugs and also borrowed from St. John's Hospital in Augusta a recently acquired portable cardiac monitor and resuscitator so as to be able to combat the arrhythmia, if necessary, by electrical as well as chemical means. At about 4:00 A.M. the general experienced another dull substernal pain, and the local cardiologist placed him under an oxygen tent and gave him another painkiller and a sedative. In the morning, following the arrival from Washington of Dr. Mattingly and Colonel Parmley, and after a review of the laboratory reports, the cardiologists reached a consensus: the patient had suffered some angina pains but there was no evidence of infarction, and since his condition was stable and the arrhythmia was under control, the primary concern was for continued observation and an effort to prevent an actual heart attack. At 11:30 A.M. this favorable report went out to the press, which was clamorous for news and was growing rapidly because of an influx of reporters from Austin, where they had been covering Lyndon Johnson's gallbladder operation."[21]

During the next twenty-four hours the signs remained stable. The physicians nonetheless maintained a very careful watch, to the extent that Mattingly carried a walkie-talkie so he could be reached when he was away from the suite. Eisenhower was annoyed by the monitor at his bedside, so the Signal Corps wired up an oscilloscope in an adjoining room to record the EKGs. It was there, at 3:00 P.M. on 10 November, that Colonel Parmley, while talking with Mamie and John, noticed an increase in the ST segment elevation, indicative of coronary ischemia. He entered the general's room and learned that he had just begun to feel discomfort. Suddenly the pain became severe, and despite a painkiller and oxygen by face mask, it persisted for about forty-five minutes, accompanied by a rise in blood pressure to 190/120. Mattingly arrived and found the patient markedly apprehensive. But soon thereafter, when the general asked what was happening, it became apparent that he had suffered amnesia during the acute phase of the attack, the result of some inexplicable neurological deficit.[22]

The physicians suspected from the EKG that this episode of anginal pain was an infarction of the inferior lateral myocardium, but the readings were inconclusive. The laboratory tests showed an elevation in the enzyme levels, however, which confirmed their suspicions—they had been witness to the heart attack taking place. They waited two days before informing Eisenhower of his condition, and he accepted the news in his usual matter-of-fact style. But the doctors remained fearful because there were indications that his coronary disease had moved beyond the left anterior descending artery, the source of the problem in 1955, to involve the circumflex artery and possibly the right coronary artery.[23]

The facilities at Fort Gordon were not adequate for the intensive care of a coronary patient, so the team decided to move Eisenhower to Walter Reed as soon as possible. In the meantime, they brought in a medical officer, nurses, and equipment from Washington in order to provide around-the-clock monitoring. Mattingly had a crucial role because of his longtime knowledge of the case, and, quite unexpectedly, Paul White called from Florida to ask if he could stop by to see the general. Eisenhower was still disturbed by what he perceived as White's "publicity seeking," but he acceded to a visit on 13 November, and the Bostonian examined him with his gold stethoscope. One member of the former team, Howard Snyder, could not be present. "To face the shock of the realization that the infirmities of the aging processes caused me to fall by the way, especially in this urgent situation, was humiliating," he wrote with deep sadness. "Since November 1945 there has not been an emergency of any nature, whether because of illness, injury, or serious upset in statecraft, when I have not been close to your side. During all these years I have always been present to shoulder the responsibilities of any emergency in your days and nights." This time, too, he had wanted to be there, "if for no other reason than [that] I believe I could have helped to reassure Mamie." But he had to be content with his promise, plaintively delivered: "I have been there in spirit every moment."[24]

This period of convalescence was shorter than after the first attack—slightly over five weeks as compared with seven in Denver—but still longer than normal because of the doctors' concern about the widespread, multivessel nature of the atherosclerotic disease. The "armchair" treatment was by this time established practice, and the patient was sitting on the side of his bed on 15 November, in a chair the next day, and for prolonged periods five days later. On 22 November he left by train for Alexandria, Virginia, and the following day traveled by helicopter to Walter Reed. His recovery in the hospital was remarkably free of complications; there were several instances of transient chest pain, but they were determined to be non-cardiovascular in origin, and there were occasional "skipped beats" but never more than three per minute. At the end of the third week Eisenhower was able to take his first steps, and by 18 December he was well enough to leave for Gettysburg. His prescribed regimen was not unlike that of a decade earlier—a progressive but gradual increase in activities, a diet moderately low in fat, and a stable weight between 165 and 170 pounds.[25]

The prognosis after this heart attack was not as bright. Indeed, the staff at Walter Reed had determined that when the Eisenhowers left by train on 28 December for their winter sojourn in Palm Desert, Colonel Parmley should accompany them. He would be on hand for any emergencies, and he could also make contact with the various military establishments to assure continued and proper medical care. The general knew, as well, that the situation was now more threatening because the insidious disease obviously was still at work. There was a popular understanding that, as in baseball, the third strike meant an out, and with this illness one was always at bat. John concluded that although his father showed no outward signs of worry, the "recognition of mortality existed beneath the surface." He began to make plans to "simplify his estate" and, in the meantime, "to follow his doctors instructions to the letter," as he always had.[26]

In mid-January 1966 Dr. Mattingly entered the following in his diary: "It is now a 'wait and see' situation as to how the coronary disease progresses after the second infarction. Hope for improvement, but we are not optimistic." The cardiologists could presume reasonably that since atherosclerosis had occluded two major arteries, it was everywhere in the coronary system, and they were expecting the appearance of such symptoms as angina, dyspnea, and congestive heart failure. But even they could not have foreseen the striking change the most recent attack would bring about—a progressive deterioration not only of the cardiovascular function but of the gastrointestinal system as well. Colonel Parmley found that the care of the general now constituted nearly a full-time job.[27]

Eisenhower had no intention of giving up his active life. He continued writing *At Ease,* he met regularly to advise President Johnson about the war, and he gave support to Republican politicians. He also meant to keep playing golf. On 8 January 1966 he and Mamie, accompanied by the Allens, left for Palm Desert on a special train assembled at Harrisburg. Their trip was uneventful, but as Ike increased his activities during what he thought would be a pleasant rehabilitation, he had a bout of arthritis, with pain in the neck and left knee and swelling in his wrists and fingers. These complications forced him to curtail his golf to some extent, and worries about his heart made his vacation even less enjoyable. In January he had an episode of dyspnea, and on several occasions he had epigastric and substernal distress lasting between five and ten minutes, usually after a meal or with exercise, and alarming enough to prompt him to take nitroglycerine tablets.[28]

The Eisenhowers returned to Gettysburg in late April, and on 4 May Ike entered Walter Reed for the treatment of his joint problems. The next day, shortly after a pleasant dinner with guests, he had a "little heartburn" and asked the nurse for some peppermint water. She then left, and he took two nitroglycerine tablets without getting any relief. He called her again, and she gave him an oxygen mask and called the doctor, who found him with severe substernal pain, shortness of breath, a pulse of 110, and blood pressure of 190/110. Colonel Parmley proceeded on the supposition that his patient had suffered another myocardial infarction, but during the next several days neither the tests nor the symptoms verified such a diagnosis, and the physician concluded that the episode was due to prolonged ischemia with minimal damage to the heart.[29]

On 25 May, still in the hospital, Ike had another ten-minute period of substernal pain while he was eating ice cream and watching television. He took two nitroglycerine tablets, asked for oxygen, and appeared to Mamie to be anxious. As before, the cardiovascular examinations gave no evidence of a heart attack, but Colonel Parmley concluded that he "is now beginning to have episodes of coronary insufficiency manifested primarily as angina." Two days later, he released the general to return to Gettysburg, with his arthritis greatly improved and his cardiac status stable, and with a warning to eat a smaller evening meal and to abstain from golf for at least two weeks.[30]

In mid-July Eisenhower returned to Walter Reed for an overnight follow-up and revealed that during his one-mile morning walk he sometimes had to stop because of shortness of breath and tightness in the throat, but without pain. He also mentioned that on several occasions he experienced "indigestion" lasting about ten minutes after his evening meal, which was not relieved by nitroglycerine. As if to provide a demonstration, on the night of admission he developed a substernal discomfort that would not respond to nitroglycerine, oxygen, or an antacid, and that required morphine for relief. During the next week he had almost daily substernal discomfort, and on 25 July he returned for further cardiovascular and abdominal evaluations, which led Dr. Parmley to conclude that he was suffering from two processes: "One was clearly that of angina pectoris, but this seemed to be relatively infrequent except when triggered by the second and the main cause of his symptoms, an apparent dyspepsia, the etiology of which is not clearly delineated. The possibility of an esophagitis was one of primary consideration." The most the doctor could do at the time was to add to his patient's medication a long-acting nitrite for the angina, and an old remedy for the stomach which Dr. Snyder had used during the White House days.[31]

During the next several months, Ike improved to the extent that he was able to participate in the election campaign and make his usual fall trip to Georgia. But his angina and dyspepsia did not go away, and during his travel he had to seek assistance from hotel physicians and, in one instance, from a fire rescue team. At Augusta he had anginal pain in the wake of either too much exercise or excitement, as on one occasion during the jubilation after Cliff Roberts made a hole in one. Throughout these months Colonel Parmley had come to believe that the gallbladder might be aggravating, and perhaps inducing, the anginal pain. He finally convinced Eisenhower to undergo the requisite studies on 20 November, and they showed poor function and five large and four small gallstones, leading to a diagnosis of chronic inflammation of the gallbladder.[32]

Having discovered the likely culprit, Colonel Parmley approached somewhat gingerly the obvious conclusion—surgery—the more so because even the surgeons were apprehensive about the risk. A consultant from Johns Hopkins University admitted that gallbladder surgery was an exceedingly difficult problem because of the president's age, vascular condition, mild emphysema, and worsening angina, but he recommended it, nonetheless, because the patient was a "vigorous man" for his years. Tom Mattingly, who agreed, argued for surgery while the patient's heart was still in a stable state with better reserve than it would have in the future. The doctors explained the risk to Ike, who gave his consent and insisted that General Heaton perform the operation. On 12 December 1966, in a procedure lasting one hour and forty-five minutes, the surgeons removed nineteen stones. The general's recovery was excellent and uncomplicated, and two days after Christmas he returned again to his Gettysburg farm.[33]

After the operation Parmley and Mattingly decided not to reinstitute anticoagulant therapy because the danger of hemorrhage would outweigh the potential benefits; they advised Ike that he could play no golf, except putting and chipping, until mid-March of the coming year. They also hoped he would decide against his habitual winter trip to California. Despite his stable condition at the moment, his condition had deteriorated throughout the year, and his chronic angina posed a constant threat. But Mattingly would not make such a recommendation unless the general personally asked him about it, for as he noted in his diary, "I have learned from the past that he does not appreciate voluntary advice."[34]

The Eisenhowers did not want to spend the winter at Gettysburg, and on 4 January 1967 they left Harrisburg for California on their special train with their staff and Colonel Parmley, who preferred not to let his patient travel so far alone. The early stages of the trip were routine and enjoyable, but when the train began to ascend to the Mofatt Tunnel west of Denver and reached an elevation of 6,000 feet, the general experienced a crescendo type of angina. Mamie, who had always believed that altitude was a threat to the heart, panicked—so much so that the doctor had to confine her to her room under sedation.

As the engineer raced as rapidly as possible toward the summit of 12,500 feet, Parmley remained secluded with the general in his compartment for several hours, hoping to offer him reassurance. He administered oxygen, nitroglycerine, and, when that provided no relief, a painkiller. During these hours Ike became nostalgic and talked of his experiences—from his years in the Philippines to the steps he had taken to end the Korean War. He reminisced about the pleasant days of trout fishing in Colorado and the gourmet delight of eating the catch, freshly fried over the open fire, with friends all around. Most touchingly, he recalled the death from scarlet fever of his four year-old son, Icky, and his own sense of total helplessness during his son's illness. He described the frustration he had felt when the medical personnel barred him from the pediatric ward at the hospital, and his attempts to pull himself up with his hands on the outside of the building so he could look through the window to gain a view of his child. When Parmley explained that doctors had changed the practice that had hurt him so much, so as to encourage parents to be with their sick children, Eisenhower seemed pleased.[35]

The sojourn in California began happily, with an enthusiastic crowd on hand to greet the Eisenhowers at San Bernardino, but the remainder of the year left little room for celebration. At Palm Desert two events worried the physicians. The first, at the end of February, was Ike's initial frank episode of congestive heart failure, which although it responded well to treatment, indicated further deterioration of his cardiovascular condition. The other, on 3 April, was a transient ischemic cerebrovascular event, reminiscent of the small stroke in 1957. It occurred on the golf course, and Ike's friend Freeman Gosden reported it to his secretary. There were no lasting effects, but in Washington General Heaton was so concerned that he sent Colonel Parmley back to California in the guise of a casual visitor, hoping not to alarm the Eisenhowers. The colonel's informal observations convinced Heaton that Ike had no residual dysfunction, but he nonetheless arranged for a physician to accompany him on the train back to Gettysburg.[36]

The remainder of 1967 brought no further cardiovascular incidents—no congestive failure, no arrrythmias except for occasional skipped beats, and only short periods of angina promptly relieved by nitroglycerine. But Ike's gastrointestinal problems required seven hospitalizations. No sooner had he returned home than he had severe abdominal pain with diarrhea and vomiting, and on 7 May he had to rush by ambulance to Walter Reed, where the specialists suspected a recurrence of his ileitis or complications from his gallbladder surgery. During the next six months, he suffered similar problems—the worst being a fourteen-hour siege in August—which the doctors could diagnose only in such vague terms as "acute gastroenteritis" and "irritable bowel syndrome," and which, apart from the inherent danger, concerned them because once again they served as a trigger for short periods of angina.[37]

Ike could still enjoy golf, and he and Mamie decided to leave Gettysburg before Christmas in order to visit the Eisenhower center in Abilene on their way to Palm Desert. Prior to their departure, they passed another milestone when they decided to will their farm to the government. They were not prepared for the poignant and wrenching moments they would have to go through on 29 November, when Horace Busby and Stewart Udall, two emissaries from President Johnson, arrived in Gettysburg to receive the deed. The emissaries arrived by helicopter in mid-afternoon, with the sun shining but the wind so cold that the general had been asked to remain inside. He emerged, nonetheless, and Busby observed that "the state of his health is all too obvious and the concern of his staff for his well-being is not misplaced." They went to the glassed-in porch retreat where the two old folks, Mamie explained, had been "observing quiet hour"—she by playing solitaire and watching television, he by painting with his oils.

"Our conversation was cordial and simple," Busby recalled, "no ceremonies, no signing, no onlookers. The calm, I soon learned, was deceptive. For both of them, it was an emotional moment, most especially for Mrs. Eisenhower. I felt uneasy, as though Secretary Udall and I were men from the bank foreclosing on the farm." The general began talking to the secretary, mostly about his friend Alton Jones, who had purchased some adjacent land to prevent its commercial development and then had donated it to the United States. Mamie talked with Busby, mostly about the meaning the farm had for her. "Repeatedly, her eyes welled with tears as she talked," he noticed. "She had not, as the General said, wanted to sign the deed. Her explanation to me: 'After fifty-one years of doing it, I thought I was through, but now I am back in a government house again.' Her emotions of the afternoon, however, ran more deeply; it was very clear to me that heavy on her heart and mind was the question whether, after they departed the following day for California, they would ever return together."

Mamie went on to explain that she associated the porch with Ike's recovery from his illnesses when he was president. After his heart attack, she had called an architect from Denver and arranged to have the porch enclosed so there would be a sunny and cheerful place for Ike. After the ileitis surgery, he again did most of his recuperating at Gettysburg. "My son tells me," she revealed, "the farm and the porch have lengthened Ike's life twice already"; she added very softly, "I don't suppose you could ask for more." Mrs. Eisenhower also told with emotion of their plan to visit Abilene to see the site and the chapel where they would be buried, noting that Ike had told her when he was a first lieutenant, "Mamie, I don't know where or when I'll die, but I want you to promise me that wherever you bury me, it won't be Arlington Cemetery." She recounted in some detail how she had had the body of their first son removed from the original grave for reburial at the plot in Abilene, "so we can all be together again."

After Mamie became quiet, Ike recounted with "extraordinary affection" various stories about his friend Pete Jones, who had died accidentally in 1962. Then there were photographs, a tour of the house, and the walk to the helicopter, with the general going along, even without his hat and coat. Busby sensed the special meaning of the situation and the depth of the Eisenhowers' feelings. In an attempt to offer solace, he mentioned President Johnson's personal comment that someday he and Lady Bird might have to make the same decision. When Busby returned to Washington, he thanked the president for the opportunity to have shared in what he had felt was a "quiet but unforgettable moment."[38]

Mamie's deepest fears about the future were justified. The Eisenhowers left by train the next day for Palm Desert, accompanied by a physician because Colonel Parmley still considered Ike's cardiovascular condition "fragile." They never returned together to Gettysburg. They planned to stop in Abilene to see the Meditation Chapel, the news of which prompted Tom Mattingly to write in his diary that it was "perhaps a bad omen as to the approaching year." The general did become "upset," John Eisenhower reported, "an emotion brought on not by concern for himself, but by the sight of the tiny plaque on the floor where the body of my older brother had been placed." There were no medical problems until the last part of

Strolling with Secretary of the Interior Stewart Udall minutes after signing over his Gettysburg farm to the U.S. government. (Courtesy Dwight D. Eisenhower Library)

the trip, when a stomach disorder diagnosed as "acute gastroenteritis" caused Ike some weakness and triggered an increasing angina that required ten nitroglycerine pills over a period of eight hours.[39]

Upon arrival in California on 2 December, the doctors gave the general a physical examination, which "demonstrated a very well developed and extremely well preserved male, looking considerably younger than his seventy-seven years"; administered several EKGs, which denied any serious cardiovascular problem; and confined him to bed on a liquid diet. Mamie called John to tell him his father had some kind of ailment and that his spirits were "low." But he improved gradually and on 11 December was able to go to his office and to socialize. He also shot his first hole in one on the par three golf course he was allowed to play, gloating that it was the "thrill of a lifetime."[40]

Until late April Eisenhower had no stomach problems, and only mild exertional angina that still allowed him to play some golf and enjoy his vacation. On 25 and 26 April, however, he experienced several bouts of angina and dyspnea that would not respond to nitroglycerine, and on the night of 27 April he had another such episode. He felt well enough to play golf the following morning, with no pain or shortness of breath, but after lunch he had a period of prolonged chest pain relieved only by a painkiller. Several EKGs indicated arrhythmias and conduction abnormalities, and the next day physicians took him by helicopter to the March Air Force Base Hospital with a diagnosis of a new heart attack, his third. From Washington Colonel Parmley and Colonel Robert J. Hall, who was soon to replace him, rushed by jet aircraft to California, concerned about the runs of ventricular tachycardia. The general's cardiac rhythm stabilized over a period of several weeks, however, after treatment with lidocaine, procainamide, quinidine, and digitalis, and on 14 May he was well enough for transfer to Walter Reed on "Air Force One," sent by President Johnson to facilitate the air evacuation. Before Eisenhower left he made a final request—that the authorities give his nurses several days of leave when they arrived in Washington.[41]

Eisenhower remained at Walter Reed from 14 May 1968 until his death some ten months later, during which time the doctors continuously monitored him with an EKG oscilloscope. For much of this period he was able to sit up, move around his room, walk the length of the corridor in Ward 8 several times a day, and talk to visitors. But every time he improved, another siege of one kind or another struck him down. On 15 June, while walking in the hall, he suffered intense substernal pain that required morphine for relief and turned out to be his fourth heart attack. He had several "shaky" days, and for ten days he was under constant treatment for various arrhythmias, but his usual and remarkable recuperative powers returned, after which he was able to resume sitting up for brief periods several times a day. But this attack, which the doctors considered of greater magnitude than the one in April, made a difference. Julie Nixon reasoned that it "marked the beginning of the period when Mamie and her family had to stand by and watch as Ike, for the first time in his life, found that he no longer could control his own destiny." Indeed, the day after the attack she wrote in her diary, "David is heartbroken because he pictures his grandfather as a maverick who would like to ride off in the hills and die with his boots on."[42]

Julie Nixon was perceptive. Since 1955 Ike had taken charge of his illness by changing his style of life, restricting his diet, and stilling his anger. Even after the 1965 attack, he could believe reasonably that his own behavior could affect his condition. But the third attack had moved him to the limits of survival for even the most fortunate of men, and the fourth, coming exactly seven weeks later, implied an escalating deterioration. More than ever before he was dependent now upon whatever measures the doctors could bring to bear. And he was more dependent upon Mamie, who moved into a tiny sitting room and bedroom near his suite. For weeks at a time she would not leave the hospital, and she refused to return to the farm without him. "Whenever Ike went away," she once said, "the house sagged. When he came home, the house was alive again." For the time being she made the hospital her home, and from her room she guarded her husband from noise and stress.[43]

One of the first to see him was Richard Nixon, who stopped by on 15 July for an hour-long chat about election-year politics. This time Ike wanted to be certain there could be no misunderstanding about where he stood, and a few days later he met with a half dozen reporters in the east lounge of his hospital suite to give his former vice president a preconvention endorsement. He arrived in a wheelchair wearing a blue dressing gown with words stitched on the pocket, "FEELING GREAT AGAIN." But as he walked the last six or seven steps to his desk, the newsmen could not help but notice that he was some twenty pounds lighter than the robust man they remembered. He seemed even more frail on the evening of 5 August, the opening day of the National Republican Convention, when he put on a business suit and went to the living room of Ward 8 to tape a television message for the delegates assembled in Miami. Mamie had worried about the emotional strain involved in the occasion. "After 1955," she explained, "whenever Ike gave a speech, I always sat there in utter dread that he would have a heart attack on the air." But she went along with the doctors, who, after carefully considering the pros and cons, decided that to deny him the opportunity to "speak his piece" would create more tension and stress than to let him go on with it. This particular speech was important to him—as a testament not only to his party but to his own survival.[44]

It was also a turning point. At 6:00 the following morning, Eisenhower entered a period of nearly a month that made all of his previous cardio-vascular episodes seem inconsequential in comparison, and that made the doctors fear that he could die at any time. It began with a crushing chest pain unrelieved by nitroglycerine and requiring morphine, oxygen, lidocaine, and heparin. On 7 August he felt a dull aching sensation in his chest and underwent intermittent fibrillation. The EKG and enzyme readings indicated another heart attack—number five—which was accompanied by blood-clotting complications requiring leg wrapping and passive and active motion. He was in no condition on 9 August to hear Richard Nixon tell the full and expectant galleries in Miami of his desire, for a number of reasons, to win this election: "First a personal one. General Eisenhower, as you know, lies critically ill in the Walter Reed Hospital tonight. I have talked, however, with Mrs. Eisenhower on the telephone. She tells me . . . there is nothing he lives more for, and there is nothing that would lift him more than to win in November. And I say, let's win this one for Ike."[45]

For the next week, antiarrhythmic drugs worked reasonably well, but then Eisenhower's condition took a new course accompanied by heroic measures on the part of a supremely dedicated staff, including a standby team skilled in defibrillations and resuscitations. Heading the staff was cardiologist Robert J. Hall, who had received his training at Walter Reed when Mattingly was chief of cardiology, and who was Heaton's choice to tend to Ike after the return of cardiovascular problems in 1965. Dr. Hall, in his clinical record, described the frightening new development in its early hours and in all its intensity:

At 1320 hours on 16 August 1968 electrocardiographic monitoring revealed the sudden onset of ventricular tachycardia which rapidly deteriorated into ventricular fibrillation. Closed chest cardiac massage was instituted immediately and an anesthesiologist supported ventilation within a brief period thereafter. In somewhat over 120 seconds the patient was defibrillated with 400 watt-seconds transthoracic DC shock. . . . He regained consciousness rapidly but required intravenous phenobarbital and pentothal to control mental confusion and hyper-irritability. An intravenous was started by insertion of a plastic cannula percutaneously into the left external jugular vein. . . . By 1800 hours, after the effects of intravenous sedatives had abated, it was evident that no acute brain damage had been sustained. The patient was completely alert and had complete recall of all events immediately up to the onset of the attack.[46]

The former president was the beneficiary not only of a dedicated staff but of a major advance—the coronary care unit—which brought together in one area the specialized equipment and skilled personnel able to challenge sudden death resulting from electrical failure of the heart. Scientists had begun research on this problem in the 1920s, inspired and supported by the Consolidated Edison Company, which was concerned about the increasing number of its linemen killed by accidental electrocution. The researchers knew that an electric shock could cause ventricular fibrillation, and they discovered that it was possible to restore a rhythmic beat by delivering an alternating-current countershock to the heart, which physicians did in the 1940s during surgery and in the 1950s by external application. During the 1950s, groups from Harvard and Johns Hopkins developed defibrillating equipment, the best of which had a capacitor synchronized with the EKG so a direct-current shock could be delivered at the safest period of the cardiac cycle. They also designed a reliable electronic monitoring machine that "would not get bored or distracted or walk out of the room seconds before an unpredictable episode of cardiac arrest." In 1962, at Bethany Hospital in Kansas City, the first coronary care unit opened.[47]

The onset of the severe arrhythmia marked the beginning of a cataclysmic period lasting for nine days. In the early morning hours of 17 August, the ventricular tachycardia returned, and shortly after eight o'clock, in the middle of a conversation, Eisenhower lost consciousness and went into convulsive movements. With the monitor screen indicating ventricular fibrillation, the physicians began external cardiac massage together with mouth-to-mouth resuscitation. Suddenly the patient was pulseless, and the doctors were able to return his regular heart rhythm only after sixty seconds had elapsed and only by means of three 400 watt-seconds direct-current discharges. Since the drug of choice, lidocaine, appeared ineffective in controlling the recurring episodes of fibrillation, Dr. Hall used bretylium tosylate, an experimental antiarrhythmic drug developed in England, which he administered deep into the muscles every three hours.[48]

When the news of Eisenhower's deteriorating condition reached the press and the medical community, it brought forth suggestions for even more heroic treatment. The famous Texan cardiac surgeons Michael Debakey and Denton Cooley approached their military colleagues about the possibility of resorting to surgery as a means of improving the blood supply to the heart muscle. The conceivable options were coronary bypass surgery and heart transplant (for which twenty healthy Americans offered their hearts); both procedures were in their infancy, and neither was feasible. The military physicians, including Dr. Mattingly, discussed the possibility of a heart transplant among themselves and with the Eisenhower family, and agreed unanimously that "age, associated cerebral disease, diabetes mellitus, prostatism, ileitis and gastrointestinal bleeding on heparin all make such a consideration untenable." Mamie indicated that Ike realized he could not withstand a transplant and that he wanted his remaining days to be a peaceful time with his family.[49]

The situation seemed even more threatening on the afternoon of 17 August, when the president's heart went into fibrillation on three separate occasions, two of them requiring direct-current countershocks. Defibrillation was necessary again just before midnight, and there was a progressive increase in the erratic behavior of his heart. Morning brought no surcease from the assaults, as Dr. Hall recorded: "At 0655 ventricular fibrillation lasting 18 sec. was terminated with direct-current countershock. This was preceded by three short bursts of self-terminating rapid ventricular tachycardia-fibrillation at 0440, 0545, and 0552 hrs." Because of this flurry of arrhythmias and the need for defibrillation, the doctors concluded that bretylium was ineffective, and they discontinued the drug.[50]

By this time the physicians felt a sense of hopelessness, as is evident in Dr. Hall's record: "Bretylium does not seem to be suppressing ventricular fibrillation and ventricular premature contractions any better than the previous agents. Fear we are dealing with an irreversible ischemic area with a state of 'status electrical angina.' Do not know how to reverse the course." The doctors would not give up on the general, however, and early in the afternoon of 18 August they resorted to another method they thought might control the arrhythmias; they attached him to a table-model artificial pacemaker and passed a catheter enclosing a casing wire down his left jugular vein into the atrium. They hoped the pacemaker would overcome the abnormal impulses, but they had to discontinue it after five hours, during which time there were two additional episodes requiring defibrillation.[51]

During the next seven days, the patient continued to suffer persistent fibrillations, with many of the salvos terminating spontaneously after a few seconds but with five of them requiring countershock. On 24 August Dr. Hall decided to give bretylium another chance, and whether as a result of the drug or for some unknown reason, Ike's condition began to stabilize. By 29 August he was feeling and eating progressively better; on 9 September he was able to sit up in bed and dangle his feet; on 15 September he was able to sit in a chair for the first time in a month; and during the subsequent weeks he gradually regained his strength and progressed to sitting up in a chair three times daily for thirty minutes each. He still had occasional irregular beats but only one brief incidence of atrial fibrillation.[52]

Altogether Ike endured dozens of bursts of fibrillation, with his pulse racing at between 250 and 300 beats per minute, and although most of the episodes were brief and self-terminating, fourteen required electrical defibrillation to keep him alive. As his heart ran amok, he was in and out of consciousness, usually aware of a dull ache in his chest, often cold and clammy, and always desperately weak. He faced death with every salvo, and although he survived, he would never be the same again, for as one of the doctors noted: "It is scarcely an exaggeration to state that he 'died' fourteen times." Now his life was solely in the hands of the physicians and, even more frightening, completely dependent upon the efficacy of their drugs and machines.[53]

The clinical record gives a stark sense of the frantic and sustained efforts of the medical team during this extraordinary period, as the physicians juggled the drugs and applied the shocks so as to prevent their patient from dying, but it gives little indication of his response—although later he admitted thinking, "I might cash in my chips." Clearly he wanted to stay alive. "He was terribly, terribly grateful to these boys," General Heaton recorded, "who, the minute this started fibrillating, were in there and defibrillated." Heaton, who tried to give Ike hope by talking to him about playing golf again, was convinced that he understood the "lingering and ultimate seriousness of the situation," a truth evident in his patient's question to General Gruenther, "Have I turned into a vegetable yet?" Heaton recognized, as well, that Ike's intellectual functions and his interest in current events seemed not to have suffered, and through it all he was calm and uncomplaining. As Dr. Hall recorded at one of the darkest moments, in the aftermath of several defibrillating shocks, "His humor, wit, and cooperativeness persist unabated, courageous in living and dying."[54]

Dr. Hall could not deceive himself about the condition of Eisenhower's heart. At the end of August, even though he was able to control the arrhythmias (he continued the bretylium until late January), he noted that his patient became fatigued after the slightest exertion. "This degree of lack of 'coronary reserve' is distressing," the cardiologist continued, "and an ill omen regarding potential for recovery and rehabilitation. Believe that the recovery process will be delayed and fear that a sequence of difficulties yet lie ahead. I suspect that the degree of overall coronary involvement must be severe." Hall's concern was that "seven" heart attacks had so weakened the heart muscle that it would not be able to pump sufficient amounts of blood, a condition widely known as congestive heart failure.[55]

And yet, the general began to regain strength and spirit. David Eisenhower and his fiancé, Julie Nixon, visited in early October and found him lying flat in bed with his head slightly raised. "He was so thin and wasted under the army-issue sheet," Julie wrote. "The blueness of his eyes was startling in the dead-white face." But he was feisty: "As soon as we said hello, Ike gave us a huge grin and whipped open his hospital smock, exposing his Nixon 'buttons.' He had stuck Nixon decals on the electrodes attached to his chest." He also was relatively optimistic, as he expressed to Bill Robinson on 11 October: "As of now, I feel quite well, although I am still confined to my bed. The doctors say I am making steady progress, so I am still hopeful that one of these bright days I will be able to get around and mingle with my old friends, even though I think the verdict will be that I will never again play golf."[56]

On his seventy-eighth birthday, 14 October, Ike had a visit from the army's new chief of staff, General William Westmoreland, and that afternoon the nurses wheeled him to a raised window where he could listen to the army band present a special salute. As he waved a small flag with five white stars against a field of red, the band played "Army Blue," "The Yellow Rose of Texas," and "The Caissons Go Rolling Along." Two days later he was boasting to Bill Robinson of further improvement: "The doctors keep me in bed most of the time, but I am permitted to sit up three times a day for forty-minute periods each. This permission includes an opportunity for me to take about four or five steps to my chair over by the window. They still believe that I will make even greater improvement, but because of the duration of my illness, they do not suggest that I will be out of the hospital very shortly. I am sure that I will still be here until after the election."[57]

Mamie never gave up hope that Ike would go home again, and she became a zealot at conserving his energy. She controlled his visitors, allowing no more than two at a time and for no more than ten minutes, and she censored potentially disturbing news or television programs, including his favorite, the army-navy football game. On Thanksgiving Day she arranged for members of the Eisenhower and Nixon families to share a single course of the hospital's turkey dinner with Ike; Julie and David shared the fruit cup, Barbara Eisenhower and Pat Nixon the pumpkin pie, and so on. Her protectiveness still was not enough to satisfy Tom Mattingly, who resented anyone—especially politicians—who caused the slightest stress for his former patient. On one occasion he stopped by to visit the general, found numerous other visitors waiting in the VIP suite, and was so upset that he immediately left the hospital.[58]

Throughout the autumn months Eisenhower's condition remained stable; he had occasional angina and abdominal discomfort, but he regained enough strength to sit up for an hour several times a day and to walk short distances. His improvement did not hold, however, and the early winter months brought recurring episodes of gastrointestinal distress. At 3:50 A.M. on 21 February 1969, a severe pain to the right of the umbilicus was so sharp as to awaken him. X-rays gave evidence of a small bowel obstruction. The doctors tried to decompress him with intravenous fluids and the "much detested nasogastric tube," but the distention increased. On 23 February they decided that surgical intervention was necessary and consulted with the cardiologists, including Dr. Mattingly, who noted in his diary: "It did not require a cardiologist to inform the group that the survival of the contemplated surgery and the postoperative period was unlikely, but the survival from an unrelieved intestinal obstruction was nil; therefore, one should accept the risk of surgery." Eisenhower, fearless as always, was prepared, and as the attendants wheeled him down the hall, he grinned and gave the "thumbs-up" sign.[59]

At 9:20 that Sunday evening the surgical team, headed by General Heaton, explored the abdomen and located two large adhesive bands producing a complete small bowel obstruction some eighteen inches from the previous ileitis bypass. They freed the bands without difficulty and then were able to look at the area of original anastomosis of 1956, which they were surprised to find had remained widely open and functional, with an opening approximately the size of the surgeon's thumb. The patient withstood the two-and-one-half-hour procedure with no change in the blood pressure and with little arrhythmia, which elated General Heaton, but over the next several days he suffered from lethargy, drowsiness, and some hallucinations. The latter were worrisome, but a neurological consultant advised that there was no apparent damage. There was increasing dyspnea and bronchopneumonia, and a return of intermittent atrial fibrillation, but on 1 March the doctors recorded an improvement in Eisenhower's mental and physical status.[60]

John Eisenhower visited shortly after the operation and detected the first words approaching despair that his father had ever uttered. "It's an eerie

Visiting with Nixon at Walter Reed two months before his death.
(Courtesy Dwight D. Eisenhower Library)

feeling to have them hit you with one thing and then another," Ike told him. "Well," John replied, "now that you've had that intestinal blockage taken out, you ought to start feeling better. Maybe now you can gain some weight." "God, I hope so," Eisenhower sighed. In fact, he remained weak, seemingly unable to overcome the nearly ten days he had gone without oral nourishment, and he appeared deathly ill. When President Nixon stopped by after his return from a trip to Europe, he was shocked at the deterioration of Ike's condition during a period of less than a month; he noted: "Looked like a corpse—waxen face."[61]

On 8 March Ike sat on the edge of his bed for the first time since his surgery. Within a week he was sitting in a chair for brief periods and, in his doctor's opinion, "showing evidence of gradual improvement in mood, mentation, and physical tolerance to exercise." But these isolated signs were deceptive. There could be no recovery this time, simply because his heart was no longer able to function as a pump. The final deterioration began on 14 March, when he suffered lower chest pain, followed by intermittent breathlessness and arrhythmias. During the next ten days he had pulmonary congestion, intermittent atrial fibrillation, tachycardia, and persistent dyspnea—to the extent that he became acutely short of breath merely by sitting in bed to eat a light supper. On 26 March he began the day with considerable pulmonary edema, and later, in the words of Dr. Hall, he was "considerably restless, dyspneic, and very agitated. Would fall asleep during a conversation only to reawaken with a startle. Morphine required for comfort and dyspneas." The following morning, Dr. Hughes informed Paul White of the situation. "The general remains in a state of constant left ventricular failure despite the use of all applicable therapeutic measures," he wrote. "We cannot help but feel that his myocardial reserve is just about gone, and certainly this must be true if it parallels his general state of increasing weakness."[62]

The family began gathering on 25 March, apprised by the doctors of the gravity of the circumstances. They found that Ike already had been making his arrangements, aware that little time remained. He had asked the Reverend Billy Graham to speak with him of spiritual matters. He had ordered a dozen copies of John's book, *The Bitter Woods*, which he asked John to sign and give to the members of the caring medical staff. He began giving last-minute instructions to his son, such as "Be good to Mamie." He said his good-byes, and with President Nixon, who praised him generously for his monumental role in bringing safety to America and the world, he opened his eyes, lifted his head from the pillow, thanked him for honoring him with such words, and then raised his hand in a final salute. He clearly was at peace with himself, telling John on the evening of 27 March that the sooner the end arrived the better.[63]

That evening he slept fitfully, uncomfortable even with his head and chest elevated. At 7:00 A.M. he was especially restless, with "deep anxious respiration" and a blood pressure of 76/70. At 8:20 A.M. Dr. Hughes called John Eisenhower to tell him that the end would be coming soon. Forty minutes later, with John, Barbara, and David at his bedside, the general barked an order to lower the shades, followed by a command to lift him up and another to lift him higher. Then he turned to his son and spoke softly, "I want to go. God take me." The doctor gave him a sedative, and he lost consciousness. For the next two hours he dozed off and on and was still obviously "air hungry." Dr. Hall suspected that Ike had developed a massive pulmonary embolus; Hall wrote in his clinical record that by 11:30 A.M. he "had had progressive and rapid deterioration. He was having difficulty breathing and was agitated, and during waking periods he was severely air hungry. The doctor gave him morphine, and from this point on he appeared slightly more comfortable and dozed. At 12:35 P.M., on 28 March 1969, with Mamie holding his hand, all cardiac and respiratory activity ceased, and the oscilloscope above his bed registered its telltale straight line. The doctors pronounced him dead.[64]

The tough old soldier finally had fallen before the dread disease. Many years before the great Osler had issued his warning: "A man is as old as his arteries." The pathologist at autopsy was more specific in describing what he had found: "coronary atherosclerotic occlusive disease, multifocal, severe, with multiple recanalized thrombi." In layman's terms, the three arteries that fed blood to the heart were virtually closed; the interior linings of all of them were marked by thickening, fibrosis, and calcification that in some points had reduced the canals to pinpoint size.[65]

Overall the atherosclerosis was so extensive that it was a wonder the general had survived for the past year. The right coronary artery was in the best condition and, despite substantial thickening, was unob-structed throughout. In contrast, the left anterior descending artery, the renowned "widow-maker" that covered the front side of the left ventri-cle, was severely occluded shortly beyond its origin; in various sections it was narrowed to 10 percent of normal. As described in the autopsy protocol, "The intima [innermost layer] in one particular section has a small amount of attached thrombus of recent vintage, and the lumen of the vessel consists of multiple small channels surrounded by loosely arranged connective tissue suggesting recanalization." The circumflex artery, serving primarily the back side of the heart, was even worse; it showed thickening almost immediately at its origin, and in several sec-tions it had no opening whatever.[66]

This process of coronary occlusion, after a near lifetime of insidious and relentless advance, had taken its toll against the heart muscle itself, the myocardium. Indeed, the pathologists found no congenital or developmen-tal abnormalities, and no valvular or myocardial disease, except that resulting from the coronary atherosclerosis. The sustained interference with the blood supply had led to the death or extensive damage of the normal heart muscle, to the point that there remained, as Dr. Hughes explained to Paul Dudley White, "a very scarred myocardium with extensive areas of calcification throughout the wall of the left ventricle and septum and a laminated, partially calcified clot about the size of a Ping-Pong ball occupying the apex of the left ventricle."[67]

The pathologists also detected a large aneurysm at the anterior (front) wall of the left ventricle near the apex (blunt rounded end of the heart), attached to which was a multilayered yellow-white thrombus. "Only a thin shell of cardiac tissue remains at the site of the thrombus attachment," they noted, but they could not determine the age of the aneurysm. Mattingly wrote in his health history that "it becomes difficult to determine the exact age of the process," but he decided that because of its thin, fibrotic, and calcified wall, it predated the myocardial damage of 1968 or 1965; he claimed later that the pathologist at autopsy had agreed that it existed since 1955. The pathologists did not speculate in their official report, and it is impossible to know whether Mattingly was right. The presumptive evidence suggests that he was not. In 1955 he had been impressed by the results of a large study of 102 cases of ventricular aneurysm (from 1954), in which 88 percent of the patients died within five years, 70 percent succumbing to congestive heart failure. Eisenhower survived for thirteen and a half years.[68]

The physicians who served Eisenhower during these later years were understandably proud of their ability to keep him alive for so long. "There was the satisfaction that, with our help and the grace of God," Dr. Mattingly wrote, "we had provided the general with an additional four years." They were also sensitive to those critics who charged that they had kept Ike alive, with immense suffering for him and at great expense to the public, when they knew he could never return to the type of life he had once enjoyed. Dr. Hughes rejoined that he and his colleagues had made it possible for the general to experience some things dear to his heart—the election of Nixon, the marriage of his grandson, and the appointment of his son as ambassador to Belgium. And, too, he rationalized, they had provided exactly the same heroic-type treatment to seventy other patients in the coronary care unit.[69]

In truth, the experience of both the doctors and their patient was exceptional, for reasons expressed by General Heaton: "In the lives of some men and women there comes the opportunity to serve the mighty. Such has been our good fortune and high privilege. Our lives are much richer in the finer things of life because of this association with him. This great world figure had a style, a presence, a personality, a forcefulness of mind, a strength and grace of spirit that set him apart."[70]

9

The Meaning

❖ ❖ ❖ ❖ ❖ ❖ ❖ ❖ ❖ ❖ ❖ ❖ ❖ ❖ ❖

Cardiacs are curious people. They have had a bump not only to their heart but to their ego. In the bookkeeping of life, each cardiac knows that he might have been counted out.

So he lies immobilized, taken from all his importance and greatness. So he thinks, and curiously most of his thinking is about himself. . . .

It is an illness which must give even the churl a sense of history, if nothing else, his own history.

—*George Sokolsky, "Decisions Are Difficult"*

I began this writing as a record of a heart attack and a struggle to recover from it. I assumed that I could not recover until I could account for the reasons for the heart attack, and the one that hit me seventeen years earlier.

I now begin to think that the introspection, however pseudoclinical, is useless, or anyway illusory, that it is silly to think I can understand the reasons for these implosions of mine (anger and so on). A heart attack is a mysterious event. Life does not often have reasons; heart attacks do not necessarily have explanations. . . .

We have to be content with the simple-physical: Smoking, bad diet, stress, and heredity are the principal causes, everyone guesses. But no one understands heart attacks very well.

—*Lance Morrow,* Heart: A Memoir

In the weeks following the president's heart attack in 1955, thousands of Americans sent letters to Denver and Washington, as if through a surge of devotion they could express their years of affection. Many of them went further; they offered help, each with a special prescription, drawing upon a national storehouse of remedies and remembrances. They presented articles and books; they described diets, vitamins, and drugs; they advised about overwork and exercise, especially golf; and they shared the details of their own suffering and survival. Some of them combined their urge to help the president with a desire to act against the dread disease, as one of them proposed to him on 30 September from Liberal, Kansas:

> It is the feeling of this writer that your illness may have called to your attention a crusade that is truly worthy of your steel—a crusade against heart trouble in America. . . .
>
> As the late great president brought a halt to the crippling deaths by infantile paralysis through his long campaign which stirred up the nation against polio and brought the vaccines that may eventually curb it, so I hope that your illness will align you against heart trouble, will place you at the helm of an army of Americans who want to fight against it and lack only a great leader to defeat it.[1]

The desire to enlist Eisenhower in such a crusade came easily to a generation intimately aware of Franklin Roosevelt's unending efforts to find a cure for infantile paralysis. Through the Warm Springs Foundation, the Birthday Balls, the National Foundation for Infantile Paralysis, and the March of Dimes, FDR's "whole objective," as he put it in 1937, was "to make the country as conscious about polio as it is about TB." At all times he eagerly used his name and position to further his cause, even when it appeared exploitative. He was always conspicuously at the forefront, unquestionably the commander in the battle against polio. Only four months before his death, as his armies were closing out the Germans in World War II, he declared, "We face formidable enemies at home and abroad"; of the one at home, he continued, "Victory is achieved only at great cost—but victory is imperative on all fronts. Not until we have removed the shadow of the crippler from the future of every child can we furl the flags of battle and still the trumpets of attack. The fight against infantile paralysis is a fight to the finish, and the terms are unconditional surrender."[2]

The fight ended for the most part on Eisenhower's watch, brought to a near finish in 1955 by the success of the Salk vaccine; but even before the victory celebration there was a national outcry for another battle. Bruce Barton, the famous advertising executive and national chairman of the American Heart Association for nine years, explained: "The president's illness has, of course, made the whole country heart-conscious in a way that neither the American Heart Association nor the medical associations could have achieved in a generation." The proposals for a historical replay, however, for a different president to confront a different disease, found an implacable opponent in the White House. Eisenhower considered his illness a private misfortune, not a public event; and he honestly believed there were limits to what the government could afford, to what science could achieve, and especially to what doctors could accomplish, whether in the laboratory or in the clinic. He refused to lead the crusade, so the contemporary impact of his heart attack was muted. His illness did elicit a new relationship between the White House and the press, and it did provide the American people with their first detailed educational seminar on coronary heart disease, thereby introducing them to the more positive outlook of the experts. The most important legacy of his misfortune, however, and what makes it timeless, was the president's personal—and private—response to his disease.[3]

"The first time in history that the public immediately knew the full truth about a presidential illness," wrote two observers of medicine and politics, "was during the Eisenhower administration." They were right about their history, and older Americans in 1955 had knowledge of three examples of deception. In 1893 Grover Cleveland, informed that he had cancer of the mouth, sneaked away to a friend's yacht in New York harbor, where he had part of his jaw removed while sailing along the Atlantic seaboard. He conceived of his condition as his own business and politically dangerous, so he conspired with his physicians and close associates to lie to the press— so successfully that the cover-up lasted for twenty-four years. In 1919 Woodrow Wilson suffered a massive stroke that completely paralyzed the left side of his body, impaired his speech and vision, altered his personality, and altogether made him incompetent to hold office. But for the last seventeen months of his presidency, his doctor and his wife were able to deny his disability and cover for the frail, reclusive invalid. Finally, toward the end of World War II, Franklin Roosevelt was suffering from hypertensive heart disease and cardiac failure, but he showed no interest in or curiosity about his declining and threatening condition; his physician told the public that he was in relatively good health. Roosevelt died suddenly from a stroke, and it was twenty-five years before most of the truth about his health became known.[4]

Each of these cases was different, but in all of them responsible men in the White House assumed that a president's health problems—however serious or debilitating—were a private matter. Eisenhower broke with that tradition, dramatically. "There was no attempt to hold back details," wrote *Business Week* at the time, "to play down the seriousness of the attack, or throw a cloud of secrecy over the whole thing." Even though the president hedged his original directive about telling the "whole truth"—in order to protect himself politically—the difference was real. The American people knew with considerable specificity in this case that there was a heart attack, that there was surgery for ileitis, and that there was a transitory language impairment that the press described as a small stroke. And the break from the past was lasting; as a scholar noted in 1987, the Eisenhower-Hagerty policy of openness created "a model for presidential health news coverage that would remain essentially unchanged to the present." Indeed, it is inconceivable that a president today would try to cover up any illness that might have consequences for his ability to govern.[5]

Eisenhower made the decision to inform the people about his condition, and the doctors eagerly took that opportunity to inform them about his disease.

"It may seem paradoxical to say that your heart attack had a constructive value to the American people," David Lawrence (one of Eisenhower's favorite journalists) wrote to the president in mid-November 1955, "but, when we recently printed in our magazine some interviews with leading heart specialists, we received numerous requests for reprints, many to be distributed to the executives of companies requesting them. The amount of education through the nation's press on the subject of the human heart has been truly remarkable, and the quantity of it has been unprecedented. Because of your illness, the American people are better educated on the heart and its ailments than they ever have been before." The journalist was correct, because in early 1955 most Americans had known almost nothing about coronary disease. For six or seven years they had heard reports that it was killing more of them than ever before, that many of its victims were hard-driving businessmen, and that science was on the way to finding a cure; but they were ignorant of the most rudimentary facts about the disease.[6]

The enormous interest following the president's attack led to an unparalleled flood of knowledge that constituted the nation's first serious inquiry into its most devastating disease. There were dozens of articles with explanations of how a heart attack occurs and feels, many of them with illustrations of the "wonderful pump" that kept people alive, depicting the coronary arteries, the clot, or thrombus, that caused the infarction, and the areas of damage. All of the major news magazines provided substantial information about the factors responsible for the disease, the drugs and surgical techniques available for treatment, the studies and experiments in progress, and the chances for prevention and recovery. The coverage was so extensive that Dr. H. M. Marvin, a former president of the AHA, exclaimed: "Such jawbreaking medical terms as atherosclerosis and myocardial infarction are being bandied around by laymen in homes, shops, and offices."[7]

The immediate effect of the spate of information was fear, but it soon gave way to the more positive view put forth by experts on the heart, especially Paul Dudley White. The widespread acceptance of his thesis—"As a rule it isn't necessary to sit for the rest of one's life on a porch and watch the birds, bees, and butterflies go by"—had an immediate, practical effect. It meant that the "cardiac cripple" was a thing of the past. One of White's patients even chided him, in good humor, for having told reporters that his idle, protected life was all "hooey and that I could even shovel snow. What a letdown! . . . You sure spoiled it, the life of Riley, what a memory. Back to the old grind." Eisenhower was the most visible symbol of the new approach, and his ability to serve a second term sent a powerful message. The full extent of the historic change in attitudes was evident in the comments of the *Washington Daily News,* two days after his attack, which expressed such certainty, but were so completely wrong: "The American people will never vote for a man of Ike's age (sixty-five next month) who has had a heart attack. Lyndon Johnson (majority leader of the Senate) is only forty-seven—eighteen years younger than the president—and he had a heart attack last July. . . . Now Lyndon and his friends know that his White House chances are gone forever. A congressman, a senator, or a governor with a heart condition can be reelected, but never a president."[8]

The burst of knowledge did not bring about a meaningful change in people's behavior because the experts were so noncommittal, even confused, about the causes of heart attacks. The doctors were forthright in advising their fellow citizens to generously support more private and public spending for medical research, but they were reluctant to ask them to change their eating and smoking habits. The doctors' uncertainty about behavior provided a reason—or an excuse—for the people at large to avoid doing anything until the scientists came forth with more definite answers. Delay was especially attractive because of the majestic expectations of the time, which no one expressed better than the renowned science writer William Laurence. In a June 1956 article in *Collier's* he predicted, with the authority of two Pulitzer Prizes behind him, the coming of a "great golden era" because "vast armies of scientific workers are getting ready." He sensed "a feeling of victory" in the air, hastened because President Eisenhower's heart attack had mobilized wide public support for the fight against this "enemy of mankind." Ten years from now, he assured his readers, "we will be ten or twenty years younger."[9]

After his heart attack Dwight Eisenhower felt he could not afford to wait ten years for the scientists to find a treatment for his disease. He had sent a check to the Heart Fund from his hospital bed, but he was skeptical about quick results, telling a group of Republican leaders that it was a "fallacy" to believe that "a cascade of taxpayers' dollars will guarantee progress in research" or "that dollars alone can produce discoveries." Since he had decided that he would not sit "on a porch," he took charge of his life with a program of preventive medicine so sophisticated, so determined, and so effective that it would please the most demanding cardiologist of the 1990s.[10]

The initial academic interpretations of Eisenhower's response to his illnesses have relied heavily upon Dr. Mattingly's dire contention that he had three heart attacks by 1955 and lived with a ventricular aneurysm thereafter. They accord Ike only a minimal, passive role in his own health care in one instance, or portray him as a self-destructive personality in another. "Somehow the president survived," wrote historian Robert Ferrell. "He not only survived his second term but lived another eight years. How he managed to do this is impossible to know. . . . But Eisenhower . . . possessed a great deal of resolution, and in some way, his resolve, his steely ability to 'take it,' together with sheer luck and with an assist, he might have said, from Providence, enabled him to defy the statistics that his brother Milton so thoughtfully had kept from him."[11]

Political scientist Robert Gilbert delves into psychology to suggest that Eisenhower was so neurotic as to actually want to bring about his illnesses rather than work to control them. His severe inner conflicts led to "self-hate" and to "repeated instances of self-destructive behavior"—his decision to seek the presidency after the 1949 illness, which was "foolhardy" unless "he welcomed that danger"; his decision to run for a second term after the heart attack, knowing that four more years could be fatal; his decision to go to the NATO conference following the stroke, which "seems to have demonstrated a well-defined death wish"; and his decision to continue campaigning after the episode of "ventricular fibrillation" in 1960, "thereby risking physical calamity." He concludes that "although the pressures of high office undoubtedly contributed to his frequent and life-threatening illnesses, he may have accepted—indeed, subconsciously desired—those illnesses as punishments for the error of his ways."[12]

There is nothing mysterious or neurotic about Eisenhower's health history. He took control of his health care because he was unwilling to rely on "sheer luck" or "Providence," and because he loved life. He was ready to play the cards God dealt him because he never doubted the game was worth playing. He was fortunate because his physicians, especially White and Snyder, explained his heart attack as having its probable cause in his own culpability. Their model of disease causation was speculative and filled with question marks, but he seized upon the few opportunities it offered because he believed that every individual was responsible for the decisions that would help him keep alive and well. So he made his choices, and sacrifices, as to tobacco, diet, exercise, emotions, and even to golfing and fishing in the Rockies.

He was extraordinary because of his aggressive and affirmative commitment to his regimen. He was resolute, for example, when he stopped smoking; he explained to Cliff Roberts that it was a matter of "willpower and self-control." He admitted in 1964 that although he was frustrated in his first attempt to stop, he finally decided to "make a game of the whole business" and try a "positive approach," which he did until he had "won the battle." When Clare Boothe Luce asked him how he quit so decisively, he looked at her "with absolute disgust" and replied: "I simply gave myself the order." He perceived of his dieting in terms of reason and responsibility. Toward the end of his second term he explained to a group of AMA doctors that maintaining a balanced diet was as difficult, and important, as holding to a balanced budget. "There are some useless items of food all of us crave and often eat, no matter unwisely, . . ." he argued, but "we must conduct ourselves with a wary eye on the consequences" or suffer "ruined" health. "The choice is ours," he concluded, "and we must act with clear mind and resolution."[13]

Eisenhower did in the 1950s what experts are asking Americans to do today—make rational choices to protect their health because there are limits to what others can do for them. He did it better than the vast majority of his countrymen, then or now, and his survival for thirteen years after the 1955 heart attack—to the age of seventy-eight—is presumptive evidence of the wisdom of the choices he made. The *way* in which he lived his life during that time is an even greater lesson. In 1958 Frances Burns of the *Boston Globe,* writing to Dr. Snyder to praise the president's "courageous attitude toward physical difficulties," noted, "It gives others in his age bracket needed spine stiffening." She was overstating Eisenhower's impact on others because so few were aware of his daily activities, but she was on the mark about his courage.[14]

After Eisenhower's death, there were thousands of eulogies paying homage to the man, the soldier, and the president. Some of them have a historic ring. Who, in seeking to know the man, can improve upon the final words he spoke to Mamie shortly before he died, which President Nixon cited in his memorial comments from the Capitol rotunda: "I have always loved my wife. I have always loved my children. I have always loved my grandchildren. And I have always loved my country." Who, in seeking to remember the beloved supreme commander, can forget the touching cartoon by Bill Mauldin, with the rows of crosses stretching endlessly to the horizon and the caption "IT'S IKE HIMSELF, PASS THE WORD." And who, in seeking to understand his presidency, can ignore the eventual judgment of his foremost biographer, rendered after giving fair attention to his failures: "Eisenhower gave the nation eight years of peace and prosperity. No other president in the twentieth century could make that claim. No wonder that millions of Americans felt that the country was damned lucky to have him."[15]

There is another Eisenhower who has gone unnoticed—the aging and ailing warrior struggling against chronic disease. It was the longest battle he ever fought, and he was able to share some of his suffering with Mamie and Dr. Snyder. But for the most part he had to deal with his illness alone—through more than thirteen years of examinations, tests, and readings, hundreds of venipunctures, more than a dozen threatening hospitalizations, fourteen defibrillating shocks, five myocardial infarctions, three surgeries, and an immeasurable number of frightening pains, startling skips, touches of worry, and flashes of fear. For this struggle, as much as those he commanded in war and managed from the White House, he deserves another eulogy, perhaps of the sort given many years later by a physician on behalf of his own chronically ill patients. "It has always seemed to me," wrote Dr. Arthur Kleinman of the Harvard Medical School, "that there is a kind of quiet heroism that comes from meeting these problems and the sentiments they provoke, of getting through them each day, of living through the long course with grace and spirit and even humor."[16]

Dwight David Eisenhower was that kind of hero.

Notes

❖ ❖ ❖ ❖ ❖ ❖ ❖

Key to Abbreviations

ACWD	Ann C. Whitman Diary, Eisenhower Library, Abilene, Kansas
AHA	American Heart Association Archives, Dallas, Texas
AWF/AS	Ann Whitman File, Administrative Series
AWF/DDE:D	Ann Whitman File, Dwight Eisenhower Diary
AWF/LM	Ann Whitman File, Legislative Meeting Series
AWF/NS	Ann Whitman File, Name Series
BPP	Bruce Barton Papers, State Historical Society of Wisconsin
DDE/GF	Eisenhower General File
DDE/OF	Eisenhower Office File
DDE/PPF	Eisenhower Personal File
DDE/PPP	Eisenhower Post-Presidential Papers
DPP	Drew Pearson Papers, LBJ Library, Austin, Texas
EL	Eisenhower Library
EP	Eisenhower Pre-Presidential Papers
HS/EL	Dr. Howard Snyder Papers, Abilene, Kansas
HS/W	Dr. Howard Snyder Papers, Laramie, Wyoming
HSP	Dr. Howard Sprague Papers, Boston, Massachusetts
HSTL	Harry S. Truman Library, Independence, Missouri
JHP	James Hagerty Papers, Eisenhower Library
LBJL	Lyndon Baines Johnson Library, Austin, Texas
OH	Oral History
PDWP	Dr. Paul Dudley White Papers, Boston, Massachusetts
PPP	Public Papers of the President
TMP	Dr. Thomas Mattingly Papers, Eisenhower Library
WRGH	Walter Reed General Hospital

Introduction

1. Leonard Scheele to Howard Snyder, 10 October 1955, HS/W; *Newsweek,* 14 November 1955, 124.

2. Robert H. Ferrell, *Ill-Advised: Presidential Health and Public Trust* (Columbia, 1992), 109.

3. Myron K. Jordan, "Presidential Health Reporting: The Eisenhower Watershed," *American Journalism* 4 (1987): 147, 156; Fred Greenstein, *The Hidden-Hand Presidency* (New York, 1982).

4. Newsweek, 10 October 1955, 98; Notes on Legislative Leadership Meeting, 7 July 1959, AWF/LM.

5. Arthur Kleinman, *The Illness Narratives: Suffering, Healing and the Human Condition* (New York, 1988), 49; Osler, cited in René Dubos, *Mirage of Health* (New York, 1959), 143.

6. Associated Press bulletin, 18 January 1993; *Newsweek,* 15 February 1993, 23; and *Austin American-Statesman,* 4 April 1993.

CHAPTER 1
The Nation's Number One Killer

1. Paul Dudley White, "Medical Practice 40 Years Ago and Now," *Dow Medical College Magazine* 2, no. 2 (April 1952): 13; J. O. Leibowitz, *A History of Coronary Heart Disease* (Berkeley, 1970), 3-48.

2. Brian Livesley, "The Resolution of the Heberden-Parry Controversy," *Medical History* 19 (1975): 158-168; Leibowitz, *History of Coronary Heart Disease,* 85-86.

3. Leibowitz, *History of Coronary Heart Disease,* 99, 102; Dorothy Fisk, *Dr. Jenner of Berkeley* (London, 1959), 68.

4. Albert S. Hyman, Aaron E. Parsonnet, and David Riesman, *The Failing Heart of Middle Life* (Philadelphia, 1932), 138-139, 342.

5. On Sumner see Walter G. Shotwell, *Life of Charles Sumner* (New York, 1910), 375-378; Edward L. Pierce, *Memoir and Letters of Charles Sumner,* vol. 3 (Boston, 1893), 565; Pierce, *Memoir and Letters of Charles Sumner,* vol. 4 (Boston, 1893), 597; Joseph Taber Johnson, "Angina Pectoris, Illustrated by the Case of Charles Sumner," *Boston Medical and Surgical Journal* 15 (October 1874): 372.

6. William Osler, *Lectures on Angina Pectoris and Allied States* (New York, 1897), 32, 34-36, 142; Osler, "The Lumleian Lectures on Angina Pectoris, Lecture I," *Lancet* 1 (1910): 699.

7. Ibid., 698; William Osler, "The Lumleian Lectures, Lecture 2," *The Lancet* 1 (1910): 839.

8. Richard Middleton, "Captain of the Men of Death," *Atlantic Monthly,* July 1932, 111; Paul Dudley White, "Deadly Disease No. 1," *Hygeia,* 18 (February 1940); 104.

9. Robert K. Murray, *The Harding Era* (Minneapolis, 1969), 448–449; *Washington Post*, 29 July 1923; personal memorandum in Edgar Eugene Robinson and Paul Carrol Edwards, eds., *The Memoirs of Ray Lyman Wilbur, 1875–1949* (Stanford, Calif., 1960), 378–380, 382; *San Francisco Examiner*, 3 August 1923; and *Washington Post*, 3 August 1923.

10. Richard Ross, "A Parlous State of Storm and Stress: The Life and Times of James B. Herrick," *Circulation* 67 (1983): 957; James B. Herrick, *Memories of Eighty Years* (Chicago, 1949), 196; and Herrick, "An Intimate Account of My Early Experience with Coronary Thrombosis," *American Heart Journal* 27 (January 1944): 1–17.

11. Stanley J. Reiser, *Medicine and the Reign of Technology* (Cambridge, 1978), 100, 97–98, 107, 109; Herrick, *Memories of Eighty Years*, 196; Paul Dudley White in "A Transcript of the '20th Anniversary Program,'" American Heart Association 1968, 2–4, AHA; and "Samuel A. Levine," *Harvard University Gazette*, 11 February 1967.

12. Timothy Leary, "Pathology of Coronary Sclerosis," *American Heart Journal* 10 (February 1935): 328–337; Samuel A. Levine, *Clinical Heart Disease* (Philadelphia, 1951), 109–121; and W. Bruce Fye, "Ventricular Fibrillation and Defibrillation: Historical Perspectives with Emphasis on the Contributions of John MacWilliam, Carl Wiggers, and William Kouwenhoven," *Circulation* 71 (May 1985): 860, 862.

13. R. W. Scott, "Clinical Aspects of Arteriosclerosis," *American Heart Journal* 7 (February 1932): 304; Harry D. Piercy, "The Doctor's Answer," *William Feather Magazine*, April 1940, 11; and Paul Dudley White, "The Reversibility of Heart Disease," *Illinois Medical Journal* 86 (July 1944): 1.

14. Howard B. Sprague, "A Yankee Appraisal of the American Heart Association," n.d., 10, HSP.

15. David Rutstein to Carleton Chapman, 9 March 1963, HSP; Tinsley Harrison to H. M. Marvin, 23 September 1967, HSP; and William Moore, *Fighting for Life: The Story of the American Heart Association 1911–1975* (Dallas, 1983), 48.

16. John Gunther, *Taken at the Flood: The Story of Albert D. Lasker* (New York, 1960); Elmer Bobst, *The Autobiography of a Pharmaceutical Pioneer* (New York, 1973); and "Fanning the Fire," *Time*, 30 August 1948.

17. U.S. Congress, Senate, *Hearings of the Subcommittee of the Committee on Labor and Public Welfare*, 80th Cong., 2d sess., 8–9 April 1948, 29–32, 40, 104, 127; U.S. Congress, House, *Hearings before the Committee on Interstate and Foreign Commerce*, 80th Cong., 2d sess., 5–6 May 1948, 78, 96, 98, 128.

18. President's Commission on Heart Disease, Cancer and Stroke, *A National Program to Conquer Heart Disease, Cancer and Stroke*, vol. 2 (Washington, D.C., 1965), 26; American Heart Association, *Proceedings: First National Conference on Cardiovascular Diseases* (New York, 1950), 79–86.

19. Oglesby Paul, "Background of the Prevention of Cardiovascular Disease," *Circulation* 80 (July 1989): 210–211; Levine, *Clinical Heart Disease*; Ernst

P. Boas and Norman F. Boas, *Coronary Artery Disease* (Chicago, 1949); and H. M. Marvin, T. Duckett Jones, Irvine A. Page, Irving S. Wright, and David D. Rutstein, *You and Your Heart* (New York, 1950).

20. Daniel Steinberg, "The End of the Cholesterol Controversy," *Circulation* 80 (October 1989): 1072-1073; Paul White and Ashton Graybiel, "Diseases of the Heart," *Archives of Internal Medicine* 57 (April 1936): 28-31; and Marvin, et al., *You and Your Heart,* 115.

21. *New York Times,* 11 January 1950; Howard B. Sprague, "Environmental Influences in Coronary Disease in the United States," *American Journal of Cardiology* 16 (July 1965): 110; Paul Dudley White, "The Prevention of Heart Disease," *Virginia Medical Monthly,* 17 February 1930, 23-24; and Levine, *Clinical Heart Disease,* 81-82.

22. Helen Flanders Dunbar, *Mind and Body: Psychosomatic Medicine* (New York, 1947), 126-130, 138- 139; Paul Dudley White, "Heart Disease—Then and Now," *Hygeia,* October 1933, 952.

23. U.S. Congress, House, *Health Inquiry: Hearings before the Committee on Interstate and Foreign Commerce,* 83d Cong., 1st sess., 1-3 October 1953, 29; Boas and Boas, *Coronary Artery Disease,* 310; and Catherine Marshall, *A Man Called Peter* (New York, 1951), 214.

CHAPTER 2
The Man Who Felt Like Tarzan

1. Dwight D. Eisenhower, *At Ease: Stories I Tell to Friends* (Garden City, N.Y., 1967), 353-354.

2. Kenneth S. Davis, *Soldier of Democracy: A Biography of Dwight Eisenhower* (New York, 1945), 78-80.

3. Eisenhower, *At Ease,* 2, 7, 96-97; Harvey Green, *Fit for America* (New York, 1986), 219-258.

4. Stephen E. Ambrose, *Eisenhower: Soldier, General of the Army, President-Elect, 1890-1952* (New York, 1983), 48-50; Merle Miller, *Ike the Soldier* (New York, 1987), 30-32.

5. John Gunther, *Eisenhower: The Man and the Symbol* (New York, 1952), 34; Eisenhower, *At Ease,* 23; Miller, *Ike the Soldier,* 139, 166; Patton to DDE, 9 July 1926, EL; and Richard M. Nixon, *Six Crises* (Garden City, N.Y., 1962), 132.

6. Eisenhower, *At Ease,* 16; Miller, *Ike the Soldier,* 31; and Green, *Fit for America,* 249.

7. Mattingly, "Gastrointestinal System: Part One," 3, TMP; Eisenhower, *At Ease,* 353.

8. Mattingly, "GI System, Part One," 3-4, TMP.

9. Ibid. 5-6.

10. Miller, *Ike the Soldier,* 257; Mattingly, "GI System: Part One," 7, TMP.

11. Mattingly, "GI System: Part One," 7, TMP; DDE conversation with Snyder, 13 August 1959, HS/EL.

12. Piers Brendon, *Ike: His Life and Times* (New York, 1986), 67; Miller, *Ike the Soldier*, 313-314; John S. D. Eisenhower, ed., *Dwight D. Eisenhower, Letters to Mamie* (New York, 1978), 30 May 1944, 183.

13. John Eisenhower, *Letters to Mamie*, 8; 20 January 1943, 85; Robert H. Ferrell, ed., *The Eisenhower Diaries* (New York, 1981), 137; Miller, *Ike the Soldier*, 756; and Kay Summersby Morgan, *Past Forgetting* (New York, 1976), 244-245.

14. Dwight D. Eisenhower, *Crusade in Europe* (Garden City, N.Y., 1948), 132; Miller, *Ike the Soldier*, 399.

15. Harry C. Butcher, *My Three Years with Eisenhower* (New York, 1946), 247; Ambrose, *Eisenhower: Soldier*, 275-276; and John Eisenhower, *Letters to Mamie*, 20 February 1944, 168.

16. Eisenhower, *Crusade in Europe*, 305; Miller, *Ike the Soldier*, 528-529; John Eisenhower, *Letters to Mamie*, 20 October 1942, 170; 12 August 1943, 139; 23 January 1944, 166; DDE to John Eisenhower, 18 August 1943, 1344, EP; and Nixon, *Six Crises*, 131-132.

17. Miller, *Ike the Soldier*, 435; John Eisenhower, *Letters to Mamie*, 6 April 1943, 115; 2 December 1943, 157; 20 April 1944, 177.

18. DDE to Walter Bedell Smith, 30 August 1946, EP.

19. Ferrell, *Eisenhower Diaries*, 230; Ambrose, *Eisenhower: Soldier*, 414-415; Snyder, "Consultation Request and Report on Mamie Doud Eisenhower," 4 January 1946, HS/EL.

20. Snyder, "Summary of the Year 1945," 1-10, HS/EL; DDE to Sol Bloom, 15 November 1945, note 2, EP.

21. On Snyder see *Current Biography*, February 1955, 42-44.

22. Snyder, "Summary of the Year 1946," 22, HS/EL.

23. Ibid., 2, 12-13, 19, 40, 46; Snyder, "Summary of the Year 1947," 82, HS/EL.

24. DDE to Walter Bedell Smith, 30 August 1946, EP; Snyder, "Summary of the Year 1947," 72, HS/EL.

25. DDE to Smith, 30 August 1946, EP; Snyder, "Summary of the Year 1946," 40, HS/EL.

26. DDE to Walter Bedell Smith, 7 December 1946, and note 4, EP; DDE to Amon Giles Carter, 22 November 1946, EP; DDE to John Eisenhower, 14 November 1946, EP; DDE to Kenyon Ashe Joyce, 25 November 1946, EP; and DDE to Hal L. Mangum, 14 January 1947, EP.

27. DDE to Kenyon Ashe Joyce, 25 November 1946, EP; DDE to William R. Boyd, 4 December 1946, note 5, EP; DDE to Walter Bedell Smith, 7 December 1946, note 4, EP; and *New York Times*, 7 December 1946.

28. Snyder, "Summary of the Year 1947," 51-53, HS/EL; DDE to David Preswick Barr, 28 January 1947, note 1, EP.

29. David Barr, "History of Dwight D. Eisenhower, General," 24 January

1947, and Barr to Snyder, in Snyder, "Summary of the Year 1947," 54–58, HS/EL.

30. Snyder, "Summary of the Year 1947," 67, HS/EL.

31. Ibid., 61; *New York Herald Tribune,* 6 February 1947.

32. Snyder, "Summary of the Year 1947," 71, 76, 82–83, HS/EL; DDE to Walter Bedell Smith, 10 December 1947, EP.

33. DDE to John Montgomery Mahon Jr., 15 November 1946, EP; DDE to Milton Eisenhower, 9 December 1947, EP; and DDE to John Sheldon Doud, 31 January 1947, EP.

34. Snyder, "Summary of the Year 1946," 12–13, 29, 41, 46, HS/EL; Snyder, "Summary of the Year 1949," 128, HS/EL; "Electrocardiograph Report," WRGH, 21 June 1946, TMP; "Electrocardiographic Report," New York Hospital, 24 January 1947, TMP; and James S. Taylor, "Consultation Request and Report," 20 November 1947, TMP.

35. Emmet John Hughes, *The Ordeal of Power* (New York, 1963), 154; Miller, *Ike the Soldier,* 90.

36. Miller, *Ike the Soldier,* 90–91, 217; Peter Lyon, *Eisenhower: Portrait of the Hero* (Boston, 1974), 79.

37. Ferrell, *Eisenhower Diaries,* 52; John Eisenhower, *Letters to Mamie,* 15 September 1942, 41.

38. Merriman Smith, *Meet Mister Eisenhower* (New York, 1954), 225; John Eisenhower, *Letters to Mamie,* 11 February 1943, 93; Omar N. Bradley and Clay Blair Jr., *A General's Life* (New York, 1983), 133; and Kay Summersby, *Eisenhower Was My Boss* (New York, 1948), 28, 29, 113, 137, 278, 289.

39. Snyder, "Summary of the Year 1946," 19, HS/EL; Snyder, "Summary of the Year 1947," 52, 90, HS/EL.

40. Ferrell, *Eisenhower Diaries,* 145–146.

41. Ibid., 157–158; DDE to Henry H. Arnold, 14 March 1949, EP.

42. *New York Herald Tribune,* 26 March 1949; *New York Times,* 26, 29, and 31 March, 13 April, 12 and 15 May 1949; Smith, *Meet Mister Eisenhower,* 228–229; and Memorandum, Fernsworth to Drew Pearson, "Ike's Health," 9 June 1956, DPP.

43. Eisenhower, *At Ease,* 332–333, 354–355.

44. Snyder, "Summary of the Year 1949," 116, HS/EL.

45. Ibid., 117, 120, 128, 151.

46. Snyder to Herbert Black, 13 April 1949, HS/EL.

47. Mattingly, "General Health Status of Dwight D. Eisenhower," 80–82, TMP; Mattingly, "Cardiovascular System: Part One," 40–41, TMP.

48. Mattingly, "General Health Status," 81, TMP; Mattingly, "CV System: Part One," 22, 25–26, TMP.

49. Mattingly, "CV System: Part One," 27–32, 42–44, TMP.

50. Mattingly, "General Health Status," 82–83, TMP.

51. Robert H. Ferrell, *Ill-Advised: Presidential Health and Public Trust* (Columbia, 1992), 63, 65; Robert E. Gilbert, *Mortal Presidency: Illness and Anguish*

in the White House (New York, 1992), 81–84, and flyleaf; and William B. Pickett, *Dwight David Eisenhower and American Power* (Wheeling, Ill., 1995), 72.

52. B. L. Malpass, "Laboratory Examinations," 29–31 March, 5 April 1949, HS/EL; Allan B. Ramsay, "Radiographic Reports," 21 and 29 April 1949, HS/EL; Joe M. Blumberg, "Miscellaneous Test or Examination," 19, 20, 21, 25, and 27 April, 1949, HS/EL. It is perfectly reasonable to believe that if Eisenhower told Clare Booth Luce that he quit smoking because he had "a little heart trouble, a little warning from my doctor," he was referring to the advice given him by the cardiologist, Colonel Taylor, who detected a "rather high" pulse rate and advised him to decrease his use of cigarettes. John Gunther reported that Ike told him he quit smoking because of his pulse. Gunther, *Eisenhower,* 28–30.

53. B. L. Malpass, "Request for Electrocardiograph," 4 April 1959, HS/EL; Mattingly to Charles Leedham, 15 January 1984, TMP; Mattingly, "CV System: Part One," 29, TMP; and Oglesby Paul to author, 25 January 1993.

54. Ernst P. Boas and Norman F. Boas, *Coronary Artery Disease* (Chicago, 1949), 310; John Fogarty in *Federal Security Agency: Hearings before the House Subcommittee of the Committee on Appropriations,* 82d Cong., 1st sess., 1 March 1951.

55. *Hearings before the House Committee on Interstate and Foreign Commerce,* 80th Cong., 2d sess., 6 May 1948, 122.

56. DDE to Lewis Johnson, 30 March 1949, EP; DDE to John Hoen, 31 March 1949, EP; DDE Diary, 19 March 1949, note 4, EP; DDE Diary, 7 April 1949, notes 1, 2, EP; and Bradley and Blair, *A General's Life,* 501.

57. Snyder to Herbert Black, 13 April 1949, HS/EL; DDE to James Stack, 16 May 1949, EP; DDE to Louis Johnson, 20 April 1949, EP; and DDE to Everett E. Hazlett, 27 April 1949, EP.

58. DDE to Jerome A. Franklin, 12 May 1949, EP; DDE to Ed Dudley, 12 May 1949, prepresidential name file, EL; and DDE to James Stack, 16 May 1949, EP.

59. Robert L. Schulz to Mattingly, 25 January 1983, TMP; Mattingly, "CV System: Part One," 27, TMP; Mattingly to Charles Leedham, 15 January 1984, TMP; F. A. Spencer to Drew Pearson, 15 and 26 November 1955, DPP; and Tyler Abell, ed., *Drew Pearson, Diaries 1949–1959* (New York, 1974), 350.

60. DDE to Laurence Hansen, 11 April 1949, EP; DDE Diary, April 1949, EP; DDE to Hazlett, 27 April 1949, EP; DDE to Frederick Coykendall, 3 April 1949, EP; DDE to Clark Clifford, 5 April 1949, EP; and DDE to Walter B. Smith, 11 April 1949, EP.

61. DDE to Hal Mangum, 12 November 1946, EP; Snyder, "Summary of the Year 1949," 128, HS/EL.

62. Ambrose, *Eisenhower: Soldier,* 489. For an excellent discussion of Eisenhower's balancing of duty and ambition, see Chester J. Pach Jr. and Elmo Richardson, *The Presidency of Dwight Eisenhower* (Lawrence, Kans., 1991), 1–27, 118.

63. Ferrell, *Ill-Advised,* 53; Pickett, *Dwight David Eisenhower and American Power,* 82; Gilbert, *Mortal Presidency,* 140.

64. Bryce Harlow, "The 'Compleat' President," in *The Eisenhower Presidency,* ed. Kenneth W. Thompson (Lanham, Md., 1984), 162.

65. Eisenhower, *At Ease,* 16, 281–282.

66. DDE to John Eisenhower, 18 August 1943, EP; John Eisenhower, *Letters to Mamie,* 27 October 1942, 49; 11 February 1943, 93; 7 February 1944, 167; 30 January 1945, 233; and Gunther, *Eisenhower,* 29.

67. Snyder, "Summary of the Year 1949," 123, HS/EL.

68. Eisenhower, *At Ease,* 354–355.

69. Snyder, "Summary of the Year 1950," 137, 151, HS/EL.

70. Ibid., 151, 142; "Cholesterol, 1946–1962," HS/EL.

71. DDE to Joseph Davies, 19 May 1949, EP; DDE to James Forrestal, 13 May 1949, EP; DDE to Milton Eisenhower, 13 and 27 May 1949, EP.

72. Ferrell, *Eisenhower Diaries,* 172; Snyder, "Summary of the Year 1950," 138–139, HS/EL.

73. Snyder, "Summary of the Year 1951," 163, HS/EL; DDE to George Allen, 24 February 1951, EP.

74. DDE to George Allen, 10 and 20 March 1951, 15 November 1951, 8 and 18 December 1951, EP; DDE to Clifford Roberts, 2 and 3 May 1951, EP; DDE to Robinson, 16 February 1951, note 2, EP; and DDE to Robinson, 12 July 1951, EP.

75. Edwin Goyette, "Consultation Report," 18 August 1952, HS/EL.

76. Lester David and Irene David, *Ike and Mamie* (New York, 1981), 187; *U.S. News and World Report,* 3 October 1952, 54–56.

77. David and David, *Ike and Mamie,* 20.

CHAPTER 3
Misdiagnosis and Cover-up

1. Mary Davis to Sherman Adams, 24 December 1952, DDE/OF; "President-elect Eisenhower's Remarks at Inaugural Heart Dinner," 9 January 1953, DDE/OF.

2. Irving Wright to Sherman Adams, 29 November 1952, DDE/OF; Adams to T. E. Stephens, 30 December 1952, DDE/OF.

3. "President-elect Eisenhower's Remarks at Inaugural Heart Dinner," 9 January 1953, DDE/OF.

4. PPP, 9 February 1955, 264; *Hearings, Subcommittee of the Committee on Appropriations, Department of Labor,* 83d Cong., 2d sess., 8 April 1954, 323.

5. Ellis Slater, *The Ike I Knew* (New York, 1980), 53, 57.

6. Leonard Heaton, OH, 23, EL; Maxine Davis, "He's the President's Physician," *Good Housekeeping,* August 1954, 70, 207–211.

7. Robert H. Ferrell, ed., *The Eisenhower Diaries* (New York, 1981), 191; Robert Keith Gray, *Eighteen Acres Under Glass* (Garden City, N.Y., 1967), 110.

8. Snyder to Otto Brunzell, 4 October 1954, HS/W; Ferrell, *Eisenhower Diaries*, 288.

9. DDE to Adjutant General, 8 June 1955, AWF/NS; *Washington Post*, 16 October 1955.

10. Dwight D. Eisenhower, *At Ease: Stories I Tell to Friends* (Garden City, N.Y., 1967), 353-354; Snyder to DDE, 10 March 1955, HS/EL; ACWD, 9 May 1956; and Merriman Smith, *Meet Mister Eisenhower* (New York, 1954), 161-163, 172.

11. Dwight D. Eisenhower, *Mandate for Change: The White House Years* (Garden City, N.Y., 1963) 192.

12. Ibid.; *New York Times*, 17 April 1953; *Washington Post*, 17 April 1953; Bernard Shanley, OH, 2203, EL; and Snyder to Alfred Gruenther, 26 April 1953, HS/W.

13. *New York Times*, 18 April 1953; Shanley, OH, 2203, EL; and Smith, *Meet Mister Eisenhower*, 229.

14. Smith, *Meet Mister Eisenhower*, 228-229; Snyder to Gruenther, 28 April 1953, HS/W; *New York Times*, 17 April 1953; Eisenhower, *Mandate for Change*, 192-193.

15. Mattingly, "CV System: Part One," 37, TMP; Robert H. Ferrell, *Ill-Advised: Presidential Health and Public Trust* (Columbia, 1992), 70-71; and Robert E. Gilbert, *Mortal Presidency: Illness and Anguish in the White House* (New York, 1992), 85-86.

16. Manuscript, "Ike's Health," 30 October 1953, DPP; Stephen E. Ambrose, *Eisenhower: Soldier, General of the Army, President-Elect, 1890-1952* (New York, 1983), 250-252, 274; and "Statement of Drew Pearson," 26 October 1956, DPP.

17. Tyler Abell, ed., *Drew Pearson, Diaries 1949-1959* (New York, 1974), 38, 237, 269.

18. Manuscript, "Ike's Health," 30 October 1953, DPP.

19. Snyder to Otto Brunzell, 4 October 1954, HS/W; *U.S. News and World Report*, 23 October 1953, 14; and Snyder cited in "LB" to Drew Pearson, 27 September 1955, DPP.

20. PPP, 28 October 1953, 723; manuscript, "Ike's Health," 30 October 1953, DPP.

21. Snyder to Hagerty, 22 July 1953, DDE/PPF.

22. Snyder to Gruenther, 9 July 1954, HS/W.

23. Mattingly, "CV System: Part One," 18, TMP.

24. Samuel Sandifer, "Clinical Record," 15 September 1954, HS/EL; Edwin Goyette to Mattingly, 12 October 1954, HS/EL; and Snyder to Goyette, 22 October 1954, HS/EL.

25. Goyette to Snyder, 27 October 1954, HS/EL.

26. Mattingly, "Early Associations with Dr. White, 1932-1955," 1-5, PDWP.

27. Ibid., 6-7.

28. Mattingly, "CV System: Part One," 19, TMP; Mattingly, "Consultation Sheet," 1 August 1955, HS/EL.

29. John S. D. Eisenhower, *Strictly Personal* (Garden City, N.Y., 1974), 23; Bryce Harlow, "The 'Compleat' President," in *The Eisenhower Presidency*, ed. Kenneth W. Thompson (Lanham, Md., 1984), 148.

30. Shanley, OH, 1811, 2000-2001, 2088, EL.

31. Emmet John Hughes, *The Ordeal of Power* (New York, 1963), 149.

32. Eisenhower, *Mandate for Change*, 635-636; Snyder, "Heart Attack," 1-2, HS/EL.

33. DDE to Lyndon Johnson, 23 September 1955, LBJL; Wilton B. Persons to Lyndon Johnson, 27 September 1955, LBJL; Eisenhower, *Mandate for Change*, 636-637; Snyder, "Heart Attack," 3-5, HS/EL; and ACWD, 23 September 1955.

34. Eisenhower, *Mandate for Change*, 636; Snyder, "Heart Attack," 4, HS/EL; Robert J. Donovan, *Eisenhower: The Inside Story* (New York, 1956), 360.

35. Robert Cutler, *No Time for Rest* (Boston, 1966), 307; Snyder, "Heart Attack," 5-6, HS/EL.

36. Eisenhower, *Mandate for Change*, 637; Snyder to Harry A. Bullis, 29 October 1955, HS/EL; and Snyder, "Heart Attack," 6-8, HS/EL.

37. Eisenhower, *Mandate for Change*, 637.

38. James J. Rowley to Chief, U.S. Secret Service, 26 September 1955, HS/EL; Robert J. Donovan, *Confidential Secretary: Ann Whitman's Twenty Years with Eisenhower and Rockefeller* (New York, 1988), 90; and verbatim transcript of press conference in *U.S. News and World Report*, 7 October 1955, 66.

39. Press conference in *U.S. News and World Report*, 7 October 1955, 67; *New York Times*, 25 September 1955.

40. James J. Rowley to Chief, U.S. Secret Service, 26 September 1955, HS/EL.

41. Ibid.

42. Byron E. Pollock, "Admissions Note," Fitzsimons Hospital, 24 September 1955, HS/EL.

43. On prothrombin time see H. M. Marvin, T. Duckett Jones, Irvine H. Page, Irving S. Wright, and David D. Rutstein, *You and Your Heart: A Handbook for Laymen* (New York, 1950), 188-189. On the use of anticoagulants see Samuel A. Levine, *Clinical Heart Disease* (Philadelphia, 1951), 128. For the treatment of Eisenhower see "Nursing Notes," 24 and 25 September 1955, HS/EL; and Pollock, "Narrative Summary," 8 November 1955, HS/EL.

44. Donovan, *Confidential Secretary*, 91; Hagerty Diary, 24 September 1955, JHP.

45. Hagerty Diary, 24 September 1955, JHP.

46. James J. Rowley to Chief, U.S. Secret Service, 26 September 1955, HS/EL.

47. Pollock, "Admissions Note," 24 September 1955, HS/EL.

48. Hagerty Diary, 24 September 1955, JHP; Snyder, "Heart Attack," 22, HS/EL; Slater, *The Ike I Knew,* 106–107; Snyder to Ellis Slater, 29 September 1955, HS/EL.

49. *U.S. News and World Report,* 7 October 1955, 70, 74–76.

50. "Nursing Notes," 24 September 1955, HS/EL.

51. On Hagerty see "Ike's Press Secretary," *Time,* 7 November 1955, 63; for the quotation, see Robert H. Ferrell, *The Diary of James C. Hagerty* (Bloomington, Ind., 1983), xiv.

52. Mattingly Diary, 24 September 1955, in "CV System: Part Two," 31–32, TMP; Hagerty Diary, 24 September 1955, JHP.

53. Hagerty Diary, 24 September 1955, JHP.

54. Ibid.; Eisenhower, *Mandate for Change,* 638–639.

55. James Deakin, *Straight Stuff* (New York, 1984), 25; *New York Times,* 25 September 1955.

56. Mattingly, "Interval History," 25 September 1955, HS/EL.

57. Mattingly, "Chronology of the President's Heart Attack," PDWP.

58. Hagerty Diary, 25 September 1955, JHP.

59. Ibid.

60. "Nursing Notes," 25 September 1955, HS/EL; Pollock, "Doctor's Progress Notes," 25 September 1955, HS/EL.

61. Paul Dudley White, *My Life and Medicine* (Boston, 1971), 13–16; quotation on page 19. See also the outstanding biography of White by Oglesby Paul, *Take Heart* (Boston, 1986).

62. Paul, *Take Heart,* 80–100; White, *My Life and Medicine,* 176–177; and Hagerty Diary, 25 September 1955, JHP.

63. White, *My Life and Medicine,* 178; *Washington Post* 26 September 1955; and White, note card, 25 September 1955, PDWP.

64. J. Sheedy, "Doctor's Progress Notes," 25 September 1955, HS/EL; White, *My Life and Medicine,* 180–181; Hagerty Diary, 25 September 1955, JHP; Mattingly, "CV System: Part Two," 34, TMP.

65. Mattingly, "Chronology of the President's Heart Attack," 1982, PDWP; Mattingly, "Some Details of the Activities of Dr. White During the Hospitalization," n.d., PDWP; and Mattingly to Oglesby Paul, 10 May 1982, attachment, "1st Period, Acute Heart Attack and Hospitalization Denver," PDWP.

66. Ibid.; Mattingly Diary, 25 September 1955, in "CV System: Part Two," 35, TMP.

67. J. Sheedy, "Doctor's Progress Notes," 25 September 1955, HS/EL; "Nursing Notes," 25 September 1955, HS/EL.

68. Pollock, "Doctor's Progress Notes," 26 September 1955, HS/EL; "Nursing Notes," 26 September 1955, HS/EL; White, note card, 26 September 1955, PDWP; Hagerty Diary, 25 September 1955, JHP; and Hagerty to White, 26 September 1955, DDE/PPF.

69. "Press and Radio Conference," 25 September 1955, JHP.

70. Paul H. Streit to White, 28 September 1955, PDWP; Hagerty to White, 26 September 1955, DDE/PPF; and Frances Burns to Hagerty, 23 February 1957, DDE/PPF.

71. Mattingly to Oglesby Paul, 10 May 1982, attachment, "1st Period, Acute Heart Attack and Hospitalization Denver," PDWP; White, *My Life and Medicine,* 187; and Mattingly Diary, 26 September 1955, in "CV System: Part Two," 36, TMP.

72. *New York Times,* 28 September 1955.

73. Ibid., 30 September 1955; White to Hagerty, 29 September 1955, DDE/PPF.

74. White to Snyder, 29 September 1955, HS/W; White to Snyder, 3 October 1955 with enclosed "Comments to the Press," HS/W; and White to Hagerty, 29 September 1955 with enclosed "Comments to the Press," DDE/PPF.

75. White to Hagerty, 29 September 1955, DDE/PPF; Snyder to White, 1 October 1955, HS/W.

76. *Newsweek,* 3 October 1955, 20; *Time,* 3 October 1955, 14; and *U.S. News and World Report,* 7 October 1955, 70.

77. PPP, 1956, 166-167.

78. *Time,* 10 October 1955.

79. Deakin, *Straight Stuff,* 23-24, 329.

80. Ibid., 18, 20, 37.

81. Murray Snyder to H. Snyder, 19 October 1955, HS/EL; H. Snyder to Murray Snyder, 28 October 1955, HS/EL.

82. Silas Hays to Snyder, 1 November 1955, HS/W; Snyder to Silas Hays, 4 November 1955, HS/W.

83. Hagerty Diary, 24 September 1955, JHP; Mattingly, "CV System: Part Two," 34, TMP.

84. Snyder to White, 1 October 1955, HS/W; Snyder to B. W. Hogan, 7 October 1955, HS/EL.

85. White, *My Life and Medicine,* 181; Snyder, "Heart Attack," 35, HS/EL.

86. Snyder draft statement of 13 May 1958, HS/EL.

87. ACWD, 29 September 1955.

88. Snyder, "Memorandum Made at Bedside," handwritten copy, HS/EL.

89. Mattingly, "Chronology of the President's Heart Attack," 1982, PDWP.

90. Ibid.; Mattingly, "CV System: Part Two," 8-9, TMP; Mattingly to Oglesby Paul, 9 January 1984, PDWP; Mattingly, "CV System: Part One," 37-40, TMP.

91. Synder, "Memorandum Made at Bedside," typewritten version, HS/EL.

92. On the administration of heparin see C. Luise Riehl, *Coronary Nursing Care* (New York, 1971), 146-148, 156. For the treatment of Eisenhower see Pollock, "Admission Note," 24 September 1955, HS/EL; "Coumadin Graph," 25 September 1955, TMP; "Nursing Notes," 24 and 25 September 1955,

HS/EL. Eisenhower's prothrombin time was normal upon his admission to the hospital.

93. White, note card, 25 September 1955, PDWP; Mattingly, "Chronology of the President's Heart Attack," 1982, PDWP.

94. Snyder to Dr. George Lull, 29 September 1955, HS/W.

95. Ibid., 5 October 1955, HS/W.

96. For a list of the recipients of the doctor's letter, see "General Snyder's Letter re Sequence of Events," HS/EL; Snyder to Ellis Slater, 29 September 1955, HS/W; Snyder to Dr. George Lull, 25 October 1955, HS/W; Snyder to Dr. William B. Condon, 29 September 1955, HS/EL; Condon to Snyder, 10 October 1955, HS/EL; and Snyder to Condon, 14 October 1955, HS/EL.

97. Milton Eisenhower to Snyder, 3 October 1955, HS/W; William Robinson to Snyder, 9 October 1955, HS/EL; and Leonard Scheele to Snyder, 10 October 1955, HS/W.

98. Eli Ginzberg to Snyder, 30 September 1955, HS/EL.

99. Fletcher Knebel, "Crisis," *Look*, 27 December 1955, 21–24; Mattingly, "Chronology of the President's Heart Attack," 1982, PDWP.

100. William Bragg Ewald Jr., "A Biographer's Perspective," in *The Eisenhower Presidency*, ed. Kenneth W. Thompson (Lanham, Md., 1984), 18; Donovan, *Eisenhower: The Inside Story*, 363–364.

101. Snyder, "Heart Attack," 6–7, 10–12, HS/EL.

102. Eisenhower, *Mandate for Change*, 333.

103. Mattingly, "Interval History," 25 September 1955, HS/EL.

104. Miscellaneous handwritten note, n.d., HS/EL.

105. Richard M. Nixon, *Six Crises* (Garden City, N.Y., 1962), 138.

106. Paul, *Take Heart*, 156–157.

107. William B. Bean, "Clinical Masquerades of Acute Cardiac Infarction," *Journal of the Iowa State Medical Society* 52 (December 1962): 783; Levine, *Clinical Heart Disease*, 117, 121.

108. Paul Dudley White, *Heart Disease*, 4th ed. (New York, 1951), 564–565.

109. Pollock, "Narrative Summary," 8 November 1955, HS/EL.

110. Snyder to DDE, 10 February 1965, HS/EL.

CHAPTER 4
Treatment and Recovery

1. Ernst P. Boas and Norman F. Boas, *Coronary Artery Disease* (Chicago, 1949), 347–348.

2. Jay Katz, *The Silent World of Doctor and Patient* (New York, 1984), 20; R. Houston, "The Doctor Himself as a Therapeutic Agent," *Annals of Internal Medicine* 11 (1938): 1418.

3. Harvey is quoted in Henry J. Speedby, *The 20th Century and Your Heart*

(London, 1960), title page; Samuel Levine, *Clinical Heart Disease* (Philadelphia, 1951), 278.

4. Boas and Boas, *Coronary Artery Disease*, 310.

5. For an excellent discussion of the problems facing a patient, see Sharon L. Roberts, *Behavioral Concepts and the Critically Ill Patient* (Englewood Cliffs, N.J., 1976).

6. Lester David and Irene David, *Ike and Mamie* (New York, 1981), 237–238.

7. "Nursing Notes," 1, 2, 4, 5, 18, and 30 October 1955, HS/EL.

8. Dr. William Paul Thompson quoted in Oglesby Paul, *Take Heart* (Boston, 1986), 84; Frances Burns to James Hagerty, 23 February 1957, DDE/PPF.

9. For a superb discussion of White's views about a healthy life, see Paul, *Take Heart*, 184–204; Sherman Adams, *Firsthand Report* (New York, 1961), 187–188.

10. "Doctor's Progress Notes," 25 September–5 October 1955, HS/EL; Paul Dudley White, *My Life and Medicine* (Boston, 1971), 182.

11. For a discussion of the "armchair" treatment, see Eugene B. Mozes, *Living Beyond Your Heart Attack* (Englewood Cliffs, N.J., 1959), 58–62. T. Mattingly, "Modern Management of Arteriosclerotic Heart Patients," in *Cardiovascular Disease Nursing*, ed. Capitola B. Mattingly (Washington, D.C., 1960), 103–104; and Levine, *Clinical Heart Disease*, 127.

12. White, *My Life and Medicine*, 562; Snyder, "Heart Attack," 31, HS/EL; "Nursing Notes," 28–30 September 1955, HS/EL; Mattingly, "CV System: Part Two," 19, TMP.

13. Mattingly, "Doctor's Progress Notes," 2 October 1955, HS/EL.

14. Ibid.; "Nursing Notes," 2 October 1955, HS/EL; Pollock, "Doctor's Progress Notes," 2 October 1955, HS/EL; and Mattingly, "CV System: Part Two," 20, 39 TMP.

15. Pollock, "Doctor's Progress Notes," 6 October 1955, HS/EL; "Nursing Notes," 7–9 October 1955, HS/EL; and Mattingly, "CV System: Part Two," 20, TMP.

16. Mattingly, "Doctor's Progress Notes," 8 October 1955, HS/EL; Pollock, "Doctor's Progress Notes," 9 October 1955, HS/EL; and Mattingly, "CV System: Part Two," 22, TMP.

17. Pollock, "Doctor's Progress Notes," 9 October 1955, HS/EL; White to DDE, 10 October 1955, AWF/AS.

18. J. A. Sheedy, "Doctor's Progress Notes," 10 October 1955, HS/EL; Pollock, "Doctor's Progress Notes," 15 October 1955, HS/EL; and Mattingly, "Doctor's Progress Notes," 15 October 1955, HS/EL.

19. Mattingly, "CV System: Part Eight," 2, TMP.

20. Mattingly to O. Paul, 10 May 1982, "Activities of Dr. Paul D. White . . . 24 September to 11 November 1955," 2, TMP; "Press and Radio Conference," 22 October, JHP.

21. White to Dr. Cowles Andrus, 25 October 1955, PDWP.

22. Mattingly, "CV System: Part Eight," 3–4, TMP.

23. "Nursing Notes," 21 October-9 November 1955, HS/EL; Pollock, "Doctor's Progress Notes," 5 November 1955, HS/EL.

24. "Press and Radio Conference," 7 November 1955, JHP; Dwight D. Eisenhower, *Mandate for Change: The White House Years* (Garden City, N.Y., 1963), 643; Milton Eisenhower to Snyder, 31 October 1955, HS/EL; Snyder to M. Eisenhower, 8 November 1955, HS/EL; and Snyder to Gruenther, 29 October 1955, HS/EL.

25. "Press and Radio Conference with the Doctors," 9 and 22 October 1955, JHP.

26. Stephen E. Ambrose, *Eisenhower: The President* (New York, 1984), 274.

27. Ibid., 272-273; DDE to Hazlett, 3 August 1956, AWF/NS.

28. Ann Whitman to Alfred Gruenther, n.d., AWF/AS. For the dates of each of the visits see "The President's Appointments," HS/EL.

29. "Press and Radio Conference," 7 November 1955, JHP; White, "Consultation Sheet," 10 November 1955, HS/EL; Snyder to Wilton B. Persons, 20 October 1955, HS/W.

30. Katz, *The Silent World of Doctor and Patient*, 207.

31. Richard M. Nixon, *Memoirs* (New York, 1978), 166; Dwight D. Eisenhower, *Waging Peace, 1956-1961* (Garden City, N.Y., 1965), 638-640.

32. William Bragg Ewald Jr., *Eisenhower the President* (Englewood Cliffs, N.J., 1981), 95, 251; DDE to Hazlett, 23 January 1956, AWF/NS.

33. DDE to White, 17 November 1955, AWF/AS; Snyder, "Draft Statement," 13 May 1958, HS/EL.

34. Eisenhower, *Mandate for Change*, 637, 640.

35. Ibid., 639-640; Pollock, "Doctor's Progress Reports," 2 October 1955, HS/EL.

36. Eisenhower, *Mandate for Change*, 639.

37. Snyder, "Draft Statement," 13 May 1958, HS/EL.

38. Ibid.

39. ACWD, 11 October 1955.

40. *U.S. News and World Report*, 23 August 1957, 66; Kenneth S. Davis, *Soldier of Democracy: A Biography of Dwight Eisenhower* (Garden City, N.Y., 1945), 550.

41. Robert Cutler, *No Time for Rest* (Boston, 1966), 340. For an excellent review of the relationship between Eisenhower and Hazlett, see Robert Griffith, ed., *Ike's Letters to a Friend: 1941-1958* (Lawrence, 1984), 1-12.

42. Hazlett to DDE, 5 October 1941, AWF/NS.

43. Hazlett to DDE, 17 February 1943, 17 June 1945, and 13 March 1946, AWF/NS; DDE to Hazlett, 11 October 1941 and 20 October 1943, AWF/NS.

44. Hazlett to DDE, 17 June 1945, AWF/NS; DDE to Dr. John Sheedy, 30 November 1955, AWF/DDE:D; and Hagerty Diary, 14 December 1955, JHP.

45. DDE to Lucius Clay, 21 October 1955, AWF/DDE:D; ACWD, 11 October 1955; Mamie Eisenhower to Major General and Mrs. Leland Hobbs, 14 October 1955, AWF/DDE:D; and Cutler, *No Time for Rest*, 339-340.

46. DDE to A. Gruenther, 19 October 1955, AWF/DDE:D; DDE to Max Elbin, 19 October 1955, ACWD; DDE to Floyd Odlum, 6 October 1955, AWF/DDE:D; DDE to Clifford Roberts, 30 January 1956, Hobby Papers, EL; ACWD, 26 October 1955; Shanley Diary, 2076, EL; and Snyder to Dr. George Lull, 25 October 1955, HS/W.

47. DDE to Clifford Roberts, 30 January 1956, Hobby Papers, EL; "Nursing Notes," 7 October 1955, HS/EL; and "Questions You Want to Ask Dr. White," 6 November 1955, AWF/AS.

48. Eisenhower, *Mandate for Change,* 645; Snyder, "Progress Reports," 11 November 1955, HS/EL; and PPP, 1955, 840–841.

49. Mattingly Diary, 11 November 1955, in "CV System: Part Two," 43, TMP; Mattingly to Oglesby Paul, 10 May 1982, "1st Period, Acute Heart Attack and Hospitalization Denver," PDWP; Snyder, "Progress Notes," 11 November 1955, HS/EL; "Press Conference of Mr. Hagerty upon Return from Denver," 11 November 1955, JHP; and PPP, 1955, 236.

50. Snyder, "Progress Notes," 11 November 1955, HS/EL; Eisenhower, *Waging Peace,* 649.

51. For descriptions of Eisenhower's return to Gettysburg see *Time,* 21 and 28 November 1955. Quotation is from Shanley Diary, 1597, EL.

52. Snyder, "Progress Reports," 11 November 1955, HS/EL.

53. Snyder, "Progress Reports," 17, 19, and 21–26 November 1955, HS/EL; Mattingly, "Doctor's Progress Notes," 23 November 1955, TMP; Snyder, "Progress Reports," November 25–December 4, HS/EL; Mattingly, "Doctor's Progress Notes," 10 December 1955, TMP; Mattingly, "CV System: Part Three," 10, TMP; and Mattingly Diary, 3–5 December 1955, in "CV System: Part Three," 26, TMP.

54. Mattingly, "Doctor's Progress Report," 10 December 1955, TMP; Hagerty Diary, 10 December 1955, JHP; and "Press and Radio Conference in the White House," 10 December 1955, JHP.

55. Mattingly, "CV System: Part Eight," 3–4, 5–6, 15, TMP; Mattingly to White, 29 November 1955, PDWP.

56. Mattingly, "CV System: Part Eight, 6, TMP; Mattingly to Snyder, 10 December 1955, HS/EL.

57. Mattingly to Snyder, 10 December 1955, HS/EL; Mattingly, "CV System: Part Eight," 6–7, TMP; and Mattingly, "CV System: Part Three," 5, TMP.

58. *Washington Post,* 26 September 1955; White, *My Life and Medicine,* 183; and Thomas Mattingly, "Paul White: His Influence upon an Individual, a Nation, and the World," *American Journal of Cardiology* 15 (April 1961): 506.

59. "Press and Radio Conference with the Doctors," 22 October 1955, JHP; White, *My Life and Medicine,* 187–188; and DDE to White, 28 October 1955, AWF/AS.

60. White, *My Life and Medicine,* 175; Mattingly, "Paul White," 506. For an astute discussion of White's difficult situation see Paul, *Take Heart,* 168.

61. White to Snyder, 12 November 1955, HS/W; White to DDE, 12 November 1955, AWF/AS.

62. White to Snyder, 12 November 1955, HS/W; White to DDE, 12 November 1955,AWF/AS; and DDE to White, 17 November 1955, AWF/AS.

63. Snyder to White, 21 November 1955, HS/W; White to Snyder, 21 November 1955, HS/W; and Snyder to White, 6 December 1955, HS/W.

64. Mattingly Diary, 13 November 1955, in "CV System: Part Three," 24–25, TMP; Mattingly, "Summary of White's Activities During the Period 1 Nov. 55 and 1 Mar. 56," 1986, TMP; Mattingly to White, 29 November 1955, PDWP; and Mattingly, "Why and How Did PDW Fail in Maintaining His Desirability as a Presidential Consultant," 2, PDWP.

65. Mattingly to O. Paul, 6 May 1982, TMP.

66. Snyder, "Progress Reports," 17 December 1955, HS/EL; "Press and Radio Conference with the Doctors," 17 December 1955, JHP; and White note card, 17 December 1955, PDWP.

67. White to Snyder, 18 December 1955, HS/EL.

68. Snyder to White, 23 December 1955, HS/W; Staff Secretary, Legislative Meeting Series, 12 December 1955, EL; and Robert J. Donovan, *Eisenhower: The Inside Story* (New York, 1956), 398.

69. Donovan, *Eisenhower: The Inside Story,* 397; Nixon, *Memoirs,* 168; and PPP, 1956, 191.

70. Snyder, "Progress Reports," 22–23 December 1955, HS/EL; Richard M. Nixon, *Six Crises* (Garden City, N.Y., 1962), 156.

71. Staff Secretary, Legislative Meeting Series, 12 December 1955, EL; Nixon, *Six Crises,* 156.

72. Eisenhower, *Mandate for Change,* 671; DDE to Hazlett, 4 June 1955, AWF/NS; Robert J. Donovan, *Confidential Secretary: Ann Whitman's Twenty Years with Eisenhower and Rockefeller* (New York, 1988), 90; AWF/DDE:D, 25 May 1955; Hazlett to DDE, 8 June 1955, AWF/NS; and DDE to Hazlett, 4 June 1955 and 15 August 1955, AWF/NS.

73. Hazlett to DDE, 8 June 1955, AWF/NS; Robert H. Ferrell, ed., *The Eisenhower Diaries* (New York, 1981), 290, 323; Stephen Ambrose, *Eisenhower: The President,* vol. 2 (New York, 1984), 221; and ACWD, 19 May 1955.

74. Milton Eisenhower to Snyder, 3 October 1955, HS/W; Arthur Wilson to Snyder, 25 September 1955, HS/W; Hazlett to DDE, 27 September 1955, AWF/NS.

75. Billy Graham to DDE, 8 October 1955, DDE/PPF.

76. *Business Week,* 1 October 1955, 39; *Washington Daily News,* 26 September 1955; *Look,* 18 October 1955, 33–37; *U.S. News and World Report,* 4 November 1955, 19; and Herbert S. Parmet, *Eisenhower and the American Crusades* (New York, 1972), 415.

77. L. Richard Guylay, "Eisenhower's Two Presidential Campaigns, 1952 and 1956," in *Dwight D. Eisenhower: Soldier, President, Statesman,* ed. Joann P. Krieg (New York, 1987), 27–28.

78. DDE to Hazlett, 2 March 1956, AWF/NS; PPP, 1948, 2186; and Ferrell, *Eisenhower Diaries,* 273.

79. DDE to Hazlett, 2 March 1956, AWF/NS; Cutler, *No Time for Rest,* 340.

80. DDE to Hazlett, 2 March 1956, AWF/NS.

81. Hazlett to DDE, 21 October 1955, AWF/NS; Fletcher Knebel, "How Ike Made Up His Mind," *Look,* 1 May 1956, 19-21; Eisenhower, *Mandate for Change,* 675.

82. Hagerty Diary, 13-14 December 1956, EL.

83. Ibid.

84. Ibid.

85. Ibid., 10 December 1955, EL; Mattingly to White, 15 December 1955, HS/EL; and "Press and Radio Conference in the White House," 10 December 1955, JHP.

86. Nixon, *Six Crises,* 157; DDE to Hazlett, 23 December 1955, AWF/DDE:D.

87. "The President's Appointments," 28 December 1955-8 January 1956, HS/EL.

88. Ibid.; Mattingly, "CV System: Part Three," 11, TMP; Mattingly Diary, 30-31 December 1955, in "CV System: Part Three," 2, TMP.

89. PPP, 1956, 32-38; Eisenhower, *Mandate for Change,* 675.

90. American Research Foundation to "Doctors," 24 December 1955, HS/W.

91. White to Snyder, 28 December 1955, HS/EL; White to Snyder, 1 January 1956, HS/EL; Robert Levy to American Research Foundation, 28 December 1955, HS/EL; Snyder to DDE, 2 January 1956, HS/W; and Snyder to Levy, 2 January 1956, HS/W.

92. White to F. W. Leonard, 2 January 1956, PDWP; White to Mattingly, 3 January 1956, PDWP; and White to DDE, 4 January 1956, AWF/AS.

93. *U.S. News and World Report,* 13 January 1956, 19-22.

94. Ibid., 19-29.

95. White to Snyder, 9 January 1956, HS/EL; *U.S. News and World Report,* 13 January 1956, 19-29.

CHAPTER 5
"When the Going Gets Tough, the Tough Get Going"

1. *New York Times,* 11 September 1955.

2. Ibid., 4 and 19 December 1955.

3. John Bartlow Martin, *Adlai Stevenson and the World* (Garden City, N.Y., 1978), 241.

4. *New York Times,* 8 January 1956.

5. Ibid., 4 March 1956.

6. Robert J. Donovan, *Eisenhower: The Inside Story* (New York, 1956), 396-397, 400-402.

7. Donovan, *Eisenhower: The Inside Story*, 399-400; Dwight D. Eisenhower, *Mandate for Change: The White House Years* (Garden City, N.Y., 1963), 620-681, citation on page 674. For the best discussion of the second term decision see Stephen E. Ambrose, *Eisenhower: The President*, vol. 2 (New York, 1984), 287-297, citations on pages 290-292.

8. *New York Times*, 4 March 1956.

9. *Washington Post*, 26 September 1955; "Press and Radio Conference," 25 September 1955, JHP; and White to Hagerty, 3 October 1955, DDE/PPF.

10. *Time*, 10 October 1955, 29; "Press and Radio Conference with the Doctors," 9 October 1955, JHP; and "Press and Radio Conference with the Doctors," 7 November 1955, JHP.

11. *Washington Post*, 26 September 1955; Elmer Hess to Snyder, 29 September 1955, HS/W.

12. Snyder quoted in *Minneapolis Sunday Tribune*, 16 October 1955.

13. Milton Eisenhower to Snyder, 3 October 1955, HS/W; Snyder to M. Eisenhower, 8 November 1955, HS/EL.

14. John S. D. Eisenhower, *Strictly Personal* (Garden City, N.Y., 1974), 184; Sherman Adams, *Firsthand Report* (New York, 1961), 222.

15. Ellis Slater, *The Ike I Knew* (New York, 1980), 107, 111, 115, 120, 123.

16. Oglesby Paul, *Take Heart* (Boston, 1986), 169.

17. Paul Dudley White, "The Coronaries Through the Ages," *Minnesota Medicine* 38 (November 1955): 801 (first presented at a symposium on arteriosclerosis at the University of Minnesota on 7 September 1955); "Press and Radio Conference with the Doctors," 7 November 1955, JHP; "Press and Radio Conference with the Doctors," 17 December 1955, JHP.

18. P. D. White and Edward F. Bland, "Coronary Thrombosis (With Myocardial Infarction) Ten Years Later," *JAMA* 117 (1941): 1171; F. T. Billings, B. M. Kalstone, J. L. Spencer, C. O. Ball, and G. R. Meneely, "Prognosis of Acute Myocardial Infarction," *American Journal of Medicine* (1949): 356; C. Smith, "Length of Survival After Myocardial Infarction," *JAMA* (1953): 167; and David Cole, E. B. Singian, and L. N. Katz, "The Long Term Prognosis Following Myocardial Infarction, and Some Factors Which Affect It," *Circulation* 9 (March 1954): 321.

19. *Time*, 21 November 1955, 67; White to Mattingly, 12 December 1955, 20, HS/EL.

20. Paul Dudley White, *My Life and Medicine* (Boston, 1971), 176; Mattingly to Snyder, 15 December 1955, HS/EL.

21. Mattingly to White, 15 December 1955, HS/EL.

22. Mattingly, "CV System: Part Three," 1, TMP; Mattingly to Paul, 6 May 1982, TMP; and Mattingly to Paul, 10 May 1982, with attachment, "2d Period Nov. 1955-Nov. 1956," 2, PDWP.

23. White, *My Life and Medicine*, 188; Conrad Hobbs to White, 5 December 1955, with attachment, "Open Letter to the President," HS/EL.

24. Hobbs to White, 5 December 1955, HS/EL.

25. "Press and Radio Conference with the Doctors," 17 December 1955, JHP; White, *My Life and Medicine,* 188–189.

26. White to Snyder, 18 December 1955, HS/EL; White, *My Life and Medicine,* 188–189; White to DDE, 18 December 1955, AWF/AS; and Hazlett to DDE, 27 September 1955, AWF/NS.

27. White to Snyder, 18 December 1955, HS/EL; White to DDE, 19 December 1955, HS/EL.

28. White to Snyder, 18 December 1955, HS/EL; Mattingly to Paul, 10 May 1982, with attachment, "2d Period Nov. 1955–Nov. 1956," PDWP.

29. Mattingly to White, 22 December 1955, HS/EL; Mattingly, "Why and How Did PDW Fail in Maintaining His Desirability as a Presidential Consultant," n.d., TMP.

30. DDE to White, 27 December 1955, HS/EL; Mattingly, "CV System: Part Three," 24, TMP.

31. White to Mattingly, 28 December 1955, TMP; Mattingly to White, n.d., but clearly after 30 December 1955, TMP.

32. White to DDE, 4 January 1956, HS/EL; Conrad Hobbs to PDW, 5 December 1955, HS/EL.

33. DDE to White, 14 January 1956, HS/EL; AWF/DDE:D, 19 May 1955; White, *My Life and Medicine,* 189.

34. Shanley Diary, 2095, EL; Mattingly, "Doctor's Progress Reports," 11 January, TMP; and Snyder, Mattingly, and Pollock, "Memorandum for the President," 10 January 1956, AWF/NS.

35. Ambrose, *Eisenhower: The President,* 2:295; Shanley Diary, 2118, 2095, EL.

36. AWF/DDE:D, 10 January 1956.

37. Sherman Adams, *Firsthand Report* (New York, 1961), 225–226; Eisenhower, *Mandate for Change,* 676–677; Milton Eisenhower to DDE, 16 January 1956, AWF/NS; and AWF/DDE:D, 10 January 1956.

38. Adams, *Firsthand Report,* 226; John Eisenhower, *Strictly Personal,* 185, 384–388.

39. Eisenhower, *Mandate for Change,* 676.

40. DDE to R. Pollock, 20 January 1956, AWF/NS; Pollock to Snyder, 16 January 1956, HS/EL; DDE to R. Pollock, 20 January 1956, AWF/NS; DDE to Margaret Williams, 29 January 1956, AWF/NS; and DDE to Edythe Turner, 20 January 1956, AWF/NS.

41. PPP, 1956, 160–161; Shanley Diary, 2123, EL.

42. ACW/DDE:D, 11 January 1956; DDE to Edythe Turner, 20 January 1956, AWF/NS; DDE to William Stirling, 28 January 1956, AWF/NS; and ACWD, 9 February 1956.

43. Shanley Diary, 2121, EL.

44. PPP, 1956, 187; DDE to Donald Richberg, 23 January 1956, AWF/NS; and DDE to Tex McCrary, 23 January 1956, AWF/NS.

45. DDE to Hazlett, 23 January 1956, AWF/NS; William Robinson to DDE,

30 January 1956, William Robinson papers, EL; Pre-Press Conference Briefing, 25 January 1956, AWF/NS; and DDE to Hazlett, 2 March 1956, AWF/NS.

46. Snyder to Dr. George Eusterman, 2 February 1956, HS/W; ACWD, 13 February 1956; DDE to Victor Emanuel, 7 February 1956, AWF/NS.

47. Nixon quoted in C. L. Sulzberger, *An Age of Mediocrity* (New York, 1973), 314; DDE to Hazlett, 2 March 1956, AWF/NS; Gallup polls in Fletcher Knebel, "How Ike Made Up His Mind," *Look*, 1 May 1956, 21; Shanley Diary, 2176, EL; and ACWD, 13 February 1956.

48. PPP, 1956, 229.

49. *New York Times*, 25 December 1955.

50. Eisenhower quoted in Paul, *Take Heart*, 169.

51. *U.S. News and World Report*, 20 January 1956, 61-62.

52. Mattingly to Snyder, 4 January 1956, HS/EL.

53. Ibid.

54. Ibid.; Mattingly to Paul, 6 May 1982, TMP. There is no documentary evidence pointing either way as to whether Snyder informed his patient, but it is likely that he did; he would not have deceived the president on an issue of such import. But he surely would have explained it from his own point of view. One can imagine him saying something like this: "On medical grounds, Mr. President, Tom Mattingly is worried about the possibility of an aneurysm on your heart at the point of the scar. None of the other cardiologists—Pollock, White or Lepeschkin—agree with him, nor do I. We did have the radiologists at both Fitzsimons and Walter Reed take some special tests to give us a closer look at the area, and neither Colonel Ramsey nor Colonel Lodmell found anything out of the ordinary. As you know, Tom is very conservative in all matters, and to his credit. But in this instance we believe he is worrying unnecessarily, and that your heart has healed completely."

55. Mattingly to White, n.d., but about 1 January 1956, TMP.

56. Pollock to Snyder, 16 January 1956, HS/EL.

57. Snyder to Pollock, 27 January 1956, HS/W; "Dinner Conference at General Snyder's Apartment" 18 January 1956, PDWP.

58. Mattingly to Snyder, 28 January 1956, PDWP.

59. Snyder to DDE, 4 January 1956, HS/EL; White to Mattingly, 9 February 1956, TMP.

60. White to Snyder, 21 January 1956, 23 January 1956 and attached draft, and 24 January 1956, HS/W.

61. Ibid.

62. Pollock to White, 30 January 1956, HS/EL; Pollock to Snyder, 31 January 1956, HS/EL; and Mattingly to White, 7 February 1956, HS/EL.

63. Copies of various White drafts are in PDWP.

64. Snyder to Pollock, 2 February 1956, DDE/PPF.

65. This envelope with a 6 February 1956 postmark is in PDWP.

66. Shanley Diary, 2156, EL; *New York Times*, 15 February 1956; Adams,

Firsthand Report, 228–229; and White's medical note card, "President Eisenhower, 14 February 1956," in PDWP.

67. Mattingly to Snyder, 23 February 1956, HS/W; Mattingly Diary, 14 February 1956, in "CV System: Part Three," 26, TMP.

68. Mattingly Diary, 14 February 1956, in "CV System: Part Three," 26–27, TMP; Mattingly to Snyder, 23 February 1956, HS/W; and DDE to Wilber M. Brucker, 13 February 1956, TMP.

69. *New York Herald Tribune,* 22 January 1956.

70. DDE to Wilber Brucker, 13 February 1956, TMP.

71. Shanley Diary, 2158, EL; White, *My Life and Medicine,* 189.

72. "Press Conference of James C. Hagerty," 14 February 1956, JHP.

73. Ibid.; *New York Times,* 15 February 1956.

74. "Press Conference of James C. Hagerty," 14 February 1956, JHP.

75. Ibid.; *New York Times,* 15 February 1956.

76. *New York Times,* 11 January 1956; *New York Herald Tribune,* 22 January 1956.

77. *Washington Post,* 3 October 1955; Larry Fernsworth to Pearson, 29 December 1955, DPP; and *Washington Post,* 27 February 1956.

78. Draft of newspaper column, "Dr. White," n.d., DPP.

79. DDE to Donald Richberg, 23 January 1956, AWF/NS.

80. Shanley Diary, 2158, EL; DDE to White, 15 February 1956, PDWP; and Mattingly, "Why and How Did PDW Fail in Maintaining His Desirability as a Presidential Consultant," 6, PDWP.

81. Shanley Diary, 2161, EL; DDE to Cliff Roberts, 27 February 1956, AWF/NS; *Washington Star,* 24 February 1956; and *New York Times,* 24 February 1956.

82. Fletcher Knebel, "How Ike Made Up His Mind," *Look,* 1 May 1956, 21; Donovan, *Eisenhower: Inside Story,* 403–404; Shanley Diary, 2166–2167, EL; and Herbert S. Parmet, *Eisenhower and the American Crusades* (New York, 1972), 432.

83. Shanley Diary, 2176, EL; PPP, 1956, 263–266, 274.

84. PPP, 1956, 273–279.

85. Eisenhower, *Mandate for Change,* 681; PPP, 1956, 272; and DDE to Hazlett, 2 March 1956, AWF/NS.

86. Eisenhower, *Mandate for Change,* 678–680; DDE to Hazlett, 2 March 1956, AWF/NS; Richard M. Nixon, *Six Crises* (Garden City, N.Y., 1962), 154; and DDE to Tex McCrary, 23 January 1956, AWF/NS.

87. DDE to Hazlett, 2 March 1956, AWF/NS.

88. Ibid.; Hazlett to DDE, 1 March 1956, AWF/NS; and James David Barber, *Presidential Character* (Englewood Cliffs, N.J., 1985), 136.

89. DDE to Brigadier General William R. Gruber, 16 November 1955, AWF/NS.

90. Dr. Charles M. Gruber to DDE, 25 October 1955, DDE/PPF; Carl F. Wente to DDE, 14 October 1955, DDE/PPF; Charles S. Mason to DDE, 18

October 1955, DDE/PPF; and *U.S. News and World Report,* 7 October 1955, 55–59.

91. Frank Leahy to DDE, 14 October 1955, DDE/PPF.

92. Snyder to DDE, 30 January 1956, HS/EL; Ann Whitman to Snyder, 12 February 1956 and 27 January 1956, HS/EL; and DDE to Cliff Roberts, 30 January 1956, Hobby Papers, EL.

93. Johnson to DDE, 18 September 1955, LBJL; *Newsweek,* 7 November 1955, 35; and *Life,* 16 January 1956, 34–35.

94. DDE to Hazlett, 2 March 1956, AWF/NS.

95. Adams, *Firsthand Report,* 221; Eisenhower, *Mandate for Change,* 670–681; and DDE note, February 1956, AWF/NS.

CHAPTER 6
The Politics of Illness

1. John Bartlow Martin, *Adlai Stevenson and the World* (Garden City, N.Y., 1978), 210–211.

2. Ibid., 225; William Robinson to DDE, 12 June 1956, William Robinson papers, EL.

3. Martin, *Stevenson and the World,* 213, 227, 270, 275, 314.

4. Ibid., 346, 382–383.

5. Ibid., 213, 358.

6. Marquis Childs, *Eisenhower: Captive Hero* (New York, 1958), 224; *New York Herald Tribune,* 4 May 1956.

7. Stephen E. Ambrose, *Eisenhower: The President,* vol. 2 (New York, 1984), 298–299, 326.

8. Robert B. McLean, "Leonard D. Heaton—Military Surgeon," *Military Medicine* 147 (September 1982): 717–727.

9. Snyder to Mrs. Walker, 24 March 1956, HS/EL; Snyder to Dr. Albert Belisle, 21 May 1956, HS/W.

10. Snyder to White, 27 April 1956, HS/W.

11. PPP, 1956, 473–474; Snyder to White, 9 May 1956, HS/W; and Mattingly, "Activities of Dr. White as Civilian Consultant . . . 14 Feb. 56 to 28 Oct. 56," TMP.

12. Mattingly to White, 22 May 1956, PDWP; White to Snyder with attached "Comments for the Press as of May 25, 1956," 29 May 1956, HS/EL; White to Mattingly, 28 May 1956, TMP; Mattingly to White, 4 June 1956, HS/EL; and Snyder to White, 4 June 1956, HS/W.

13. White to Mattingly, 7 June 1956, HS/EL.

14. Mattingly, "Doctor's Progress Notes," 12 March 1956, and "Consultation Sheet," 11 May 1956, HS/EL.

15. Snyder, "Ileitis Operation," 2, 4, HS/EL; Leonard Heaton, OH, 35, EL;

"Report of Examination," 12 May 1956, AWF/AS; and *U.S. News and World Report,* 22 June 1956, 31.

16. Snyder, "Ileitis Operation," 3, HS/EL; "Report of Examination," 12 May 1956, AWF/AS.

17. Snyder, "Ileitis Operation," 3, HS/EL.

18. Snyder, "Bedside Notes," 8 June 1956, HS/EL; Snyder, "Ileitis Operation," 5-6, HS/EL; and ACWD, 8 June 1956 and 8 June-16 July 1956.

19. Snyder, "Ileitis Operation," 7-8, HS/EL.

20. Ibid., 15-16; Snyder, "Bedside Notes," 8 June 1956, HS/EL.

21. Snyder, "Bedside Notes," 8 June 1956, HS/EL; Snyder, "Ileitis Operation," 18-20, HS/EL; Leonard Heaton, Isidor Ravdin, Brian Blades, and Thomas J. Whelan, "President Eisenhower's Operation for Regional Enteritis: A Footnote to History," *Annals of Surgery* 159 (May 1964): 662-663; and Heaton, OH, 37, EL.

22. Snyder, "Ileitis Operation," 20-22, HS/EL.

23. DDE to Ravdin, 10 October 1956, AWF/AS; Heaton, OH, 38, EL; Snyder, "Bedside Notes," 8 June 1956, HS/EL; Snyder, "Ileitis Operation," 23, HS/EL.

24. Snyder, "Ileitis Operation," 26-28, HS/EL.

25. Ibid., 29-30; Heaton OH, 40-42, 61, EL; ACWD, 9- 11 June 1956.

26. Snyder, "Ileitis Operation," 26, HS/EL.

27. Heaton et al., "President Eisenhower's Operation for Regional Enteritis," 664-665; Heaton, OH, 53, EL; and *Time,* 16 July 1956, 66.

28. *New York Times,* 10 June 1956; James Deakin, *Straight Stuff* (New York, 1984), 14, 31-32.

29. ACWD, 8 June-16 July 1956; Transcript, Heaton News Conference, 9 June 1956, DPP; and *Washington Post,* 14 June 1956.

30. Deakin, *Straight Stuff,* 32; *Washington Post,* 10 June 1956.

31. *Editor and Publisher,* 23 June 1956; Associated Press bulletin and United Press bulletin, 19 June 1956, DPP.

32. *Time,* 16 July 1956, 66.

33. *Washington Star,* 14 June 1956; United Press Bulletin, 19 July 1956; *New York Times,* 13 June 1956; and Senator Pat McNamara to Editor, *Washington Star,* 21 July 1956, DPP.

34. Robert Allen to Drew Pearson, 13 June 1956, DPP.

35. Tyler Abell, ed., *Drew Pearson, Diaries 1949-1959* (New York, 1974), 362; "J. A." to Pearson, 12 June 1956, DPP; and *Washington Post,* 9 June 1956.

36. William Harlan Hale, "The Facts About Ileitis," *Reporter,* 28 June 1956, 6; Standard cited in Fletcher Knebel, "The President's Doctor," *Look,* 18 September 1956, 89-90; and *Washington Post,* 14 June 1956.

37. Harold Dingman, *Risk Appraisal* (Cincinnati, 1946), 248; Zetzel quoted in Hale, "The Facts about Ileitis," 6; and *Time,* 16 July 1956.

38. *U.S. News and World Report,* 22 June 1956, 30-31; *Time,* 16 July 1956, 66;

Heaton et al., "President Eisenhower's Operation for Regional Enteritis," 661–666; and Heaton, OH, 56–57, EL.

39. *Reporter,* 28 June 1956, 6; *U.S. News and World Report,* 22 June 1956, 31.

40. *Washington Post,* 9 June 1956; *Washington Star,* 14 June 1956; MacNamara cited in Myron K. Jordan, "Presidential Health Reporting: The Eisenhower Watershed," *American Journalism* 4, no. 3 (1987): 153; and *Newsday,* 12 June 1956.

41. Martin, *Adlai Stevenson and the World,* 340; Walter Johnson and Carol Evans, eds., *The Papers of Adlai E. Stevenson,* vol. 6 (Boston, 1972), 156; and PPP, 1956, 630, 636.

42. *Washington Post,* 1 August 1956; David Rutstein, "Doctors and Politics, *Atlantic Monthly,* August 1956, 32–35.

43. Rutstein, "Doctors and Politics," 32–35.

44. Ibid.

45. PPP, 1956, 627–629, 635.

46. PPP, 1956, 669–670, 697, 722, 727.

47. Snyder to White, 6 August 1956, HS/W; White to Robert Levy, 31 July 1956, DDE/PPF; White to Snyder, 2 August 1956, HS/W; and Snyder to White, 6 August 1956, HS/W.

48. White to Snyder, 17 August 1956, HS/W; Ravdin to DDE, 13 August 1956, DDE/PPF; DDE to Ravdin, 17 August 1956, DDE/PPF; Snyder, "Progress Reports," 29 August 1956, HS/EL; Snyder to Ann Whitman, 18 September 1956, AWF/AS; and Ravdin to DDE, 14 September 1956, AWF/AS.

49. DDE to Ravdin, 18 September 1956, AWF/AS.

50. Ibid.

51. Heaton, OH, 47–48, EL; Mamie Eisenhower to Slater, 15 June 1956, EL; and Snyder to Gruenther, 5 July 1956, HS/W.

52. Minutes of Legislative Meeting, 10 July 1956, EL.

53. Heaton, OH, 50–51, EL; Snyder to Gruenther, 9 July 1956, HS/W.

54. Richard M. Nixon, *Six Crises* (Garden City, N.Y., 1962), 168; Heaton, OH, 48–50, EL; and Snyder to Gruenther, 5 and 9 July 1956, HS/W.

55. Snyder to Gruenther, 29 July 1956, HS/W; Snyder, "Progress Reports," 19 July 1956, HS/EL; and Emmet John Hughes, *The Ordeal of Power* (New York, 1963), 176.

56. Snyder to Gruenther, 29 July 1956, HS/W; Hughes, *Ordeal of Power,* 172.

57. Snyder to Gruenther, 29 July 1956, HS/W; Snyder, "Progress Reports," 6 August 1956, HS/EL; ACWD, 28 July 1956; Mattingly, "Doctors' Progress Notes," 1 and 10 August 1956, TMP; and Mattingly, "CV System: Part Eight," 9, TMP.

58. Hughes, *Ordeal of Power,* 198.

59. Porter McKeever, *Adlai Stevenson* (New York, 1989), 376–377.

60. Richard M. Nixon, *Memoirs* (New York, 1978), 178; Martin, *Adlai Stevenson and the World,* 336, 382–383; and McKeever, *Adlai Stevenson,* 365, 369–370, 374, 379.

61. Ellis Slater, *The Ike I Knew* (New York, 1980), 136; Hughes, *Ordeal of Power,* 198.

62. DDE to Hazlett, 2 November 1956, AWF/NS; Hughes, *Ordeal of Power,* 198.

63. Hughes, *Ordeal of Power,* 177, 193, 199, 202.

64. Snyder, "Progress Reports," 27 September 1956 and 4, 9, and 18 October 1956, HS/EL; Robert J. Donovan, *Confidential Secretary: Ann Whitman's Twenty Years with Eisenhower and Rockefeller* (New York, 1988), 109.

65. *Newsweek,* 17 September 1956, 39.

66. White to DDE, 23 June 1956, AWF/AS; DDE to White, 14 July 1956, PDWP; and DDE to White, 11 July 1956, AWF/AS.

67. Dr. James A. Halsted to White, 13 June 1956, PDWP; White to Halsted, 18 June 1956, PDWP; and Halsted to White, 8 July 1956, PDWP.

68. White to Snyder and attached paper, 12 June 1956, HS/W.

69. Ibid.; White to Hagerty, 1 October 1956, PDWP.

70. White to Hagerty, 1 October 1956, PDWP.

71. White to Hagerty, 2 October 1956, PDWP; Hagerty to White, 3 October 1956, PDWP; and White to Hagerty, 3 October 1956, PDWP.

72. White to DDE, 3 October 1956, PDWP; DDE to White, 10 October 1956, PDWP; White to Hagerty, 11 October 1956, PDWP; White to Hagerty, 12 October 1956, PDWP; White to Frances Burns, 16 October 1956, PDWP; and White to Hagerty, 16 October 1956, HS/W.

73. Paper is attached to White to Hagerty, 16 October 1956, HS/W; see also White et al., "A Completed Twenty-five Year Follow-up Study of 200 Patients with Myocardial Infarction," *Journal of Chronic Diseases* 4 (October 1956): 415–422.

74. Hagerty to Snyder, n.d., DDE/GF.

75. "Reminder Note," n.d., HS/W; White to Hagerty, 12 October 1956, JHP.

76. White, "Reflections on Receiving a Blakeslee Award of the American Heart Association," 28 October 1956, JHP.

77. Abell, *Drew Pearson, Diaries,* 366; John Ingle to Pearson, 15 October 1956, DPP.

78. Pearson, "Letter of Record," 5 November 1956, DPP; *Washington Post,* 27 October 1956; and Pearson column, DPP.

79. Associated Press Bulletin, 28 October 1956, DPP; *New York Post,* 27 October 1956; *Grants Pass Courier,* 30 October 1956; and Abell, *Drew Pearson, Diaries,* 455.

80. L. Renzel to Pearson, 28 October 1956, DPP; Pearson, "Letter of Record," 5 November 1956, DPP.

81. *Oceanside Blade Tribune,* 28 October 1956; Abell, *Drew Pearson, Diaries,* 379.

82. *Oceanside Blade Tribune,* 28 October 1956.

83. Dwight D. Eisenhower, *Mandate for Change: The White House Years* (Gar-

den City, N.Y., 1963), 646; Eisenhower, *Waging Peace, 1956-1961* (Garden City, N.Y., 1965), 58.

84. Hughes, *Ordeal of Power*, 212; press release, "Report of Examination," 28 October 1956, JHP; and Mattingly, "Consultation Sheet," 28 October 1956, TMP.

85. Snyder, "Progress Reports," 5 and 6 November 1956, HS/EL.

86. Martin, *Adlai Stevenson and the World*, 390; Donovan, *Confidential Secretary*, 100.

87. Hughes, *Ordeal of Power*, 228.

88. Snyder, "Progress Reports," 25 November 1957, HS/EL; Eisenhower, *Waging Peace*, 227-228.

89. Eisenhower, *Waging Peace*, 227-228.

90. Snyder, "Progress Reports," 25 November 1957, HS/EL.

91. Ibid.

92. Ibid.; R. E. Clauson Jr., "Consultation Report," 25 November 1957, HS/EL.

93. Snyder, "Progress Reports," 25 November 1957, HS/EL.

94. Ibid.; DDE, *Waging Peace*, 228.

95. John S. D. Eisenhower, *Strictly Personal* (Garden City, N.Y., 1974), 196-197; Snyder, "Progress Reports," 26 November 1957, HS/EL; Mattingly, "Doctor's Progress Notes," 26 November 1957, HS/EL; Mattingly, "Nervous System," 8, 10, TMP; and Mattingly Diary, 25-26 November 1957, in "CV System: Part Three," 30-32, TMP.

96. Snyder, "Progress Reports," 26 November 1957, HS/EL; H. Houston Merritt to Snyder, 27 November 1957, HS/EL.

97. Merritt to Snyder, 27 November 1957, HS/EL; Mattingly Diary, 26 November 1957, in "CV System: Part Three," 32, TMP.

98. Snyder, "Progress Reports," 26 November 1957, HS/EL.

99. Deakin, *Straight Stuff*, 32-35; Robert Pierpoint, *At the White House: Assignment to Six Presidents* (New York, 1981), 35-37.

100. *New York Times*, 28 November 1957.

101. Snyder, "Progress Reports," 11 December 1957, HS/EL; Roy E. Clausen, "Consultation Sheet," 10 December 1957, HS/EL.

102. Mattingly Diary, 10 December 1957, in "CV System: Part Three," 33, TMP.

103. Eisenhower, *Waging Peace*, 229-230; Ambrose, *Eisenhower: The President*, 439-440.

104. For the background of the Twenty-fifth Amendment see John D. Feerick, *The Twenty-fifth Amendment* (New York, 1976), 52-56; for the Eisenhower quotes see Feerick, *From Failing Hands* (New York, 1965), 211; and Feerick, *Twenty-fifth Amendment*, 55.

105. Snyder, "Progress Reports," 2 August 1958 and 23 August 1959, HS/EL; Eisenhower, *Waging Peace*, 229.

106. Deakin, *Straight Stuff*, 37.

107. PPP, 1956, 269.

CHAPTER 7
The Life Apart

1. Emmet John Hughes, *The Ordeal of Power* (New York, 1963), 224-227.

2. Ibid., 227-228.

3. ACWD, 15 July 1960.

4. Stephen E. Ambrose, *Eisenhower: The President*, vol. 2 (New York, 1984), 423; Chester J. Pach Jr. and Elmo Richardson, *The Presidency of Dwight D. Eisenhower* (Lawrence, Kans., 1991), 175.

5. ACWD, 9 May 1960; George B. Kistiakowsky, *A Scientist in the White House* (Cambridge, Mass., 1976), 375; and Snyder, "Progress Reports," 16 July 1960, HS/EL.

6. Ellis Slater, *The Ike I Knew* (New York, 1980), 130.

7. Mattingly "CV System: Part Three," 22, TMP; Mattingly Diary, 1959-1960, in "CV System: Part Three," 35-36, TMP.

8. Mattingly, "CV System: Part Three," 22, TMP; Mattingly Diary, 1 May 1957, in "CV System: Part Three," 29, TMP.

9. Mattingly Diary, 25-26 November 1957, and 10 December 1957, in "CV System: Part Three," 31-33, TMP.

10. Mattingly, "Consultation Sheet," 4 January 1957, HS/EL.

11. Mattingly, "Hematopoietic System," 4-5, TMP.

12. Snyder, "Progress Reports," 8 February 1960, 6 November 1958, and 4 June 1959, HS/EL.

13. Snyder, "Progress Reports," 12 March 1957, 22 December 1960, 5 April 1959, 13 November 1958, 25 March 1959, 28 July 1958, and 17 March 1958, HS/EL.

14. Snyder, "Progress Reports," 9-10 June 1957, HS/EL; Mattingly, "Gastrointestinal System: Part Two," 18, 20, 21, TMP; Mattingly to Snyder, 10 June 1957, HS/EL.

15. Mattingly, "CV System: Part Three," 10-13, 19, TMP.

16. William W. Moore, *Fighting for Life: The Story of the American Heart Association 1911-1975* (Dallas, 1983), 78, 84, 212-213.

17. Frederick Stare to Paul White, Howard Sprague, and Samuel Levine, 4 October 1957, HSP; Frederick Stare to Howard Sprague, 6 February 1959, with attached "Statement for Guidance," HSP.

18. Ancel Keys to Frederick Stare, 10 February 1959, HSP.

19. Leonard Heaton, OH, 26, 29, 32, EL; "Cholesterol, 1946-1962," HS/EL.

20. Snyder, "Progress Reports," 21 August 1958, HS/EL.

21. Ibid., 6, 14, and 17 November 1958, HS/EL.

22. *New York Times*, 4 May 1959; Heaton cited in Mike Gorman to John Fogarty, 24 July 1959, John Fogarty papers, Providence College, Providence, Rhode Island.

23. Slater, *The Ike I Knew*, 198, 203; Snyder, "Progress Reports," 1 December 1959, HS/EL.

24. Snyder, "Progress Reports," 20 February 1960 and 6 April 1960, HS/EL.

25. Ibid., 22 April 1960, HS/EL.

26. Ibid., 23 April 1960, 28–29 April 1960, 9 August 1960, and 19 January 1961, HS/EL.

27. Ancel Keys to Frederick J. Stare, 10 February 1959, HSP; PPP, 1959, 452; and Joseph D. Beasley, *The Betrayal of Health* (New York, 1991), 170, 226.

28. On the Morris study see H. M. Marvin, T. Duckett Jones, Irvine H. Page, Irving S. Wright, and David D. Rutstein, *You and Your Heart* (New York, 1950), 148–156; Edward D. Frolich and Albert N. Brest, eds., *Preventive Aspects of Coronary Heart Disease* (Philadelphia, 1990), 182.

29. *U.S. News and World Report*, 23 August 1957; White to DDE, 23 June 1956, AWF/AS.

30. Snyder, "Progress Reports," 26 May 1959, HS/EL.

31. Statistics on golf for the first term from *U.S. News and World Report*, 23 August 1957, 61; statistics for the second term compiled from Snyder, "Progress Reports," HS/EL.

32. *U.S. News and World Report*, 23 August 1957, 60; Snyder "Progress Reports," 27 May 1959 and 8 March 1959, HS/EL; and Slater, *The Ike I Knew*, 184–185.

33. Snyder "Progress Reports," 20 August 1957, HS/EL; Slater, *The Ike I Knew*, 184.

34. Snyder, "Progress Reports," 28 May 1959, 1 September 1958, and 21 November 1959, HS/EL.

35. Ibid., 31 August 1958, and 11 April 1958.

36. *New York Times*, 26 October 1958.

37. Meyer Friedman and Ray H. Rosenman, "Association of Specific Overt Behavior Pattern with Blood and Cardiovascular Findings," *JAMA* 171 (1959): 1085–1096; Meyer Friedman and Ray H. Rosenman, *Type A Behavior and Your Heart* (Greenwich, Conn., 1974), 70–79.

38. Snyder, "Heart Attack," 32, HS/EL; Bryce Harlow, "The 'Compleat' President," in *The Eisenhower Presidency*, ed. Kenneth W. Thompson (Lanham, Md., 1984), 160.

39. Kistiakowsky, *A Scientist at the White House*, 9, 17, 91, 158, 335.

40. Snyder, "Progress Reports," 24 June 1958 and 6 April 1958, HS/EL; Slater, *The Ike I Knew*, 184.

41. Snyder, "Progress Reports," 13 January 1960, HS/EL.

42. C. D. Jenkins, "Psychologic and Social Precursors of Coronary Disease," *JAMA* 284 (1971): 312; Stephen M. Weiss, Susan Czajkowski, Sally Shumaker, and Roger Anderson, "Psychosocial Factors in Coronary Heart Disease," in *Preventive Aspects of Coronary Heart Disease*, ed. Edward D. Frolich and Albert N. Brest (Philadelphia, 1990), 137–138; and Redford B. Williams Jr. and Norman B. Anderson, "Hostility and Coronary Disease," in *Car-*

diovascular Disease and Behavior, ed. Jeffrey W. Elias and Phillip H. Marshall (Washington, D.C., 1987), 17–18.

43. Margaret A. Chesney, "Anger and Hostility: Future Implications," in *Anger and Hostility in Cardiovascular and Behavioral Disorders,* ed. Margaret A. Chesney and Ray Rosenman (Washington, D.C., 1985), 285–287; Weiss et al., "Psychosocial Factors in Coronary Heart Care," 138; Harlow, "The 'Compleat' President," 148; and ACWD, 13 July 1960.

44. *U.S. News and World Report,* 3 October 1960, 77.

45. Snyder, "Progress Reports," 2 October 1958, HS/EL.

46. Ibid., 17 March 1959.

47. Ibid., 2 October 1958.

48. Julie Nixon Eisenhower, *Special People* (New York, 1977), 203; Ambrose, *Eisenhower: The President,* 29; Julie Nixon Eisenhower, "Mamie," *Ladies' Home Journal,* June 1977, 108; and Jane Stafford, "His Heart in Your Keeping," *Mademoiselle,* February 1956, 132.

49. Slater, *The Ike I Knew,* 171, 186; Snyder, "Progress Reports," 5 April 1958, 27 May 1959, 3 September 1957, 22 January 1959, and 2 October 1958, HS/EL.

50. Snyder, "Progress Reports," 25 March 1959 and 22 April 1960, HS/EL.

51. Julie Eisenhower, *Special People,* 207; DDE to P. A. Hodgson, 19 July 1954, AWF/DDE:D.

52. Snyder, "Progress Reports," 13 November 1960, 23 August 1959, 26 October 1959, and 29 April 1959, HS/EL.

53. Ibid., 3 September 1957, 26 July 1960, and 24 March 1959.

54. Ibid., 5 and 7 April 1958, and 23 April 1959.

55. Ibid., 20 July 1958, 16 March 1958, and 11 February 1958.

56. Hazlett to DDE, 1 March 1956, AWF/NS; Kenneth S. Davis, *Soldier of Democracy: A Biography of Dwight Eisenhower* (Garden City, N.Y., 1945), 455; and Julie Eisenhower, *Special People,* 195.

57. Julie Nixon Eisenhower, "Mamie," 108; Lester David and Irene David, *Ike and Mamie* (New York, 1981), 15.

58. Wayne M. Sotile, *Heart Illness and Intimacy: How Caring Relationships Aid Recovery* (Baltimore, 1992), 77.

59. Snyder, "Progress Reports," 26 October 1959, HS/EL.

60. Dorothy Thompson, "May I Tell You About My Heart Attack?" *Ladies' Home Journal,* April 1960, 12; Clarence Randall, "The Happy Cardiac," *Harper's,* March 1959, 64, 66.

61. Hughes, *The Ordeal of Power,* 250–251; Andrei Gromyko, *Memories* (New York, 1990), 170.

62. Snyder, "Progress Reports," 13 January 1959, HS/EL; White to Snyder, 7 September 1965, HS/EL.

63. Merrill P. Anderson, "Psychological Issues in Cardiovascular Rehabilitation," in *Cardiovascular Disease and Behavior,* ed. Jeffrey W. Elias and Phillip Howard Marshall (Washington, D.C., 1987), 156– 159.

64. Arthur Kleinman, *The Illness Narratives: Suffering, Healing and the Human Condition* (New York, 1988), 47.

65. Snyder, "Progress Reports," 5 March 1958, 6 December 1957, 11 October 1958, and 11 December 1957, HS/EL.

66. Ibid., 24 January 1957 and 17–18 October 1960.

67. Marvin, *You and Your Heart*, 32–35; *Changing Times*, March 1953, 37.

68. Snyder, "Progress Reports," 22 April 1959 and 18 May 1957, HS/EL.

69. Ibid., 24–25 March 1959.

70. Marvin, *You and Your Heart*, 69–70, 81.

71. Mattingly, "CV System: Part Three," 14–15, TMP; Snyder, "Progress Reports," 10 September 1958, HS/EL.

72. Snyder, "Progress Reports," 23 October 1959 and 24 February 1960, HS/EL.

73. Mattingly, "CV System: Part Three," 15, TMP; Snyder "Progress Reports," 16 October 1958, HS/EL.

74. Snyder, "Progress Reports," 17 November 1959, 16 July 1958, and 14 November 1958, HS/EL.

75. Ibid., 3 December 1958.

76. Kleinman, *The Illness Narratives*, 267; Snyder, "Progress Reports," 31 December 1956, HS/EL.

77. DDE to Clark Gable, 7 November 1960, ACW/DDE:D.

78. Mattingly, "CV System: Part Three," 19, TMP.

79. Piers Brendon, *Ike: His Life and Times* (New York, 1986), 265; Kistiakowsky, *A Scientist at the White House*, 374.

80. Tyler Abell, ed., *Drew Pearson, Diaries 1949–1959* (New York, 1974), 546.

81. Snyder, "Progress Reports," 27 May 1959, HS/EL; Hughes, *The Ordeal of Power*, 239.

82. Alonzo L. Hamby, *Liberalism and Its Challengers* (New York, 1985), 119; William B. Pickett, *Dwight David Eisenhower and American Power* (Wheeling, Ill., 1995), 166–167. For an excellent study of Eisenhower's philosophy and policies during the second term see John W. Sloan, *Eisenhower and the Management of Prosperity* (Lawrence, Kans., 1991).

83. Fawn M. Brodie, *Richard Nixon: The Shaping of His Character* (New York, 1981), 421; Stephen E. Ambrose, *Nixon: The Education of a Politician, 1913–1962* (New York, 1987), 559; and Arthur M. Schlesinger Jr., *A Thousand Days* (Boston, 1965), 114.

84. Richard M. Nixon, *Memoirs* (New York, 1978), 222; William Bragg Ewald Jr., *Eisenhower the President* (Englewood Cliffs, N.J., 1981), 212; Tom Wicker, *One of Us: Richard Nixon and the American Dream* (New York, 1991), 242.

85. Nixon, *Memoirs*, 222.

86. Ambrose, *Eisenhower: The President*, 222; Wicker, *One of Us*, 244–245.

87. Snyder, "Progress Reports," 27 June 1960 and 26, 28, and 30 July 1960, HS/EL; Thompson, *The Eisenhower Presidency*, 159–160.

88. Snyder, "Progress Reports," 17 October 1960, HS/EL.

89. Ibid.

90. Ibid., 17 and 18 October 1960.

91. Ibid., 18, 19, and 28 October 1960.

92. Herbert S. Parmet, *JFK: The Presidency of John F. Kennedy* (New York, 1983), 17. On Kennedy's Addison's disease see Parmet, *Jack: The Struggles of John F. Kennedy* (New York, 1980), 191-192; and Joan Blair and Clay Blair Jr., *The Search for JFK* (New York, 1976), 561-574. For a thoughtful argument see also Kenneth R. Crispell and Carlos F. Gomez, *Hidden Illness in the White House* (Durham, N.C., 1988), 160-202.

93. Blair and Blair, *The Search for JFK*, 575; Peter Collier and David Horowitz, *The Kennedys: An American Drama* (New York, 1984), 241.

94. Telephone conversation, Don Cook and Walter Jenkins, 5 July 1960, LBJL.

95. Theodore Sorensen, *Kennedy* (New York, 1965), 157.

96. UPI bulletin, 3 November 1960, HS/W; ACWD, 5 November 1960.

97. Dr. John Milne Murray to Snyder, 31 August 1960, HS/W.

98. Note, "Newport Rhode Island, Dr. John Milne Murray," 5 August 1960, HS/W; ACWD, 5 November 1960.

99. Dwight D. Eisenhower, *Mandate for Change: The White House Years* (Garden City, N.Y., 1963), 639; Snyder, "Progress Reports," 4 March 1959, HS/EL.

100. Snyder, "Progress Reports," 13 February 1959, 2 March 1959, and 4 October 1960, HS/EL; Staff Secretary, Legislative Meetings Series, 30 June 1959, EL.

101. Snyder, "Progress Reports," 12 November 1960, HS/EL; John S. D. Eisenhower, *Strictly Personal* (Garden City, N.Y., 1974), 285; and Slater, *The Ike I Knew*, 230.

102. Snyder, "Progress Reports," 13 November 1960, 5 December 1960, and 13 and 19 January 1961, HS/EL.

103. John Eisenhower, *Strictly Personal*, 287; Peter Lyon, *Eisenhower: Portrait of a Hero* (Boston, 1974), 825; Dwight D. Eisenhower, *Waging Peace, 1956-1961* (Garden City, N.Y., 1965), 618-619.

104. Hughes, *Ordeal of Power*, 8.

CHAPTER 8

The Struggle to Stay Alive

1. *New York Times*, 15 July 1965.

2. Ibid.

3. John Bartlow Martin, *Adlai Stevenson and the World* (Garden City, N.Y., 1978), 693, 807; Porter McKeever, *Adlai Stevenson* (New York, 1989), 515, 544, 555-556.

4. Martin, *Adlai Stevenson and the World*, 748, 807, 849.

5. PPP, 1956, 276.

6. John S. D. Eisenhower, *Strictly Personal* (Garden City, N.Y., 1974), 293.

7. For the best general view of Eisenhower's retirement see Stephen E. Ambrose, *Eisenhower: The President*, vol. 2 (New York, 1984), 628–675.

8. DDE to Churchill, 22 April 1961, DDE/PPF; Mamie cited in Peter Lyon, *Eisenhower: Portrait of the Hero* (Boston, 1974), 333; Ellis Slater, *The Ike I Knew* (New York, 1980), 248; and DDE to B. Harlow, 11 August 1964, DDE/PPF.

9. Meyer Friedman and Ray H. Rosenman, *Type A Behavior and Your Heart* (Greenwich, Conn., 1974); William W. Moore, *Fighting For Life: The Story of the American Heart Association* (Dallas, 1983), 212–213, 222–223.

10. Mattingly, "CV System: Part Four," 1–2, TMP; Mattingly, "GI System: Part Three," 1, 7, TMP.

11. Howard Snyder to Howard M. Snyder Jr., 22 June 1962, HS/W; Snyder to DDE, 25 January 1963, HS/W; Snyder to DDE, 14 January 1963, HS/W; Snyder to Robert Woodruff, 14 August 1961, HS/W; and Snyder to DDE, 31 December 1964, HS/W.

12. White to Mattingly, 6 August 1965, HS/EL; White to Snyder, 3 September 1965, HS/EL; White to Snyder, 7 September 1965, HS/EL; White to Snyder, 5 October 1965, HS/EL; and Mattingly, "Summary of Activities of Dr. Paul D. White Related to President Eisenhower After November 1956," TMP.

13. DDE to Heaton, 30 December 1964, DDE/PPP; Mattingly, "GI System: Part Three," 1–2, TMP; Mattingly, "CV System: Part Four," 15–16, TMP; and Carl Wolnisty, "Summary of Medical Care of Dwight D. Eisenhower from 9 January Until 24 April 1963," TMP.

14. Ann Whitman to Snyder, 18 February 1962, HS/W; Snyder to DDE, 3 August 1962, HS/W; and Snyder to Ann Whitman, 12 February 1963, HS/EL.

15. Mattingly, "CV System: Part Four," 3–7, 11–12, 19, TMP.

16. Edward J. Kamin, "Doctor's Progress Notes," 16 May 1963, HS/EL; Edward J. Kamin, "Doctor's Progress Notes," 13 September 1963, HS/EL; and Mattingly, "CV System: Part Four," 5–6, TMP.

17. DDE to Charles B. Jones, 4 September 1963, DDE/PPP.

18. Loren Parmley, "Narrative Summary," 3 January 1966, TMP; Mattingly, "CV System: Part Four," 12, TMP; Mattingly, "CV System: Part Six," 2, TMP; and Carl Wolnisty to Richard Crone, 26 April 1965, TMP.

19. Slater, *The Ike I Knew*, 264–265; John Eisenhower, *Strictly Personal*, 328.

20. Mattingly, "General Eisenhower's Heart Attack, 1965," TMP; Mattingly, "CV System: Part Five," 1–2, 14, TMP; and Snyder to Cliff Roberts, 12 November 1965, HS/W.

21. Mattingly, "CV System: Part Five," 2–3, TMP.

22. Ibid., 4–6, 16.

23. Ibid., 6–8, 29.

24. Ibid., 8, 17-18; Snyder to DDE, 16 November 1965, HS/EL.

25. Mattingly, "CV System: Part Five," 9-13, TMP.

26. Ibid., 21; Parmley, "Narrative Summary," 3 January 1966, TMP; and John Eisenhower, *Strictly Personal*, 328.

27. Mattingly, "CV System: Part Six," 1-3, 8, TMP.

28. Parmley, "Cardiovascular Problems and Management During the Year 1966," 1-2, TMP.

29. Ibid., 3-6; Mattingly, "CV System: Part Six," 8, TMP; and Mattingly, "GI System: Part Three," 7-9, TMP.

30. Mattingly, "CV System: Part Six," 10, TMP.

31. Ibid., 10-12.

32. Ibid., 12-13; Mattingly, "CV System: Part Six," 6, TMP; and Parmley, "Narrative Summary," 27 December 1966, TMP.

33. Philip Tumulty, "Consultation Report," 9 December 1966, TMP; Mattingly, "Consultation Report," 9 December 1966, TMP; and F. J. Hughes, Joseph H. Baugh, Lewis A. Mologne, and Leonard D. Heaton, "A Review of the Late General Eisenhower's Operations," *Annals of Surgery* 173 (May 1971): 795.

34. Mattingly, "CV System: Part Six," 9, TMP.

35. Parmley, "Cardiovascular Status During the Year 1967," 1-2, TMP.

36. Ibid., 2-3.

37. Ibid., 2-5.

38. Horace Busby to Lyndon Johnson, 29 November 1967, Famous Names Series, LBJL.

39. Parmley, "Cardiovascular Status During the Year 1967," 5-6, TMP; Mattingly, "CV System: Part Six, 1967," 8, TMP; and John Eisenhower, *Strictly Personal*, 329.

40. Mattingly, "CV System: Part Six, 1967," 8, TMP; Major Finney, "Medical Note," 4 December 1967, TMP.

41. Parmley, "Cardiovascular Status and Complications for the Period January 1968 to Death on 28 March 1969," 1-3, TMP; John Eisenhower, *Strictly Personal*, 329.

42. F. J. Hughes to P. D. White, 7 March 1969, PDWP; Robert J. Hall, "Narrative Summary," 1969, 2-3, TMP; and Julie Nixon Eisenhower, *Special People* (New York, 1977), 189-190.

43. Julie Eisenhower, *Special People*, 190-191, 209.

44. Richard M. Nixon, *Memoirs* (New York, 1978), 307; Julie Eisenhower, *Special People*, 207; P. J. Hughes to P. D. White, 7 March 1969, PDWP.

45. Robert J. Hall, "Narrative Summary," 1969, 4-5, TMP; Nixon cited in Stephen E. Ambrose, *Nixon: The Triumph of a Politician, 1962-1972* (New York, 1989), 175.

46. Hall, "Narrative Summary," 1969, 6, TMP.

47. James Bordley, *Two Centuries of American Medicine* (Philadelphia, 1976), 492-496.

48. Hall, "Narrative Summary," 1969, 6–7, TMP.

49. Parmley, "Cardiovascular Status . . . 1968–1969," 4–5, TMP; Mattingly Diary, 19 August 1968, in "CV System: Part Six, Year 1968–69," 8–9, TMP.

50. Hall, "Narrative Summary," 1969, 7–8, TMP.

51. Ibid., 9; Parmley, "Cardiovascular Status . . . 1968–1969," 9, TMP.

52. Hall, "Narrative Summary," 1969, 10–13, TMP.

53. P. J. Hughes to P. D. White, 7 March 1969, PDWP.

54. John Eisenhower, *Strictly Personal*, 333; Leonard Heaton, OH, 74, EL; William Bragg Ewald Jr., *Eisenhower the President* (Englewood Cliffs, N.J., 1981), 252; and Parmley, "Cardiovascular Status . . . 1968–1969," 4, TMP.

55. Parmley, "Cardiovascular Status . . . 1968–1969," 5, TMP.

56. Julie Eisenhower, *Special People*, 193; DDE to Robinson, 11 October 1968, DDE/PPP.

57. John Eisenhower, *Strictly Personal*, 332–333; DDE to Robinson, 16 October 1968, DDE/PPP.

58. Julie Eisenhower, *Special People*, 193; Mattingly Diary, October 1968, in "CV Status: Part Six," 9, TMP.

59. F. J. Hughes to White, 7 March 1969, PDWP; Mattingly Diary, 23 February 1969, in "CV System: Part Six," TMP; and John Eisenhower, *Strictly Personal*, 334.

60. Hughes, et al., "A Review of the Late General Eisenhower's Operations," 796–799.

61. John Eisenhower, *Strictly Personal*, 335; Nixon, *Memoirs*, 375.

62. Hall, "Narrative Summary," 14 May 1968, 16–18, TMP; F. J. Hughes to White, 27 March 1969, TMP.

63. John Eisenhower, *Strictly Personal*, 335–336; Nixon, *Memoirs*, 379–380.

64. Hall, "Narrative Summary," 14 May 1968, 19, TMP; John Eisenhower, *Strictly Personal*, 336.

65. Mattingly, "The Cardiovascular Status as Observed at Autopsy," 1, TMP; "Autopsy Protocol, Dwight D. Eisenhower," 39–40, TMP.

66. "Autopsy Protocol," 39–40, 50–52, TMP.

67. F. J. Hughes to White, 7 March 1969, PDWP; Mattingly, "The Cardiovascular Status as Observed at Autopsy," 1–3, TMP; and "Autopsy Protocol," 37–39, TMP.

68. "Autopsy Protocol," 38–39, TMP; "Mattingly, "Summary of the Activities of White During the Period 1956–1969," 4, TMP; and Mattingly, "CV System: Part Eight," 5–6, 15, TMP.

69. Mattingly, "CV System: Part Six," 10, TMP; Parmley, "Cardiovascular Status . . . 1968–1969," 4, TMP; Hughes, et al., "A Review of the Late General Eisenhower's Operations," 799.

70. Hughes, et al., "A Review of the Late General Eisenhower's Operations," 799.

CHAPTER 9
The Meaning

1. Harry Chrisman to DDE, 30 September 1955, DDE/PPF.

2. Richard Thayer Goldberg, *The Making of Franklin D. Roosevelt* (Cambridge, Mass., 1981), 142, 156; Hugh Gregory Gallagher, *FDR's Splendid Deception* (New York, 1985), 146-152; and John R. Paul, *A History of Poliomyelitis* (New Haven, Conn., 1971), 319.

3. Bruce Barton to A. W. Robertson, 7 November 1955, BPP.

4. Kenneth R. Crispell and Carlos F. Gomez, *Hidden Illness in the White House* (Durham, N.C., 1988), 204; 67-74 (for Wilson) and 102-120, 148-154 (for Roosevelt); Edward B. MacMahon and Leonard Curry, *Medical Cover-ups in the White House* (Washington, D.C., 1987), 38-55 (for Cleveland), 56-58, 70-77 (for Wilson), and 90-102 (for Roosevelt).

5. *Business Week*, 8 October 1955, 27; Myron K. Jordan, "Presidential Health Reporting: The Eisenhower Watershed," *American Journalism* 4, no. 3 (1987): 156.

6. David Lawrence to DDE, 18 November 1955, AWF/NS.

7. H. M. Marvin, "Don't Be Afraid of Your Heart," *American Magazine*, January 1956, 21, 98.

8. "Comments to the Press," White to Hagerty, 29 September 1955, DDE/PPF; *Washington Daily News*, 26 September 1955.

9. William Laurence, "Medical Triumphs Just Ahead," *Collier's*, 8 June 1956, 25-27, 29.

10. Ann Whitman to Snyder, 12 February 1956, HS/EL; DDE to Melvin Laird, 27 July 1959, AWF/LM.

11. Robert H. Ferrell, *Ill-Advised: Presidential Health and Public Trust* (Columbia, 1992), 138.

12. Robert E. Gilbert, *The Mortal Presidency: Illness and Anguish in the White House* (New York, 1992), 140-141.

13. DDE to Clifford Roberts, 2 and 3 May 1951, EP; Luce OH, 10, EL; and PPP, 1959, 129-130.

14. Frances Burns to Snyder, 8 February 1958, HS/W.

15. Richard M. Nixon, *Memoirs* (New York, 1978), 376; Mauldin cartoon in Peter Lyon, *Eisenhower: Portrait of the Hero* (Boston, 1974), 859; Stephen E. Ambrose, *Eisenhower: The President*, vol. 2 (New York, 1984), 627.

16. Arthur Kleinman, *The Illness Narratives: Suffering, Healing and the Human Condition* (New York, 1988), 44-45.

Bibliography

❖ ❖ ❖ ❖ ❖ ❖ ❖

Three collections of papers have provided the major documentation for this study. Those of Dr. Howard McCrum Snyder at the University of Wyoming comprise primarily the doctor's extensive correspondence with friends and associates, which often includes relevant medical information. The papers of Dr. Snyder and Dr. Thomas Mattingly at the Eisenhower Library in Abilene, Kansas, taken together, constitute the most thorough body of material that we have for any president's medical history. In addition to health records so detailed as to include EKGs and cholesterol readings, as well as the clinical records for all of the president's illnesses, each of the physicians has left a personal account. Dr. Snyder left the draft chapters of a proposed health history of Eisenhower covering the period from 1945 to 1956, together with his "progress reports," a diary of important medical developments in the president's life from December 1945 to January 1961. Dr. Mattingly deposited at the library a long, narrative manuscript entitled "General Health Status of Dwight David Eisenhower," a labor of love and a magnificent contribution. The Paul Dudley White papers in the Countway Library of Medicine at the Harvard Medical School are excellent for White's lifelong efforts to educate the public about coronary disease, and very thorough with regard to his participation in the care of the president.

Abell, Tyler, ed. *Drew Pearson, Diaries 1949-1959*. New York: Holt, Rinehart and Winston, 1974.

Adams, Sherman. *Firsthand Report*. New York: Harper and Row, 1961.

Allbutt, Clifford. *Diseases of the Arteries, Including Angina Pectoris*. London: Macmillan, 1915.

Ambrose, Stephen E. *Eisenhower: Soldier, General of the Army, President-Elect, 1890-1952*. New York: Simon and Schuster, 1983.

———. *Eisenhower: The President*. Vol. 2. New York: Simon and Schuster, 1984.

―――. *Nixon: The Education of a Politician, 1913-1962.* New York: Simon and Schuster, 1987.

―――. *Nixon: The Triumph of a Politician, 1962-1972.* New York: Simon and Schuster, 1989.

Anderson, Merrill P. "Psychological Issues in Cardiovascular Rehabilitation." In *Cardiovascular Disease and Behavior,* edited by Jeffrey W. Elias and Phillip Howard Marshall, 156-159. Washington, D.C.: Hemisphere, 1987.

Barber, James David. *Presidential Character.* Englewood Cliffs, N.J.: Prentice-Hall, 1985.

Bean, William B. "Clinical Masquerades of Acute Cardiac Infarction." *Journal of the Iowa State Medical Society* 52 (December 1962): 781-783.

Beasley, Joseph D. *The Betrayal of Health.* New York: Times Books, 1991.

Billings, F. T., B. M. Kalstone, J. L. Spencer, C. O. Ball, and G. R. Meneely. "Prognosis of Acute Myocardial Infarction." *American Journal of Medicine* 7 (1949): 356-357.

Blair, Joan, and Clay Blair Jr. *The Search for JFK.* New York: Berkeley, 1976.

Boas, Ernst P., and Norman F. Boas. *Coronary Artery Disease.* Chicago: Year Book, 1949.

Bobst, Elmer. *The Autobiography of a Pharmaceutical Pioneer.* New York: David McKay, 1973.

Bordley, James. *Two Centuries of American Medicine.* Philadelphia: Saunders, 1976.

Bradley, Omar N., and Clay Blair Jr. *A General's Life.* New York: Simon and Schuster, 1983.

Brendon, Piers. *Ike: His Life and Times.* New York: Harper and Row, 1986.

Brodie, Fawn M. *Richard Nixon: The Shaping of His Character.* New York: Norton, 1981.

Butcher, Harry C. *My Three Years with Eisenhower.* New York: Simon and Schuster, 1946.

Chesney, Margaret A. "Anger and Hostility: Future Implications." In *Anger and Hostility in Cardiovascular and Behavioral Disorders,* edited by Margaret Chesney and Ray Rosenman, 285-287. Washington, D.C.: Hemisphere, 1985.

Childs, Marquis. *Eisenhower: Captive Hero.* New York: Harcourt Brace, 1958.

Cole, David., E. B. Singian, and L. N. Katz. "The Long Term Prognosis Following Myocardial Infarction, and Some Factors Which Affect It." *Circulation* 9 (March 1954): 321-323.

Collier, Peter, and David Horowitz. *The Kennedys: An American Drama.* New York: Summit, 1984.

Crispell, Kenneth R., and Carlos F. Gomez. *Hidden Illness in the White House.* Durham, N.C.: Duke University Press, 1988.

Cutler, Robert. *No Time for Rest.* Boston: Little, Brown, 1966.

David, Lester, and Irene David. *Ike and Mamie.* New York: Putnam, 1981.

Davis, Kenneth S. *Soldier of Democracy: A Biography of Dwight Eisenhower.* Garden City, N.Y.: Doubleday, Doran, 1945.

Davis, Maxine. "He's the President's Physician." *Good Housekeeping*, August 1954, 70, 207–211.

Deakin, James. *Straight Stuff*. New York: William Morrow, 1984.

Dingman, Harold. *Risk Appraisal*. Cincinnati: National Underwriter, 1946.

Donovan, Robert J. *Eisenhower: The Inside Story*. New York: Harper and Row, 1956.

———. *Confidential Secretary: Ann Whitman's Twenty Years with Eisenhower and Rockefeller*. New York: Dutton, 1988.

Dubos, René. *Mirage of Health*. New York: Harper and Row, 1959.

Dunbar, Helen Flanders. *Mind and Body: Psychosomatic Medicine*. New York: Random House, 1947.

Eisenhower, Dwight D. *Crusade in Europe*. Garden City, N.Y.: Doubleday, 1948.

———. *Mandate for Change: The White House Years*. Garden City, N.Y.: Doubleday, 1963.

———. *Waging Peace, 1956–1961*. Garden City, N.Y.: Doubleday, 1965.

———. *At Ease: Stories I Tell to Friends*. Garden City, N.Y.: Doubleday, 1967.

Eisenhower, John S. D. *Strictly Personal*. Garden City, N.Y.: Doubleday, 1974.

———, ed. *Dwight D. Eisenhower, Letters to Mamie*. Garden City, N.Y.: Doubleday, 1978.

Eisenhower, Julie Nixon. *Special People*. New York: Simon and Schuster, 1977.

———. "Mamie." *Ladies' Home Journal*, June 1977, 108.

Elias, Jeffery W., and Phillip H. Marshall, eds. *Cardiovascular Disease and Behavior*. Washington, D.C.: Hemisphere, 1987.

Ewald, William Bragg, Jr. *Eisenhower the President*. Englewood Cliffs, N.J.: Prentice-Hall, 1981.

———. "A Biographer's Perspective." In *The Eisenhower Presidency*, edited by Kenneth W. Thompson, 15-37. Lanham, Md.: University Press of America, 1984.

Feerick, John D. *From Failing Hands*. New York: Fordham University Press, 1965.

———. *The Twenty-Fifth Amendment*. New York: Fordham University Press, 1976.

Ferrell, Robert H., ed. *The Eisenhower Diaries*. New York: Norton, 1981.

———. *The Diary of James C. Hagerty*. Bloomington: Indiana University Press, 1983.

———. *Ill-Advised: Presidential Health and Public Trust*. Columbia: University of Missouri Press, 1992.

Fisk, Dorothy. *Dr. Jenner of Berkeley*. London: Melbourne, 1959.

Friedman, Meyer, and Ray H. Rosenman. "Association of Specific Overt Behavior Pattern with Blood and Cardiovascular Findings." *Journal of the American Medical Association* 171 (1959): 1085–1096.

———. *Type A Behavior and Your Heart*. Greenwich, Conn.: Fawcett, 1974.

Frolich, Edward D., and Albert N. Brest, eds. *Preventive Aspects of Coronary Heart Disease*. Philadelphia: Davis, 1990.

Fye, W. Bruce. "Ventricular Fibrillation and Defibrillation: Historical Perspectives with Emphasis on the Contributions of John MacWilliam, Carl Wiggers, and William Kouwenhoven." *Circulation* 71 (May 1985): 858-865.

Gallagher, Hugh Gregory. *FDR's Splendid Deception.* New York: Dodd, Mead, 1985.

Gilbert, Robert E. *The Mortal Presidency: Illness and Anguish in the White House.* New York: Basic Books, 1992.

Goldberg, Richard Thayer. *The Making of Franklin D. Roosevelt.* Cambridge, Mass.: Abt Books, 1981.

Gray, Robert Keith. *Eighteen Acres Under Glass.* Garden City, N.Y.: Doubleday, 1967.

Green, Harvey. *Fit for America.* New York: Pantheon, 1986.

Greenstein, Fred. *The Hidden-Hand Presidency,* New York: Basic Books, 1982.

Gromyko, Andrei. *Memories.* New York: Doubleday, 1990.

Griffith, Robert, ed. *Ike's Letters to a Friend: 1941-1958.* Lawrence: University Press of Kansas, 1984.

Gunther, John. *Eisenhower: The Man and the Symbol.* New York: Harper, 1952.

———. *Taken at the Flood: The Story of Albert D. Lasker.* New York: Harper, 1960.

Guylay, L. Richard. "Eisenhower's Two Presidential Campaigns, 1952 and 1956." In *Dwight D. Eisenhower: Soldier, President, Statesman,* edited by Joann P. Krieg, 21-30. New York: Greenwood, 1987.

Hale, William Harlan. "The Facts About Ileitis." *Reporter,* 28 June 1956, 4-6.

Hamby, Alonzo L. *Liberalism and Its Challengers.* New York: Oxford University Press, 1985.

Harlow, Bryce. "The 'Compleat' President." In *The Eisenhower Presidency,* edited by Kenneth W. Thompson, 145-162. Lanham, Md.: University Press of America, 1984.

Heaton, Leonard, Isidor Ravdin, Brian Blades, and Thomas J. Whelan. "President Eisenhower's Operation for Regional Enteritis: A Footnote to History." *Annals of Surgery* 159 (May 1964): 661-666.

Herrick, James B. "An Intimate Account of My Early Experience with Coronary Thrombosis." *American Heart Journal* 27 (January 1944): 1-17.

———. *Memories of Eighty Years.* Chicago: University of Chicago Press, 1949.

Houston, R. "The Doctor Himself as a Therapeutic Agent." *Annals of Internal Medicine* 11 (1938): 1418-1420.

Hughes, Emmet John. *The Ordeal of Power.* New York: Atheneum, 1963.

Hughes, F. J., Joseph H. Baugh, Lewis A. Mologne, and Leonard D. Heaton. "A Review of the Late General Eisenhower's Operations." *Annals of Surgery* 173 (May 1971): 793-799.

Hyman, Albert S., Aaron E. Parsonnet, and David Riesman. *The Failing Heart of Middle Life.* Philadelphia: Davis, 1932.

Jenkins, C. D. "Psychologic and Social Precursors of Coronary Disease." *Journal of the American Medical Association* 284 (1971): 307-317.

Johnson, Joseph Taber. "Angina Pectoris, Illustrated by the Case of Charles Sumner." *Boston Medical and Surgical Journal* 15 (October 1874): 372.

Johnson, Walter, and Carol Evans, eds. *The Papers of Adlai E. Stevenson.* Vol. 6. Boston: Little, Brown, 1972.

Jordan, Myron K. "Presidential Health Reporting: The Eisenhower Watershed." *American Journalism* 4 (1987): 147-158.

Katz, Jay. *The Silent World of Doctor and Patient.* New York: Free Press, 1984.

Kistiakowsky, George B. *A Scientist at the White House.* Cambridge, Mass.: Harvard University Press, 1976.

Kleinman, Arthur. *The Illness Narratives: Suffering, Healing and the Human Condition.* New York: Basic Books, 1988.

Knebel, Fletcher. "Crisis." *Look,* 27 December 1955, 21-24.

———. "How Ike Made Up His Mind." *Look,* 1 May 1956, 19-21.

———. "The President's Doctor." *Look,* 18 September 1956, 88-91.

Larson, Arthur. *Eisenhower: The President Nobody Knew.* New York: Scribner, 1968.

Laurence, William. "Medical Triumphs Just Ahead." *Collier's,* 8 June 1956, 25-27, 29.

Lear, Martha Weinman. *Heartsounds.* New York: Simon and Schuster, 1980.

Leary, Timothy. "Pathology of Coronary Sclerosis." *American Heart Journal* 10 (February 1935): 328-337.

Leibowitz, J. O. *A History of Coronary Heart Disease.* Berkeley: University of California Press, 1970.

Levine, Samuel A. *Clinical Heart Disease.* Philadelphia: Saunders, 1951.

Lewis, Sir Thomas. *Diseases of the Heart.* New York: Macmillan, 1933.

Livesley, Brian. "The Resolution of the Heberden-Parry Controversy." *Medical History* 19 (1975): 158-171.

Lyon, Peter. *Eisenhower: Portrait of the Hero.* Boston: Little, Brown, 1974.

MacMahon, Edward B., and Leonard Curry. *Medical Cover-ups in the White House.* Washington, D.C.: Farragut, 1987.

Marshall, Catherine. *A Man Called Peter.* New York: McGraw-Hill, 1951.

Martin, John Bartlow. *Adlai Stevenson and the World.* Garden City, N.Y.: Anchor Press/Doubleday, 1978.

Marvin, H. M. "Don't Be Afraid of Your Heart." *American Magazine,* January 1956, 21, 98.

Marvin, H. M., T. Duckett Jones, Irvine H. Page, Irving S. Wright, and David D. Rutstein. *You and Your Heart.* New York: Random House, 1950.

Mattingly, Thomas. "Modern Management of Arteriosclerotic Heart Patients." In *Cardiovascular Disease Nursing,* edited by Capitola B. Mattingly, 103-104. Washington, D.C.: Catholic University of America Press, 1960.

———. "Paul White: His Influence upon an Individual, a Nation, and the World." *American Journal of Cardiology* 15 (April 1961): 505-507.

McKeever, Porter. *Adlai Stevenson.* New York: William Morrow, 1989.

McLean, Robert B. "Leonard D. Heaton—Military Surgeon." *Military Medicine* 147 (September 1982): 717–727.

Middleton, Richard. "Captain of the Men of Death." *Atlantic Monthly,* July 1932, 111–117.

Miller, Merle. *Ike the Soldier.* New York: Putnam, 1987.

Moore, William W. *Fighting for Life: The Story of the American Heart Association 1911–1975.* Dallas: American Heart Association, 1983.

Morgan, Kay Summersby. *Past Forgetting.* New York: Simon and Schuster, 1976.

Morrow, Lance. *Heart: A Memoir.* New York: Time Warner, 1995.

Mozes, Eugene B. *Living Beyond Your Heart Attack.* Englewood Cliffs, N.J.: Prentice-Hall, 1959.

Murray, Robert K. *The Harding Era.* Minneapolis: University of Minnesota Press, 1969.

Nixon, Richard M. *Six Crises.* Garden City, N.Y.: Doubleday, 1962.

———. *Memoirs.* New York: Grosset and Dunlap, 1978.

Osler, William. *Lectures on Angina Pectoris and Allied States.* New York: Appleton, 1897.

———. "The Lumleian Lectures on Angina Pectoris, Lecture I." *Lancet* 1 (1910): 697–702.

———. "The Lumleian Lectures on Angina Pectoris, Lecture II." *Lancet* 1 (1910): 839–844.

———. "The Lumleian Lectures on Angina Pectoris, Lecture III." *Lancet* 1 (1910): 973–977.

Pach, Chester J., Jr., and Elmo Richardson. *The Presidency of Dwight D. Eisenhower.* Lawrence: University Press of Kansas, 1991.

Parmet, Herbert S. *Eisenhower and the American Crusades.* New York: Macmillan, 1972.

———. *Jack: The Struggles of John F. Kennedy.* New York: Dial Press, 1980.

———. *JFK: The Presidency of John F. Kennedy.* New York: Dial Press, 1983.

Paul, John R. *A History of Poliomyelitis.* New Haven, Conn.: Yale University Press, 1971.

Paul, Oglesby. *Take Heart.* Cambridge, Mass.: Harvard University Press, 1986.

———. "Background of the Prevention of Cardiovascular Disease." *Circulation* 80 (July 1989): 206–214.

Pickett, William B. *Dwight David Eisenhower and American Power.* Wheeling, Ill.: Harlan Davidson, 1995.

Pierce, Edward L. *Memoir and Letters of Charles Sumner.* Vols. 3 and 4. Boston: Roberts, 1893.

Piercy, Harry D. "The Doctor's Answer." *William Feather Magazine,* April 1940, 11.

Pierpoint, Robert. *At the White House: Assignment to Six Presidents.* New York: Putnam, 1981.

Randall, Clarence. "The Happy Cardiac." *Harper's,* March 1959, 64–66.

Reiser, Stanley J. *Medicine and the Reign of Technology.* Cambridge: Cambridge University Press, 1978.

Riehl, C. Luise. *Coronary Nursing Care.* New York: Appleton Century Crofts, 1971.

Roberts, Sharon L. *Behavioral Concepts and the Critically Ill Patient.* Englewood Cliffs, N.J.: Prentice-Hall, 1976.

Robinson, Edgar Eugene, and Paul Carrol Edwards, eds. *The Memoirs of Ray Lyman Wilbur, 1875-1949.* Stanford, Calif.: Stanford University Press, 1960.

Ross, Richard. "A Parlous State of Storm and Stress: The Life and Times of James B. Herrick." *Circulation* 67 (May 1983): 955-959.

Rutstein, David. "Doctors and Politics." *Atlantic Monthly,* August 1956, 32-35.

Schlesinger, Arthur M., Jr. *A Thousand Days.* Boston: Houghton Mifflin, 1965.

———. *Robert Kennedy and His Times.* Boston: Houghton Mifflin, 1978.

Scott, R. W. "Clinical Aspects of Arteriosclerosis." *American Heart Journal* 7 (February 1932): 304.

Shotwell, Walter G. *Life of Charles Sumner.* New York: Crowell, 1910.

Slater, Ellis. *The Ike I Knew.* New York: Privately printed, 1980.

Sloan, John W. *Eisenhower and the Management of Prosperity.* Lawrence: University Press of Kansas, 1991.

Smith, C. "Length of Survival After Myocardial Infarction." *Journal of the American Medical Association* 151 (1953): 167-168.

Smith, Merriman. *Meet Mr. Eisenhower.* New York: Harper, 1954.

Smith, S. Calvin. *Heart Patients: Their Study and Care.* Philadelphia: Lea and Febiger, 1939.

Sokolsky, George. "Decisions Are Difficult." King Features Syndicate, 25 January 1956.

Sontag, Susan. *Illness as Metaphor.* New York: Farrar, Straus and Giroux, 1977.

Sorensen, Theodore. *Kennedy.* New York: Harper and Row, 1965.

Sotile, Wayne M. *Heart Illness and Intimacy: How Caring Relationships Aid Recovery.* Baltimore: Johns Hopkins University Press, 1992.

Speedby, Henry J. *The 20th Century and Your Heart.* London: Centaur Press, 1960.

Sprague, Howard B. "Environmental Influences in Coronary Disease in the United States." *American Journal of Cardiology* 16 (July 1965): 106-113.

———. "Environment in Relation to Coronary Artery Disease." *Archives of Environmental Health* 13 (1966): 4-12.

Stafford, Jane. "His Heart in Your Keeping." *Mademoiselle,* February 1956, 132.

Steinberg, Daniel. "The End of the Cholesterol Controversy." *Circulation* 80 (October 1989): 1070-1078.

Sulzberger, C. L. *An Age of Mediocrity.* New York: Macmillan, 1973.

Summersby, Kay. *Eisenhower Was My Boss.* New York: Prentice-Hall, 1948.

Thompson, Dorothy. "May I Tell You About My Heart Attack?" *Ladies' Home Journal,* April 1960, 12-18.

Thompson, Kenneth W., ed. *The Eisenhower Presidency.* Lanham, Md.: University Press of America, 1984.

Weiss, Stephen M., Susan Czajkowski, Sally Shumaker, and Roger Anderson. "Psychosocial Factors in Coronary Heart Disease." In *Preventive Aspects of Coronary Heart Disease,* edited by Edward D. Frolich and Albert N. Brest, 137–138. Philadelphia: Davis, 1990.

White, Paul Dudley. "The Prevention of Heart Disease." *Virginia Medical Monthly,* 17 February 1930, 1–26.

———. "Heart Disease—Then and Now." *Hygeia* 11 (October 1933): 877–880, 950–952.

———. "Deadly Disease No. 1." *Hygeia* 18 (February 1940): 104–108.

———. "The Reversibility of Heart Disease." *Illinois Medical Journal* 86, no. 1 (July 1944): 1–5.

———. *Heart Disease.* 4th ed. New York: Macmillan, 1951.

———. "Medical Practice 40 Years Ago and Now." *Dow Medical College Magazine* 2, no. 2 (April 1952): 13–17.

———. "The Coronaries Through the Ages." *Minnesota Medicine* 38 (November 1955): 801–808.

———. *My Life and Medicine.* Boston: Gambit, 1971.

White, Paul Dudley, and Edward F. Bland. "Coronary Thrombosis (With Myocardial Infarction) Ten Years Later." *Journal of the American Medical Association* 117 (1941): 1171–1173.

White, Paul Dudley, and Ashton Graybiel. "Diseases of the Heart." *Archives of Internal Medicine* 57 (April 1936): 27–34.

White, Paul Dudley, David W. Richards, and Edward F. Bland. "A Completed Twenty-five-Year Follow-up Study of 200 Patients with Myocardial Infarction." *Journal of Chronic Disease* 4 (October 1956): 415–422.

Wicker, Tom. *One of Us: Richard Nixon and the American Dream.* New York: Random House, 1991.

Williams, Redford B., Jr., and Norman B. Anderson. "Hostility and Coronary Disease." In *Cardiovascular Disease and Behavior,* edited by Jeffrey W. Elias and Phillip H. Marshall, 17–18. Washington, D.C.: Hemisphere, 1987.

Index

❖   ❖   ❖   ❖   ❖   ❖   ❖

Adams, Sherman, 83–84, 117, 124,
    129, 131, 148–149, 162, 171, 173,
    186, 193, 196, 199, 241, 249
Adenauer, Konrad, 213
Allbutt, Clifford, 7
Allen, George, 54, 71, 102, 151, 174,
    304
Allen, Robert, 215
Alsop, Joseph, 184, 187, 190, 219
Alsop, Stewart, 184, 187, 190, 202, 219
Alvarez, Walter, 200
Ambrose, Stephen, 19, 49, 203, 285
American Heart Association (AHA),
    2, 5, 14, 57–58, 83, 255–256, 264,
    296, 325–326
American Heart Journal, 14
American Medical Association
    (AMA), 11, 114, 152, 214, 255,
    298, 330
American Research Foundation poll,
    152–154
Anderson, Robert, 102, 292
Andrus, Cowles, 78, 121, 140–142
Angina pectoris, 8–11, 13, 87
    Eisenhower and, 305–307, 311, 318
*Angina Pectoris and Other Allied
    States* (Osler), 10
Annals of Internal Medicine, 190
Annals of Surgery, 217
Armstrong, George, 102
Arnold, Thomas, 10
At Ease: Stories I Tell to Friends, 19,
    40, 43, 296, 304

Atlantic Monthly, 218

Baker, Russell, 178
Ball, George, 295
Barkley, Alben, 83
Barr, David, 34, 51
Barton, Bruce, 325
Battey, Louis, 301
Beach, George, 24
Ben-Gurion, David, 237
Berry, Frank, 102
Bitter Woods, The (John Eisenhower),
    320
Black, Herbert, 42, 44, 47
Black, Jim, 262
Blades, Bryan, 210–211, 237
Bliss, Raymond, 102
Blount, Gilbert, 78
Boas, Ernst, 16, 18
Boas, Norman, 16, 18
Boone, Joel, 99
Boston Globe, 117, 232, 331
Brooklyn Eagle, 73
Brownell, Herbert, Jr., 149
Burns, Frances, 117, 232, 331
Burton, Hal, 218
Busby, Horace, 308–309
Bush, George, 2
Business Week, 147, 327
Butler, Paul, 214

Calver, George, 215
Cantor, Eddie, 156

Carnegie, Andrew, 83
Carroll, Pete, 68, 126, 148
Casals, Pablo, 83
Chamberlain, Francis, 78
Changing Times, 277
Childs, Marquis, 202
Churchill, Winston, 296
Clark, Bob, 73
Clausen, R. E., Jr., 240–242, 244
Clay, Lucius, 60, 145, 193
Cleveland, Grover, 326
Clinical Heart Disease (Levine), 16
Clinton, Hillary, 5
Collier's, 329
Condon, William, 102
Connally, John, 288
Connor, Fox, 37
Cooley, Denton, 314
Coronary Artery Disease (Boas), 16
Coronary heart disease, 1, 7–15, 296,
    313–314
  causes of, 16–17, 87, 159, 255–256,
    275–276
  changing perceptions of, 254–255,
    274–275, 326–329
  deaths from, 3, 15–16
  fear of, 18, 46–47
  personality type and, 17, 161,
    264–267, 279, 296
  See also Angina pectoris; Heart
    attack of 1955
Cover-up
  of ileitis, 207–208
  of 1955 heart attack, 72, 85, 99–102
  of 1949 illness, alleged, 42–50
  White and, 91
Craig, May, 92
Crohn, Burrill, 207, 217–218
Cronkite, Walter, 296
Cutler, Robert, 71, 83, 102, 130–131,
    148

da Vinci, Leonardo, 7
Davis, T. J., 148

Deakin, James, 93–94, 155
DeBakey, Michael, 259, 314
Detroit Free Press, 214–215
Dewey, Thomas E., 57, 79, 149
Donovan, William, 15
Donovan, Robert, 57, 106–107, 143,
    158
Doud, Elivira, 82, 105–108
Drummond, Roscoe, 150
Dudley, Ed, 48
Dulles, Allen, 292
Dulles, John Foster, 71, 124, 173, 245,
    290
Dunbar, Helen Flanders, 17, 247
Durant, Henri, 166

Eden, Anthony, 239
Editor and Publisher, 213
Edwards, India, 288
Eisenhower, Barbara
    (daughter-in-law), 317, 320
Eisenhower, David (grandson), 317,
    320
Eisenhower, Dwight David
  abdominal surgury of, 306–307,
    318–319
  ambition of, 26, 49, 195, 199
  athletics and, 20–22, 276
  autopsy of, 321–322
  campaign of 1956 and, 203, 219,
    223, 227–229, 236–239
  cholesterol and, 52, 144, 257–261,
    298
  courage of, 198, 316
  death of, 320–321, 331–332
  depression and, 129, 143, 223, 225,
    249, 291
  diet and, 52, 171, 257–260
  election of 1960 and, 284–292
  fear of being invalid of, 20,
    129–131
  gastrointestinal problems of,
    18–19, 23–28, 30–35, 39–50,
    61–63, 254, 307–308, 310

general health of, 19-20, 23,
  26-27, 34-36, 64-65, 69-70,
  253-254, 299-300, 310-316,
  320-322
golf and, 23, 53, 61, 261-264
heart attacks of, in retirement,
  301-304, 311-318, 321
as hero, 4, 332
hidden-hand presidency and, 3
hypertension and, 27, 32, 38,
  53-55, 66-68, 278-280
ileitis and, 40, 219-223
motivation of, 194-196, 198-199
1953 illness and, 61-63
1949 illness and, 39-50
personal responsibility for health
  of, 23, 26-27, 29, 49-50, 54-55,
  257, 311-312, 329-331
the press, management of, 3, 34,
  49, 150, 191-192, 203, 220-222,
  239, 326-328
preventive medicine and, 4-5, 50,
  53-55, 60-61, 248-250, 254, 257,
  267-268, 282, 298-299, 329
publications of, 19, 40, 43, 296, 304
retirement and, 295-296, 298,
  304-310
second term performance of,
  248-250, 283-284, 291-292
smoking and, 27, 35, 36, 44, 50-54,
  330
stress and, 33, 36, 49
stroke of, 239-246
temper and, 32, 37-38, 56, 68-70,
  129, 162, 263-268, 272-274, 298
twenty-fifth amendment and,
  245-246
war against disease and, 57-58,
  324-326
See also Eisenhower, Mamie; Heart
  attack of 1955; Heaton,
  Leonard; Mattingly, Thomas;
  Nixon, Richard; Pearson, Drew;
  Second term decision; Slater,

Ellis; Snyder, Howard; White,
  Paul Dudley; Whitman, Ann
Eisenhower, Ida (mother), 69
Eisenhower, John (son), 84, 119-120,
  133, 162, 174, 178, 225, 241-242,
  269, 310, 318-320
  on father, 37, 68, 273, 295, 304, 309
Eisenhower, Julie Nixon
  (granddaughter-in-law), 273,
  311, 317
Eisenhower, Mamie Doud (wife), 23,
  28-29, 37-38, 56, 60, 66, 71,
  119-120, 146, 292
  as caretaker in retirement,
    295-297, 300, 312-317, 331
  as caretaker in second term, 248,
    268-272, 276-281, 291-292
  election of 1960 and, 285, 287, 291
  health problems of, 29, 52, 76, 271
  husband's ileitis and, 208, 211,
    223, 235
  husband's 1955 heart attack and,
    72, 76, 79, 82, 84, 97-100,
    105-112, 116, 122-123, 126,
    134-135, 140
  husband's stroke and, 241, 245
  as irritant to husband, 56, 272-274
  relationship with husband and,
    32, 38, 269-270, 272-274
  second term decision and, 162,
    174, 193
Eisenhower, Milton (brother), 57, 76,
  78, 104, 123, 140, 145-146, 149,
  161, 173-174
  on election of 1956, 146
Eisenhower: Inside Story (Donovan),
  158

Ferrell, Robert, 44, 50, 329
Fleeson, Doris, 218
Folliard, Edward, 188
Foote, Emerson, 15
Forrestal, James, 39-40
Forster, Francis, 242, 244

Fothergill, John, 8
Friedman, Meyer, 264, 296

Gable, Clark, 281–282
Garroway, Dave, 160
Gilbert, Robert, 44, 50, 329–330
Ginzberg, Eli, 104
Gofman, John, 16
Goodpaster, Andrew, 239–240
Gosden, Freeman, 307
Goyette, Edwin, 55, 66–67
Graham, Reverend Billy, 146, 320
Gray, Gordon, 282
Griffin, Martin, 74, 77, 82
Gromyko, Andrei, 275
Gruber, Bill, 196
Gruenther, Alfred, 47, 62, 66, 102, 128, 151, 316
Gunther, John, 51

Hagerty, James, 60, 73, 75–77, 124, 142, 160, 193
  background of, 79, 82–83
  disclosure policy and, 64–65, 80, 85, 93, 191, 203
  Eisenhower's ileitis and, 212–216, 219, 222, 231–232, 235–236
  Eisenhower's stroke and, 244
  See also Heart attack of 1955
Hall, Leonard, 102, 147, 193, 284
Hall, Robert, 311, 313–316, 320
Hammill, James, 242
Harding, Warren, 11–12, 99
Harlow, Bryce, 68, 265, 267
Harper's, 275
Harvey, William, 114
Hays, Silas, 95, 102
Hazlett, Everett "Swede," 47, 272
  Eisenhower and, 194, 198
  heart attack of, 130–131
  See also Second term decision
Healing and the Mind (Moyers), 5
Hearst, William Randolph, 83
Heart attack of 1955

aneurysm and, 122, 136–138, 165, 204, 322
"armchair treatment" of, 118–122, 127–129
coumadin use for, 118, 135, 252–253
differing accounts of, 73, 81, 88–89, 91–99
doctors' disagreements about, 120–121, 128–129
Eisenhower's arrythmia after, 151, 276–279, 286
Eisenhower's recovery from, 113–145, 151–152, 329–330
Eisenhower's response to, 275–276, 281–282
Hagerty and, 73–77, 79–93, 95
Mattingly as consultant on, 91, 99–101, 117, 119–122, 127, 135–144
misdiagnosis of, 2, 90–112
Nixon and, 76, 84, 120, 124, 133, 151
Pollock as cardiologist for, 74–77, 88, 96, 100–105, 111, 117, 119–122, 128
press coverage of, 75–78, 80–82, 91–94
questions about, 82–86, 88, 91–92, 100–101, 108
Snyder's role and, 73–94, 125, 128–129, 135–144
White as consultant on, 83, 91, 117–122, 125, 129, 133, 138–144
See also Eisenhower, Mamie
Heart Disease (White), 16, 83
Heaton, Leonard, 136–137, 141–142, 144, 186, 250–253, 257, 259
  background of, 204
  Eisenhower in retirement and, 297–300, 306, 313, 318–322
  Eisenhower's ileitis surgery and, 210–214, 217, 221, 224–225
Heberden, William, 8

Herrick, James, 12, 109
Herter, Christian, 292
Hess, Elmer, 102
Hobbs, Conrad, 166–167, 182
Hobby, Oveta Culp, 102
Hogan, B. W., 102
Holiday Magazine, 156
Hope, Bob, 262
Hughes, Emmet, 69, 155, 226, 228, 239, 247–248, 283
Hughes, F. J., 320, 322
Humphrey, George, 149
Hunter, John, 8

Ileitis (Crohn's disease), 63, 201, 207, 218
    Democrats and, 214–215, 219, 222
    See also Eisenhower, Dwight; Eisenhower, Mamie; Hagerty, James; Heaton, Leonard; Pearson, Drew; Snyder, Howard

Jenkins, Walter, 288
Jenner, Edward, 8
Johnson, Edwin, 197
Johnson, Lyndon, 296, 302, 308, 311
    and heart attack of, 70, 141, 156, 197–198, 200, 288, 297, 328
Joliffe, Norman, 258
Jones, Pete, 102
Journal of Chronic Diseases, 232
Journal of the American Medical Association, 12, 164, 222

Katz, Jay, 125
Katz, Louis, 256
Kennedy, John, 284, 287–290, 292
Kennedy, Robert, 288
Keys, Ancel, 256, 260
Kistiakowsky, George, 249, 265
Kleinman, Arthur, 4, 332
Knebel, Fletcher, 105

Knowland, William, 149, 186

Ladies' Home Journal, 274
Lasker, Albert, 15
Lasker, Mary Woodward, 14–15, 255
Laurence, William, 329
Lawrence, David, 150, 154, 327
Lax, Henry, 294–295
Leahy, Frank, 197
Lear, Martha Weinman, 293
Leedham, Charles, 43–45, 48
Lepeschkin, Eugene, 120, 141
Levine, Samuel, 16–17, 78, 109, 114, 255
    "armchair method" of, 117–118
Levy, Robert, 153
Lewis, Thomas, 83, 113
Life, 198
Lodmell, Elmer, 136–138, 207
Look, 105
Luce, Clare Booth, 44, 330
Lull, George, 102
Lynn, Doss, 279
Lyons, John, 210–211, 237

MacArthur, Douglas, 25, 37
McCrary, Jinx, 176
McCrary, Tex, 176
Macfadden, Bernarr, 20, 23
McIntyre, Ross, 42, 99
McNamara, Pat, 214, 218
Mademoiselle, 269
Marshall, Catherine, 18
Marshall, George C., 27, 29, 37
Marvin, H. M., 16, 328
Master, Arthur, 157
Mattingly, Thomas, 2
    background, 42, 67–68, 250–251, 282, 286
    diagnosis of aneurysm and, 204, 251–252, 322
    disputes with White and, 141–142, 164–170, 206
    Eisenhower in retirement and, 297–309, 314–318, 322

Mattingly, Thomas *(continued)*
  Eisenhower's ileitis and, 209-211, 237
  on Eisenhower's 1949 illness, 42-49, 63, 77
  Eisenhower's stroke and, 241, 244
  See also Heart attack of 1955; Second term decision
Mauldin, Bill, 331
Merritt, Houston, 242-244
Minton, Sherman, 197
Mitchell, James, 102
Moaney, John, 74, 134, 261, 269, 271
Moley, Raymond, 1
Montgomery, Bernard, 125
Montgomery, Robert, 227
Morris, J. N., 261
Morrow, Lance, 324
Moyers, Bill, 5
Muhammad V (King of Morocco), 239, 241

National Heart Institute, 15
New England Journal of Medicine, 217
Newsday, 218
Newsweek, 3, 91
New York Herald Tribune, 21, 35, 40, 65
New York Sun, 21
New York Times, 21, 40, 155, 189, 293
Nixon, Patricia, 284-285, 317
Nixon, Richard, 3, 28, 147, 149, 193, 202, 203, 227, 238, 245, 312-313, 319-320, 331
  on Eisenhower, 23, 143-144, 177, 194, 225, 319
  on election of 1960, 284-291
  See also Heart attack of 1955
Norstad, Lauris, 47

Oceanside (California) *Blade-Tribune,* 236

Osler, William, 4-5, 10-11, 13, 17, 57, 161, 247, 321

Page, Irvine, 256
Parmley, Loren, 293, 300-307, 309, 311
Parry, Caleb Hillier, 8
Patton, George, 23, 63
Paul, Oglesby, 108-109
Pearson, Drew, 2, 63-64, 184, 190-191, 245, 283
  Eisenhower's ileitis and, 215-218
  election of 1956 and, 234-236
Pepper, Claude, 15
Persons, Wilton, 102, 193, 225-226
Pickett, William, 44, 50
Pollock, Byron, 81-82, 84, 86, 118, 128-129, 137, 174, 205. *See also* Heart attack of 1955; Second term decision
Powell, George, 96, 117, 132
Preventive medicine, 60, 204, 297
Pruitt, Francis, 207, 209, 240, 252-253

Ramsay, Allen, 122, 137-138
Randall, Clarence, 274-275
Ravdin, Isador, 210-211, 221-223, 237
Rayburn, Sam, 200
Readers' Digest, 157
Reagan, Ronald, 2
Reed, Daniel, 197
Reporter, 216
Reston, James, 155-159, 184, 190
Roberts, Clifford, 54, 85, 102, 151, 176, 306, 330
  heart attack of, 197
Robinson, William, 54, 85, 102, 104, 176, 200, 317
Roosevelt, Franklin, 2, 4, 42, 63, 64, 94, 202, 218, 219, 283, 325-326
Roosevelt, John, 289
Roosevelt, Theodore, 20
Rosenman, Ray, 264, 296
Rowley, James, 73-74, 77

Russek, Henry, 264
Rutstein, David, 219-222

St. Louis Post Dispatch, 93
Salinger, Pierre, 289
Sawyer, Charles, 11
Scheele, Leonard, 1, 15, 104
Schlesinger, Arthur, Jr., 202
Schulz, Robert, 44
Schweitzer, Albert, 83
Second term decision
    cardiologists and, 152-154
    Democrats and, 200-203
    Eisenhower and, 145, 151, 158,
        173-178, 186-199, 248-250,
        282-283
    Hazlett and, 146, 149, 167, 176,
        195
    historians and, 155
    Mattingly and, 165, 179-182,
        185-188
    Pollock and, 174-181, 184-185
    the press and, 188, 190, 192
    Snyder and, 3, 160-163, 178-189,
        193, 196
    White and, 3, 156, 159-171, 178,
        181-183, 187-192, 196
    See also Eisenhower, Mamie
Shakespeare, William, 1
Shanley, Bernard, 62, 69, 172, 175
Sheedy, John, 75, 96, 117
Six Crises (Nixon), 284
Slater, Ellis, 78, 102-103, 151,
        162-163, 227, 250, 259, 270, 296,
        300
    on Eisenhower, 262, 266
Slim, William, 28
Smith, Merriman, 19, 43, 79-80
Smith, S. Calvin, 113
Smith, Walter "Beetle," 26
Snyder, Howard, 2, 248, 331
    background, 30, 35, 59
    commitment to Eisenhower, 59-60
    criticism of, as doctor, 60

as doctor to Mamie Eisenhower,
    29-30, 52, 60
Eisenhower's ileitis and, 208-211,
    213, 225-233, 237, 239
Eisenhower's 1949 illness and,
    40-50
Eisenhower's stroke and, 240-244
election of 1960 and, 285-289
papers of, 41-42, 297
press management by, 35, 50, 55,
    64-65, 78, 81-82, 85, 203-205,
    221-222, 228-229
relationship with Eisenhower and,
    60, 250, 268, 281, 291
second term special role of,
    248-258, 263-280, 283
service after retirement of, 297,
    299-303, 305
See also Heart attack of 1955;
    Second term decision; White,
    Paul Dudley
Snyder, Howard, Jr., 102
Snyder, Murray, 73, 75-78, 81, 92, 94-95
Sokolsky, George, 324
Sprague, Howard, 7, 255
Sprague, John, 197
Stamler, Jeremiah, 256
Standard, Samuel, 216
Stare, Frederick, 155
Stevenson, Adlai, 149, 193
    campaign of 1956 and, 200-202,
        218-219, 226-229, 238-239
    death of, 293-295
Stirling, Bill, 175
Summersby, Kay, 26, 38, 273
Sumner, Charles, 9

Taylor, James, 36, 51
Taylor, Maxwell, 265
Thompson, Dorothy, 274
Time, 91, 93, 156, 164, 217
Times (London), 294
Tkach, Walter, 209
Tree, Marietta, 293

Truman, Harry, 39–40, 58, 202
Turner, Edythe, 175

Udall, Stewart, 308
U.S. News and World Report, 55, 64, 91, 147, 150, 153–154, 179, 196, 267, 290

Vanderbilt, Cornelius, 84
Vinson, Fred, 127
von Neumann, John, 192

Wall Street Journal, 297
Warren, Earl, 149
Washington Daily News, 328
Washington Post, 188, 216
Washington Star, 297
Weeks, Sinclair, 156
Westmoreland, William, 317
Wheaton, Anne, 243
White, Paul Dudley, 2, 250, 261, 290
  biography of, 83–84
  on coronary disease, 7, 16–18, 87, 109–110, 117, 164, 190, 202, 204–206, 230, 232–233, 255, 328
  as educator, 86–87, 139
  Eisenhower's ileitis and, 210–211

election of 1956 and, 229–234
defense of Snyder, 89–93
press and, 189–190, 200, 205, 221, 229–234
relations with Eisenhower and, 139, 143, 169, 229–230, 233–234, 251, 256–257, 297–298, 302, 322
writings of, 16, 83, 190, 230, 232–233
See also Heart attack of 1955; Mattingly, Thomas; Second term decision
Whitman, Ann, 73–76, 177, 208, 212, 238, 239, 248–249, 269, 290
  on Eisenhower, 124, 267, 298
  relations with Eisenhower, 69, 73
Wicker, Tom, 285
Wilson, Arthur, 146
Wilson, Woodrow, 2, 80, 94, 218–219, 326
Wolf, Stewart, 264
Woodruff, Bob, 102
Wright, Irving, 256

You and Your Heart (Marvin), 16

Zetzel, Louis, 217